THE PITTSBURGH THEOLOGICAL MONOGRAPH SERIES

General Editor
Dikran Y. Hadidian

26

Candid Questions Concerning Gospel Form Criticism

Erhardt Güttgemanns

CANDID QUESTIONS CONCERNING GOSPEL FORM CRITICISM

A Methodological Sketch of the Fundamental Problematics of Form and Redaction Criticism

by

ERHARDT GÜTTGEMANNS

translated by

William G. Doty

THE PICKWICK PRESS
Pittsburgh, Pennsylvania

1979

226.06
G987c

LIBRARY
ATLANTIC CHRISTIAN COLLEGE
WILSON, N. C.

Translated with the author's approval from
Offene Fragen zur Formgeschichte des Evangeliums:
Eine methodologische Skizze der Grundlagenproblematik
der Form- und Redaktionsgeschichte
2nd, corrected, edition
Munich: Chr. Kaiser Verlag, 1971 [c. 1970];
additions by the author, 1978.
Beiträge zur evangelische Theologie,
Theologische Abhandlungen, ed. Ed. Wolf, volume 54.

Library of Congress Cataloging in Publication Data

Güttgemanns, Erhardt.
    Candid questions concerning Gospel form criticism.

    (The Pittsburgh theological monograph series ; 26)
    Translation of the 2d, corr. ed. of Offene Fragen zur
Formgeschichte des Evangeliums.
    Includes bibliographical references.
    1. Bible. N.T. Gospels—Criticism, Form. I. Title.
II. Series.
BS2555.2.G7613   226'.06'7   79-10167
ISBN 0-915138-24-7

Copyright© 1979 by
THE PICKWICK PRESS
5001 Baum Boulevard
Pittsburgh, PA 15213

CONTENTS

NOV 0 4 1979

79-1099

iii

Translator's Preface

A. "In All Candor...".

Some of the dictionary synonyms for the "offen" of the German title of this work, *Offene Fragen...*, gather a semantic range that only limps through the working the author and I agreed upon, *Candid Questions....* *Offen* means first of all "open", as in "an open letter", i.e., a writing programmatically slanted toward concerned readers who may not be the explicit correspondence partners. It also carries overtones of "frank, sincere", and the book is certainly such: It honestly expresses exasperation with a methodological ostrich-ism that has ducked its head into the sand more frequently, ignored non-religious scholarship more completely, and pooh-poohed criticism from other academic disciplines more effectively, than now seems credible, given recent developments that have opened biblical studies toward literary-critical and other methodologies.

Offen leads on to "exposed", and the scope of Dr. Güttgemanns' treatment has meant that he has had to leave his flanks exposed at more than one juncture here, insofar as exhaustive argumentation and documentation have not been possible. *Offen* also leads to "overt", as "overt hostility", which is less politely repressed in continental academic debate than it is on this side of the Atlantic. The author alludes to the controversy surrounding this book in his Epilogue; he has not shared there the painful acrimonies of the debate, but perhaps I may just indicate that the book was often misread as an "overt" attack from a mindless debaser of the scriptural tradition-- which Erhardt Güttgemanns certainly is not.

Our term also contributes to commercial phrases: an *offene Rechnung* is an outstanding or unsettled account; some of those overtones resound where the "candid questions" are aporia that have been recognized (as by Bultmann, see Ch. #13), but remain *unresolved*. A "public, manifest", aspect is also present, and altered as *öffentlich*, so are the connotations of "publicized, publicity". Again the author's intention, as I see it: to drive exegesis out into the open, public, no-holds-barred agora, where self-conscious, explicit, even aggressive, debate may chase away at least some of the phobias adhering to interdisciplinary studies, where it may garner some of the delights of re-approaching sanctified texts by seeing them warped and woofed as tapestries belonging to the multiform *richesse* of Western literature, and not merely as patchwork snippets hidden in a cabineted *hermeneutica sacra*.

The approach comes no more easily than the diction--and this is a very dense, technical, and complicated work indeed. But it promises many openings as it challenges accepted scholarly truisms. Often practicing a hermeneutics of deceit, it asks us to re-examine many of our assumptions, particularly form-critical assumptions. (Note the way some of the traditional diction is exposed here: "sociological setting", often merely by consistently being set apart by quotation marks, constantly plays upon the tension between Gunkel's original usage, and what came to be made of it.) We are led to the German Romantics, to subsequent folkloristics, and later, even to gestalt psychology!

The book is *not* a work in structuralist linguistics, although it maps some of the linguistic background Güttgemanns will work from as he develops (primarily in the journal he edits and publishes in Bonn, *Linguistica Biblica*) his "generative poetics". It *is* a full-scale attempt toward exegetical accuracy, focused upon methodological aporias that have too often been shoved into the "must resolve...someday!" files. And it does attempt (Ch. 8):

> to re-integrate the atomistically-splintered methodologies once again into a unity which will do justice to the unity of the linguistic phenomenon, 'text'.

Hence one of the key aims of the book; as expressed in Chapter #5, the author is working:

> toward a more careful and more productive methodological development of form criticism by overcoming its stagnation and its unnecessary isolation from the linguistic and sociological disciplines.

But something more than that is attempted as well--or we might say, "form criticism is something more than that", in that Güttgemanns' style of exegesis, only anticipated here (the reader must follow *Linguistica Biblica* and its associated publications to see what I mean), touches much more than what is usually thought of as the "form" in form criticism.

When in 1970 I first read the second edition of this book, in German galleys, I suggested to an American publishing firm that the work surely ought to be translated. That did not happen then, and I later accepted Pickwick's request to translate it myself only hesitantly. Now I am glad I did, and wish the book the widest possible "candid" reception!

B.   On the Translation.

My method of translating this book is a departure from that followed in *Semeia* 6 (1976): *Erhardt Guttgemanns' "Gen-*

erative Poetics", where I had the excellent collaboration of
Norman R. Petersen, and where we were concerned not only to
be accurate with respect to Dr. Güttgemanns' original essays,
but so far as possible to work within translation conventions
of international discussions of structuralist linguistics.
Here I am not any less concerned with accuracy, but the material pre-dates the later involvement with Generative Poetics
and developments in structuralist analysis, and I have worked
alone, except that the author read and approved the English
translation. He has also supplied additional footnotes reflecting recent discussion (indicated in the footnotes by
[+1978: ...]), and an Epilogue--these have sometimes been extensively reworked by the translator.

I have preferred to present a translation that will carry
the English reader through the extremely compressed style,
finding ways of altering the German syntax so as to incorporate quotations within the structure of sentences and para-
graphs, as the author so frequently does. Any first-year
student of German knows the ways German can express in a com-
pound word what English can only express in a string of words;
that problem is exacerbated here in that the author refers to
disciplines and terms unfamiliar to many biblical critics, or
makes his own neologisms--saving space in German, but certainly not in English!

And finally, the translation has not been taken to the
stage one normally takes a translation, i.e., moving from a
literal to a "free" rendition in polished English style. It
seemed more important to have the technical developments the
author presents in his own patterns of expression than literary English (which would have increased the length of the
translation substantially, by the way). Page numbers in the

original are indicated in brackets throughout, and anyone who wishes greater gracefulness for her or his own purposes is encouraged to adapt the translation accordingly. This is *a working translation* of an important critique of the form-critical method, meant for use by scholars and students.

Some specific aspects:

1. Translation of New Testament passages are those of the literal translation I prefer for working with the Greek text, the *New American Standard Bible: New Testament* (La Habra, CA: The Lockman Foundation, 1963), or my own.

2. I have generally *not* followed the customary practice of splitting the German writer's long dependent clauses into series of short English sentences with repeated subject. This makes for turgid English prose, but requires only that the reader carry forward the primary subject in her or his head.

3. Some conventions used:

    a. *Gestalt/en* has been anglicized consistently: "gestalt/s".

    b. *Ur:* usually "pre + substantive/adjective" (Urliteratur = pre-literature), but sometimes anglicized (ur-historical) where the technical nuance would not otherwise be clear. *Urchristlich:* consistently "primitive Christian".

    c. *Gesetzmässigkeiten:* "regularities", etc., seemed too weak, so I have mostly used "laws", which in turn is rather too strong an expression.

    d. *Sitz im Leben:* consistently "sociological setting" (as throughout my *Contemporary New Testament Interpretation*, 1972, justified there).

e. *Kleinliteratur:* left in German, as explained in a page-note in Chapter #3.

f. *-geschichte*, in compounds, presents the usual problems; when one component is emphasized by the author, I have used, for example, form-*historical* or *traditio*-historical; otherwise form, redaction, motif, and literary *criticism*, but tradition *history*, as is customary, though inaccurate.

g. *Soziologisch* is simply "sociological" here, but the usage background is often a Comte-ian contrast between the collective and the individualistic rather than the more recent and less-philosophical American usage, where theoretical sociology receives a minor emphasis within the data-oriented academic discipline.

C. Technical Matters.

1. All words/phrases within quotation marks, and most hyphenated constructions, represent the author's own usage; however many originally-hyphenated constructions (e.g., hermeneutisch-theologisch) are divided by *and* (hermeneutical and theological).

2. Although English translations of works quoted here are frequently available, all translations in this work, with the exception of some extended citations from Latin and Greek texts, are the translator's.

3. The author's typographic emphasis is followed except for italicizing names of scholars in the text and the notes. Footnote sequence is sometimes out of numerical order, to accommodate the changes from German to English sentence structure.

4. The Table of Contents is complete, down to sub-sub-sections, to facilitate reference; given the mass of 1579 footnotes in the original text, it has not been possible to manage an Index.

5. Bibliographic citations are considerably reduced in this translation: I have cited only the actual edition quoted, and omitted references to series. Since the footnote numbers correspond exactly to those in the German edition, such information can be obtained readily. Many of the earlier works pertaining to form criticism, especially English-language works, are listed in full among the 238 entries in my own bibliographic survey, "The Discipline and Literature of New Testament Form Criticism," *Anglican Theological Review* 51 (1969) 257-321. Abbreviations in the notes mostly follow *Die Religion in Geschichte und Geganwart*, 3rd ed.

6. There are many cross references within the footnotes; in order to expedite publication, we have introduced the author's *original paginations in brackets*: "See above, p. [29]" therefore refers to the page numbers given in brackets in the text, not to the pages of this translation.

I am grateful to the author for his contributions, and for a virtual archive of additional materials supplied over a several-year period; to editor Dikran Y. Hadidian, of Pickwick Press, for his patience; and to my wife, Joan T. Mallonee, for help in clarifying parts of the English text.

Quincunx, Amherst, MA

William G. Doty
August 1978

Foreword to the First Edition

This book is one of the studies of the gospels announced
in my dissertation. From the first I have thought of it as a
project needing to be supplemented by additional essays. As
such it only brings to light some of the aspects of a new conception of a New Testament theology that is oriented toward
form criticism and that reflects hermeneutical theory, upon
which I have been working now for several years. As "aspects"
of a new conception, therefore, this work cannot promise exhaustive treatment. And above all, this self-limitation both
in terms of my presentation and in terms of the references to
theological and secular and scientific bibliography, is also
due to the insufficient preparation of readers for the methodologies and modes of inquiry in this book. The scientific
advance that we seek must not be loaded down with too much
ballast in the hold.

To be sure, this book is not for those readers to whom
scientific theories and hypotheses in N. T. theology have become such second nature that they can easily avoid consciousness of the problem and their own scruples with respect to the
possibilities of knowing and describing the primitive Christian
history. To such readers these pages will bring little joy,
since seemingly everything that seems certain to them is
brought into question here. I regret that I must contradict
so many people in this book--especially my own teachers. Can-
dor toward all fronts and the growing acceptance of Franz Overbeck's conception of a primitive Christian "pre-literature"
[Urliteratur] with its "darkness with respect to the primitive
historical period" seems to me to be quite appropriate to a

1

period in which traditio-historical reconstructions are apparently not bounded by fantasy. Whoever does not dare to inquire about the bases of his own premises may accuse me of historical scepticism; in this respect I feel myself in good company.

This book is the consistent development of form-critical argumentation that is already to be found in my dissertation, where I rejected a traditio-historical *argumentum e silentio* [argument from silence]. This further development of my earlier work is, to be sure, carried out by means that have been a surprise even to me. Although I saw earlier the clear necessity of a connection between form criticism and hermeneutic, my deeper affinity to Ernst Fuchs--seen in purely external terms--came about through concentration upon linguistics and [p. 14] literary criticism. This occurred entirely by chance, such as, for instance, reading a book by Harald Weinrich concerning systems of grammatical tenses. It was in this context that the question of christological thought patterns emerged anew, and that happened in a manner that was totally different from anything I had expected.

This book consciously plays, in its manner of presentation, with the double subterranean meanings of its title. It is directed both to the candid [offene] opening up of aporia with respect to "gospel form criticism", and with respect to frank questioning of positions we have all been taught. So both the book's frankness, and the need for these studies to be supported further are rooted in its subject matter. I am concerned about the practise of a theology conscious of its own problems that calmly sets the aporia to the side and does not reflect upon them with the same intensity that is granted to the hastiest of "solutions". Not hypothesis-construction, but consciousness of problems and preparedness for constant revision are the marks of rigorous scientific method even for the historian.

This book was written in an atmosphere of unrest with respect to the neo-positivist splintering of N. T. studies that seems to disavow the fact that Rudolf Bultmann once developed a theological exegesis for Karl Barth's proposals that astonished his teachers, and which united exegesis and hermeneutics into an indivisible whole. "Pure historical criticism!"--again today this is the slogan of many exegetes. In a peculiar way the present situation is a variation of that earlier situation, since now the historical-critical method is used as a weapon against too extensive use of hermeneutics in N. T. studies, and the traditional boundaries of the disciplines are stressed. The right to establish appropriate boundaries for the theological disciplines is only established by the universal problematics of the subject matter treated in each instance; and only it can judge the adequacy of scientific description. The "purely historical" is always transmitted by language, and is only understandable by means of linguistic processes. It must therefore be referred to a linguistic critique of "historical reason", that amplifies the traditional humanistic hermeneutics by linguistic data, and in the process also causes modifications. In such a situation the estranged sisters, hermeneutics and linguistics, confront one another again in the exegesis of texts that are "given".

This volume could hardly have been written and completed without the unselfish help of Professor Hans-Georg Geyer, who, after several long and difficult years of library management, took me on as his assistant without respect to my area of academic study, and who shared with me his rich knowledge of philosophy and the history of ideas as well as his openness to unaccustomed areas of research; he gave me strength and cour-

4

age to complete this study. That he also did justice to the
completed work greatly encouraged me [p. 15] in my endeavors.
I also remember gladly the numerous technical discussions with
Professor Johannes Botterweck (Catholic Theological Faculty of
Bonn), Professor Johann Knobloch, Professor Helmut Gipper
(Sprachwissenschaftliches Institut, Bonn), Professor Gerold
Ungeheuer (Institut für Kommunikationsforschung und Phonetik,
Bonn), Dr. Manfred Beller (Germanistisches Seminar Bonn, Abteilung für Vergleichende Literaturwissenschaft), and Professor Hans-Dieter Bastian (Pädagogische Hochschule Rheinland,
Abteilung Bonn). I first learned the correct nature of many
interdisciplinary relationships in these discussions. Above
all, Professor Botterweck and Professor Bastian sacrificed
much time for me; and they are also to be thanked for supporting me wholeheartedly in another respect. Professor
Ernst Wolf readily accepted my book in his series and also
supported me in other ways during the past few years; I am
grateful to him as well as to the [original] publisher, Chr.
Kaiser Verlag, for careful printing. My self-effacing par-
ents made possible this publication by their own sacrifices;
the leadership of the Evangelische Kirche im Rheinland also
contributed a subvention. Karla Maasshoff read the proofs;
together with Erich Ott and myself, she compiled the index--
that work will be appreciated by the reader [not included
here--W.G.D.]. I dedicate the book to my wife, who in recent
years has patiently carried an overload of hindrances on my
part and given me time for the leisure of reflection.

Bonn-Röttgen, March 1970   Erhardt Güttgemanns

Foreword to the Second, Corrected, Edition

I am pleased that my "candid" questions have found such strong echoes. Five months after the first edition I can make a few corrections and add to the bibliographic references. It is good to see, especially in Catholic Old Testament exegesis, a tendency to correlate form criticism and linguistics (cf., e.g., B. W. Richter, *Die sogennanten vorprophetischen Berufungsberichte*, 1970; Richter, "Formgeschichte und Sprachwissenschaft," *ZAW* 82 [1970] 216-25). My mother was not able to experience the success of the book, so I dedicate the second edition to her memory.

Bonn-Röttgen, November 1970   E. G.

PART I. THE CURRENT RESEARCH SITUATION

Introductory Remarks

This work represents only a selection of a further and
much more inclusive study concerning the christological relevance of the gospel form. This relevance has been emphasized
repeatedly by E. Käsemann in connection with the recently-re-
vived question about the "historical Jesus", and it has been
made the nodal point of the so-called "post-Bultmannian revision" of N. T. theology. Chapter #1 pursues these connections
by tracing the horizons of Käsemann's theses concerning the
christological relevance of the gospel form in the history of
research and of theology. In the process it will also become
clear that the problem set out by Käsemann cannot really be
dealt with within the relatively-proscribed limits of the traditional theological disciplines, since Käsemann's theses are
demonstrably not only obtained analytically and exegetically,
but are also guided by definite dogmatic and hermeneutical
interests that could only be analyzed by a study of their
appropriateness that steps beyond the boundaries of the disciplines for the sake of the subject involved. The essential
necessity for such a complex reworking of the problem indicated is rooted both in methodology and in the history of
theology.

A *methodological* necessity follows from the recognition
that there are certain form- and redaction-critical theses
bound up with the conception typologically represented by
Käsemann, and these concern an evaluation of the gospel-form
in favor of a theological relevance of the "historical Jesus"

7

that is part of the methodological foundations of form and redaction criticism. We must therefore reflect upon these foundations anew. Can the gospel-form really be used in the ways
E. Käsemann, G. Bornkamm, E. Schweizer, and others affirm,[1]
namely to support a particular christological position within
the contemporary debate about christology? It is part of the
nature of this question that both in its answer, as well as
in the methodological analysis of this answer, the boundaries
between [p. 18] traditional historical-critical exegesis, hermeneutical reflection, and one's own systematic and theological position dissolve into one another. It would seem to me
to be entirely improper, given this problematic situation
(which will be described more exactly below), to plead for a
"purely exegetical" discussion of the theme, and to screen
out all questions situated on the other side of an apparently
"objective" description as simply not belonging to N. T. theology. A conception that pursues a definite methodological
intention, as does the one to be discussed here, can only be
methodologically studied with respect to its propriety, its
boundaries, and even its methodological miscarriages: "The
question concerning the inner content of the N. T. is in fact
a *systematic* question, which is valid to begin with so far as
N. T. theology is concerned."[2] To be sure there are also many
"purely exegetical" facts, which must be stated against E.
Käsemann. But these facts require signifying, as do all "historical" details, if they are to be utilized in a particular
design for a N. T. theology. However, the propriety of such
signifying is to be thrashed out methodologically. In other
words: Our attempt concerns *the methodological foundations
of that N. T. theology* which earned its right to exist through
R. Bultmann's epochal work.

The necessity from the point of view of the *history of
theology* has thereby already been touched upon. With respect

to the history of research, an analysis of our situation concerning N. T. theology, and especially concerning a corresponding christology,[3] results in my opinion in the pressing conclusion that in our "post-Bultmannian era" (J. M. Robinson) it
is fundamentally possible only to hold to the unity of historical analysis and theological interpretation attained in Bultmann's entire corpus, and so to modify it so that it is appropriate to the new types of questions that have appeared in the
meanwhile.[4] Everything else seeking to remedy our everlasting
methodological aporias, such as neopositivistic statistics,[5]
would seem to me to be a regression into a "pre-Bultmannian
era", which the spiritual and theological level already attained should forbid.[6] [p. 19] If therefore following R.
Bultmann's proposed N. T. theology, we even attempt a modified
and certainly in many respects revised presentation of N. T.
theology or its parts,[7] we may actually attain to new insights
only by a methodological discussion of the foundations of such
a presentation, if Bultmann's turn toward hermeneutics is still
to be generally obligatory for us. Today it is certain "that
we will not succeed by means of classifying the exegetical disciplines as 'historical' instead of 'systematic' theology,
since that classification itself has become a *thema probandum*
[thesis to be proved, justified]."[8]

At this point in the history of research, however, we are
faced not only with the dismantling of a methodologically fragmented position, but also with the construction of a positive
alternative. In these circumstances, what methodological criteria can be decisive for this construction? They can only result from that analysis of the history of research that thoroughly investigates the bases for what I consider to be the
restrictiveness of form and redaction criticism, and that simultaneously seeks to provide revisions leading out of such
restrictiveness by reference to the methodological framework

of form and redaction criticism, namely to general linguistics
and literary criticism. J. Barr's criticism of a linguisti-
cally-naive theology, while temperamental and not always appropriate,[9] as well as R. W. Funk's proposals, provide an indication[10] that the time is ripe for such revision to be attempted.

Granted, initial attempts at revision will be plagued
with many uncertainties concerning methodology and authorship
so long as general linguistics and literary criticism are
pushed onto the dark back shelves of theology, and until dilettantism has been overcome by the strenuous efforts of all
concerned. Some may regard our necessarily longer expositions
concerning this aspect of our subject--materials questioning
the restrictiveness of form criticism in N. T. theology in
terms of linguistics and literary criticism--as a still hypothetical contribution to methodological foundations of a positive [p. 20] reconstruction after the negative dismantling.
However, after long reflection it appeared to me to be the
most appropriate means of initiating work on a N. T. theology
that is oriented to linguistic phenomena.[11]

Moreover, this approach results in what I consider to be
a healthy distancing vis à vis those theses and premises that
appear to belong to the self-understood aspects of our exegesis, without our noticing how questionable they are from logical, cognitive-theoretical, linguistic, literary critical, and
finally also hermeneutical, viewpoints. If in this manner
questions arise that turn back toward questions concerning
the legitimacy of prevailing opinions within N. T. theology,
the intentions of this work will be fully satisfied.

The specific types of questions and problems to be confronted in such an expanded form-critical founding of a N. T.
theology will be indicated briefly in #3. Of course the completion of the methodological sketch presented there remains

for now a promise to be kept, since in many ways it makes too much of a demand upon the reader. Persons familiar with the situation will be aware how foreign and unaccustomed this new questioning is in light of the present place of form criticism in both N. T. and O. T. theology. Hence it seemed to me advisable to take up here only aspects of the new questioning that have been thoroughly worked through; they are treated sequentially and in their hypothetically significant aspects in the excurses, holding for a later monograph the ideas that take us too far from our immediate subject.[12]

For such reasons, the selection from the more complex methodological foundation of a N. T. theology presented in this book is limited to one major problem concerning the synoptic gospels developed by redaction criticism. This problem will be gradually worked through and sketched in its full acuteness in Part II, ##4-8, under the theme "The Oral and the Written". It will thereby be shown [p. 21] that the thesis in contemporary gospel form criticism concerning the traditio-historical continuity between oral and written materials is freighted with many more difficulties than is generally known and recognized. In that discussion we will point once more to the still unexplained nature of the gospel form.

In Part III this form will be methodologically connected with "gestalt" theory, in terms of the leading question: *To what extent* is the gospel form a literary "gestalt"?

Part IV presents a variation of this question: *Of what* is the gospel a literary "gestalt"? Is it an expansion of the kerygma, or should it be more adequately "derived" in some way other than by genealogy and tradition history?

Naturally, the self-conscious limitations of this work only allow me, if I may be permitted an archaeological analogy, to cut an exploratory trench through a very complex region. Hence the questions and the bibliography treated are determined by these limitations. Materials not dealt with here must await the anticipated monograph. Above all especially theological questions about the theologies of the synoptic writers, can first be discussed when prior questions about form-critical methodology are clarified. These selections from the larger enterprise are dedicated solely to this clarification, without relinquishing the long-range goals.

Notes to Introductory Remarks

1. Cf. nn. 1-18 in section #14 below.

2. E. Fuchs, *Marburger Hermeneutik*, 1968, 83.

3. Such an analysis is presented in E. Güttgemanns, *Der leidende Apostel und sein Herr*, 1966, 44ff., 386ff.

4. On the inherent Bultmann-criticism, cf. E. Güttgemanns, review of W. Schmithals, *Die Theologie Rudolf Bultmanns*, 1966, in *TheolPract* 3 (1968) 87-100.

5. Against neo-positivism, also H. Conzelmann, *EvTh* 22 (1962) 230f. On the rights and boundaries of the historical method cf. Güttgemanns, *Der leidende Apostel*, 388ff.

6. The view of the position of New Testament studies produced by such a standpoint is shown in E. Güttgemanns, "Literatur zur Neutestamentlichen Theologie," *VF* 12/2 (1967) 38-87.

7. Cf. R. Schnackenburg, *Neutestamentliche Theologie*, 1963 (original French ed., 1961); H. Conzelmann, *Grundriss der Theologie des Neuen Testaments*, 1967; K. H. Schelkle, *Theologie des Neuen Testaments*, vol. I, 1968.

8. Fuchs, *Marburger Hermeneutik*, 91.

9. J. Barr, *Bibelexegese und moderne Semantik*, 1965 (orig. English ed., 1961). Cf. also F. Ferré, *Language, Logic and God*, 1961. Further literature is cited below in section #2, nn. 55f.

10. R. W. Funk, *Language, Hermeneutic, and Word of God*, 1966. Cf. also P. M. van Buren, *The Secular Meaning of the Gospel Based on an Analysis of Its Language*, 1963; C. Michalson, *Worldly Theology*, 1967, 41ff.; D. O. Via, *Die Gleichnisse Jesu*, 1970.

11. A hermeneutically-clarified New Testament theology is a "language school of faith". Cf. E. Fuchs, *Hermeneutik*, 1958-2nd ed., 96ff.

12. In the planning stages: a publication with the theme "form criticism and linguistics", in which for the first time

all possible interconnections between the related disciplines
might be extensively presented, so that the universal horizons
of the program would be clearer. Cf. also E. Güttgemanns,
"Sprache des Glaubens--Sprache der Menschen. Probleme einer
theologischen Linguistik," *VF* 14/2 (1969) 86-114; Güttgemanns,
"Linguistische Probleme in der Theologie. I.," *LB* 8 (1970) 18-
29. [+1978: Preparation for the projected publication was
aided by a grant of DM 180.000 from the Deutsche Forschungs-
gemeinschaft for a large scale research project, "Generative
Poetics of the New Testament". Results of this research were
published in articles in *Linguistica Biblica*, and in mono-
graphs in the series Forum Theologiae Linguisticae, starting
in November 1970. In the process of the research, the aims
shifted to "new frontiers", making necessary a revision of
my original plans referred to in this note.]

#1. The Relevance of the Gospel Form in the
        Present Situation of the History of Theology

1. The "Post-Bultmannian" Era.

J. M. Robinson characterized the new phase in post-war
German theology dialectically as "post-Bultmannian": "On the
one hand there is the fact that this movement was developed by
Bultmann's students, evidence that it would scarcely have been
conceivable without Bultmann's mode of inquiry, his methodology, and the results of his research. On the other hand the
inheritance of such a critical and free spirit as Bultmann's
cannot be preserved otherwise than by a critical revision of
his own position."[1] Such critical revision mostly concerns
three major theological complexes.[2]

(a) The Hermeneutical Problematics.

The result of the controversy about R. Bultmann's program of demythologizing[3] was initially a development of a
lively interest in hermeneutics,[4] an interest that led--at
first, to be sure, gradually and partially--to new positions
in hermeneutics that have truly led to progress.[5] Therefore
it is today still [p. 23] generally undecided as to whether
we already find ourselves, with respect to historical and
analytical exegesis, meaningfully within a "post-Bultmannian"
phase (since N. T. studies always remains aware, precisely in
its analytical work, of the necessity of hermeneutical reflection produced by the task of theological interpretation), or
whether there is not a noticeable tendency in exegetical mono-
graphs and essays to consider the "historical" method to be

15

hermeneutically neutral and presuppositionless.[6] At any rate
it must still be shown more clearly how far the hermeneutical
consciousness prevailing since Bultmann is in each case introduced into exegetical work.[7]

(b) The Christological Problematics.

The christological problem immediately arises in the
controversy concerning demythologization. Already R. Bultmann himself introduced the question whether a Christian understanding of existence, an eschatological posture, was possible without Christ.[8] J. Schniewind took up this problem in
asking "how the events of the cross and the resurrection were
necessary for such an eschatological posture. If [Bultmann]
turns away from the uniqueness of Jesus and understands the
Christ event solely from the standpoint of our historical and
personal existence, are not the Christ events simply symbols
or stimulating concepts?"[9] K. Barth regarded Bultmann as having apparently affirmed this question, at least *de facto*, and
therefore raised the reproach of docetism,[10] a reproach that
has since been taken up repeatedly.[11] That is [p. 24] also
the central issue of the newly revived question concerning
the "historical Jesus", which is at the center of christological interests.[12]

(c) The Revision of Eschatology.

The "post-Bultmannian" revision appears to be endangered
as much by eschatology as by christology.[13] Although R. Bultmann considers the mythical eschatology of the N. T. to be
"finished" by the simple fact of the delay of the parousia[14]
and so formulates the concept of the "eschatological event"
in such a way as to include not only the elemental Christ
event of Jesus' death and resurrection, but also the *existen-*

tielle alteration of the self-understanding made possible by
the actual alteration of temporality,[15] the revision of this
concept has been subject to criticism,[16] insofar as the historical *ephapax* of the saving event and the *extra me* that lies
in historic uniqueness threatens to be lost in the eternal
timelessness of the *nunc stans*.[17] While eschatology is interested in the contingency and teleology of the course of
time,[18] and "in historical being the flowing of the course of
time from the past to the future is constantly a given,"[19]
Bultmann's concept lacks any durational character of time,[20]
so that not only is the saving history and therewith the assimilation of the Jesus-history to the history of the theologically thematized Old Testament lost,[21] but also the hope,
which maintains, carries, and draws faith forward,[22] as well
as the proleptic of history and the being which is analogous
to it[23] and the [p. 25] future aspect of Christian faith,
propagated in Jewish and primitive Christian apocalyptic,
namely the universal victory of grace in the christocracy
that leads to theocracy.[24] So it is not to be doubted that
this series of questions--above all following Bultmann's own
procedure--[25] has been dealt with more and more in terms of
the systematic schema "history and eschatology".[26]

2. Theological Interest in the Historical Jesus.

Theological interest in the "historical Jesus" remains
today at the center of christological problematics.[27] This
interest is widely understood as a necessary bulwark against
the docetism evidently threatening in R. Bultmann's works,
and against the feared evaporation of the historical figure
of Jesus into an ahistoric myth or a transhistorical idea.[28]
E. Käsemann initially in 1953 revivified the debate that had
certainly never died down completely,[29] and shortly thereafter, in a second lecture that contained a critique that was

partly damaging to Bultmann, stimulated reconsideration of the arguments brought forth by both sides.[30] Not needing to report his arguments here in detail, we can restrict our discussion to the aspect that is central to Käsemann, and that which must remain, within the framework of our theme, at the forefront, namely the christological relevance of the gospel form.

[p. 26] This relevance is summarized by E. Käsemann in the thesis: "Without the gospels, the gospel would not remain what it is. Kerygma becomes, except where it is not also narrated, the proclamation of an idea, and except where it is always narratively won anew, a historical document."[31] According to this thesis, the moment of "narrative", which characterizes the gospel form, is the bulwark against both (gnostic) docetism as well as against (Ebionitic) historicism.

The theological appeal to the "historical Jesus" is therefore attempted here in such a manner as to exclude intentionally a relapse into a historistic understanding of reality. The gospel is not to be reduced to the "historical Jesus",[32] since this product of the Enlightenment has shown itself to be a *fata morgana* [mirage].[33] Since the N. T. does not recognize such a Jesus in and for himself[34] and the "historical Jesus" is only accessible by means of reconstruction,[35] the dissolution of history into *bruta facta*[36] as well as the relapse into an objectivizing thought[37] that seeks to establish faith by objective historical means[38] are excluded.

3. Connections between Theological Interest and the Gospel-Form: E. Käsemann.

Since the "history" of primitive Christianity has been transmitted solely in the kerygma,[39] a historical verification of the kerygma in the sense of liberal hermeneutics is

impossible.[40] According to his own intentions, E. Käsemann's
appeal to the "historical Jesus" should by no means be a relapse into historicism, since he respects the primitive Christian view that a manner of questioning directed only to the
"historical Jesus" is an abstraction.[41]

Rather the appeal to the "historical Jesus" is directed
against a possible docetism, insofar as Käsemann criticizes
R. Bultmann's historical scepticism,[42] which would lead to
resignation and disinterest in the earthly Jesus.[43] Such a
position overlooks the fact that the kerygma of the N. T.
reckons the earthly Jesus as one of its own criteria,[44] insofar as there is in the gospels a kerygmatic recourse to the
form of the message. [p. 27] "The key to our problem as a
whole lies not in the historical Jesus issue as such, and as
an isolated alternative to the kerygma, but it is the kerygmatic recourse to the form of the message, following which
enthusiasm, mythological presentation, and dogmatic reflection
were successful in their own ways, as can be seen in the primitive Christian hymns."[45] Therefore the narrative form of the
gospel documents the continued theological relevance of Jesus'
history, so that the question about the "historical Jesus" is
identical with that concerning the theological relevance of
the gospel-form.[46]

Disinterest in the earthly Jesus, on the other hand, also leads to a disinterest in the gospel-form,[47] so that the
writing of the gospels remains for R. Bultmann "in the last
analysis an inconceivable and superfluous variation of the
kerygma".[48] Since the relationship to Jesus' history is best
preserved in the gospels,[49] which by their form emphasize the
ephapax and the contingency of the eschatological event,[50] and
which by means of the past character of what is related emphasize the prevenience of God's act and the *extra nos* of salvation,[51] memory of the earthly Jesus remains necessary in the

framework of the gospel.[52] Therefore the form of the gospel
possesses central christological relevance,[53] because even today it represents theological positions that are not to be
given up. "Recourse to the form of the message of the gospels, to the narrative of the Palestinian proclaimer to the
'once' in contrast to the 'once-for-all times', to historicizing [p. 28] presentation in the framework of the kerygma, and
last but not least to the Jesus who passed through Palestine,
ensues as a theologically relevant reaction, accepted and
maintained by the church, a reaction which had to do with the
unavailability of the Christ, of the Spirit, of faith. The
presence of Christ and of the Spirit in the church may not be
misused in such a fashion that they are dissolved into the
eschatological self-understanding of believers. The precedence of the Lord before his congregation and believers can
and even must be expressed temporally. Present eschatology
without this retrospective view toward the past of salvation
is delivered without defense to enthusiasm, and anthropology
and ecclesiology cannot be distinguished from, or appropriately separated from, christology."[54] This summarizing quotation
demonstrates once again in conclusion the inner connections
between the three main elements of the "post-Bultmannian" revision we sketched above, represented here by E. Käsemann.

4. E. Käsemann's Historically and Analytically
    Unproven Dogmatic Premises. (A Preliminary
    Summary Toward a More Extensive Hermeneuti-
    cal Analysis.)

We cannot undertake here the task of developing a comprehensive analysis of the reconceptualizing of the christological problem outlined by E. Käsemann. We will presuppose such
an analysis, however, and refer here to its results with respect to Käsemann's dogmatic premises,[55] which obstruct our

viewing of the historical phenomenon of the gospel-form in contemporary research.[56]

(a) The Confusion of "Historical" and "Material" Questions.

E. Käsemann cannot close the gap in R. Bultmann's distinction between the "historical" and the "material" question within the christological problematics,[57] because he confuses or conflates the *existentielle* question (intended by Bultmann as the "material" question) about the truth of the identity asserted by kerygma and faith between the literally [p. 29] really-present Lord and the earthly Jesus[58] and the *history of ideas* question about the continuity and discontinuity between the "historical" Jesus and the Christian community. This is seen, for example, in his thesis that the material question develops "indeed out of the encounter with the historical phenomenon",[59] and therefore the historical question and the material question may not be as sharply distinguished as Bultmann suggests.[60] This confusion of categories corresponds to the lack of a categorical distinction between the "historical" Jesus and the "earthly" Jesus,[61] since interest in the real human Jesus is *immediately* identified with "historical" interest in Jesus on the one hand,[62] while on the other it is associated with interest in the gospel-form.[63]

(b) Narrative "History" as the Understanding of Reality Most Appropriate to the Material.

This connection implies the postulate that the "narrative form" of the gospel represents the understanding of Jesus' reality most appropriate to the materials: *"History" must be narrated, if it is to remain "history"!*[64] In this postulate the distinction already necessary in form criticism between the narrative form of the history of Jesus and the form of the reflection about the history of Jesus is converted into a hermeneutical scale of values: The only necessary form of reference appropriate to Jesus' earthly reality is tied *a priori* to "narrative". Thereby, somewhat as in J. Schniewind's hermeneutics,[65] the gospels have the uppermost place on the christological scale of values: they become the hermeneutical canon for propinquity to Jesus' reality.

(c) The Interpretive Circle between "History" and "Narrative".

The principal correlation of Jesus' "history" and the moment of "narrative" is not univocal in its meaning. Since other [p. 30] forms also--such as fairy tale, saga, legend, novella, or even myth--serve "narrative",[66] it is a *petitio principii* [begging the question], without extensive examination of the various understandings of reality that in each case differentiate the so-called "elementary forms",[67] to recognize solely in the moment of "narration" an indication of "history", if the concept of "history" is to be made precise and opposed to myth.[68] With such *a priori* procedure the gospels' actual understanding of reality is concealed by modern premises.

(d) The Ideal and Typological Conception of Docetism.

To these modern premises belong also the schematic antithesis of "myth" and "history" which has gradually developed since the Enlightenment, and which was based on the avoidance of docetism. This denies to myth any relationship to reality, since from the beginning it historistically narrows the concept of reality.[69] In this manner not only the concept of docetism, but also the concept of myth has been used in an idealistic and typological manner, and not by means of extensive analysis of concrete historical phenomena.[70] "Myth" is no longer a formal concept,[71] but the quintessence of an "ahistorical" and hence docetic understanding of reality. The attempt to determine whether such a *petitio principii* featuring a historical concept of reality can be analytically proved at all in concrete myths, is given up, so that no "historical" legitimacy is attributed to myth of antiquity. But besides this it remains entirely questionable to me whether the assumption of the real presence must not, given similar premises, be devalued as myth, in which case the foundations [p. 31] of Word of God theology are finally not applicable.[72] In spite of its avoidance in liberal hermeneutics, its influence is nonetheless determinative in that the essential premises of the renewed questioning about the "historical Jesus" cannot be dissolved from it without causing a fundamental crisis.

(e) "History" as a Criterion for the Kerygma.

Dependence upon liberal hermeneutics is also seen, in my opinion, in the way E. Käsemann at least *de facto* utilizes "history" as the criterion for the interpretation of Jesus in the kerygma.[73] In order to be able to judge the kerygma by means of this criterion at all, understanding must be separated from "history", which therefore makes "history" into a series of *bruta facta*. Since Käsemann certainly wants to avoid such a solution, since the elements of tradition and interpretation belong unalterably to history,[74] the exposed rudiments of liberal hermeneutics show through in the doubled concept of "history" that simultaneously becomes apparent.

24

"History" that is only possible in its unity with the history
of understanding, however, is made *de facto* into a criterion
to be contrasted with understanding.

(f)   The History of Ideas as an Answer
to the Material Question.

Another aspect corresponding to liberal hermeneutics is
that E. Käsemann makes Jesus' "history" into the criterion of
kerygma and faith insofar as he attempts to prove the identity
of the really-present Lord with the concrete human Jesus, that
is *asserted* by primitive Christian faith in the kerygma, by
means of historical analysis of a *history-of-ideas* continuity
or even discontinuity established by means of historical analysis.[75] Out of the asserted identity an identity is developed
on the sly that is not proved (or at least not provable) by
faith, since the historical analysis is not in any case essentially an enterprise of faith. Since Käsemann certainly wants
to avoid this result, he does not himself attain to R. Bultmann's enjoined clarification of the theological relevance of
the historical question for the *fulfillment* of faith, on account of his unmanageable liberal heritage.

[p. 32] (g)   The Confusion of the Material
Prae with Linear and Temporal Pre-Temporality.

The identification of the material *prae* of grace with the
linear and temporal *prae* of "history" is remarkable and in
need of interpretation.[76] Unless we are to assume an actual
salvation history or special history in the past,[77] and therefore arbitrarily designate a "divine" history within general
history, under these premises *every* historical past must also
possess a material *prae*. Thereby the historical past becomes
the dimension that orients all of existence in a materially

primary way. And so just in the center of E. Käsemann's proposal we confront once again the basic historical dogma according to which the historically conceivable and thereby
temporally-past reality becomes *the* actual reality.[78]

5.   The Methodology Offered in this Situation.

E. Käsemann's "post-Bultmannian" revision of the christological problem may be considered a summary and high-water-
mark of the newly reawakened question concerning the "historical Jesus". Even if his attempt--as presented above--is not
effected without crucial dogmatic premises, Käsemann desires
to be understood decidedly as a historian.[79] Therefore it is
not enough to engage in a purely hermeneutical discussion of
his objections and those of numerous others against R. Bultmann. To be sure, such a discussion is necessary, since a
central hermeneutical problem is involved. However since
Käsemann, at least in his intentions, establishes his position by means of historical argumentation, it is necessary
to study analytically his theses concerning the christological relevance of the gospel form.

In the course of my reflections on the methodological aspects of such an analysis, I decided to confront Käsemann's
thesis with particular standards of general linguistics and
literary criticism, in order to question the tenability of
the theses from their standpoint. The *hermeneutical* controversy concerning the [p. 33] christological relevance of the
form-critical phenomenon of the gospel finally concerns the
methodological foundations of the *linguistic* (grammatical and
literary-critical) phenomena utilized one way or another in
exegesis to establish one's own *theological and dogmatic* position; in other words it concerns the secular and scientific
verifiability of the debate in which at least one side argues

79-1099   ATLANTIC CHRISTIAN COLLEGE
LIBRARY
WILSON N. C.

"historically". Clarification of the methodological foundations of a definition of the gospel form that is sufficiently
linguistic and literary-critical is therefore accentuated in
this book. In light of the foundational problematics already
indicated, it would appear to me self-deceptive simply to let
the so-called "historical material" speak for itself. Still,
on the basis of the considerations presented below, the possibility appears of organizing the "historical" material according to viewpoints newly obtained from the methodology.
Purely for practical and economic reasons this new analysis
will be presented in a special investigation, which will go
beyond the bounds of this work. However this much can be
stated in advance: If such an investigation were to come to
results essentially different from the position represented
by E. Käsemann, then at least at this point the "post-Bultmannian" revision would be fundamentally shaken.[79a] And if
at the same time hermeneutical examination also reached a
different result, it would be entirely open as to where further development of R. Bultmann's hermeneutic would lead in
the history of theology, unless we want to be confronted unexpectedly by a retrenchment.

Naturally the avoidance of such a retrenchment also en-
tails the avoidance of a sharp separation between the his-
torical-analytical and the hermeneutical examination of the
theses presented,[80] since the issue concerns indeed the hermeneutical and theological relevance of the analytical results. A theological material content of the N. T. ought of
course to be studied and presented as a historical dimension.
However since we must subsequently complete the objective
theological execution of thought in this historical dimension,
if we are actually to attain understanding of the intended
material content, the necessary theological analysis can only
be conceived together with a decided theological questioning,

and that to be sure of a sort that neither exegetes the historical results while ignoring theological interpretation nor remains historical analysis without theological interest.

The best way to resolve the problem is to [p. 34] incorporate the history of understanding into historical analysis so that we enter into dialogue with the understanding coming to us from the texts, and hence clarify our own pre-understanding in the encounter with understanding that is also available elsewhere.[81] In this way we respect the origination of understanding in the understanding transmitted by the text, and so appreciate the text as a dimension pre-given and pre-ordered to our understanding, in order to safeguard therein the hermeneutically-clarified historical interest.

From these considerations comes the task of studying the christological relevance of the gospel form with the aid of questions that are reflective in every respect. Since in the investigation the issue is the understanding of Jesus' reality objectivized in the gospel-form, the investigation cannot be a "pure form-critical" one that attends only to stylistic and formal characteristics. Rather these characteristics are to be analyzed as "signs" of the christological understanding,[82] so that the form-critical results are theologically and hermeneutically evaluated. The central aspect of this evaluation, namely the understanding of time that acquires a gestalt in the gospel form, is shaped in dialogue with E. Käsemann. Therefore our guiding perspective will be this question: *Is the gospel form the linguistic "gestalt" of a particular christological understanding of time?* Naturally we can only attempt partial answers to this question, given the restricted framework of the present portion of the more complex content already mentioned.[83] However the developmental possibilities of the preliminary answer given here will in themselves provide enlightenment to those familiar with the subject.

Notes to #1

1. J. M. Robinson, *Kerygma und historischer Jesus*, 1960, 10.

2. Cf. J. B. Cobb, "The Post-Bultmannian Trend," *JBR* 30 (1962) 3-11; J. M. Robinson, "Basic Shifts in German Theology," *Interpretation* 16 (1962) 76-97; R. E. Brown, "After Bultmann, What?", *CBQ* 26 (1964) 1-30; P. J. Cahill, "Rudolf Bultmann and Post-Bultmann Tendencies," *CBQ* 26 (1964) 153-78; C. F. H. Henry, "The Theological Situation in Europe: Decline of the Bultmann-Era?", *ChrTo* 8 (1964) 1089-92, 1154-56.

3. On the boundless literature cf. the references in G. Bornkamm, "Die Theologie Rudolf Bultmanns in der neueren Diskussion," *ThR* 29 (1963) 33-141 (reprinted in *Geschichte und Glaube* 1, Ges. Aufs. vol. 3, 1968, 173-275). Cf. also J. Macquarrie, *The Scope of Demythologizing*, 1960, 95ff.

4. Cf. the brief summary in G. Ebeling, "Hermeneutik," *RGG*-3rd ed., vol. 3 (1959) 256-58, as well as J. M. Robinson, "Die Hermeneutik seit Karl Barth," in *Die neue Hermeneutik*, J. M. Robinson and J. B. Cobb, eds., 1965, 13-108.

5. Here we could cite, for instance, the efforts directed toward a "New Hermeneutic". Along with philosophical efforts (H.-G. Gadamer, E. Betti), we might mention attempts to correlate M. Heidegger's philosophy with theological reflections. Cf. H. Ott, *Denken und Sein*, 1959; J. M. Robinson, "Heilsgeschichte und Lichtungsgeschichte," *EvTh* 22 (1962) 113-41; *Der spätere Heidegger und die Theologie*, J. M. Robinson and J. B. Cobb, eds., 1964. On W. Pannenberg's "universal history conception", cf. the literature cited in E. Güttgemanns, *Der leidende Apostel*, 53, n. 1, and 55, n. 11. On the new attempts after Bultmann generally, cf. G. Bornkamm, *ThR* 29 (1963) 80-101.

6. I believe myself in the position to diagnose such tendencies. Cf. Güttgemanns, *Der leidende Apostel*, 46ff.

7. Not only Fuchs, but above all Marxsen, is working toward such purposes; cf. *Einleitung in das Neue Testament*, 1963. Cf. however the criticism of P. Vielhauer in *ThR* 31 (1965/66), 137-48.

8. R. Bultmann, in *Kerygma und Mythos*, vol. 1, H.-W. Bartsch, ed., 1954-3rd ed., 31ff.

9. J. Schniewind, *ibid.*, 99.

10. K. Barth, *Rudolf Bultmann*, 1952, 22.

11. Cf. for instance H. Thielicke, in *KuM* I, 166f., 174f.; E. Käsemann, in *Die Freiheit des Evangeliums und die Ordnung der Gesellschaft*. 1952, 151; Käsemann, *Aufsätze*, vol. I, 199-203; N. A. Dahl, *KuD* 1 (1955) 124, 129; P. Althaus, *Das sogenannte Kerygma und der historische Jesus*, 1958, 10, 15; G. Koch, *ZThK* 57 (1960) 260; J. Jeremias, in *Der historische Jesus und der kerygmatische Christus*, H. Ristow and K. Matthiae, eds., 1960, 17f.; K. Schubert, in *Der historische Jesus und der Christus unseres Glaubens*, 1962, 10; J. R. Geiselmann, *Jesus der Christus*, vol. I, 1965, 34; O. Cullmann, *Heil als Geschichte*, 1965, 30, 73.

12. Cf. below, p. [25f.]

13. Cf. H. Schlier, *EvTh* 8 (1948/49) 463f. = *Die Zeit der Kirche*, 1956, 149f.

14. Bultmann, *KuM*, vol. I, 18.

15. Cf. *ibid.*, 27ff.

16. Cf. for instance Schniewind, *ibid.*, 100ff.; H. Ott, *Geschichte und Heilsgeschichte in der Theologie Rudolf Bultmanns*, 1955; J. Körner, *Eschatologie und Geschichte*, 1957; G. Hasenhüttl, *Der Glaubensvollzug*, 1963, 79-81, 91-95, 129-31; G. Greshake, *Historie wird Geschichte*, 1963; G. Bornkamm, *ThR* 29 (1963) 134ff.; W. Schmithals, *Die Theologie Rudolf Bultmanns*, 1966, 129ff., 306ff. Cf. Güttgemanns, *Der leidende Apostel*, 386-412.

17. Cf. Schniewind, *KuM*, vol. I, 102ff.

18. Cf. *ibid.*, 105f.

19. *Ibid.*, 106.

20. Cf. H. Ott [cited in n. 16], 116; Ott, in *Kerygma und Mythos*, vol. 4, H.-W. Bartsch, ed., 1955, 117; W. Kreck, *Die Zukunft des Gekommenen*, 1961, 71f.

21. Cf. O. Cullmann, *Christus und die Zeit*, 1948-2nd ed.; Cullmann, *Heil als Geschichte*, 1965. J. M. Robinson, in

"Heilsgeschichte und Lichtungsgeschichte," *EvTh* 22 (1962) 113-41; *Interpretation* 16 (1962) 91ff.; and "The Historicality of Biblical Language," in *The Old Testament and Christian Faith*, B. W. Anderson, ed., 1964, 124-58, wants to modify the heilsgeschichtliche conception in the sense of the later Heidegger: The issue concerns "historicality" as the fusion of historicity and historicalness.

22. Cf. J. Moltmann, *Theologie der Hoffnung*, 1964.

23. Cf. W. Pannenberg, "Heilsgeschehen und Geschichte," *KuD* 5 (1959) 218-37, 259-88; *Offenbarung als Geschichte*, W. Pannenberg and others, eds., 1961; Pannenberg, "Hermeneutik und Universalgeschichte," *ZThK* 60 (1963) 90-121; Pannenberg, *Grundzüge der Christologie*, 1964, 47ff.

24. Cf. E. Käsemann, "Die Anfänge christlicher Theologie," *ZThK* 57 (1960) 162-85 (= *Aufs.*, vol. 2, 82-104); and "Zum Thema der urchristlichen Apokalyptik," *ZThK* 59 (1962) 257-84 (= *Aufs.*, vol. 2, 105-31).

25. R. Bultmann, *Geschichte und Eschatologie*, 1964-2nd ed. (orig. Engl. ed., 1955).

26. Cf. on this G. R. Edwards, "Opportunity for Interdependence," *Interpretation* 18 (1964) 285-303.

27. There is still no carefully discriminating survey of the vast literature. However cf. J. M. Robinson, *Kerygma und historischer Jesus*, 1960; R. Bultmann, *Das Verhältnis der urchristlichen Christusbotschaft zum historischen Jesus*, 1961-2nd ed. Cf. also the studies in P. Biehl, "Zur Frage nach dem historischen Jesus," *ThR* 24 (1957-58) 54-76; P. Althaus, *Der gegenwärtige Stand der Frage nach dem historischen Jesus*, 1960; E. Lohse, "Die Frage nach dem historischen Jesus in der gegenwärtigen neutestamentlichen Forschung," *ThLZ* 87 (1962) 161-74; J. M. Robinson, "The Recent Debate on the 'New Quest'," *JBR* 30 (1962) 198-208; Sch. M. Ogden, "Bultmann and the 'New Quest'," *JBR* 30 (1962) 209-18; H. Anderson, "Existential Hermeneutics," *Interpretation* 16 (1962) 131-55.

28. Cf. n. 11 above.

29. E. Käsemann, "Das Problem des historischen Jesus," *ZThK* 51 (1954) 125-53 (= *Aufs.*, vol. 1, 187-214).

30. Käsemann, "Sackgassen im Streit um den historischen Jesus," *Aufs.*, vol. 2, 31-68.

31. *Ibid.*, 95.

32. Cf. *ibid.*, 56.

33. Cf. Käsemann, *Aufs.*, vol. 1, 235.

34. Cf. *ibid.*, 194.

35. Cf. *ibid.*, 235.

36. Cf. *ibid.*, 191, 194f.

37. Cf. Käsemann, *Aufs.*, vol. 2, 43.

38. Cf. Käsemann, in *BEvTh* 15, 150; *Aufs.*, vol. 1, 236; *Aufs.*, vol. 2, 43.

39. Cf. Käsemann, *Aufs.*, vol. 1, 192.

40. Cf. *Aufs.*, vol. 2, 53.

41. Cf. *Aufs.*, vol. 1, 195.

42. Cf. Käsemann in *BEvTh* 15, 150; *Aufs.*, vol. 1, 189, 235; *Aufs.*, vol. 2, 42.

43. Cf. Käsemann, *Aufs.*, vol. 1, 195, 213. Cf. also Ch. W. F. Smith, "Is Jesus Dispensable?", *AnglThR* 44 (1962) 263-80.

44. Cf. Käsemann, *Aufs.*, vol. 2, 53.

45. *Ibid.*, 66. The historical sequence narrative-tradition--hymns--letters is indeed here an analytically unproven premise; only so could one refer to a "recourse". But how can the uniqueness of the hymns not be determined by their form and "sociological setting" (in the sociological sense!), next to which in *the same* community other forms with another "sociological setting" should have been present, so that we distinguish several structurally determined linguistic fields from one another, but cannot make tradition-historical distinctions? *De facto* an *argumentum e silentio* is used here, for it has not been proved that the presumed community has used *only* the hymns. The structurally determined linguistic fields studied in linguistics represent the main objection against the usual tradition-historical splitting-up of the materials. Cf. below, p. [198ff.].

46. Cf. *ibid.*, 61: The history of Jesus is only faith-
fully maintained where narrative and repetition are the motives for the writing of gospels.

47. Cf. *ibid.*, 47: "For it seems to me that no one
writes a gospel but finds the gospel form inadequate, if
one is not concerned about the earthly Jesus."

48. *Ibid.*, 61.

49. Cf. Käsemann, *Aufs.*, vol. 1, 192f.: The relationship of the N. T. writings to the history of Jesus is sharply
distinguished. "It is especially noteworthy that only the
gospel serves the Christ-message in the framework of the history of the earthly life of Jesus.

50. Cf. on this *ibid.*, 195-99.

51. Cf. *ibid.*, 202f.; *Aufs.*, vol. 2, 67.

52. *Ibid.*, 68.

53. Similarly also J. P. Martin, "Beyond Bultmann,
What?", *ChrTo* 6 (1961) 188-91; D. T. Rowlingson, "The Gospel-
Perspective and the Quest of the Historical Jesus," *JBR* 33
(1965) 329-36.

54. Käsemann, *Aufs.*, vol. 2, 66.

55. For a fresh grounding of my interpretation of Bultmann, cf. the inherent criticism in Güttgemanns, *TheolPract*
3 (1968) 87-100. There I have especially emphasized the significance of the real presence for Bultmann's theology.

56. Precisely with regard for the dignity of the historical I have included the following hermeneutical excursis
within the framework of this book.

57. Cf. the extensive treatment in Güttgemanns, *Der
leidende Apostel*, 388-93.

58. Cf. *ibid.*, 393-403.

59. Käsemann, *Aufs.*, vol. 2, 43.

60. Cf. *ibid.*, 42f.

61. Cf. Käsemann, *Aufs.*, vol. 1, 213: To be sure, no
Life of Jesus can be reconstructed; but at the same time we

need not concede, "that because of this situation we must give in to resignation and scepticism and allow ourselves to be disinterested in the *earthly* Jesus" (my emphasis). *Ibid.*, 195: Primitive Christianity's conception of the in-separability of its own history of faith from the history of Jesus, and its rejection of the abstraction of a purely "historical Jesus" "may not, naturally, lead us to press the question concerning the *earthly* Jesus in spite of the precarious-ness of such a question, in so far as it is raised in isolated fashion, and in spite of the difficulty of answering it" (my emphasis).

62. Cf. on the contrary W. Kreck, "Die Frage nach dem historischen Jesus als dogmatisches Problem," *EvTh* 22 (1962) 460-78.

63. Cf. above, p. [26ff.]

64. Cf. above, p. [26].

65. Cf. Güttgemanns, *Der leidende Apostel*, 383ff.

66. Cf. O. Cullmann's concession, *Heil als Geschichte*, 75, 118f. Cf. my criticism, *VF* 12/2 (1967) 46f.

67. Cf. A. Jolles, *Einfache Formen*, 1965-3rd ed., orig. 1930.

68. Cf. Käsemann, *Aufs.*, vol. 2, 54: To be sure, the dominant feature of the gospels is "the kerygmatic interest. However they express it in the form of the gospels which as such have not the form of preaching, but of reporting." Thereby an antithesis between the kerygmatic and the histori-cizing tendencies of the gospels is set up, one which comes quite clearly from the premise that the form of the gospel is "history", not kerygma.

69. I have worked on the single proof in terms of the theme "'Mythos' and 'History' as Categories in the Under-standing of Reality" in another essay. Because of the rea-sons cited, I must remain dependent upon that work in the framework of this book.

70. Cf. P. Weigandt, *Der Doketismus im Urchristentum und in der theologischen Entwicklung des 2. Jahrhunderts*, Theol. Diss. Heidelberg, 1961.

71. Its determination is explored by M. Dibelius, *Die Formgeschichte des Evangeliums*, 1959-3rd ed., 265ff. It is

wrong to object too quickly that we no longer have to do with a "formal" concept, since in such a manner form and content would be separated. Cf. below, pp. [65ff., 161ff.]. Nonetheless there remains here a terminological aporia. [+1978: It seems to me to be one of the sad things in the history of research that Bultmann could not relate his concept of myth to that of C. Lévi-Strauss, who developed a "myth-formula" in logical terms. A correlation of Bultmann's concept with that of Lévi-Strauss' would prove the former to be totally untenable.]

72. Cf. below, p. [63ff.].

73. Cf. the quotation in n. 68.

74. Cf. Käsemann, *Aufs.*, vol. 1, 190ff.

75. Cf. above, p. [28f.].

76. Cf. above, p. [27f.].

77. So O. Cullmann, *Heils als Geschichte*, 1965. For criticism, see Güttgemanns, *VF* 12/2 (1967) 44-49.

78. Cf. the suggestion below, p. [107ff.]

79. Cf. Käsemann, *Aufs.*, vol. 2, 105 n.; 107, n. 2 from the previous page; *ZThK* 62 (1965) 147f.

79a [+1978: During my research it became very clear that e.g. the smallest content units of narrative, the so-called "motifemes", are universals, so that differences between the gospels and other narratives are hardly *semantic*; they can be only *pragmatic*. Cf. Güttgemanns, "Erzählstrukturen in der Fabel von Wolfgang Amadeus Mozarts 'Zauberflöte'. Ein Beitrag zur Heiterkeit der Kunst und zum 'historischen Jesus," *LingBibl* 31 (1974) 1-42.]

80. Cf. in more detail Güttgemanns, *Der leidende Apostel*, 46ff.

81. Cf. Fuchs, *Aufs.*, vol. 1, 93f., 99; G. Ebeling, *Wort und Glaube*, 1960, 333f.

82. On the linguistic concept of "sign", cf. below, p. [41f.].

83. The foregoing reflections therefore surround the program-horizon of a more complex questioning, as well as

solution of the problems. That the solution is only suggested in this book has to do with the hermeneutical situation which in my opinion is constantly to be experienced, one which can first be attained after clarification of essential preliminary questions in a number of approaches to a new breakthrough in the history of research.

#2. *The Fundamental Victory of Form Criticism in Germany.*[1]

1. Form Criticism in Germany: Victory or Stagnation?

The contemporary situation of German research on the gospels[2] can be characterized by the fundamental victory of the form-critical approach.[3] On the basis of suggestions by H. Gunkel,[4] F. Overbeck,[5] and finally J. G. Herder and the "romantic school",[6] the foundations for the approach were laid and individual analyses tested by K. L. Schmidt,[7] M. Dibelius,[8] R. Bultmann,[9] and others.[10] [p. 36] Subsequently, criticism arose both with respect to fundamentals and to specific aspects,[11] and it has continued right up to the present, especially from the Roman Catholic side.[12] However this criticism has scarcely had an impact on exegetical practice in Germany.[13]

Due to the fragmentary character of the perspective of each study, it is difficult to analyze the contemporary situation in detail. At any rate it is scarcely too hasty to judge that the form-critical approach is by and large recognized and consolidated in Germany. All shades of German research on the gospels utilize form-critical insights to a greater or lesser degree, although occasionally these are ascribed to the development of a particular school; and there have been no new fundamental proposals, if we pass over A. N. Wilder[14] and G. Schille[15] and do not consider the new genres, [p. 37] "Christ-stories"[16] and "missionary or regional legends".[17] Is form criticism more or less moribund?[18]

H. Conzelmann, on the basis of a similar analysis of the
situation, does indeed suggest: "If we glance at the present
activity in N. T. studies, we may be impressed by a certain
stagnation of form-critical work. The method is, on the one
hand, still treated as the developments of a school, but on
the other hand it is watered down into a formal and aesthetic
way of regarding texts."[19]

Such stagnation may be due to two causes: First, the
method may have reached certain natural limits because of its
own inner nature; its possibilities exhausted, its results so
generally accepted that no one thinks about further developments. Second, the stagnation may be determined by a shift-
ing of research onto other methods and directions, so that
certain aspects of the form-critical method are left to develop on their own, such as the question about the hermeneutical relevance of form-critical findings.[20] The two causes
complement one another and partly determine each other.

[p. 38] Now it can certainly be asked, in view of certain signs of uncertainty and purely half-hearted participa-
tion, whether there is in the general awareness an acknowledged reception and affirmation of the principles originally
determinative for form criticism, or rather a well-meaning
tolerance that by no means thinks of itself as decisively
tied to the form-critical method. At any rate W. Klatt, in
his very informative work on H. Gunkel, substantiates a
break between Gunkel and today's form critics. This break
consists in the fact "that we utilize in theology today an
exegetical method for which the theological presuppositions
that came to light with it and have always accompanied it
are no longer fully shared".[21] Klatt rightly refers in this
connection to the remarkable fact that the form-critical
method did not disappear with the revolution in the history
of theology brought about by dialectical theology that

threatened its foundations, but has proved itself to be a
method that is independent[22] of the world-view connected to
the history of religions school.[23] Although Klatt takes this
development as the occasion to refer programmatically to the
new theology of the history of religions originating in the
circle around W. Pannenberg which is associated with form
criticism (= tradition history),[24] and hence gives to theology a renewed linking of form criticism and the history of
religion under *theological* auspices,[25] his analysis of the
situation in the history of theology with reference to the
humanistic and metaphysical roots of central form-critical
principles is more accurate than Klatt apparently realized.[26]
What if somehow the stagnation of form criticism diagnosed by
Conzelmann were unconsciously related to the tensions between
these roots and today's more positivistic and formalistic attitude,[27] so that it would be an indication of an unacknowl-
edged separation between contemporary form criticism and its
own foundations in the humanities? I state this question
here without any thetic intention; it must be seen in the
course of the work whether or not the educated guess is correct. However if such a hunch is correct, [p. 39] one question must be asked, namely as to which contemporary foundations might replace the older ones. Perhaps sociology as the
methodological foundation of a series of linguistically-related disciplines? Chapter #3, below, will explore this
possibility further.

   2. Is Form Criticism Merely an Ancillary Dis-
       cipline to Historical Research?

It can scarcely be denied that even in Germany N. T.
studies is often reluctant to grant that the form-critical
method has developed a distinctive and fundamentally *theo-*

logical value in its reference to history and thereby to the safe-guarding of Christianity as a "historical religion".[28] Above all on the Roman Catholic side--especially since the Encyclical *Divino afflante Spiritu* of Pope Pius XII (1943)[29] --there has been a gradual revision of the originally sharply critical or at least sceptical attitude toward the form-critical method,[30] not without inner struggles,[31] since only careful regard for the *forma dicendi* and the *genus litterarum* as a contemporary accommodation of the biblical authors[32] could confirm the historical value of the sources. With respect to the historical truth of the gospels, the form-critical method has been almost a duty, at least since *Instructio de historica Evangeliarum veritate*, issued 21 April 1964 by Pope Paul VI:[33]

> In order to put the abiding truth and authority of the Gospels in their full light, [the Catholic exegete] will accurately adhere to the norms of rational and Catholic hermeneutics. He will diligently employ the new exegetical aids, above all those which the historical method, taken in its widest sense, offers to him....As occasion warrants, the interpreter may examine what sound elements are contained in the 'Form-Critical method' that can be used for a fuller understanding of the Gospels. But let him be wary, because scarcely admissible philosophical and theological principles have often come to be mixed with this method, which not uncommonly have vitiated the method itself as well as the conclusions in the literary area. Others begin with a false idea of faith, as if it had nothing to do with historical truth--or rather were incompatible with it. Others deny the historical value and nature of the documents of revelation almost *a priori*. Finally, others make light of the authority of the apostles as witnesses to Christ, and of their task and influence in the primitive community, extolling rather the creative power of that community. All such views

> are not only opposed to Catholic doctrine, but
> are also devoid of scientific basis and alien
> to the correct principles of historical meth-
> od.[34] Unless the exegete pays attention to
> all these things which pertain to the origin
> and composition of the Gospels and makes
> proper use of all the laudable achievements
> of recent research, he will not fulfil his
> task of probing into what the sacred writers
> intended and what they really said.[35]

In this statement of function, the form-critical method
is devalued from status as a key discipline for the linguistic shape of biblical texts to being merely an ancillary discipline to historical research. What is to be determinative-
ly convincing in this respect would be something like the
certainty of the gospels as "history" in the statement of S.
Gonzales de Carrea, O. F. M. Cap.: "The gospels are and contain history. But the measure of this historicity and of the
historical intention of the evangelists cannot be deduced *a
priori*.[36]

J. Jeremias seems to ascribe a similar, purely ancillary
value to the form-critical method. He gives five reasons for
considering scepticism as unjustified--especially R. Bultmann's scepticism with respect to eliciting genuine Jesus-
materials from the synoptic tradition:[37, 38] Literary criticism takes us back to the stage [p. 41] of oral transmission;
form criticism gives us insight into the origin and development of the transmission; historical work on the period [of
the N. T.] discloses to us Jesus' environment; research on
Jesus' mother tongue deepens our knowledge of that environment; and discovery of the eschatological character of Jesus'
message creates a protective defense against a psychologizing
modernization of Jesus.[39] It is striking in this argument
that form criticism is not listed as the central method for
the study of the linguistic phenomenon of the "text", but as
one method among many others, and that it is utilized only in

terms of historical concern for the *ipsissima verba* [the
actual words] of Jesus.[40] E. Käsemann has so comprehensive-
ly and appropriately dealt with the theological and hermeneutical implications of this concern[41] that I can be satisfied
here with closer analysis of Jeremias' evaluation of the form-
critical method.

Indeed Jeremias has a notion that the usefullness of form
criticism can be compared with the usefulness of the archaeological reconstruction of strata to the historian. The essential significance of form criticism consists for him in "that
it helps us to identify a hellenistic layer that has been deposited over an older Palestinian transmission".[42] K. G. Kuhn
correctly judges the methodology of a book by Jeremias when he
suggests:[43] The author proceeds "like an excavator who wants
to break through the superimposed levels to the original level,
which is the only important one".[44]

However it can certainly be asked whether, in such an
application of the form-critical method, the linguistic phenomenon, for which the method is designed is recognized in
its own right. Is the linguistic form essentially a *reference* to the history lying behind it?[44a] It is amazing that
the language or the linguistic signs (*signa*) are repeatedly
related to the *facta* and the *res* directly, even though already Aristotle understood the *signum-res* schema within the
framework of his doctrine of affects as a spiritual process,
and this was taken up into Christian hermeneutics and tied to
the doctrine of the multiple meanings of scripture by Augustine:[45] That which is vocalized is a symbol [p. 42] of the
psychic affects; that which is written is a sign of that
which is vocalized.[46] What is indicated by the verbal sign
(*semeion*) is therefore essentially something related to the
soul and spirit (*pathēmata*), a psychic replication (*homoiōma*)
of the *res* (*pragma*).[47] The linguistic *signum* has no immediate

reference to the *res*, but only an indirect one by means of the linguistically-shaped understanding (*noēma*) of humankind.[48] Linguistic matters (*onoma, heēma*) stand for matters of thought (*noēma*): *Stat aliquid pro aliquo* [the one takes the place of the other].[49] Similar ideas are found in the work of F. de Saussure, the founder of modern structural linguistics,[50] as well as in the linguistic discipline that is associated with W. v. Humboldt.[51]

Christian theology is hardly unfamiliar with the linguistic problem touched here, and indeed it was the major object of the controversy about universals in the Middle Ages:[52] Every linguistic sign is something general, a universal concept (*universale*); but the *res* signified by the *signum* (*universale*) is, on the other hand, something individual, at any rate so long as we are not talking about "ideal" concepts (for example freedom, justice, love, etc.). We have a right to signify the various types of *res* with *one signum* only when the *res* that are so combined [p. 43] have something in common that makes them comparable, in other words, when they are related by analogy. The linguistic principle of analogy is the presupposition for universals. As is well known, there were three standpoints in the related controversy: objective idealism (Platonism; *universalia sunt* ante *res*), critical realism (Aristotelianism; *universalia sunt* in *rebus; universalia sunt realia*), and nominalism (*universalia sunt* post *res; universalia sunt nomina*). These three positions reappear once again in contemporary linguistics in modified form.

From these linguistic problematics of the principle of analogy and linguistic generalization, discovered long ago, theological hermeneutics can learn the following: *Within* language there is *never* a *res bruta* (in Kantian terms: a "Ding an sich"), something lacking any linguistic realization, a non-understood, non-spiritually shaped *res*.[53] Within a linguistic context the *res* is always spiritually shaped, always somehow understood by means of language, and spiritually appropriated by means of "naming". *Within language there are only facta per principium analogiae linguisticae interpretata*, since already the phenomenon of linguistic concepts presupposes the functioning of the principle of analogy. The "fact-"concept often appealed to in the contemporary christological debate has not been reflected upon from a linguistic viewpoint and miscarries in terms of the principle of analogy that lies at the basis of every linguistic phenomenon.

Wouldn't it be better if a linguistically-instructed theology would evaluate the linguistic signs and gestalten, and therefore the forms and genres also,[54] not as "sources" for history, but as "signs" of an understanding,[55] which in our case is to be more precisely stated as christological understanding? I raise the question here only in order to indicate the hermeneutical relevance of a linguistic fructifying of form criticism.[56] In spite of our self-limitation in this book, it will be demonstrated that this is a meaningful question.

Notes to #2

1. Cf. the accounts in O. Cullmann, "Die neuen Arbeiten
zur Geschichte der Evangelientradition," (originally in French,
1925) in *Vorträge und Aufsätze*, K. Fröhlich, ed., 1966, 41-89;
M. Goguel, "Une nouvelle école de critique evangelique: la
'form- und traditionsgeschichtliche Schule'," *RHR* 94 (1926)
114-60; M. Dibelius, "Zur Formgeschichte der Evangelien," *ThR*
1 (1929) 185-216; J. Schniewind, "Zur Synoptiker-Exegese,"
ThR 2 (1930) 129-89, above all 161-89; K. Grobel, *Formgeschichte und Synoptische Quellenanalyse*, 1937, 5ff.; V. Taylor, *The Formation of the Gospel Tradition*, 1957-6th ed.
(orig. 1933), 9ff., 22ff.; G. Iber, "Zur Formgeschichte der
Evangelien," *ThR* 24 (1957/58), 283-338; Iber, "Neuere Literatur zur Formgeschichte," in M. Dibelius, *Formgeschichte*, 1961-
4th ed., 302-12; K. Koch, *Was ist Formgeschichte?*, 1967-2nd
ed.; H. Zimmermann, *Neutestamentliche Methodenlehre*, 1967,
128ff.

2. For a presentation of a certain consensus consult G.
Bornkamm, "Evangelien, formgeschichtlich," *RGG*-3rd ed., vol.
2, 1958, 749-53.

3. So also W. Klatt, *Hermann Gunkel: Zu seiner Theologie der Religionsgeschichte und zur Entstehung der formgeschichtlichen Methode*, 1969, 11, with reference to the general
situation. (Dissertation, 1966, is occasionally cited.)

4. Cf. below, p. [154ff.].

5. Cf. below, p. [106f.]. [+1978: It is doubtful that
the relation between form criticism and Overbeck is as recti-
linear as was formerly supposed. Cf. J.-C. Emmelius, *Tendenz-
kritik und Formengeschichte*, 1975. Emmelius was a pupil of P.
Vielhauer, and attained to quite other results concerning Overbeck's point of view when he utilized all the relevant unpublished manuscripts.]

6. Cf. below, pp. [120ff., 126ff.].

7. K. L. Schmidt, *Der Rahmen der Geschichte Jesu*, 1919;
Schmidt, "Die Stellung der Evangelien in der allgemeinen Lit-
eraturgeschichte," in *Eucharisterion*, vol. 2, 1923, 50-134;
Schmidt, "Formgeschichte," *RGG*-2nd ed., vol. 2, 1928, 638-40;
Schmidt, "Geschichtsschreibung II," *ibid.*, 1115-1117; Schmidt,
"Fondement, but et limites de la méthode dite la 'Formgeschich-

te' appliquée aux Evangiles," *RHPhR* 18 (1938) 1-26; Schmidt,
Kanonische und apokryphe Evangelien und Apostelgeschichten,
1944.

8. M. Dibelius, *Die Formgeschichte des Evangeliums*,
1919, [1961-4th ed.], ed. G. Bornkamm; Dibelius, *Geschichte
der urchristlichen Literatur*, 1926, two vols.; Dibelius, "The
Structure and Literary Character of the Gospels," *HThR* 20
(1927) 151-70; Dibelius, "Evangelienkritik und Christologie,"
1935, in *Botschaft und Geschichte*, vol. 1, G. Bornkamm, ed.,
in assoc. with H. Kraft, 293-358. Cf. also Dibelius, *Die ur-
christliche Ueberlieferung von Johannes dem Täufer*, 1911.

9. R. Bultmann, *Die Geschichte der Synoptischen Tradition*, 1921, 1957-3rd ed. with supplement; Bultmann, *Die Erforschung der synoptischen Evangelien*, 1925, 1960-3rd ed.; Bultmann, "The New Approach to the Synoptic Problem" *JR* 6 (1926)
335-62; Bultmann, "Evangelien, gattungsgeschichtlich," *RGG-*
2nd ed., vol. 2, 1928, 418-22.

10. Cf. for instance M. Albertz, *Die synoptischen Streitgespräche*, 1921; Albertz, "Zur Formgeschichte der Auferstehungsberichte," *ZNW* 21 (1922) 259-69; Albertz, *Die Botschaft
des Neuen Testaments*, vol. I/1, 1947; G. Bertram, *Die Leidensgeschichte und der Christuskult*, 1922; Bertram, "Die Bedeutung
der kultgeschichtlichen Methode für die neutestamentliche Forschung," *ThBl* 2 (1923) 25-36; P. Fiebig, *Der Erzählungsstil
der Evangelien im Lichte des rabbinischen Erzählungsstils un-
tersucht*, 1925; Fiebig, *Rabbinische Formgeschichte und Geschichtlichkeit Jesu*, 1931.

11. Cf. E. Fascher, *Die formgeschichtliche Methode*, 1924;
L. Köhler, *Das formgeschichtliche Problem des Neuen Testaments*,
1927; B. S. Easton, *The Gospel before the Gospels*, 1928; V.
Taylor, *Formation*, 9ff.; E. B. Redlich, *Form Criticism: Its
Value and Limitations*, 1939; B. P. W. Stather Hunt, *Primitive
Gospel Sources*, 1951, 103ff.; H. Riesenfeld, *The Gospel Tradi-
tion and its Beginnings*, 1957; W. S. Taylor, "Memory and the
Gospel Tradition," *ThToday* 15 (1958/59) 470-79; G. Schille,
"Der Mangel eines kritischen Geschichtsbildes in der neutesta-
mentlichen Formgeschichte," *ThLZ* 88 (1963) 491-502.

12. Cf. H. Dieckmann, "Die formgeschichtliche Methode und
ihre Anwendung auf die Auferstehungsberichte," *Scholastik* 1
(1926) 379-99; E. M. Braun, *Où en est le problème de Jésus?*,
1932, 215-65; D. E. Florit, "La 'Storia delle Forme' nei vangeli in rapporto alla dottrina cattolica," *Bibl* 14 (1933) 212-
48; Florit, *Il metodo della "Storia delle Forme" e sua appli-
cazione al racconto della Passione*, 1935; F.-X. Peirce, "Form

Criticism of the Synoptics," *EcclRev* 93 (1935) 85-97; E.
Schick, *Formgeschichte und Synoptikerexegese*, 1940; P.
Benoit, "Réflexions sur la 'formgeschichtliche Methode',"
RB 53 (1946) 481-512; S. Muñoz Iglesias, "Géneros literarios
en los Evangelios," *Estudios Bíblicos* 13 (1954) 289-318; A.
Wikenhauser, *Einleitung in das Neue Testament*, 1956-2nd ed.,
182-99; J. Leal, S.J., "Forma, historicidad y exégesis de las
sentencias evangélicas," *Estudios Eclesiásticos* 31 (1957) 267-
315; X. Léon-Dufour, S.J., "Bulletin d'exégèse du Nouveau
Testament: Formgeschichte et Redaktionsgeschichte des Evangiles synoptiques," *RechSR* 46 (1958) 237-69; Anonymous (J.-J.
Weber), "Formgeschichte. Wert und Grenze dieser Methode für
das Neue Testament," *HerKorr* 17 (1962-63) 425-29; R. Schnackenburg, "Zur formgeschichtlichen Methode in der Evangelienforschung," *ZKTh* 85 (1963) 16-32.

13. An orientation to the reaction in Anglo-Saxon lands
is provided by K. Emmerich, "Die formgeschichtliche Betrachtung der Evangelien in der englischen theologischen Literatur," *Kirchenbl. ref. Schweiz* 98 (1942) 2-4. Specific criticism: V. Taylor, *The Formation of the Gospel Tradition*, 1933,
1957-6th ed.; E. B. Redlich, *Form Criticism*, 1948-2nd ed.,
34ff.; R. P. Casey, "Some Remarks on Formgeschichtliche Methode," in *Quantulacumque: Studies Presented to K. Lake*, 1937,
109-116.

14. Cf. A. N. Wilder, *The Language of the Gospel*, 1964.

15. Cf. G. Schille, "Das Leiden des Herrn," *ZThK* 52
(1955) 161-205; "Die Topographie des Markusevangeliums, ihre
Hintergründe und ihre Einordnung," *ZDPV* 73 (1957) 133-66;
"Bemerkungen zur Formgeschichte des Evangeliums (I). Rahmen
und Aufbau des Markus-Evangeliums," *NTS* 4 (1957/58) 1-24; "II.
Das Evangelium des Matthäus als Katechismus," *ibid.* 101-14;
"III. Das Evangelium als Missionsbuch," *NTS* 5 (1958/59) 1-11;
"Der Mangel eines kritischen Geschichtsbildes in der neutestamentlichen Formgeschichte," *ThLZ* 88 (1963) 491-502; "Zur
Frage der ersten christlichen Gemeindebildung," *FF* 37 (1963)
118-21; *Anfänge der Kirche*, 1966; "Erwägungen zur urchristlichen Kirchenbildung," in P. Wätzel and G. Schille, eds.,
Theologische Versuche, 1966, 66-83; "Der Beitrag des Evan-
gelisten Markus zum kirchenbildenden (ökumenischen) Gespräch
seiner Tage," *KuD* 12 (1966) 135-53; and "Die Topologie und
die christliche Gemeindebildung," *FF* 40 (1966) 151-53.

16. Cf. G. Bornkamm, *RGG*-3rd ed., vol. 2, 1958, 752:
The stories are characterized by the fact "that they are
molded by faith from the start, and express faith--often by
use of legendary motifs--even when they connect to historical

givens and present themselves as reports (Baptism, Temptation, Ascension, Infancy Narratives in Matthew and Luke, Resurrection Accounts, *et al.*)".

17. Cf. G. Schille, *ZDPV* 73 (1957) 137ff.; Schille, *Anfänge der Kirche*, 64ff. Some examples would be: Mark 5:1-20, 7:24-30, 8:22-26, 10:46-52; Luke 19:1-10; Matthew 8:5-13; Luke 10:38-42, 17:11-19, *et al.* We cannot here discuss the way these initial points have been developed further--partly in a way full of fantasy--toward a tradition-historical differentiation of a Jewish congregation in Bethany, one in Emmaus, one in Jericho, a Jordanian baptist-group, a Joseph-tradition, a North-Galilean circle, a Decapolis congregation, and a Cana congregation (cf. Schille, *Anfänge der Kirche*, 160ff.).

18. Cf. L. J. McGinley, *Form-Criticism of the Synoptic Healing Narratives*, 1944, 154. [+1978: This should be a signal: W. Schmithals told me a few months ago (August 1977) that he now denies form criticism in the gospels more or less totally. What remains if this is already granted?!]

19. Conzelmann, *VF* 7 (1956/57) 151f. Similarly, Iber, *ThR* 24 (1957/58) 285. Cf. Bornkamm, *Aufs.*, vol. 3, 16.

20. Cf. E. Fuchs, *Hermeneutik*, 1958-2nd ed., 177ff.; Güttgemanns, *Der leidende Apostel*, 34-36, 291-94; R. W. Funk, *Language, Hermeneutic, and Word of God*, 1966, 224ff.

21. Klatt, *op. cit.*, 13.

22. Cf. p. [161ff.].

23. Cf. Klatt, *op. cit.*, 13f.

24. Cf. *ibid.*, 5f.; Klatt, *VF* 10 (1960/62, 1963/65) 201f.

25. Klatt considered this undertaking promising and apparently untouched by the crisis in dialectical theology, since W. Pannenberg's universal-historical conception lay *behind* Neo-Kantianism from a history of ideas perspective (cf. Diss., 389), i.e. the Neo-Kantianism that had wrongly distinguished between "historical" and "theological" (*ibid.*, 6). I will not be able to discuss in this connection this argumentation, which in my opinion appears to be tautological.

26. For substantiation, cf. below, p. [126ff.].

27. Also Klatt, Diss., 6 n. 12, criticizes the formalistic direction of contemporary form-critical studies.

28. Cf. C. H. Dodd, *History and the Gospel*, 1960 (orig. 1938), 11ff.

29. Cf. the extract in H. Denzinger and K. Rahner, *Enchiridion Symbolorum*, 1957-31st ed., No. 2294.

30. Cf. the bibliography given in Zimmermann, *Ntl. Methodenlehre*, 17 n. 1, as well as in R. Schnackenburg, "Der Weg der katholischen Exegese," *BZ* 2 (1958) 161-76; J. L. McKenzie, "Problems in Hermeneutics in Roman Catholic Exegesis," *JBL* 77 (1958) 197-204; D. M. Stanley, S.J., *ThSt* 20 (1959) 565-70; L. Alonso-Schökel, S.J., "Genera litteraria," *VD* 38 (1960) 3-15; H. Haag, "Zum Verhältniss Exegese-Dogmatik," *ThQ* 142 (1962) 1-22; W. M. Abbott, "Pius XII's Encyclical on Bible Study," *Bible-Today* 1 (1963) 439-43; P. G. Duncker, O.P., "Biblical Criticism," *CBQ* 25 (1963) 22-33; C. Kearns, O.P., "The Present Situation in Catholic Gospel Exegesis," *IrEccl Rec* 99 (1963) 289-309.

31. Cf. J. A. Fitzmyer, S.J., "A Recent Roman Scriptural Controversy," *ThSt* 22 (1961) 426-44; S. Schulz, "Die römisch-katholische Exegese zwischen historisch-kritischer Methode und lehramtlichem Machtanspruch," *EvTh* 22 (1962) 141-56; B. Brinkmann, "Die Glaubwürdigkeit der Evangelien als hermeneutisches Problem," *ZKTh* 87 (1965) 61-98.

32. Cf. Denzinger, *op. cit.*, 687f.

33. Cf. the text in *VD* 42 (1964) 113-20. Cf. C. M. Martini, "Adumbratur quomodo complenda videatur argumentatio pro historicitate Evangeliorum synopticorum," *VD* 41 (1963) 3-10; C. Kearns, O.P., "The Instruction on the Historical Truth of the Gospels," *Angelicum* 41 (1964) 218-34; A. Bea, S.J., "La storicita dei vangeli sinottici," *Civilta Cattolica* 115 (1964) 417-36; J. A. Fitzmyer, S.J., "The Biblical Commission's Instruction on the Historical Truth of the Gospels," *ThSt* 25 (1964) 386-408; J. Bukovski, "La verdad historica de los evangelios," *Revista Biblica* (Buenos Aires) 27 (1965) 167-78; G. Gamba, S.D.B., "Considerazioni in margine alla poetica dei Vangeli," *Rivista Biblica* (Italiana) 13 (1965) 289-302.

34. *VD* 42 (1964) 114f. [In place of the original Latin quoted by Güttgemanns, I have used the translation by Joseph A. Fitzmyer, S.J., in Augustin Cardinal Bea, S.J., *The Study of the Synoptic Gospels: New approaches and outlooks*, 1965,

which was originally published in *Theological Studies* 25 (1964) 402-8. - W.G.D.]

35. *Ibid.*, 117. [See note on translation in n. 34 - W.G.D.]

36. S. Gonzales de Carrea, O.F.M. Cap., "El método histórico-redaccional en los evangelios sinopticos," in *Naturaleza y Gracia* (= *NatGrac*) 11 (1964) 225 (translation: "The gospels are history, contain history. But the measure of this historicity, of the historical intention of the evangelists cannot be deduced *a priori*.") Cf. also J. Leal, S.J., art. cited in n. 12 above; A. Descamps, "De historiciteit van de synoptische evangeliën," *CollBrugGand* 6 (1960) 145-62; A. Vögtle, "Die historische und theologische Tragweite der heutigen Evangelienforschung," *ZKTh* 86 (1964) 385-417; M. Zerwick, S.J., "Historicidade dos Evangelhos," *RevCultBib* 1 (1964) 89-104; J. Alonso-Díaz, "Fidelidad y libertad histórica de los Evangelistas," *CultBib* 23 (1966) 3-10; A. Quacquarelli, "Il riflessi storici negli schemi letterari dei Vangeli," *RivistBib* 14 (1966) 279-93; M. Sabbe, "De historische zin van de Bijbel," *CollBrugGand* 11 (1965) 116-33. Cf. also #13, n. 83, below.

37. Cf. above, p. [26f.].

38. J. Jeremias, "Der gegenwärtige Stand der Debatte um das Problem des historischen Jesus," in H. Ristow and K. Matthiae, eds., *Der historische Jesus und der kerygmatische Christus*, 1960, 12-25, especially pp. 20-23.

39. I have shown in *VF* 12/2 (1967) 43, that on the contrary the categories of "consistently eschatological" interpretation are seemingly psychological. Cf. also below, p. [95f.].

40. Cf. also J. Jeremias, "Kennzeichen der ipsissima vox Jesu," 1954, now in *Abba*, 1966, 145-52.

41. Cf. Käsemann, *Aufs.*, vol. 2, 32-41.

42. Jeremias, *Der histor. Jesus*, 21.

43. Cf. Jeremias, *Die Abendmahlsworte Jesu*, 1960-3rd ed.

44. K. G. Kuhn, *ThLZ* 75 (1950) 400.

44a [+1978: In this case a text is understood as an "icon", i.e., a mirror-reflection, of history. This implies

a Leninist theory of perception and knowledge: mental phe-
nomena--such as texts--are a superstructure (Ueberbau) above
matter, which is ontologically prior to spirit. Cf. L. O.
Resuikow, *Erkenntnistheoretische Fragen der Semiotik*, 1968.]

45. Cf. Augustine, *De doctrine christiana* I-III (Migne
P. L. 34, 15-122) and on that, G. Ebeling, *RGG*-3rd ed., vol.
3, 1959, 249. - The linguistic theory of signs, semiotics,
will likewise be treated in the anticipated special publication. Cf. however R. Gätschenberger, *Zeichen, die Fundamente
des Wissens*, 1932; K. Bühler, *Sprachtheorie*, 1965-2nd ed.;
E. Benveniste, "La structure du signe linguistique," *Acta
Linguistica* 1 (1939) 23ff.; E. Lerch, "Vom Wesen des sprachlichen Zeichens," in *ibid.*, 145ff.; W. Bröcker and J. Lohmann,
"Vom Wesen des sprachlichen Zeichens," *Lexis* 1 (1948) 24ff.;
A. Nehring, "The Problem of the Linguistic Sign," *Acta Linguistica* 6 (1950) 1ff.; Nehring, *Sprachzeichen und Sprechakte*,
1963.

46. Cf. Aristotle, *De interpretatione* I.16a.4: "Spoken
words are the symbols of mental experience and written words
are the symbols of spoken words." (W. D. Ross, ed., *The Works
of Aristotle*, vol. 1, 1928, transl. E. M. Edghill.)

47. *Ibid.*, 11.7ff. "...all men have not the same speech
sounds, but the mental experiences, which these directly sym-
bolize, are the same for all, as also are those things of
which our experiences are the images."

48. *Ibid.*, 11.12f.: "Nouns and verbs, provided nothing
is added, are like thoughts without combination or separation...." My attention was called to this connection by A.
Korzybski's *General Semantics*. Cf. S. I. Hayakawa, *Semantik*,
1967-2nd ed., 232ff., 263ff., 281ff.

49. Cf. Bühler, *Sprachtheorie*, 40f.

50. Cf. F. de Saussure, *Cours de linguistique generale*,
Ch. Bally, A. Sechenaye, A. Riedlinger, eds., 1967-new ed.
(orig. 1916), 97ff., 158ff.

51. Cf. B. L. Whorf, *Sprache, Denken, Wirklichkeit*, 1968-
4th ed. (orig. 1963), P. Krausser, ed.; L. Weisgerber, *Von
den Kräften der deutschen Sprache*, I. *Grundzüge der inhaltbezogenen Grammatik*, 1962-3rd ed.; II. *Die sprachliche Gestaltung der Welt*, 1962-3rd ed.; III. *Die Muttersprache im Aufbau
unserer Kultur*, 1957-2nd ed.; Weisgerber, *Die vier Stufen in
der Erforschung der Sprachen*, 1963 (Sprache und Gemeinschaft,
vol. 2, L. Weisgerber, ed.); Weisgerber, *Das Menschheitsge-*

setz der Sprache als Grundlage der Sprachwissenschaft, 1964
(orig. 1951). Cf. also the presentation of H. Basilius, "Neo-
Humboldtian Ethnolinguistics," *Word* 8 (1952) 95-105, and in
the publication planned.

52. Cf. J. Klein, "Universalienstreit des MA," *RGG*-3rd
ed., vol. 6, 1962, 1151-57; E. Heintel, "Einige Gedanken zum
Universalienproblem," *Studium Generale* 18 (1965) 509-18, as
well as J. Reiners, *Der aristotelische Realismus in der Frühscholastik*, Diss. Bonn, 1907; Reiners, *Der Nominalismus in der
Frühscholastik*, 1910. On linguistics in general cf. J. Pin-
borg, *Die Entwicklung der Sprachtheorie im Mittelalter*, 1967.

53. Cf. E. Heintel, "Herder und die Sprache," in J. G.
Herder, *Sprachphilosophische Schriften*, E. Heintel, ed., 1964-
2nd ed., xv-lxvii.

54. For substantiation, see below p. [53].

55. To be sure this contradicts Barr, *op. cit.* However
that very servicable book, because of its one sided reliance
on a positivistic-formalistic direction of structural linguistics, has some evident weaknesses at this point. Cf. L.
Alonso-Schökel, S.J., "Teologia biblica y linguistica," *Bibl*
43 (1962) 217-23; Th. Boman, *Das hebräische Denken im Vergleich mit dem griechischen*, 1968-5th ed., 194-213.

56. Cf. also L. Alonso-Schökel, S.J., "Hermeneutics in
the Light of Language and Literature," *CBQ* 25 (1963) 371-86;
Alonso-Schökel, "La Biblia como obra literaria," *Cultura
Biblica* 20 (1963) 131-48; "El proceso de la inspiracion:
Hablar y escribir," *Bibl* 46 (1965) 269-86; "The Function of
Language in the Scriptures," *Continuum* 3 (1965) 22-32; and
Sprache Gottes und der Menschen, 1968 (orig. English ed. 1965).

#3. Sociology as the Methodological Foundation of Form Criticism and of Linguistics and Literary Criticism Generally.

1. Form Criticism's Understanding of Sociology.

According to H. Conzelmann, form criticism represents: "the acceptance of a *sociological* approach: A text is only understood when the narrating community is drawn into the exegesis, when its 'sociological setting' ['Sitz im Leben'] has been recognized (naturally such an approach is only appropriate for particular texts, namely those of a pre-literary type)."[1] In the conflict between individualistic and sociological concepts of history, form criticism has, as a matter of fact, opted for the sociological position[5]--in contrast to scholars like A. Jülicher[2] and J. Weiss[3] each of whom is a significant forerunner of form criticism:[4] If the form truly betrays something about its origins, the application of an anti-individualistic, sociological inquiry is possible,[6] one in which individual personalities disappear behind the materials.[7] "The so-called form-critical approach does not ask, to the extent that literary criticism [Literarkritik--what English-speaking criticism refers to as source criticism, W.G.D.] did, who wrote this or that source; rather form criticism talks about the community out of whose collective life the primitive Christian literature, and especially the gospels, were composed."[8]

The sociological inquiry encompasses all the essential points of form-critical conceptuality. The search for the "sociological setting" is "not directed toward the individual occurrence that in each case is foundational to the narrative, but toward the typical, permanent sociological condition...to which the narrative points".[9] The "'sociological setting' [p. 45] refers to a societal reality which has become customary through its use in a particular culture and which plays such a definite role for speakers and hearers or writers and readers that the utilization of a particular linguistic genre becomes necessary".[10] Therefore the style which is impressed by a particular "sociological setting" and which belongs to a particular form is "not a matter of aesthetic fancy but a matter of sociological fact".[11] We may never forget "that form and style are more than the raiments available for idiosyncratic use by the narrator in which he can clothe his account, but rather they are a function of the life of the community, an index of its needs and interests, a moment of its history".[12] "Inquiry from the point of view of cultic history" (G. Bertram)[13] shares with form criticism an anti-individualistic, sociological emphasis: "it is not the personality of the individual evangelist...that determines the formalizing of the material, but rather the collective, the congregation, that creates particular genres."[14] M. Dibelius' "proclamation" is also a sociological category; he refers to "the theologically and sociologically significant circumstances in which the spiritual activity of the Christian community bursts forth".[15] Hence the most important concepts of form criticism are concerned with "illuminating the interrelation between style, form, and genre on the one hand, and the life of the primitive Christian congregation on the other".[16]

Occasionally M. Dibelius also utilized sociological arguments when referring to details of the evaluation of the history of primitive Christianity. In his opinion the "sociological nature of the congregation" ruled out the possibility of genuinely scholarly work in the oldest congregations.[17]

Dibelius likewise sought to explain the process of Christianity's transition from the Palestinian area into the hellenistic world as a change of sociological structure: "The gospel message presupposes, both spiritually and socially, Galilean agriculture." "A completely different situation prevailed when Christianity entered the hellenistic world. It gradually altered its sociological structure, became a state religion, and slowly engaged the upper classes; its eschatological hope was relocated or subsided. Since the sociological and eschatological restrictions over against the world became weaker, Christianity suffered [p. 46] pressure to become like the world", as can be observed in the Christian literary genres.[18] Palestinian Christianity's estrangement from the world, "determined by the eschatological faith and the sociological character of the congregations",[19] yielded to openness to the world and adaptation to it.

It may be remarked in passing that this historical sketch strikes me as rather hypothetical, since as far as I can see we can say nothing with certainty concerning the sociological structure of the early churches beyond the quite general reference to the "galilean fishermen" and passages like I Cor 1: 26-31; it would be best not to sketch whole historical canvases on the bases of conjectures alone.[20] However another matter is much more important.

To be sure one must respect the relativity of this new orientation to the philosophy of history within the history of research.[21] However as concerns a decided option in the *philosophy* of history, there are always sociological premises to form-critical research, even if this option when used by someone like Dibelius has not been made philosophically explicit. At any rate its roots lie in A. Comte's attack on the metaphysical foundations of the scientific disciplines and his simultaneous "positive" re-foundation of them.[22]

Hence the option for a sociological conceiving of the hypothetical premises of a form-critical interpretation of the
empirical material, concerns from the beginning a particular
philosophical and hermeneutical attitude to precisely this
material, which in contrast to the other attitude has the
particular feature of being devoted to the criteria of factu-
ality, usability, certainty, and exactness as the four primary
features of "genuine", i.e., "positive" philosophy[23] of the
empirical side of the material. Just these hermeneutical implications of the sociological conception of form criticism--
sometimes all too quickly forgotten--have indeed been the
primary hindrances causing the initial hesitancy of older
exegesis rather than rapid acceptance: "The researcher's
positive or negative attitude to a new method is always more
or less consciously determined by the acceptance or rejection
of the sociological conception."[24]

     With respect to the sociological conception of the form-
critical method, [p. 47] N. T. research today stands, in my
opinion, at a decisive turning point. Insofar as M. Dibelius'
conceptual model is related to theses of J. G. Herder or older folkloristics,[25] it cannot be considered today, in view of
the crisis in more recent folkloristics and its revision of
the mostly metaphysical foundations of the principles of
Herder and the "romantic school", to be operating in a completely neutral realm.[26] New Testament studies should not
take too lightly the scientific revolution taking place in
folkloristics;[27] it should not minimalize it by asserting
today--in contrast to the period when form criticism was being established--that the self-understandability of the general reference to the phenomenon of analogy in German folkloristics is irrelevant because the hypothetical assessment
in the circular method of form criticism[28] has become so certain by its verification in the entire synoptic material that

it no longer needs renewed reflection about methodological
foundations and their justification. Indeed it could be that
the stagnation of form-critical research diagnosed by H. Conzelmann[29] represents the calm before the storm that should be
evaluated as an indication of a crisis already initiated in
its own territory--this would be the case if the impression
of certainty begins to disappear when we look at the results
of the general scientific and theoretical situation of form
criticism. As I see it we are faced with a renewed and more
critical conflict concerning the appropriateness of a decidedly sociological foundation of form criticism, which will lead
in some manner to a modified approach within the history of
research, especially with respect to the synoptic gospels.
W. Marxsen has already initiated this conflict with his thesis concerning the discontinuity of form and redaction criticism and his reference to the tension between the sociological
conception of form criticism and redaction criticism's interest in the more individual factors.[30] The almost unilateral
rejection of this thesis indicates, in my opinion, that this
is not a passing fashion but a decisive problematic for future
gospel research. However [p. 48] commentary on this prolepsis
of the wider course of events must be omitted here, where we
are only concerned to call attention to the importance of the
decision for a sociological understanding of form criticism
in the general consciousness.

If the option for a sociological understanding is still
to be valid today, and given the crisis in folkloristics and
the present realization that metaphysical implications of essential methodological premises cannot simply be assumed uncritically, I see only *one* possibility that will stand up well
in the conflict between an individualistic and a sociological
classification of the N. T. forms, namely to direct our attention beyond the traditional boundaries of the disciplines of

the humanities to the sociological orientation of general linguistics and literary criticism. The following materially necessary over-stepping of the boundaries is to be comprehended
in terms of the fundamental indications argued in our introductory remarks to this volume.

   2.   General Linguistics as the Scientific and
        Theoretical Foundation of the Humanities,
        and the Linguistic Tasks of Theology.

   Since all the disciplines in the humanities make some
sort of reference to "linguistic" phenomena,[31] general linguistics[32] is the scientific and theoretical foundation of
all the humanities.[33] Since language is the carrier and medium of understanding,[34] and since understanding can be regarded as the methodological foundation of the humanities,[35]
the common foundation of literary criticism and linguistics
is to be found in the hermeneutical [p. 49] center of understanding:[36] "consideration of the nature of poetry[37] demands
prior consideration of the nature of language."[38] This methodological connection between literary criticism (and therefore of form and redaction criticism) and linguistics forces
us to the course of action adopted here.

   Although scholars in the exegetical disciplines have
frequently referred to philological foundations,[39] one unique
fact can be determined if we regard the details of their works
critically: The lack of a fundamental linguistic training, at
least on the part of most German exegetes, works to the disadvantage of methodological integrity, above all in lexicographic and conceptual investigations, but also in endeavors
in the history of religion and motif-criticism. Therefore J.
Barr was fundamentally correct in raising the reproach that
in their theses various exegetes "stubbornly disregard linguistic matters well known in the linguistic usage of the

Hebraic and Greek Bible, and distort the results".[40] The
sweeping lack of knowledge of linguistic methodology has
far-reaching consequences not only for philological analysis
oriented to a single term, but also especially for descrip-
tions oriented to the morphology of larger linguistic structures, and hence, for example, for form and redaction criticism and the history of religion. Therefore Barr concludes
his criticism with this challenge: "Only by a direct and
systematic treatment of the significative function of language generally conceived, can false interpretive methods in
theology be held in check."[41]

3. The Sociological Foundations of Structural
    Linguistics (Ferdinand de Saussure, and
    Others)[41a]

Although to my knowledge linguistics seems to have exercised a greater influence in the fields of Germanic and Romance language studies, and in English and Slavic studies than
in biblical and exegetical studies, [p. 50] unfortunately it
can only be stated with reference to the humanities generally,
that especially since 1900[42] linguistics has remained a scientific stepchild[43] in spite of many fruitful initiatives.[43a]
That is probably partly due to the fact that the everyday self-
understandability of our speaking, the abundance of the available lexicographic and grammatical resources,[44] and the inclination to positivism[45] at the same time that there was a
disinclination against apparently too-powerful influences on
linguistics from quasi-metaphysical language philosophy,[46]
all seduced us into a hermeneutical naivete that thought of
the phenomenon of language as being readily accessible or in
most cases sufficiently studied by philologists. Nevertheless
language is *the* fundamental hermeneutical problem![47]
     Modern linguistics can hardly be conceived of without the

decisive influences of F. de Saussure (1857-1913).[48] At least since his work, linguistics distinguishes two fundamental aspects within language, for which currently de Saussure's French terminology is retained [also in English!, W.G.D.]: The phenomenon of language [*Sprache*] (*langage*)[49] [p. 51] has a sociological aspect (*la langue*) and an individual aspect (*la parole*).[50]

As *language* [*Sprache*] (*langue*) it is a transindividual, purely-psychic, sociological *system* of distinct signs which correspond to distinct spiritual ideas,[51] a system *"qui ne connaît que son ordre propre"*,[52] since it is ontologically pre-given to speaking [*Sprechen*] (*parole*), although speaking presupposes language historically and hermeneutically:[53] Language and speaking form one circle of meaning.[54]

As *speaking* (*parole*), a linguistic phenomenon is an individual, psycho-psychic, occasional *act*,[55] which is ordered according to the laws and structure of language (*langue*),[56] that is, language "insofar as it is actualized by a speaker in a particular moment".[57]

If we co-ordinate the "speech acts" ["Sprechhandlungen", "Sprechakte", and "Sprechereignisse"] with *parole*,[58] we can use "language events" ["Sprachereignisse"] for the aspect of *langue*,[59] i.e., "language events" as events in the objective sphere of language that allows reality to appear *as* reality, because it is ontologically prior, as the linguistic forming power, to every "speech event" ["Sprechereignis"].[60] This co-ordination demonstrates the cross connection between linguistics or metalinguistics and the so-called "new hermeneutic" in N. T. exegesis, as represented for instance by E. Fuchs,[61] although it has been asserted [p. 52] that in the "new hermeneutic" the specific linguistic problematics has been insufficiently regarded,[62] and a somewhat differently utilized concept put forward.

That the distinction between a linguistics of *langue* and
a linguistics of *parole* thereby described implies difficult
methodological problems with respect to individual details,
can here only be briefly indicated. For instance, it provokes the question whether language (*langue*) can be derived
on the one hand exclusively from the speech act (*parole*), that
is, from the speaking *zoon politikon*,[63] if on the other hand
we should be able to investigate *langue* actually separated
from *parole*.[64] Does speaking humankind constitute language
(*langue* = mother tongue) by means of concrete speech acts,
which give expression to the sensual apperception of non-linguistic reality?[65]--the consequence would be an orientation of
linguistic psychology to experimental psychology.[66] Or is
there also an influence upon language (*langue*) addressed and
expressed by the non-linguistic object or subject matter acting simultaneously with the speaker, so that language does not
operate completely arbitrarily, according to Th. Hobbes' theory of convention or agreement,[67] but is also an aspect of the
spiritual "gestalt" of the subject matter being affected by
that which is linguistically perceived?--in this case linguistic psychology would also be mobilized by the object![68]

Such inquiries are certainly something other than purely
theoretical and abstract; rather they have concrete influences
upon the form-critical method. One aspect of the differentiation of *langue* and *parole* is especially important for our form-
critical and theological investigation, namely the sociological
trend in understanding language as structure (*langue*), corresponding to the sociological trend of form criticism or serving as its reduction to the linguistic foundation [p. 53] of
form criticism:[69] As it is not, for form criticism, a con-
crete-individual speech-situation or a single person (speaking a *parole*) who is held responsible for the origination or
specification of a form, but rather a sociologically-deter-

mined collective language-situation, so for the French school of sociology that is connected with A. Comte (but also extensively in linguistics),[70] language (*langue*) is "a collective manifestation, which like every higher spiritual activity cannot be studied on the basis of the individual alone".[71] Language as a system (*langue*) is not the object of individual psychology, but of cultural psychology in W. Wundt's sense:[72] "Although it is in close relationship to certain manifestations of the individual consciousness, it is tied like myth, custom, law, and art to social life. The isolated individual would never attain to the creation of a language."[73]

Also belonging to language as structure (*langue*) are language-formations or language-works,[74] i.e., in literary-critical perspective, the forms and genres. In this sense the forms are, as structurally determined genres, a manifestation of *langue*, not of *parole*, although the single concrete expressions of the form, and therefore the textual "evidences" for the single forms, as concrete manners of manifestation of general sociological laws, are to be accounted absolutely to *parole*.[75] This means methodologically *that the forms must be analyzed fundamentally according to the principles of the linguistics of langue*, not according to the principles of the linguistics of *parole*: Do stylistic peculiarities of fixed forms[76] possess a defineable structural value (*valeur*)[77] within form as structure (*langue*), or do they actually belong to an individual's style, and therefore to *parole*? Do fixed terms [p. 54] in fixed forms have a structural value (*valeur*)?, i.e., Is their "significance" tied to a fixed structure, that of the form?[78] At this point questions of this type can only be indicated, but the indication is sufficient to establish the methodological relevance of the linguistics of *langue* for biblical form criticism, and to show in which respect form criticism's sociological disposition could be

justified by an alliance with linguistics, with respect to the
crisis of the folkloristic entanglement. At the same time
such questions prepare the way for our thesis that only an
alliance of form criticism and linguistics can deal with the
problem renewed by W. Marxsen, namely the problem of the more-
sociological or more-individual integration of the form of the
gospels and their style.[79] Only such an alliance could solve
the problem on a material and above all empirical and positivistic level,[80] if this level is truly to be regarded as the
principle of historical-critical exegesis.[80a]

4. The Structural Value (*Valeur*) of All
   Linguistic Phenomena.

The structural contours that are widely accepted in
subsequent modern linguistics are connected to the methodological distinction we have just sketched. Following F. de
Saussure's description of *langue* as a language-system having
its own *structure*,[81] linguists transferred their interest from
the positivistic analysis of individual linguistic phenomena
to the analysis of the structure of *langue*:[82] The philological and atomistic study of statistics of details was super-
seded by a type of morphology closely related to syntax; lexi-
cography, morphology, and syntax form a methodological whole.[83]

[p. 55] According to de Saussure's methodological clarification a word (term)[84] can no longer be studied semantical-
ly[85] as an isolated element in itself.[86] "Each element must
be regarded within its functional value in the framework of
the structural system"; that means the end of atomic semasiology and the beginning of the synoptic, functional, and structural method.[87] The word (term) is embedded in various structural matrices (*langue*), i.e., in phonological, etymological,
contextual, morphological, and other structures.[88] Thereby

linguistics recognizes the merely *relative* semantic autonomy of the word (term);[89] in a "structuralist approach"[90] not only is the lexical morphology of the word (term) studied,[91] but also its syntactic morphology,[92] in short, its structural syntax.[93]

Within the language structures each word has the *valeur* that co-determines and alters its "significance", i.e., a functional value of signification determined by the language-system.[94] In the case of an entire fabric of structures--as for instance in the case of the forms of literature[95]--a word (term) has in many instances a unique *valeur* for each individual structure,[96] and this is as true for the realm of *langue*[97] as it is for the realm of *parole*.[98]

In this manner a large number of structural connections is obtained [p. 56] for a word:[99] "On the level of discourse the word is a part and an element of a context, and on the level of language, a part and an element of the linguistic systems of structure and value."[100] Such a language-system can, for example, be implicit in a fixed rule for the sequence of words,[101] or in a word combination that has become conventional,[102] which must be analyzed as the linguistic context of a word.[103]

Hence language (*langue*) consists not only of semantemes and morphemes,[104] but also of asemantemes,[105] of systememes[106] and their "fields" and the synsemantica functioning in these "fields";[107] in short, language consists of the various *valeurs* of a term, which are determined by the system of conventions of *langue*,[108] and which constitute the context of signification of the term.[109]

Hence analysis of the "significance" of a linguistic phenomenon corresponding to the language structure[110] will both study the functions (*valeurs*) of the specific structural elements of a *langue*,[111] and also distinguish carefully between just this structural *valeur* and its lexicographic and effective reduction and abstraction.[112] Here A. W. de Groot's warning statement must be taken seriously: "A doctrine of meaning without a structural theory of the meaning is...nowadays inconceivable."[113]

[p. 57] This excursus concerning some of the essential foundations of structural linguistics was necessary to avoid leaving the suggestions concerning the value of linguistics for form criticism completely without content, and the assertion that the common methodological foundations of both linguistically-related disciplines is in sociology without any rationale. Unfortunately I must forego here any more precise presentation and testing of what I consider to be possible and requisite inquiries within form criticism that are specifically linguistic; I will save them for an anticipated monograph. Here, initially, we have made only necessarily sketchy reference to the sociological inquiry formulated in the disciplines that are related to form criticism. In the course of this book, however, it will be seen at several points just how much is to be learned from this sketch, even given our rather limited assignment (cf. the conclusion, #15, Section 8).

5. The Connections between Form Criticism and the Sociology of Literature.

(a) Connections between Form Criticism and Literary Criticism.

Consideration of general and comparative literary criticism[114] and above all of the sociology of literature[115] is part of a contemporary reorientation of the sociological conception of form criticism. The methodological connection between literary criticism, [p. 58] and hence form and redaction history, and linguistics, has become inescapable in the contemporary research of linguistically-related studies.[116] If N. T. studies are yet today the result of F. Overbeck's programatic statement of the secular character of the historical and form-critical attitudes,[117] then there is, at any rate, no *theological* right to forbid our glancing at the related disciplines in the humanities, and N. T. studies can only attempt to reintegrate into form criticism the secular character of the linguistic and literary-critical methods.[118]

It is only natural that there will be many specific difficulties in attempting such a re-integration as is presented here as an initial attempt, since such an understanding will often strain one's powers to their utmost. Hence a good deal may and must remain hypothetical. However this hypothetical character can only be regarded as a call to shared work on the path that has been indicated, in which case certain self-corrections will result from the hypotheses themselves. Here it will suffice to have indicated the fundamental possibility of the expansion of the methodological horizon on the basis of F. Overbeck's program for a secular presentation of the history of the primitive Christian literature.

One possible objection to appropriating literary-critical methods and results, and especially those of the sociology of literature, would be a reference to the special character of "Kleinliteratur"--which may not be confused with or assimilated to literature proper.* However this objection is im-

---

*I have left Kleinliteratur in German, since there is no exact English equivalent. Kleinliteratur (as opposed to Grossliteratur, or literature-proper) refers to folk products not intended primarily for publication, minor folk genres, etc., as opposed to what is self-consciously literature, and to formal literature proper. W.G.D.

proper for two reasons. First so-called "oral literature" is also naturally an object of literary criticism,[119] and therefore is a phenomenon comparable to "Kleinliteratur". [p. 59] Second, there is no opposition whatsoever between form criticism and literary criticism, "since form and genres are manifested in higher literature, i.e., in the works of individual authors and poets, just as in anonymous Kleinliteratur, even though the forms and genres may be partly different ones".[120] In order to obtain greater distinction between form and literary criticism, R. Bultmann distinguishes between "literature" in the narrower sense, and "literature" in the wider sense: To the former "belong only those writings in which the *forms* have taken on independence and have their own laws, in which not only *what* is being said, but above all *how* it is said is significant". However "literature" also has a further meaning, "because it encompasses here not only the written, but also the oral word".[121] Bultmann's description corresponds completely to literary criticism's contemporary self-understanding, so that the objection mentioned above is finally only a secondary matter, of a purely terminological nature. Therefore there is a thoroughly positive relation between form and literary criticism:[122] The goal of form criticism is a primitive-Christian literary criticism.[123] To be sure it has not yet been completely realized.[124]

(b) The Sociological Understanding of Forms as a Counterbalance to the Aesthetic Understanding.

As already indicated, the actual representatives of form criticism understand the sociological arrangement of the material as being in tension with its aesthetic evaluation.[123a] The style which characterizes a genre is "not a matter of aesthetic fancy but a sociological fact"; "it has its origins in particular historical situations which are thereby typical".[125]

Analysis of genres serves historical research rather than aesthetics,[126] precisely because it illuminates the sociological processes in the development of primitive Christianity.[127] The anti-individualistic, sociological view is not to be confused with the aesthetic. "That would have to be evaluated on the basis of the relatively [p. 60] expert perfection that is possible, and hence have to distinguish between popular and educated style, between collective and individual art. Many stimulating ideas can be derived from such a position; however they would always be supplementary, either presupposing or completely ignoring scientific findings. Scientific results would be gained by the aesthetic approach to the gospels only if it brings about comparative analysis of the forms of other religious literature and attempts to develop an aesthetic for religious texts."[128] Consequently form criticism is a decidedly sociological rather than an aesthetic method.

This ties form criticism to the newer tasks of the sociology of literature.[129] Since sociology holds to the fundamental principle of value-free judgment,[130] since the sociology of literature in particular "regards the literary work not as an artistic but as a social phenomenon, there is for it no possibility of aesthetic evaluation".[131] The aesthetic and the sociological may not be conflated and an attempt made "in analogy to the possibility of regarding an aesthetic object as a social phenomenon, to regard the pure social phenomenon aesthetically".[132] As a science oriented to social, intersubjective acting or behavior, the sociology of literature is "not interested in the literary work as an aesthetic object; rather literature is significant to it only insofar as there are within literature specifically interpersonal actions involved. Therefore the sociology of literature deals with humans who are acting within the literature; its object is the interactions of the persons who participate within the literature."[133]

According to this definition of the task by H. N. Fügen, the sociology of literature belongs along with linguistic behaviorism[134] to the broader context of behavioristics. Its object is "an interpersonal acting completed within and for literature which on closer inspection shows itself to be a complex of forms of interpersonal behavior. This complex of behavioral forms cannot be scientifically and clearly specified without its being related to the corresponding aspects of social reality."[135] Behavior proper to literature involves a type of "cultural model"[136] which, as a sociological law similar to *langue*, determines individual behavior:[137] "Literary behavior ruled by the cultural model precedes the individual, and the individual cannot depart from it without stepping outside the sphere of literature. This is to a certain extent the culturally-objectified side of the social phenomenon of literature."[138]

In specific applications, the sociology of literature has not progressed nearly so far as sociological and structural linguistics; "it is also lacking agreed-upon and binding methods and determination of goals".[139] Therefore an actually productive enrichment of form criticism by stepping outside the traditional disciplinary boundaries cannot presently be recognized at first glance. However there has been sociological research concerning form and style which has sought "the social preconditions for the origination, growth, decline, and neglect of particular genres, forms, and styles".[140] H. N. Fügen, for example, has proposed a sketch of Western developments using this format.[141] Caution toward having form criticism simply work by analogous steps must be suggested, however, since these studies for the most part have had little reference to "Kleinliteratur" as the object of the sociology of literature, at least not at the present time.

Such caution should not be taken to indicate that there can be absolutely no further connections between form criticism and the sociology of literature today. The oral and written character of genres and problems related to the traditions between both are also related to the issue of behavioral forms found in discussing literature in the widest sense.[142] Since this complex of issues poses particular difficulties for form and redaction criticism, the work at hand is restricted to this extract from what is currently underway in the sociology of literature; this will be expanded later.[143]

[p. 62] 6. Form Criticism: History of Language Events or of Speech Events? (A Quarrel with the Anti-Sociological Criticism of the Form-Critical Method by the So-Called "New Hermeneutic".)

(a) "Freedom to the Word" or Linguistic Regularity?

Today to be sure one must mention the specifically theological problem caused by the sociological expansion of form criticism we have surveyed. The main question is whether the sociological conception of form criticism, and especially the concept of the "sociological setting", is sufficiently appropriate to the actual content of the N. T. considered as a word event.[144] After all, the sociological approach reckons with a certain regularity of the linguistic process, which dismisses form, or at least only leads to form concurrently. Isn't there something lost thereby, something that might be called in N. T. terms (Ro 8:15, Gal 4:6f.)--as E. Fuchs does--"freedom to the word"?[145] If the genuine appearance of the forms actually depends upon "freedom to the word", then it is freedom and not the law that sets the word free. How far may theology, which indeed sees the question of truth presupposed by this N. T. assertion,[146] take the law methodologically into account, as in the form of sociological regularities?--this be-comes a theological problem corresponding to a particular meth-odology for specific exegetical studies. Indeed traditional form criticism implies with its "sociological setting" the thought that every word has its time, or better: that we *must* have time for the word in order *to be able* to speak our own word.[147]

But when is this time given to us? If we want to trust the facts of the N. T. this time is only permitted us at a particular "place", described by the time-indicator *en Christō*.[148] So the N. T. modulates When? into Where?:[149] Where is time for the word given us? There, for example, where to us Jesus' proclamation as permission for freedom at the same time raises permission in language,[150] where the crucified modulates into the word of the cross with permis-sion for all people to believe,[151] [p. 63] where therefore the "language event"[152] addresses the believer as one already encompassed by love and so finds his being-for-the-neighbor permitted[153] or "is granted entrance into God's presence".[154]

According to this train of thought that E. Fuchs develops, freedom toward our word is granted to us only where our lan-guage is in analogy to God's language in Jesus,[155] where therefore our word co-responds to the nature of language, which is permission.[156] Here we have to do with a language-understanding "for which the word signifies the gain of free-dom and the freedom of gain".[157]

Within such a hermeneutic, oriented to the facts of the N. T.,[158] it is appropriate to reject an all-too-sociological orientation of form criticism,[158a] and to regard the creation of the gospel-form not only as a sociological process, but as "a genuine occurrence of being in language itself".[158b] Hence the decisive hermeneutical step is "similarly as in the ques-tion about the How? of understanding to the question about the

Where? of that which is to be understood".[159]

H.-D. Bastian, especially, has raised sharp protest
against such a decidedly theological view of linguistic phenomena.[160]   He formulates his statements in a self-consciously
provocative manner as an attack on the widely prevalent Theology of the Word. This theology is linguistically naive;[161]
its "speaking about the uniqueness of the proclamation is a
myth, which receives its nourishment from the unclear sources
of a verbal doctrine of transsubstantiation".[162]   On the basis
of mathematical and cybernetic information theory one can only
judge: "The sermon is precisely not effective *ex opere opera-
to*."[163]   The unobserved [p. 64] loss of effect of linguistic
truth is to be explained today by means of cybernetics:[164]
ignoring the structural and functional laws of the communication process leads to the death of the kerygma as a linguistic
form.[165]   This leads to the thesis: "Without linguistic exer-
tion the transmission of the gospel to modern persons will
simply not succeed."[166]   "A form criticism of ecclesiastical
speech will therefore not be able to avoid concerning itself
seriously with 'knowledge of communications media'."[167]   "The
dogmatic theorem 'proclamation' would have to be deciphered in
concrete, applicable forms of speech if its communicative
power were to be analyzed."[168]   But even if hermeneutics, in
the light of Ro 10:17, is inseparably tied to cybernetics:
"Faith is a specific function of the activation and processing of information."[169]   "The message concerning God's acting
does not exist at all without the physically graspable fact,
that is without the human signal as its bearer."[170]   Therefore
we need a methodology "that critically teaches what is and
what is not possible in communication systems--what is real
and what simply fantasized."[171]   "The linguistic possibilities
of Christians are precisely as extensive as those of any
speaking person."[172]   "There are no other informational and

communicational media available to the church that are not
elsewhere available, just as the means of communication are
by no means fundamentally different."[173]   The category "Word
of God" is not an ecclesiastical super-weapon![174]

I cannot, within the framework of this book, go into the
field of mathematical and cybernetic information theory thereby drawn into theological polemics and above all into homi-
letics,[175] and can only refer again to the intended publication mentioned above.[175a]   But it is certainly clear that
Bastian in his own way denies the truth question which theologians understand as being implied by the N. T. references:
What happens in language is not experienced from the mythological and metaphysical expressions of the N. T., to which E.
Fuchs constantly refers, but from modern information-theory.
If N. T. theology [p. 65] does not latch onto this argument,
it has negatively decided against not only the truth value of
the N. T. theology, but also fundamentally against its own
theological right to exist; at most it would be an archival
science.

At least Bastian's proposal has the merit of having
called attention to a lasting aporia: Is the appropriately
sufficient method for study and description of the N. T.
language phenomenon to be studied by means of modern linguistics in the widest sense, as in form criticism, or also by
means of the N. T.'s own understanding of this language phenomenon? We will certainly have to guard against an all too
simple alternative and to seek out a means of bringing together the satisfactory aspects of each standpoint in a hermeneutical and linguistic discussion. Neither an absolute
rejection of the N. T. expressions concerning language phenomena because they are "mythological and metaphysical" is
possible, nor a hermeneutics that accepts in linguistics *only*
the so-called "language events" that rob history of its power

but ignores the continually present regularity of the "speech events". Such a conception would represent a dialectic of law and gospel dissolved into an enthusiast's conception of history![176] To support this assertion we engage the reflections of E. Jüngel which are connected with those of E. Fuchs.

(b) The Identity of "Form" and "Content" in "Language Event".

In the framework of his hermeneutical work E. Jüngel has presented a methodological consideration of the relationship between eschatology and form criticism,[177] in which he also reflects upon the problematics of the "sociological setting". In the process he rejects the traditional conception of form criticism especially with respect to the breaking of the circle between "form" and "content".

The distinction between "form" and "content" is in this connection influenced by idealism; it is not appropriate to the facts, since in the eschatological parables of Jesus (Mt 13:44-46, 13:47f., 13:24-30; Mk 4:26-29, 4:30-32//Mt 13:31f.// Lk 13:18f.; Lk 11:5-8, 16:1-7, 15:11-32; Mt 20:1-15; Lk 10:30-35)[178] the proclaimed *basileia* cannot be separated as "content" from the [p. 66] parable-"form"; rather, in the completion of the parable the *basileia* itself occurs "linguistically": *"form" and "content" are identical in the linguistic event of the parable.*[179] To separate them for the purposes of conceptualization is actually inappropriate.[180]

The traditional, form-critically-oriented exegesis of the parables[181] has not observed this fact stringently enough, according to Jüngel: "Although the content of the text is certainly not to be made responsible for its form, even so analysis of the form is made fruitful for the understanding of the content of the text."[182] This hermeneutical function of form criticism however is only meaningful when to the hermeneutical

accessibility of the "content" by means of the "form"--indeed
as "form"--there is a corresponding ontological determination
of the "form" by means of the "content" in the manner of a
circle: "Insofar as something enters language *in* a linguistic form, it enters language more primally (ontologically) *as*
this linguistic form."[183] "For if form and content create a
primal unity, we would not only have to make the form responsible for the content, but likewise the content responsible
for the form of a transmitted language event."[184]

Such ideas are not new as such, but they are new within
their contemporary hermeneutical context. It was already
fundamentally clear in H. Gunkel's methodological clarification of form-critical principles that the form and the content of a work of art are not totally separable.[185] And also
in modern literary criticism, as seen for instance in the Russian formalists (V. Šklovskij, B. Eichenbaum, B. Tomaševskij,
R. Jakobson, V. Žirmunskij, J. Tynjanow),[186] the separation
of "form" and "content" is avoided: "It is the ideal of interpretation...to synthesize the contents and form of the
poetic work as clearly and as fully in consciousness as possible by constant interrelation of form and content."[187] In
the aesthetic structure of a literary work "form" and "material" have formed a complete unity.[188] As concepts placed
next to one another, on the other hand, they are used only
by a few; "already by the most careful [p. 67] separation of
the concepts the work of art is simply divided into two components".[189]

The disputed question arising between Jüngel and the in-
herited understanding of form criticism becomes to what extent
the "content" is determined by its "setting" in society, that
is by sociological needs, and to what extent it is self-deter-
mined. Jüngel appeals to R. Bultmann's concession that it is
not correct "to ask *only* about purpose and needs, since a spir-

itual possession also objectifies itself without any special
purpose".[190] Jüngel therefore concludes: "that which desires
to be expressed in language can or must enter language of itself; consequently the linguistic form *at least* is *also* determined by that which is itself entering language."[191]

In Jüngel's marked narrowing of the generalization of a
concession made by Bultmann in passing lies the entire problem. It lets itself be clothed in the question whether then
every realization of a linguistic form may already *a priori*
be taken to represent a "language event".[192] Only if this
question is to be unconditionally affirmed, is it methodologically permitted to focus on something prior to the sociological questioning by emphasizing the eschatological language
event,[193] which is thought to constitute the realm of sociological phenomena first and foremost.[194] Only if it can be
said unconditionally and without exception for any individual
case that in the new questioning "the eschatological *extra nos*
of the *basileia* must be regarded" as that moment constituted
in the form-critical genres in Jesus' proclamation "which desires to become *Word*",[195] can the possibility be denied that
in the individual case it has not finally been the "form" that
has determined the "sociological setting". In other words:
only when "form" and "content" *actually* are identical in the
individual instance in the "language event", can we differentiate the "historical location" of the transmission from its
"ontological place of origin",[196] which as the divine language
history of Jesus' love [p. 68] is determined by Jesus' "behavior",[197] and so is identical as "language event" with the occurrence of the kingdom of God.[198] If however in a single
case a "language event" may be presupposed, if something not
only "wants to, can, or must enter language",[199] but actually
has been actualized in language; or differently: if the gospel *has* replaced the law,[200] that can no longer determine a

generally accessible method, but only one which occurs at the locus of the language event.[201]   To be sure, Jüngel's view has its moments, but we must repeat again the question,[202] whether in his case the category of the "language event" has not all too often and all too rapidly concealed the difficulties of the individual occurrence, since the planes of method and existence, objectivized representation, and believing inclination are no longer distinguished as they were by R. Bultmann.[203]

Notes to #3

1. H. Conzelmann, *Schweizer. Theol. Umschau* 29 (1959) 55.

2. Cf. A. Jülicher, review of G. Bertram, *Die Leidensgeschichte...*, *ThLZ* 48 (1923) 9-11.

3. J. Weiss, *Das älteste Evangelium*, 1903, 350, representing the thesis "that Mark composed his work on the basis of his sketch of Peter and by including other traditions". Cf. below, p. [243ff.].

4. Cf. Fascher, *Formgesch. Methode*, 42 n. 1, 45ff.

5. Cf. *ibid.*, 231f.; Cullmann, *Vorträge*, 60ff.

6. Cf. Dibelius, *ThR* 1 (1929) 187f.

7. Cf. Bertram, *Leidensgeschichte*, 10: "However we do not have before us particular authorial individualities in the gospels; rather the individual personalities disappear here behind the materials."

8. K. L. Schmidt, in *Eucharisterion*, vol. 2, 89.

9. G. Iber, *ThR* 24 (1957/58) 322. Cf. also below, p. [167f.].

10. Koch, *op. cit.* (2nd ed.), 35f.; partly in italics in the original.

11. K. L. Schmidt, *RGG*-2nd ed., vol. 2, 1928, 639, in italics in the original. Cf. also Dibelius, *Formgesch.*, 7.

12. Iber, *op. cit.*, 326.

13. Cf. above #2, n. 10. R. Bultmann, *ThLZ* 50 (1925) 315, rejects a cult-historical *method*.

14. M. Dibelius, *RGG*-2nd ed., vol. 3, 1929, 1338.

15. Iber, *op. cit.*, 310.

16. *Ibid.*, 308.

17. M. Dibelius, *ThR* 1 (1929) 194.

18. *Ibid.*, 215f.

19. *Ibid.*, 215.

20. Schick, *Formgesch.*, 261, criticizes a one-sided sociology of religion. On sociology of religion in general, cf. G. Mensching, *Soziologie der grossen Religionen*, 1966; and *Soziologie der Religion*, 1968-2nd ed.

21. Cf. Schmidt, in *Eucharisterion*, vol. 2, 89.

22. Cf. A. Comte, *Rede über den Geist des Positivismus*, transl., introduced, and ed. by I. Fetscher, 1966-2nd ed. (orig. 1956).

23. Cf. *ibid.*, 85-87.

24. Cullmann, *Vorträge*, 60. [+1978: As a consequence of his philosophical presuppositions, P. Vielhauer even denied (orally) that Dibelius had spoken of a "collective", although these are clear quotations. Cf. n. 14 above.]

25. Cf. below, p. [120ff.].

26. See the evidence below, p. [126ff.].

27. The attempt to do this is still too large-scale, in light of the fantasy-production of Th. Boman, *Die Jesus-Ueberlieferung im Lichte der neueren Volkskunde*, 1967. For criticism, see below, p. [150ff.].

28. Cf. Bultmann, *Syn. Trad.* [German ed.], 5: "What is essential...is the insight that in the form critical work... one has to do with a circularity. Conclusions about the motives of the community life are to be derived from the forms of the literary transmission, and from the community life the forms are to be clarified. There is no method for making the first steps toward regulating or proscribing the necessary interchange and the simultaneous relationship of both approaches."

29. Cf. above, p. [37].

30. Cf. below, p. [73ff.].

31. Religious studies, theology, and philology proceed from "texts" or have their center in them. Philosophy thinks by means of language and aligns itself in the history of philosophy objectivized in "texts". History works with "sources", etc.

32. No associations with worldview or norms should be attached to this foreign word. In the present work, at any rate, it is used as a briefer term in the sense of being a collective concept for all possible directions, for whose presentation in full we must once again refer to the special publication being planned.

33. Cf. W. Porzig, *Das Wunder der Sprache*, 1957-2nd ed., 7: "Linguistics is...the fundamental science for all of the humanities in the same sense in which mathematics is the fundamental science for the natural sciences."

34. Cf. bibliography above, #2, n. 51.

35. Cf. W. Dilthey, *Einleitung in die Geisteswissenschaften*, 1883; W. Windelband, *Geschichte und Naturwissenschaft*, 1894; H. Rickert, *Die Grenzen der naturwissenschaftlichen Begriffsbildung*, 1913; Rickert, *Kulturwissenschaft und Naturwissenschaft*, 1921.

36. Cf. F. Schultz, in *Philosophie der Literaturwissenschaft*, E. Ermatinger, ed., 1930, 4: "In each case and for each beginning point onward literary criticism shares with philology, however this may be defined from time to time, the problem of understanding, the hermeneutical direction."

37. In our use of the quotation, "poetry" only represents the linguistic gestalts of literary criticism.

38. H. Seidler, *Die Dichtung*, 1965-2nd ed., 21.

39. Concerning the hermeneutical problematics of philological exegesis, cf. E. Betti, *Allgemeine Auslegungslehre als Methodik der Geisteswissenschaften*, 1967, 261ff.

40. Barr, *op. cit.*, 7. On its limitations, cf. #2, n. 55 above.

41. Barr, *op. cit.*, 292.

41a Both of the following sections attempt to meet the reproach correctly raised against J. Barr by Th. Boman, *Das hebräische Denken im Vergleich mit dem griechischen*, 1968-5th ed., 194f., namely that a linguistic criticism of exegetical-theological judgments should not remain without a positive presentation of the linguistic principles that are formative for this criticism. The same is true for the remaining linguistic-literary-critical sections of this book.

42. Cf. the overview in K. Baldinger, *Die Semasiologie*, 1957, 10-39.

43. Cf. *ibid.*, 3.

43a [+1978: For me it is a puzzle in the history of research why, for example, Wilhelm Dibelius' work *Englische Romankunst*, 1910, which influenced the Russian Formalists, was never discussed between Wilhelm and his cousin Martin Dibelius. The history of form criticism would have developed quite differently, if an early contact had taken place. Cf. R. Breymayer, *LingBibl* 15/16 (1972) 38f.]

44. These resources can lead, for instance, to naiveté in the task of translation unless a language should be thought of as being essentially an aggregation of elements that can be catalogued. Against the schematism of traditional grammar, cf. G. Ipsen, *IJ* 11 (1926/27) 4: "What is set out in our dictionaries as meanings are mostly vapid abstractions, insufficient class concepts empty of content, which are supposed to comprehend a majority of concrete meanings; they seek the substantial genre-characteristic in place of the governing unity of the sense wherein a skillful multiplicity is compressed into simplicity. On such paltry grounds every struggle toward a doctrine of meaning is useless." Cf. also M. Regula, *Grundlegung und Grundprobleme der Syntax*, 1951; J. R. Kantor, *An Objective Psychology of Grammar*, 1952-2nd ed.; H. Kronasser, *Handbuch der Semasiologie*, 1968-2nd ed., 21f.; L. Weisgerber, *Vom Weltbild der deutschen Sprache*, vol. 2, 1954-2nd ed., 6ff.; W. Porzig, *Das Wunder der Sprache*, 1967-4th ed., 94.

45. K. Vossler, *Positivismus und Idealismus in der Sprachwissenschaft*, 1904; E. Rothacker, *Logik und Systematik der Geisteswissenschaften*, 1965, 26ff.; A. Neubert, *Semantischer Positivismus in den USA*, 1962.

46. One thinks for instance of E. Husserl, *Logische Untersuchungen*, 1913-21; L. Wittgenstein, *Tractatus Logico-Philosophicus*, 1921, in *Schriften*, vol. 1, 1963-2nd ed., 7ff.; M. Heidegger, *Unterwegs zur Sprache*, 1959. Cf. the presentation of K. O. Apel, "Wittgenstein und das Problem hermeneutischer Verstehens," *ZThK* 63 (1966) 49-87; E. Albrecht, *Sprache und Erkenntnis*, 1967, 71-79; G. Pitcher, *Die Philosophie Wittgensteins*, 1967.

47. Cf. H.-G. Gadamer, *Wahrheit und Methode*, 1960, 361ff.

48. F. de Saussure, *Cours de linguistique générale*, Ch. Bally, A. Sechehaye, A. Riedlinger, eds., 1967-new ed.

49. It is a manifestation of the specifically-human capacity to create a language (langue); *ibid.*, 26.

50. Cf. *ibid.*, 37.

51. *Ibid.*, 26, 33.

52. *Ibid.*, 43.

53. *Ibid.*, 37: "la langue est nécessaire pour que la parole soit intelligible et produise tous ses effets; mais celle-ci est nécessaire pour la langue s'établisse; historiquement, le fait de parole précède toujours."

54. *Ibid.*: "Il y a donc interdépendence de la langue et de la parole; celle-là est à la fois l'instrument et le produit de celle-ci."

55. Cf. *ibid.*, 30: "l'exécution n'est jamais fait par la masse; elle est toujours individuelle, et l'individu en est toujours le maître."

56. A. Martinet, *Eléments de linguistique générale*, 1960, 30f., emphasized therefore that the *parole* has no organization independent of the *langue*; it only concretizes the organization of *langue*.

57. G. Neumann, *RGG*-3rd ed., vol. 6 (1962) 265.

58. Cf. K. Bühler, *Sprachtheorie*, 48ff.; F. Kainz, *Psychologie der Sprache*, vol. 1, 1967-4th ed., 18.

59. Cf. A. Reichling, *Het woord*, 1935, 435: "The object of linguistics is the language events in all their relations." It does "not only have to do with the study of the language events alone; other aspects belong to its field of study."

60. Cf. Heidegger, *op. cit.*, 166: "The Being of each thing that is dwells in the word. Therefore the expression holds true that Language is the house of Being." *Ibid.*, 165: "Something *is* only where the appropriate and therefore proper word names something as being and so constitutes the respective Being as such." *Ibid.*, 227: The word lends "first presence, that is, Being, wherein something appears as Being". [I have not made the technical distinctions in English Heidegger makes with Sein/Seiend here. W.G.D.]

61. Cf. E. Fuchs, "Das Sprachereignis in der Verkündigung Jesu, in der Theologie des Paulus und im Ostergeschehen," in Fuchs, *Aufs.*, vol. 1, 281-305; Fuchs, "Was ist ein Sprachereignis?", in Fuchs, *Aufs.*, vol. 2, 424-30; Fuchs, *Marburger Hermeneutik*, 1968, 227ff. Cf. also J. C. Weber, "Language-Event and Christian Faith," *TheolToday* 21 (1965) 448-57; R. W. Funk, *Language*, 20ff., 47ff.

62. So A. N. Wilder, in W. Klassen and G. F. Snyder, eds., *Current Issues in New Testament Interpretation*, 1962, 48; Barr, *Bibelexegese*, 274ff.; H.-D. Bastian, *Verfremdung und Verkündigung*, 1967-2nd ed., 6f.; Bastian, *EvTh* 28 (1968) 50f.; Bastian, *Theologie der Frage*, 1969, 234f., 256f., 324f.

63. Cf. for instance the polemics in Kainz, *op. cit.*, 13ff., against the language-creative folk soul. *Ibid.*, 23: Linguistic psychology has only to consider "what happens in the acts and processes of the speaking and language-understanding individual."

64. Cf. de Saussure, *op. cit.*, 31: "La langue, distincte de la parole, est un objet qu'on peut étudier séparément."

65. Cf. H. Dempe, *Ueber die sogenannten Funktionen der Sprache*, Diss. Jena, 1929, 24: "It is recognized...that language can only arise from speaking, that speaking for its part must presuppose language. Doubtless it could be stated that language produces its own presupposition."

66. Cf. Kainz, *op. cit.*, 35-54.

67. So de Saussure, *op. cit.*, 26: "la langue est une convention, et la nature du signe dont on est convenu est indifférente."

68. Cf. Kainz, *op. cit.*, 59-66.

69. I will have to put off a comprehensive presentation in the framework of this excursis. But see below, p. [174ff.].

70. Cf. G. Ipsen, *IJ* 11 (1926/27) 8f. On language psychology (sociolinguistics), see M. Cohen, *Pour une sociologie du langage*, 1956; A. Capell, *Studies in Socio-Linguistics*, 1966; *Readings in the Sociology of Language*, ed. J. A. Fishman, 1968.

71. Kainz, *op. cit.*, 12.

72. Cf. W. Wundt, *Völkerpsychologie*, vol. 1, 1911-12-3rd ed., summarized by Kainz, *op. cit.*, 12-15.

73. Kainz, *ibid.*, 12.

74. Cf. Bühler, *Sprachtheorie*, 48ff.

75. On this dialectics, see below pp. [134f., 143].

76. I am thinking, for instance, of the utilization of tenses (see below #14, n. 31), of the stylistic distinction of "paradigm" and "novella" emphasized by Dibelius, *Formgesch.*, 66ff., of the peculiar characteristics of the controversy discourses (cf. Bultmann, *Syn. Trad.*, 39ff.), of the style of the statements of eschatological law (cf. *ibid.*, 138ff.; E. Käsemann, "Sätze heiligen Rechtes im Neuen Testament," in *Aufs.*, vol. 2, 69-82), of the stylistic use of relatives and participles in "hymns" (cf. E. Norden, *Agnostos Theos*, 1956-4th ed., 166ff., 201ff., 383ff.), and others.

77. See below, p. [54ff.].

78. This question presupposes that "significance" and "meaning" are not to be separated as "content" from the "form", but that the linguistic form of the linguistic-structural context is the linguistic sign. See below, pp. [65ff., 161ff.].

79. See below, p. [76 ff.].

80. I cannot here go into the problem of positivism in linguistics. See, however, the bibliography in n. 45.

80a This level is to be sure not that which I consider hermeneutically adequate; but in the strong inclination of many exegetes to "purely historical" procedure, linguistics is offered as a means of agreement between it and that interpretation which is mostly considered *too* hermeneutical and hence rejected. In other words linguistics is the field for the "language school of faith" in which positivistic exegesis would have to answer to its own aporias if it were to be entirely consistent.

81. Cf. de Saussure, *op. cit.*, 24, on *langage*: "A chaque instant il implique à la fois un système établi et une évolution", that is, *langue* and *parole*.

82. Cf. Baldinger, *Semasiologie*, 8-10, 15-19.

83. Cf. de Saussure, *op. cit.*, 185.

84. Linguistic technical term; Romance loan word; plural: term(s). Related designations are lexeme and moneme. Cf. M. Pei, *Glossary of Linguistic Terminology*, 1966, 145f., 165f.

85. There are various designations for the science of research on words: semantics, semantic; semasiology, semasiological; semiology (semeology), semiological; sematology, sematological. Cf. H. Kronaser, *Handbuch*, 29; St. Ullmann, *The Principles of Semantics*, 1957-2nd ed., 4f.

86. Differently F. Heerdegen, *Grundzüge der Bedeutungslehre*, 1890.

87. Baldinger, *op. cit.*, 19.

88. Cf. K. Ammer, *Einführung in die Sprachwissenschaft*, vol. 1, 1958, 62.

89. Cf. Baldinger, *op. cit.*, 21-24. The "relative semantic autonomy" means the fact that a single word can only bear "significance" restricted to itself; the context will then make it more definite. Cf. H. Weinrich, *Linguistik der Lüge*, 1966, 15ff.

90. Cf. St. Ullmann, *Principles*, 54ff.

91. Cf. *ibid.*, 49f.

92. Cf. *ibid.*, 52-54.

93. Cf. A. W. de Groot, *Structuureele syntaxis*, 1949.

94. Cf. de Saussure, *op. cit.*, 116: "la langue est un système de pures valeurs que rien ne détermine en dehors de l'état momentané de ces termes." Cf. *ibid.*, 155ff.

95. Language as *langue* is a superstructure; cf. Kainz, *op. cit.*, 274ff.

96. Cf. de Saussure, *op. cit.*, 114f.

97. G. Guillaume, *L'architectonique du temps dans les langues classiques*, 1945, 12f., who distinguishes the *valeur* of morphological phenomena within the *parole* from that within the *langue*.

98. Cf. St. Ullmann, *Words and Their Use*, 1951, 17: "The sound, the word and the syntactic construction are the three units of connected speech." Therefore a linguistic analysis of the *parole* must investigate simultaneously all three elements.

99. Cf. de Groot, *op. cit.*, 10.

100. Baldinger, *op. cit.*, 24.

101. Cf. de Groot, *op. cit.*, 53f. The word sequence can be the object of analysis in so-called tagmatics (a part of syntax). Cf. Ammer, *Einführung*, vol. 1, 91f.

102. Cf. St. Ullmann, *Words*, 34: "Words do not live in isolation in the language system. They enter into all kinds of groupings held together by a complex, unstable and highly subjective network of *associations*."

103. Cf. Ammer, *op. cit.*, 62: The thesis of the contextual connection of the words means "that many words first have any meaning at all in that they become clear in a particular context".

104. Usually one understands by semanteme the "significance" of a term-carrying unit, by morpheme the lexical-syntactic variation.

105. Since for example proper names within the *langue* do not serve the signification context but identify an individual or something individual, they are called asemantemes. Cf. St. Ullmann, *Semantics*, 1964-2nd ed., 74. Otherwise attention to the valeur of the asemanteme is very important exegetically. Cf. E. Güttgemanns, "CHRISTOS in 1. Kor. 15,3b--Titel oder Eigenname?", *EvTh* 28 (1968) 533-54.

106. So Guillaume, *op. cit.*, 9, 11.

107. Bibliography on this research: #10, n. 1, below.

108. Cf. de Saussure, *op. cit.*, 157: "La collectivité est necéssaire pour établir des valeurs dont l'unique raison d'être est dans l'usage et le consentement général; l'individu à lui seul est incapable d'en fixer aucune."

109. Cf. *ibid.*, 158.

110. Cf. St. Ullmann, *Principles*, 65-82.

111. Cf. St. Ullmann, *Semantics*, 23ff.; G. Frey, "Formale Strukturen in der Sprache," *EvTh* 28 (1968) 357-72.

112. Cf. F. Rundgren, *Erneuerung des Verbalaspekts im Semitischen*, 1963, 53: "We must distinguish precisely between the pure objective-lexical significance of a morphological category, which for example can be defined as type of action, and the structurally determined worth (*valeur*) of the respective category in the system of language (*langue*)." (Italics in original.)

113. de Groot, *op. cit.*, 9.

114. Cf. A. L. Jellinek, *Bibliographie der vergleichenden Literaturgeschichte*, 1903; L.-P. Betz, *La littérature comparée*, 1904-2nd ed., ed. F. Baldensperger; F. Baldensperger and W. P. Friedrich, *Bibliography of Comparative Literature*, 1950; K. Wais, ed., *Forschungsprobleme der Vergleichenden Literaturgeschichte* (1.) 1951; (2.) 1958; M. F. Guyard, *La littérature comparée*, 1951; N. P. Stallknecht and H. Frenz, eds., *Comparative Literature*, 1961; E. Frenzel, *Stoffe der Weltliteratur*, 1962; Frenzel, *Stoff-, Motiv- und Symbolforschung*, 1963; H. Rüdiger, "Vergleichende Literaturwissenschaft, -geschichte (Komparatistik)," in *Kleines literarisches Lexikon*, 4th ed., vol. 3, ed. H. Rüdiger and E. Koppen, 1966, 430-35; U. Weisstein, *Einführung in die Vergleichende Literaturwissenschaft*, 1968. The standard work today is R. Wellek and A. Warren, *Theorie der Literatur*, 1966; a very rich bibliography *ibid.*, 279-310.

115. Cf. L. L. Schücking, *Soziologie der literarischen Geschmacksbildung*, 1961-3rd ed.; W. Ziegenfuss, "Kunst," in A. Vierkandt, ed., *Handwörterbuch der Soziologie*, 1931, 301-38; A. L. Guérard, *Literature and Society*, 1935; H. Read, *Art and Society*, 1956-3rd ed.; D. Daiches, *Literature and Society*, 1938; W. Witte, "The Sociological Approach to Literature," *Modern Language Review* 36 (1941) 86-94; C. Lessing, *Das methodologische Problem der Literatursoziologie*, Diss. Bonn, 1950; H. D. Duncan, *Language and Literature in Society*, 1961-revised ed.; R. Escarpit, *Das Buch und der Leser*, 1966-2nd ed.; G. Lukács, *Schriften zur Literatursoziologie*, 1968-3rd ed.; H. N. Fügen, *Die Hauptrichtungen der Literatursoziologie und ihre Methoden*, 1968-3rd ed.; E. Koppen, "Literatursoziologie," in *Kleines literar. Lexikon*, 237f.; J. L. Aranguren, *Soziologie der Kommunikation*, 1967; H. N. Fügen, ed., *Wege zur Literatursoziologie*, 1968. Further bibliography in H. D. Duncan, *op. cit.*, 143-214; H. N. Fügen, *Hauptrichtungen*, 204-25.

116.   Cf. L. Alonso-Schökel, S.J., "Hermeneutics in the
Light of Language and Literature," *CBQ* 25 (1963) 371-86.
Specifically linguistic studies appear only rarely in literary criticism. See however R. S. Crane, *The Languages of
Criticism and the Structure of Poetry*, 1953; H. Sörensen,
"Littérature et linguistique," in *Théories et Problèmes* (*Or-
bis litterarum*, Suppl. II), 1958, 182-97; S. R. Levin, *Linguistic Structures in Poetry*, 1962; H.-P. Bayerdörfer, *Poetik
als sprachtheoretisches Problem*, 1967; J. Ihwe, "Linguistik
und Literaturwissenschaft," *LB* 3 (1969) 30-44. Further bibliography *ibid.*, 36-43.

117.   Cf. below, p. [106].

118.   It is necessary to speak of a *re*integration since the
unity of form criticism (literary history) and linguistics was
already presupposed by J. G. Herder and H. Gunkel. Cf. below
pp. [120ff., 154ff.]. [+1978: A few years later I also de-
tected that F. Schleiermacher, as well as Chr. H. Wilke, had
clear systems of linguistic, semiotic, and exegetical methods.
Cf. E. Güttgemanns, "Die synoptische Frage im Lichte der
modernen Sprach- und Literaturwissenschaft," *LingBibl* 29/30
(1973) 2ff. So I am convinced today that nearly all that I
have learned during my studies of "introductions" is only a
very narrow viewpoint of a much broader field.]

119.   See the bibliography cited in #7, n. 234, below.

120.   Bultmann, *ThLZ* 50 (1925) 317.

121.   Bultmann, *RGG*-2nd ed., vol. 3 (1929) 1676.

122.   Cf. Fascher, *formg. Methode*, 228-31.

123.   Cf. Dibelius, *Geschichte der urchristlichen Literatur*,
1926, 2 vols.

123a   [+1978: I have learned from Dan O. Via, *The Parables*,
1967, that the parables, for example, possess an "aesthetic autonomy" which makes them independent of "sociological" condi-
tioning. Furthermore, form criticism seems to regard the
"aesthetic" dimension of texts as being only a "surface" phenomenon like "style". What if "style" and the "aesthetic" dimension were already elements of the "deep" structure? Then
there would be another point for a revision of form-critical
concepts.]

124.   Cf. H. Conzelmann's indication that "we...still do
not have a traditio-historical introduction to the N.T.,"
EvTh 25 (1965) 4 n. 16.

125. K. L. Schmidt, *RGG*–2nd ed., vol. 2, 1928, 639.

126. Cf. R. Bultmann, *ThLZ* 50 (1925) 317: "Genre analysis is useful not to aesthetics but to historical research, and the appearance of mixed forms 'shows that different historical motives can be at work simultaneously."

127. Cf. above, p. [44ff.] on the resulting historical perspective.

128. M. Dibelius, *ThR* 1 (1929) 188.

129. Cf. the overview in Fügen, *Hauptrichtungen*.

130. Cf. *ibid.*, 56.

131. *Ibid.*, 41.

132. *Ibid.*, 40.

133. *Ibid.*, 14.

134. Cf. for instance L. Bloomfield, *Language*, 1967–rev. ed.; C. Morris, *Signs, Language and Behavior*, 1946; B. F. Skinner, *Verbal Behavior*, 1957. Cf. also A. Neubert's presentation in *Semantischer Positivismus*, 61-66, 72-79.

135. Fügen, *op. cit.*, 106.

136. Cf. *ibid.*, 113.

137. Cf. above, p. [49ff.].

138. Fügen, *op. cit.*, 118.

139. E. Koppen, *Kleines literar. Lexikon*, 237.

140. *Ibid.*, 238.

141. Cf. Fügen, *op. cit.*, 119ff.

142. Cf. the suggestions, *ibid.*, 110-13.

143. Cf. below, p. [119ff.].

144. Cf. G. Ebeling, *Wort und Glaube*, 1960, 203ff.

145. Cf. E. Fuchs, *Aufs.*, vol. 2, 176f. Cf. also A. N. Wilder, *The Language of the Gospel*, 1964, 21; W. C. van Unnik,

"The Christian's Freedom of Speech in the New Testament," *Bull JRL* 44 (1962) 466–88.

146. Cf. Fuchs, *Aufs.*, vol. 1, 138.

147. Cf. *ibid.*, 191.

148. For more extensive establishment of the temporal understanding of the "spatial" *en Christō*, cf. Güttgemanns, *Der leidende Apostel*, 212ff.

149. Cf. *ibid.*, 43f. Further bibliography is given there.

150. Cf. Fuchs, *op. cit.*, 290. [+1978: Today I would stress that "permission" also belongs to "speech acts" such as those analyzed by John R. Searle, *Speech Acts*, 1969. As a consequence this would mean that the opposition "law" *vs.* "freedom" is no longer pertinent. It seems to me that Fuchs depends upon the opposition of "nomothetic" sciences of "nature" *vs.* "ideographic" sciences of "ideas". This opposition has proved itself as untenable. Cf. G. H. von Wright, *Explanation and Understanding*, 1971. Therefore I would now stress more clearly that Fuchs' argumentation is only an instance of *rabies theologorum* (rage of theologians).]

151. Cf. *ibid.*, 296; similarly, *ibid.*, 305.

152. Note 61 above gives relevant bibliography.

153. Cf. Fuchs, *Aufs.*, vol. 3, 212.

154. *Ibid.*, 427.

155. Cf. *ibid.*, 308: "do we not, with our language, correspond from the first to a Yes that grants us entrance, entrance into that being in which we are then allowed to be by ourselves and yet are not alone?"

156. Cf. Fuchs, *Aufs.*, vol. 1, 283.

157. Fuchs, *Aufs.*, vol. 2, 278.

158. My relationship to the "new" hermeneutic, which is determined by immanent criticism, is presented in Güttgemanns, *Der Leidende Apostel*, 48ff.; my review of E. Jüngel, *Paulus und Jesus*, in *VF* 12/2 (1967) 52–59; and my review of J. M. Robinson and J. B. Cobb, eds., *Die Neue Hermeneutik*, in *Pastoraltheol.* 57 (1968) 353f. On this discussion, cf. also P. J. Achtemeier, "How Adequate is the New Hermeneutic?",

TheolToday 23 (1966) 101-19; R. T. Osborn, "A New Hermeneutic?", *Interpretation* 20 (1966) 400-11; P.-A. Stucki, "Herméneutique et Dialectique," *RevThéolPhil* 99 (1966) 121-29.

158a   Cf. for instance Fuchs, *Aufs.*, vol. 3, 6; *Marburger Hermeneutik*, 1968, 81f.

158b   Cf. Fuchs, *Hermeneutik*, 1958-2nd ed., 181.

159.   *Ibid.*, Ergänzungsheft, 3.

160.   Cf. bibliography, n. 62, above.

161.   H.-D. Bastian, *EvTh* 28 (1968) 50f.

162.   Bastian, *Verfremdung*, 9.

163.   *Ibid.*, 22.

164.   Cf. *ibid.*, 14f.

165.   Cf. *ibid.*, 27f.

166.   Bastian, *EvTh* 28 (1968) 51.

167.   Bastian, *Verfremdung*, 24.

168.   *Ibid.*, 58.

169.   Bastian, *TheolPract* 3 (1968) 34.

170.   *Ibid.*, 39.

171.   *Ibid.*, 38.

172.   Bastian, *Verfremdung*, 26.

173.   *Ibid.*, 21.

174.   Cf. *ibid.*, 33.

175.   Cf. C. Cherry, *Kommunikationsforschung--eine neue Wissenschaft*, 1967-2nd ed.; St. Chase, *Wörter machen Weltgeschichte*, 1955; H. Zemanek, *Elementare Informationstheorie*, 1959; W. Meyer-Eppler, *Grundlagen und Anwendungen der Informationstheorie*, 1959; C. F. v. Weizsäcker, "Sprache als Information," in Der Bayer. Ak. der schönen Künste, ed., *Die Sprache*, 1959, 33-53; Y. Bar-Hillel, *Language and Information*, 1964, espec. 221ff. (together with R. Carnap); K. Steinbuch, "Information," *EvTh* 28 (1968) 344-57.

175a   Cf. also the bibliography given in the Introductory Remarks above, n. 12.

176.   I do not intend here a criticism of E. Fuchs, but only an avoidance of a possible enthusiastic misunderstanding of his statements. E. Fuchs, *Marburger Hermeneutik*, 69ff., emphasizes the continuing estrangement of the person in the *extra se*, which is a schism between Law and Law (cf. Romans 7:22f.). Thereby the dialectic between law and gospel is safeguarded.

177.   Cf. E. Jüngel, *Paulus und Jesus*, 1962, 290-300.

178.   On the exegesis of these passages, cf. *ibid.*, 139-74.

179.   Cf. *ibid.*, 135, 295f. Discussion of these theses: Güttgemanns, *VF* 12/2 (1967) espec. 58f.

180.   Jüngel, *op. cit.*, 291f., is "...well aware of the problematics of the expressions 'content' and 'form' deriving from metaphysics. They are used here for the purpose of the discussion but are replaced by the concept of the language event in the subject matter itself".

181.   Cf. for instance A. Jülicher, *Die Gleichnisreden Jesu*, vol. 1, 1899-2nd ed., vol. 2, 1899; J. Jeremias, *Die Gleichnisse Jesu*, 1967-7th ed.

182.   Jüngel, *op. cit.*, 291.

183.   *Ibid.*, 292.

184.   *Ibid.*, 291.

185.   Cf. below, p. [161ff.].

186.   Cf. B. Eichenbaum, *Aufsätze zur Theorie und Geschichte der Literatur*, 1965, 7-52; R. Wellek and A. Warren, *op. cit.*, 120f.; E. Koppen, "Formalismus," in *Kleines literar. Lexikon*, 134f.

187.   H. O. Burger, *GRM* 32 (1950-51) 83.

188.   Cf. Wellek and Warren, *op. cit.*, 217f.

189.   *Ibid.*, 22.

190.   Bultmann, *Syn. Trad.*, 393.

191. Jüngel, *op. cit.*, 292, my emphasis.

192. Already G. Bertram, *ThBl* 6 (1927) 165, had indicated the actual form-critical problem in terms of the question "how extensively form and contents correspond, how far the contents break apart the form, or how far the form determines the contents in a direction which is foreign to them". Only if form and content are actually identical because the content can choose its own form without constraint, can we speak of a "language event". But to what extent does the history of linguistic forms approximate to utopia, where correspondence or identity of form and content is the rule?

193. Cf. Jüngel, *op. cit.*, 293ff.

194. Cf. *ibid.*, 292.

195. *Ibid.*, 295.

196. Cf. *ibid.*, 299: "The *ratio cognoscendi* for form criticism goes from the typical aspect of the location of the transmission as the Where of the tradition to the place of origination of the transmission as the Wither of the tradition that is identical with the What. The *ratio essendi* is itself the revolution underlying this movement."

197. *Ibid.*, 293, 294f.

198. Cf. *ibid.*, 295: "The eschaton enters language as eschatological word." *Ibid.*, 196: "The basileia providently enters language as parable in parable."

199. *Ibid.*, 292.

200. Does not Jüngel's variation of the "new" hermeneutic play so much with a utopian historical sketch that the might of the law (e.g., sociology) is disputed, and all events are derived from the might of the gospel? Cf. on the other hand Bastian, *Verfremdung*, 74: "The history of proclamation is always at the same time, the history of the passion, but never the history of Easter."

201. Cf. *VF* 12/2 (1967) 55: where I have demonstrated that Jüngel takes up into the scientific presentation the truth question which R. Bultmann delivered over to the existential fulfillment and encounter, so that his formulations have a homologous resonance with Bultmann's. The presentation succeeds *a priori* from the standpoint of faith.

202.   Cf. *ibid.*, 57:   The category "language event" conceals the methodologically necessary distinction between
proclamation and theology.

203.   As argued in Güttgemanns, *TheolPract* 3 (1968) 87f.,
91f.

PART II. PROBLEMS OF THE ORAL AND THE
WRITTEN, AND THEIR RELATION
TO THE GOSPEL FORM.

#4. *Form and Redaction Criticism: Continuity and Dis-
continuity*.

   1. Form and Redaction Criticism: Continuity
      within the History of Research.

From a certain perspective the redaction-critical method
represents a direct development of form criticism within the
history of research.[1] There are good reasons to doubt that
this development is totally continuous with respect to form
criticism's methodological approach. One indication of a certain precariousness is to be seen in one of M. Dibelius' considerations [discussed below, sub #4.2.(a).--W.G.D.]

   For a while Dibelius sought--as had H. Gunkel[2]--to regard the object of form criticism as a "paleontology of the
gospels"[3] (F. Overbeck), not with respect to the completed
literary works, but only the small component units, "which
are passed on in oral or written transmission, but which we
know about from books which have incorporated them. Strictly
speaking therefore the form-critical approach is only able to
find a place for such works as are collections of such small
units or which incorporate them into their text".[4]

   K. L. Schmidt similarly reflects the main viewpoint of a
"paleontology of the gospels" when he refers to "the investigation of the oral [p. 70] tradition of the materials that
have become fixed literary parts of the gospels".[5] For R.
Bultmann also the primitive Christian literature "primarily

existed only orally, and gained its written form only gradually due to the necessities of life".[6] All these remarks
provide an indication of the form critics' tendency to mis-
place their analysis by emphasizing the stage of development
preceding that of literary fixation.

However the correctness of concentrating upon the small
units themselves, or upon their pre-literary history, is not
to be acceded without further stipulations, since otherwise
a subject such as form criticism of the Pauline letters would
remain precluded--for here at least we have a case of the
larger unit comprised of smaller elements made into an *eo
ipso* "literary" work.[7] So even the "framework" of the whole,
in this case of the gospel, was from the start regarded as
the object of form-critical investigation,[8] not only in terms
of the redaction of the traditional materials in general,[9]
but also and especially in terms of the redaction and composition of the materials in the gospels.[10] These were understood as having been completed according to the same laws as
the tradition in the individual units, since form criticism
denied a *major* differentiation between the oral and the written transmission:[11] "There is no major difference between the
oral and the written transmission, and neither was the redaction of the traditional material first begun at the stage of
literary fixation." Since the composition of the gospels
"does not bring about anything new in principle, but only
completes what was already begun in the original oral tradition, it can only be regarded in organic connection with the
history of the materials prior to what is present in the gospels".[12] Programmatic remarks at the beginning of form criticism therefore give the impression: "that a redaction critical approach was already recognized as necessary [p. 71] in
the early period", although in actual practice there was

little preference given to the redactional level of the tradition.[13]

In the light of this professed form-critical intention,
therefore, it is not at first obvious why W. Marxsen regards
the redaction-critical approach as discontinuous with that of
form criticism[14] and W. Hillmann,[15] G. Iber,[16] and G. Schille
represent the redaction-critical interests of form criticism
as limited,[17] or why H. Dieckmann placed form and literary
criticism alongside one another.[18]

To be sure today the theological meaning and contents of
gospel redaction and composition press ever more strongly into the foreground,[19] something that can be understood within
the perspective of the history of research as a necessary
swing of the pendulum: [p. 71] "Following form criticism's
emphasis upon the pericope, we must once again take into account the total conception and composition of the synoptic
gospels, without thereby denying the methodology and success
of the form-critical work on the pericopes."[20]

But to begin with M. Dibelius[21] and R. Bultmann[22] emphasized theological aspects in their analysis, which was oriented to individual materials, and secondly contemporary theological evaluation of redaction proceeds with the aid of the
analytically-elicited technique for studying tradition and
stylistic peculiarities: "Not in spite of, but only using
the presupposition of the form-critical method, is it both
possible and necessary today to bring the question of the
theological concepts of the synoptic authors to the fore, a
question that could not be meaningfully *stated* without this
presupposition."[23]

There are therefore the greatest differences of degree
as regards the centrality and emphasis given to the question
of the theology of the evangelists, but no fundamental opposition.[24] Perhaps we should refer less to an "addition to

the program formulated long ago",[25] than to a shift of emphasis which without doubt has been productive: Form criticism
is primarily interested in the pericope, "while redaction
criticism desires, on the other hand, to conceptualize the
whole pattern that is now visible".[26]

[p. 73] 2. The Thesis of the Discontinuity
between Form and Redaction Criticism in the
History of Research.

(a) The Traditional Thesis of Traditio-
Historical Continuity between Tradition and Redaction.

Are we therefore to reject entirely W. Marxsen's thesis
concerning the discontinuity of form and redaction criticism?
I think that total rejection of Marxsen's thesis leads us to
overlook too quickly some definite difficulties of form-critical positions. These difficulties can be seen in M. Dibelius'
uncertainty (referred to above) about the extent to which the
form-critical method can be applied. Analysis of H. Gunkel's
procedure indicates a similar problem namely that in its beginnings form criticism, because of its use of the works of
J. G. Herder and the "romantic school" or the early folklorists, relied upon their distinctions between the oral and the
written, and hence were dependent upon a conceptual model
which was in striking tension with its own thesis concerning
the lack of traditio-historical differentiation between oral
and written transmission.[27] We might therefore suspect that
Dibelius' uncertainty is connected with this tension: Since
form criticism is actually interested only in the oral character of the forms--a definite influence through Gunkel from
earlier folkloristics, but now transformed into sociological
conceptions--and is therefore interested in the level "preceding the incorporation of the transmission into a different

aggregation, that of scripture",[28] it actually can only deal
with works constructed from the small, originally-oral units;
if then such a method is carried over to other works, their
written character—again in tension with essential premises
of form criticism!—must be de-emphasized if the thesis concerning the lack of difference between the oral and the written level is to be maintained.[29] As is the case with the
gospel tranmission as a whole, the written gospel-form is not
a product of a literary movement; the tradition "has its origin in Jesus' proclamation and in the expressions of his
church, in sermon and teaching, in mission and defence".[30]
Therefore it is not based upon any single "literary" *act* of
creation, embodied or shaped by an individual, but upon a
longer, "non-literary" originating *process* ultimately resting
in the sociological "community" based on Jesus' proclamation,
[p. 74] a process which finds its expression in the written
gospel-form. In other words: *The written character of the
gospels as well as its tradition is considered by traditional
form criticism to be a sociological phenomenon, namely a surrogate for the activities of a collective.* We should not
overlook the fact that this thesis also implies a criticism of
the aesthetics of genius,[30a] and hence stands in tension with
the romantic aesthetics of J. G. Herder, so that early form
criticism is not simply a consequence of earlier folkloristics; it is rather a further development brought about by the
introduction of the discipline of sociology, which at least
in literary respects has left up in the air its own relationship to its pre-history.[30b]

Even if W. Marxsen's comments on the relational discontinuity of form and redaction criticism[31] perhaps do not emphasize clearly enough the difficulties we have noted, they
have nonetheless disclosed a continuing problem, namely the
question as to the horizon in which we are to understand the

evangelists' *literary* work upon the mostly *oral* traditional material available to them.

This question was already evident at an early date as the question concerning the individualistic or sociological element in the form-creative process.[32] Insofar as form criticism made a decisive choice for the sociological conception,[33] following H. Gunkel,[34] it not only had to regard style and form as something impersonal and objective,[35] but also to reject the understanding of the evangelists as "authorial personalities":[36] "The gospel is in its nature [p. 75] not literature proper but Kleinliteratur, not the product of an individual writer, but a book of the people, not biography but cultic legend."[37] K. L. Schmidt comes to this judgment on the basis of a comparison of the gospels with contemporary analogies; so: the classification of the gospels as being "Kleinliteratur" and "books of the people" is also a result of comparative literary criticism. But simultaneously it is tied firmly to basic sociological perspectives, since the "book of the people" is counterposed to the "individual authorial activity". The evangelists are only *the last link in the chain of a linear development over a longer period of time*; their works are Kleinliteratur = folks-literature = the product of a collective.[38]

Since there are prior levels in the collection of the traditional material, redaction of the gospels "takes place in a line of oral tradition-history".[39] "The literary understanding of the gospels begins with the recognition that they contain collective material. The authors are only in the most minor way authors, more significantly they are collectors, tradents, redactors."[40] Their final redactional work is not to be distinguished principally from the process of tradition already present to them, since the individual element cannot be fundamentally eliminated,[41] nor are the gospel redactors independent shapers of the transmitted material "with absolute freedom, but [they are] connected to the community tradition and the needs of the church":[42] "nowhere in redaction-critical studies, even as a hint, is there a suggestion that the evangelists might have proceded purely arbitrarily in the shaping of the tradition."[43] "As exponents of their communities the evangelists are not authors who might relinquish their individuality back behind literary expression. Rather insofar as they incorporate the transmitted forms, their stylistic media are impersonal", so that we must distinguish between possible individual *dogmatic* conceptions and individualizing in the *literary* area.[44] [p. 76] This form-critical tendency to emphasize the collective tradents, that level to which basically even the evangelist, as the final compiler, belongs, is no cause for resignation. "For we know the general profile of this collective author much better than we know the personalities of the evangelists, of whom we scarcely know their names."[45]

(b) Willi Marxsen's Criticism of the Traditional Conception.

Over against this seemingly closed and inaccessible conceptual model (whose originally hypothetical character must never be forgotten), Willi Marxsen seeks to demonstrate the interior tension between the fundamental, older option for a sociological formation of the tradition and the newer understanding of the individual theological achievement of the evangelists.

Marxsen begins his reflections with the observation that as a whole "the so-called redactor always [appears] in a bad light" in form criticism. Such a judgment rests upon an antithesis between authors on the one side, and collectors, tradents, redactors on the other. But can this antithesis really be maintained absolutely, given the newer valuation of the theological achievement of someone like Luke?[46] Can we really follow R. Bultmann in affirming that the composition itself does not contribute anything new in principle, but is only the completion of what was begun with the first oral tradition?[47] "Precisely the results of form criticism contradict this assessment, however," because it ignores the variety of the forms and above all of the "sociological settings", and therefore does not diagnose a movement toward collection, but a centrifugal movement of the traditional material which does not make comprehensible the unity of the gospel-form without further clarification.[48] In such circumstances can we understand the work of the first evangelist, Mark, merely as *the final phase of anti-individualist, sociological laws*?

G. Strecker has answered this question positively, and by differentiating "between an individual *dogmatic* conception and individualizing on the *literary* level", has begun to study the issue in a new way: "As exponents of their community the evangelists are not 'authors'," but they utilize transmitted forms and furthermore impersonal stylistic means. "On the other hand it is to be emphasized that the drafting of the gospel is in each case determined by a design [p. 77] that is expressed in processing the traditional materials--by means of selection, abbreviation, and expansion."[49]

However in my opinion this differentiation is difficult to apply, since it is based upon idealism's separation of "form" and "content" already rejected by H. Gunkel:[50] But how can we judge the possibility of an individual dogmatic concept of Mark if ultimately we have direct and immediate access only to the literary phenomenon as the object of our study, something which indeed is supposed to be derived from the community exponents tied to the sociological laws? Would it not be more consistent to understand Mark not just with respect to style and form as the so-to-speak "external factor", but also with respect to his theological material as the "interior factor", as the anonymous exponent of a collective, and to deny to him each and every personal, that is, individual, theological achievement? In what ways was the evangelist in his selection, abbreviation, and expansion of the traditional materials, in short: in the design and plan of his gospel, freer, more individual than in the style, if the outline and similarly the structure belong to the formal marks of a genre, and indeed in the case of the gospel-form are to be regarded as the most decisive criteria of the genre?[51] Is it true that we can make judgments about events such as the origin of the unity of the gospel-form, rather than merely being ready to suggest hypothetical intuitions, which at any rate cannot regulate anyone in an *a priori* way? In other words: Closer reflection and more exact analysis leads us to see just how vulnerable such an argument is.

Marxsen's insistance upon the problematic aspect of the sociological premises, with respect to understanding the unity of the gospel-form, therefore pinpoints a weakness of the form-critical approach: The unity of form of something like the Gospel of Mark "is a systematically produced work, which can by no means be understood as the 'completion' of the anonymous level of the process of passing-on the tradition". Redaction that runs counter to the divergence and centrifugal tendency of the materials "cannot be explained without bringing into the picture an individual, an authorial personality, who pursues a definite goal with his work". An anti-individualistic approach to the gospels elevated to the status of scientific dogma *is not able to* "include the evangelists themselves in the picture".[52]

Therefore Marxsen attempts to appreciate Mark's individual theological [p. 78] achievement more adequately than has been possible due to the previously anti-individualistic and sociological attitude of form criticism. When contrasted with the individual elements perhaps already present in the pre-literary collections,[53] the achievement of personal shaping in the gospel's "form" "is much more significant. So far as we can tell, Mark is the first to introduce the individualistic moment into the forming and shaping of the tradition."[54] This individual achievement is to be sighted "not in the first instance in the material, but in the 'framework'". "This framework however should not now be simply historically demolished, as has almost always happened in form criticism, but it is to be redaction-critically analyzed for its 'sociological setting'."[55] The evangelists reworked the materials available to them "not as patchwork artists,...but as authorial individuals".[56]

(c) Consequences of Willi Marxsen's Criticism.

The unity of the gospel form is therefore precisely that element that we encounter initially and immediately in our analytical viewing, and that which the tradition passes on as well. Only by means of this element, that is, only by means of scientific analysis having the character of probability, do we have immediate access to the tradition residing in the gospels.[57] However that also means that we can also only gain a view of the tradition-history lying behind the present final configuration of the gospel-form insofar as the evangelist permits it by his choice and arrangement of his materials. *Our hypothetical reconstruction of the pre-history of the gospel form is always dependent upon the ways the first evangelists seized the* [p. 79] *tradition-history present to them.* The tradition passed on through Mark to Matthew, Luke, John, the

Apostolic Fathers, the apocryphal gospels, and the agrapha is of secondary significance insofar as it is excluded from Mark's gospel, or unknown to him in terms of the origin of its form. If Mark actually was the first to *create* the form, the rest of the tradition-history belongs to the history of the "literary" variations of the form, not to the history of its "pre-literary" origins, of which the "literary" level only reflects mediated reflections. In other words: We must carefully differentiate between the "pre-literary" tradition-history of the gospel-materials, and the "literary" tradition-history of the gospel-form.[57a] Only the "literary" level of the tradition is directly and immediately present to us, and that must determine the scope of our analysis of the "pre-literary" levels. Wouldn't it be better then to stick with F. Overbeck's judgment concerning the fragmentary character of "proto-literature"?[58] At any rate W. Marxsen's intention to give greater consideration to the "individualistic" moment that adheres within the gospel-form is the only means of guarding against a retrogression into J. C. L. Gieseler's hypothesis about the role of traditions,[59] which was based upon J. G. Herder's assumption of an oral protogospel which presupposed three oral sources upon which the gospels are dependent,[60] a viewpoint that recurs with typical variations even today.[61]

To avoid a possible misunderstanding of this work it should be stated expressly that the acceptance of oral tradition and also the assumption of "small units" as well as pre-Markan redactional compositions is not disputed here in the least. But the path to these "small units" and this tradition-history, up to the point of the "literary" gospel form, seems to me to be much less certain and more hypothetical than is generally recognized today. Hasn't form criticism too quickly derived the gospel genre from the tradition-history of its materials because it regarded the evangelists' work as entirely determined by the tradition? *To what extent do not only the material but also the genre border upon the oral tradition?* "Kerygma" has usually been referred to at this point, but too inclusively; we will have occasion to disagree with that in detail later.[62] In the light of these candid questions, it is indeed better to avoid hasty hypotheses concerning the oral pre-history of the [p. 80] gospel form, and to begin with the written form of the Gospel of Mark, if we want to talk about this form. In this regard redaction criticism regards the work of the evangelists as being almost entirely determined by redactional activity, since the tradition is also encompassed by redaction, and belongs to it as *selected* tradition.

The literary unity of the gospel form therefore has its own problematics independent of the study of the tradition-history of the oral materials.[63] Form criticism as previously practiced is in fact "to be expanded by a 'form criticism of the gospels'",[64] which does not mean a departure from the analytical tradition, but its modification in an altered context of research: "The gospels may not be regarded as being merely collections of acts and deeds, arranged in a more or less artistic form. The gospel, each individual gospel, is an actual literary work, a product of the individual, self-conscious, and uninterrupted activity of the evangelist who is a real *author*, not merely a compiler of disconnected traditional data."[65]

The evangelist Mark is both *auctor* and *compositor*:[66] *compositor* with respect to his choice and arrangement of materials, *auctor* with respect to the gospel genre he creates, which is also a "gestalt"-principle presupposed in the choice and arrangement of the materials.[67] As we might put it in other words, both traditio-historically and redaction-critically *the auctor of the framework is its compositor.* The *auctor* determines both the gospel form and the possibilities

of sighting the pre-history of his materials. So W. Hillmann
suggests that the contemporary task is "to demonstrate the
literary character of the synoptic gospels in terms of their
fixed and regularized composition by the evangelists; the
gospels did not come about by means of a simple process of
collection and by a mere redaction of just any sources, but
they took on the form in which they are present to us on the
basis of a unified conceptuality which has been followed consistently and has determined the choice, arrangement, and
even to a certain extent the concrete shaping of the pericopes".[68]

[p. 81] The favorite objection, that this view eliminates the boundaries between literature proper and "Kleinliteratur",[69] is on closer analysis much less compelling than
it seems; we have already dealt with it in another connection[70]
and will return to it once more below.[71] Therefore as a whole
it can be stated reasonably that in the transition from the
oral "sociological setting" to the literary "framework", there
are many more problems and difficulties than were dealt with
earlier by form and redaction criticism. Our task must now
consist of exposing these problematics as sharply as we can.

Notes to #4

1. Cf. G. Iber's report, *ThR* 24 (1957/58) 328ff.; X. Léon-Dufour, S.J., "Bulletin d'exégèse du Nouveau Testament: Formgeschichte et Redaktionsgeschichte des Evangiles synoptiques," *RechSR* 46 (1958) 237-69; J. Rohde, *Formgeschichte und Redaktionsgeschichte in der neutestamentlichen Forschung der Gegenwart*, Diss., East Berlin, 1962, in briefer form as *Die redaktionsgeschichtliche Methode*, 1965; S. Gonzales de Carrea, O.F.M. Cap., "El método histórico-redaccional en los evangelios sinopticos," *Naturaleza y Gracia* (= *NatGrac*) 11 (1964) 205-25; H. Zimmermann, *Ntl. Methodenlehre*, 214ff.

2. Cf. below, p. [155ff.].

3. K. L. Schmidt, *RGG*-3rd ed., vol. 2, 1928, 638, following Overbeck. Cf. below, #6, n. 22.

4. M. Dibelius, *ThR* 1 (1929) 187. Similarly Schick, *Formgesch.*, 20.

5. Schmidt, *op. cit.*

6. R. Bultmann, *RGG*-2nd ed., vol. 3, 1929, 1681.

7. M. Dibelius, *Geschichte der urchristlichen Literatur*, vol. 2, 1926, also does not consider himself restricted in such a manner. Perhaps "forms" and "genres" can be terminologically distinguished, the former distinguishing the smaller units, the latter the overarching form; so Zimmermann, *Ntl. Methodenlehre*, 135. But that does not make for a distinction in principle, since form criticism from its beginning desired to distinguish literary genres. Cf. Cullmann, *Vortr.*, 47.

8. Cf. Schmidt, *Rahmen*, 17: "It is valid...to explain the earliest framework of the history of Jesus, as it is to be found in Mark, in terms of itself."

9. Cf. Bultmann, *Syn. Trad.*, 347ff.

10. Cf. *ibid.*, 362ff.; K. L. Schmidt, "Der geschichtliche Wert des lukanischen Aufrisses der Geschichte Jesu," *ThStKr* 91 (1918) 277-92.

11. Cf. G. Strecker, *Der Weg der Gerechtigkeit*, 1962, 9: "The traditio-historical unity of the preliterary transmission belongs to the redactions of the gospels...as a presupposition

of form-critical work, and it is clear that the latter cannot be contrasted with the former."

12. Bultmann, *op. cit.*, 347.

13. Koch, *Formgeschichte*-1st ed., 68f.

14. Cf. W. Marxsen, *Der Evangelist Markus*, 1956, 11: Redaction criticism "is not just the continuation of form criticism. It merely made its appearance at a later date. And for its work there is much to be learned from the earlier research."

15. W. Hillmann, *Aufbau und Deutung der synoptischen Leidensberichte*, 1951, vii: "A very important procedure has seemingly been entirely overlooked in form-critical research, or perhaps too little observed, namely the living process of the way the gospel became a form, as well as the factors which definitely determine this process." Cf. also Anonymous (J.-J. Weber), *HerKorr* 17 (1962/63) 428: "Finally, form criticism commits the error of regarding the gospels as uniform collections of material."

16. G. Iber, *ThR* 24 (1956/57) 329: "But also for the person who seeks like the form critic to conceive the form and the kerygmatic contents of the congregation's transmission, the 'framework' looses its significance; for precisely what cannot be said of the framework is that it is an original witness of the first congregations. From this it is understandable why the representatives of form criticism do not pay attention to the framework." *Ibid.*, 335: "The question about the unity of the gospel writings was for form criticism only a marginal question."

17. G. Schille, *NTS* 4 (1957/58) 1: "Almost the only thing to be considered the work of the evangelist would be the 'collection' (redaction) and fixation of materials which had already been pre-formed for a long time."

18. Cf. H. Dieckmann, *Scholastik* 1 (1926) 380.

19. Cf. here the special bibliography for Mark: H. Risenfeld, "Tradition und Redaktion im Markusevangelium," in *Neutestamentliche Studien für Rudolf Bultmann*, 1954, 157-64; W. Marxsen, "Redaktionsgeschichtliche Erklärung der sogenannten Parabeltheorie des Markus," *ZThK* 52 (1955) 255-71; Marxsen, *Der Evangelist Markus*, 1956; J. M. Robinson, *Das Geschichtsverständnis des Markus-Evangeliums*, 1956; T. A. Burkill, "The Cryptology of Parables in St. Mark's Gospel," *NovTest* 1 (1956)

110

246-62; Burkill, "The Injunction to Silence in St. Mark's Gospel," *ThZ* 12 (1956) 585-604; Burkill, "St. Mark's Philosophy of History," *NTS* 3 (1956/57) 142-48; Burkill, "Concerning St. Mark's Conception of Secrecy," *HibJ* 55 (1957) 150-58; Burkill, "St. Mark's Philosophy of the Passion," *NovTest* 2 (1958) 245-71; Burkill, "Anti-Semitism in St. Mark's Gospel," *NovTest* 3 (1959) 34-54; Burkill, *Mysterious Revelation*, 1963; G. Schille (see #2, n. 15); J. Schreiber, *Der Kreuzigungsbericht des Markusevangeliums*, Diss. Bonn, 1959; Schreiber, "Die Christologie des Markusevangeliums," *ZThK* 58 (1961) 154-83; Schreiber, *Theologische Erkenntnis und unterrichtlicher Vollzug*, 1966; Schreiber, *Theologie des Vertrauens*, 1967; E. Schweizer, "Anmerkungen zur Theologie des Markus," in his *Neotestamentica*, 1963, 93-104; Schweizer, "Die theologische Leistung des Markus," *EvTh* 24 (1964) 337-55; Schweizer, "Zur Frage des Messiasgeheimnisses bei Markus," *ZNW* 56 (1965) 1-8; P. Vielhauer, "Erwägungen zur Christologie des Markusevangeliums," in his *Aufs.*, 199-214; U. Luz, "Das Geheimnismotiv und die markinische Christologie," *ZNW* 56 (1965) 9-30; E. Best, *The Temptation and the Passion: The Markan Soteriology*, 1965; A. Suhl, *Die Funktion der alttestamentlichen Zitate und Anspielungen im Markusevangelium*, 1965; S. Schulz, *Die Stunde der Botschaft*, 1967.

20. Cf. Rohde, *Redakt. Methode*, 17.

21. Cf. Dibelius, *Formgesch.*, 231ff.

22. Cf. Bultmann, *Syn. Trad.*, 370ff. Rohde's assertion, *op. cit.*, 19, that Bultmann has "designated as superfluous an investigation of the evangelist's work in detail, in view of its scanty results" is therefore incorrect.

23. G. Klein, *Die zwölf Apostel*, 1961, 16. Similarly H. Conzelmann, *ThLZ* 82 (1957) 585: "We have to do with a methodological 'advance', which for its part presupposes literary criticism and form criticism."

24. *Versus* W. Marxsen also H. Köster, *VF* 7 (1956/57, 1958/59) 178f.; G. Strecker, *ZKG* 72 (1961) 143ff.; Klein, *op. cit.*, 15ff.; Strecker, *Weg der Gerechtigkeit*, 10; G. Schille, *ThLZ* 88 (1963) 492f.; Rohde, *op. cit.*, 31f.; Rese, Diss., p. 13, n. 10; Zimmermann, *op. cit.*, 215f.

25. Schille, *ThLZ* 88 (1963) 492. Against this: Rohde, *op. cit.*, 192.

26. Schreiber, *Theol. des Vertrauens*, 10.

27. Cf. below, p. [155ff.].

28. Koch, *Formgesch.*, 69.

29. Cf. the evidence below, pp. [94f., 103ff.].

30. Bultmann, *RGG*-2nd ed., vol. 2, 1928, 420.

30a Cf. F. Brentano, *Das Genie*, 1892; H. Wolf, *Versuch einer Geschichte des Geniebegriffs in der deutschen Aesthetik des 18. Jahrhunderts*, vol. 1, 1923; E. Zilsel, *Die Entstehung des Geniebegriffes*, 1926; W. Lange-Eichbaum, *Das Genie-Problem*, 1931; Lange-Eichbaum, *Irrsinn und Ruhm*, 1967-6th ed.; P. Grappin, *La théorie du génie dans le préclassicisme allemand*, 1952.

30b M. Dibelius constantly interprets the "Kleinliteratur" explicitly as "collective art", whose formation is conditioned by "the collective, the congregation, which creates particular genres" (cf. the quotation above, #3, n. 124 and n. 14); he therefore modifies the older concept of the "folk art" in the sense of the newer sociological conceptuality.

31. Marxsen, *op. cit.*, 7-16.

32. Cf. *ibid.*, 7f.

33. Cf. above, p. [44ff.].

34. Cf. H. Gunkel, *Reden und Aufsätze*, 1913, 28: We realize: "that the author's freedom of movement in a time when the individual was relatively undeveloped, and custom has more compulsion than it does today, was only a limited freedom. Some of the O. T. authors are by no means 'authors', but rather collectors".

35. Cf. Fascher, *Formgesch. Methode*, 210: The conclusions of E. Norden's style-critical research are "that the style and the form are impersonal and objective matters taken up by humans from each other; of style in this impersonal sense we can only speak in terms of folkloristic transmission such as we ourselves know".

36. Cf. Dibelius, *Formgesch.*, 3; K. L. Schmidt in *Eucharisterion*, vol. 2, 53; Schniewind, *ThR* 2 (1930) 152f.; Rohde, *op. cit.*, 3. Differently: J. Weiss, *ThLZ* 48 (1923) 9f.

37. Schmidt, *op. cit.*, 76. Cf. *ibid.*, 125: In the process of an exact comparison of the gospels with contemporary documents it can be seen "how far from the ideal of the his-

torian working with original sources are the evangelists, even
Luke". Schmidt, in P. Barth, ed., *Jesus Christus im Zeugnis
der Heiligen Schrift und der Kirche*, 1936-2nd ed., 12: "In
the gospels the literary portrait as the object and the authorial personality as the subject of the gospel writing disappear."

38. So H. Clavier, *EThR* 9 (1934) 7.

39. G. Strecker, *ZKG* 72 (1961) 143.

40. Dibelius, *Formgesch.*, 2. In agreement: Cullmann,
Vorträge 60; Zimmermann, *op. cit.*, 137.

41. Cf. Rohde, *op. cit.*, 193: "What takes place within
the anonymous masses belongs to the concept 'popular piety',
which is not to exclude that creative religious personalities
can arise from them."

42. Strecker, *op. cit.*, 144.

43. Rohde, *op. cit.*, 193.

44. Strecker, *Weg der Gerechtigkeit*, 10. Cf. below, p.
[77].

45. Cullmann, *Vorträge*, 59.

46. Marxsen, *op. cit.*, 7.

47. Cf. above, n. 12. [+1978: Obviously Bultmann did not
even suspect that "composition" as a text-syntactic operation
is a new "network" which may give new functional values to the
tradition. May we then say so readily that there is nothing
"new" between tradition and composition?]

48. Marxsen, *op. cit.*, 8: "But it is not at all understandable in itself that this entirely disparate material
leads in the end to the unity of the gospel."

49. Strecker, *op. cit.*, 10, my emphasis.

50. Cf. below, p. [161ff.]; above, p. [65ff.].

51. Cf. below, p. [258ff.]

52. Marxsen, *op. cit.*, 9.

53. Hence Strecker's objection (*op. cit.*, 10) is deflected,
namely that its execution of the "plan" in the gospel-form is

not what distinguishes the gospel redaction "in its essentials, from the passion history; rather the various phases of the pre-synoptic transmission can be associated with dogmatic expressions, especially when the transmission not only expands upon what has been delivered, but simultaneously makes transitions from one form to another". Furthermore the conceptual model of this objection is in my opinion inappropriate: Was there then before the association with "dogmatic" expressions some sort of a so-to-speak "non-dogmatic" traditional material? Is not the traditional material the dogmatic expression itself? Otherwise it is indeed clear that here the *premise* of the traditio-historical continuity (cf. above, n. 39) is introduced. This is a matter of the methodological justification of this premise, whose hypothetical character is never to be forgotten.

54. Marxsen, *op. cit.*, 9.

55. *Ibid.*, 12.

56. So already C. F. G. Heinrici, *Der litterarische Charakter der neutestamentlichn Schriften*, 1908, 43f.

57. Cf. Marxsen, *op. cit.*, 10: "The initial matter confronting us is in fact the transmission, but that means the transmission of the evangelists, i.e., reference is to the tradition deposited in the gospels."

57a On the tension between tradition- and utilization-hypotheses, see below, p. [149f.].

58. Cf. #6, n. 22, below.

59. Cf. Marxsen, *op. cit.*, 10.

60. Cf. J. C. L. Gieseler, *Historisch-kritischer Versuch über die Entstehung und die frühesten Schicksale der schriftlichen Evangelien*, 1818. Cf. W. G. Kümmel, *Das Neue Testament*, 1958, 99.

61. Cf. below, p. [170ff.].

62. Cf. below, p. [189ff.].

63. So also S. Gonzales de Carrea, O.F.M. Cap., *NatGrac* 11 (1964) 218.

64. Marxsen, *op. cit.*, 11.

114

65. Gonzales de Carrea, *op. cit.*, 217: [I have translated
the Spanish version given in the text; Güttgemanns provides a
German translation in this note. W.G.D.]

66. Cf. G. J. Sirks, "Auctor-compositor," *NedThT* 12 (1957/
58) 81-91.

67. Cf. below, p. [184ff.].

68. Hillmann, *Aufbau*, 2. Differently: Schniewind, *ThR*
2 (1930) 164: "the reconstruction of the trains of thought
with which the exegete concerns oneself in treating Paul is a
methodological error with respect to the synoptic writers"
(partly in italics in original). Against this: Hillmann, *op.
cit.*, 3, 259: "The exterior regularity of the composition
which proceeds according to set and formal laws, makes it
clear that the outline of the synoptic gospels is of a fundamentally systematic nature."

69. Cf. Strecker, *op. cit.*, 10.

70. Cf. above, p. [75f.].

71. Cf. below, p. [94f.].

#5. *The Problematics of the Transition from the Oral "Sociological Setting" to the Literary "Framework".*

1. The Traditio-Historical Contingency of the "Sociological Setting" of the Gospel Form.

That there are, within the phenomenon of the "literary framework" of the "pre-literary" tradition, several unresolved problems that have not yet been sharply enough delineated, becomes clear when we examine more precisely the relationship of the literary "framework" to the oral "sociological setting" of the "small units".* With reference to this relationship, we already noted one important question in our discussion of W. Marxsen's work: To what extent does the "framework" characteristic of the gospel form serve the pericopes bound up within it as a new "sociological setting", within which they are utilized,[1] if the framework also simultaneously *has* a "sociological setting" within the gestalt of the gospel-form, and therefore cannot be understood as something totally individualistic, something created by the evangelist on his own? Or are the "sociological setting" of the oral pericopes and the literary "framework" to be contrasted as linguistic relations that dissolve into one another, since they are indications of the transition from the "pre-literary"

---

*"kleinen Einheiten"--this phrase, and the term Einzelstück/e, have sometimes been translated by pericope/s below when it would be awkward to translate "small" or "isolated unit/s". W.G.D.

level of the tradition? Naturally the concept "sociological
setting" receives in these questions a certain and perhaps
even decisive modification: It no longer designates as "setting in the life of the folk" H. Gunkel's understanding of
the place of the *oral* transmission of a pericope,[2] but rather
its functional and structural insertion into a *literary* context. However just that shows us that the concept "sociological setting" can by no means have been tied originally
to a literary phenomenon without a certain amount of tension,
that in other words form criticism makes a direct concession
of an essential distinction between the oral and the written
level of tradition.

As insightful as is the argument in favor of a continuous connection between form and redaction criticism in one
respect, and as much as it actually maintains an essential
aspect of the form-critical approach, it is quite unsatis-
factory in another respect. [p. 83] Form criticism analyzes
the various forms of the pericopes and thereby obtains a
plurality of "sociological settings", in which in each case
a specific form has impressed itself and has been passed along
further as tradition.[3] The laws of tradition for a particular
form, valid for a specific "sociological setting" are analyzed,
with the result that the material of the synoptic tradition is
localized in a whole series of "settings" and thereby is also
subject to the most various traditio-historical laws determined by the multiplicity of "settings".

To be sure M. Dibelius has bridged these divergences by
means of his wide-reaching derivation of the synoptic materials
from the preaching of the early church;[4] however his model has
subsequently shown itself to be too one-sided.[5] It does not
accord with the multiplicity of the forms and "sociological
settings" such as R. Bultmann has derived; it is a consequence
of the "constructive" method,[6] which is properly open to crit-

icism so far as Dibelius "derives the concepts and the history of the genres not from the analysis of the given materials but from presupposed needs of the communities".[7] In the final analysis the preaching-concept is only a quite general cipher for the fact that the synoptic material is somehow "kergymatic": "When considered more closely it is nevertheless striking how vaguely this original setting is defined and how little of the material composing our gospels can be linked with the preaching so often referred to."[8] Hence we may no longer conceal the divergencies of the synoptic materials by means of elastic concepts and "constructive" hypotheses. *The heterogeneity of the "sociological settings" remains an unquestionable fact.*

The accepted--and partly at least hypothetically still applicable--pre-literary collection of the pericopes[9] does in this respect present a problem. Since such collections are by no means completely explainable as an accumulation of similar forms,[10] it is not at all understandable *a priori* how it is that out of the collective effect [p. 84] of the most heterogeneous laws of tradition, the individual building blocks *can* coalesce at all into a new construct, one that subsequently develops its own form-critical laws. Does the new form (and with it, the new "sociological setting" also) originate as a mosaic created by simply arranging the disparate building blocks into series, or is it essentially determined by the needs of a new "sociological setting", which in turn determines the choice, arrangement, and adaptation of the materials? How is the "sociological setting" of the new construct related to the "settings" of its individual pericopes? Perhaps as the final traditio-historical consequence with respect to its pre-history? It seems to me that such a conceptual model cannot be analytically proven, if we constantly remain aware of the danger of a hypothetical construction as a whole. In

these circumstances has the process of origination of the complex form already been understood when the new construct is
described as a mosaic produced by the assimilation of separate
building blocks, i.e., understood essentially from the form-
critical implications of its materials, instead of on its own
terms, or from the implications of the new "sociological settings"? *With respect to the more complex form and the "sociological setting", is the analytical questioning still at all
relevant*, or with respect to the outline of the new construct
encompassed within itself, is "the literary analysis only
relevant at a second remove",[11] whereas the new construct
should, with respect to hermeneutics and interpretation, belong so completely to the primary principle that even the tradition belongs "primarily to the redaction"[12] in which case
each section is to be questioned as to its structural value
for the entirety of the new model?

J. Schreiber recently drew up the following consequences
for the Gospel of Mark, I think correctly: The "framework"
is the hermeneutical principle for the interpretation of the
tradition constituent to the gospel; "we must inquire about
the relation between framework and tradition. Only after we
have taken this inquiry 'as far as it will lead, and made it
the basis of criticism', is it legitimate to study the small
traditional units in isolation--unless in the meantime such
an investigation has not been shown to be superfluous!"[13]

All this means that the new "sociological setting" of the
more complex construct cannot be derived easily from the tradition-history of its smaller units; *traditio-historically it
is just as contingent as the "sociological settings" of the
smaller units.* Within the sociological conception of form
criticism a "sociological setting" is indeed a phenomenon of
the sociological composition of a collective,[14] [p. 85] which
may certainly have a pre-history; but the pre-history of the

linguistic and traditio-historical materials must not be confused with this *sociological* pre-history of the transmitters.
Naturally this is not of the same significance as the thesis
of a complete lack of relationship between the "sociological
setting" of the pericope and the "sociological setting" of
the more complex construct. But it signifies the rejection
of a traditio-historical misunderstanding of this relation,
that otherwise remains in a certain tension with the sociological foundations of the "sociological setting", because a
sociological typology cannot signify a tradition-history even
if content-bound. Naturally *one* "sociological setting" does
not always correspond to only *one* genre. For example the
following materials may have their "sociological setting" in
the primitive Christian service of worship in the wider sense,
or in "cult":[15] liturgical fragments such as the liturgy of
the Last Supper (I Cor 11:23-25; Mark 14:22-25 and parallels),[16] "hymns" (cf. Phil 2:6-11, 3:20f.; I Tim 3:16; Col
1:13-20; I Peter 2:22-24, 3:18ff.),[17] "confessions" (cf. Ro
3:25f., 4:25),[18] "formulas" (cf. Ro 10:9, I Cor 15:3-5, I
Thess 1:9f., and others),[19] prophetic phenomena such as
glossolalia (cf. I Cor 14)[20] and also, according to G.
Schille, the passion.[21] The "sociological setting" is often
distributed "among a multitude of genres that are loosely connected to each other, each of which exercises its special
function".[22] Several different genres can have a common
"sociological setting", and because of this common quality,
can be collected into a new and larger, formal construct,
[p. 86] so that the "sociological setting" of the new construct is actually determined by its constituent pericopes.
In this sense we might follow K. Koch in distinguishing
"framework genres" and "component genres" [Rahmengattungen
und Gliedgattungen].[23] As an example of the process of
collection intended here, we might list something like the

literary collection of the Psalms, which with respect to style consist of quite heterogeneous forms related to one another in various ways, but sharing a common "sociological setting" in the wider sense.[24]

But this possibility of collation of different genres as a consequence of common utilization in *one* "sociological setting" does not yet explain the adaptation of units with a different "sociological setting" into a more complex construct, whose "sociological setting" cannot any longer simply be derived from the tradition-history of its constituent parts. Were these units subordinated to the "sociological setting" of the new construct by this adaptation, or were they modified precisely by their being taken up into this "sociological setting"?

At any rate we must guard here against schematic answers and a rigid conceptual model. Moreover we cannot demonstrate for primitive Christianity a phenomenon similar to that of the Psalms; the "cultic" or "liturgical" units we listed above were never collected as "component genres" by a "framework genre", which shows that the common "sociological setting" by no means necessarily has as its consequence what is a conceivable possibility, namely collection into the "framework genre". Finally precisely what must be demonstrated is that we may understand the gospel form as having this character of a "framework genre" at all. As a whole the difficulties of a simple traditio-historical derivation of a new "sociological setting" of a more complex construct are therefore so many *that it is better to begin with its traditio-historical contingency.*

2. The Transition from the Oral "Sociological
   Setting" to the Literary "Framework".

The derivation of the traditio-historical contingency of
the "sociological setting" of a new unit signifies the maintenance of its sociological foundation in the needs and functions
of the "active subject".[25] These sociological factors determine the new construct [p. 87] so greatly, and reach so deeply
into the tradition-history of the components of the construct,
that it is here that a more consequential break takes place.

The pericopes are divorced from their previous "sociological setting" and co-ordinated to the "setting" of the new
form, by being "framed" into the newer and larger entity,[26]
so that they also must be interpreted from the standpoint of
the later form, insofar as the new form develops a history of
variations, which in the case of the gospel would be the gospels. Naturally we can also conceive of further application
of the components as independent material, so that the old
"sociological setting" has not simply been erradicated. We
can also take into account the inertia of the genres, their
"tendency to remain in operation after the sociological setting disappears", so that we may not in every case "draw in-
ferences from a utilized genre to the *simultaneous* origination
of the sociological setting that belongs to it".[27]

Hence it is possible to demonstrate something like a free
application of the Jesus-material outside the synoptic collec-
tion--even if this is only one instance--[28] especially if we
accept as new sources the mass of gnostic "gospels" at Nag
Hammadi[29] in terms of "unknown words of Jesus"[30] and in terms
of the tradition-history of "synoptic" words of Jesus,[31]
rather than assuming with W. Schrage the use of an early
Coptic bible translation by the gnostic writers.[32] But we
have all these texts, as well as the entire traditional material of the gospels [p. 88] only in their published *state*;

hence the problem is whether we may conceive this state immediately and directly as the fallout of an oral *process*, if we possess no direct empirical evidence of a strictly oral process.[32a] In the non-biblical cases where we do have such direct empirical evidence, at any rate, the assumed "precomposition" [Urfassung] of the oral linguistic monuments is seen to be only a phantom.

Form-critically, that is, structurally, something so decisive occurs in the pericope when it makes the transition to a different "sociological setting", especially the transition from an oral to a written mode of tradition, that we must practically speak of a form-critical alteration,[33] if we are not at the same time to upend the methodological form-critical foundations that predicate the sociological determination of the forms by their "sociological setting". Even if almost nothing--looking at the matter purely externally, that is, stylistically and with regard for the consistency of the words in the pericope--seems to be changed,[34] because of the plain fact of its "framework", its insertion from a "preliterary level"[35] into a larger "literary connection" with its own laws, it is subordinated to a reformulation in structural and functional respects,[36] which can lead, in some circumstances, to a radical re-interpretation of its original meaning, as D. M. Stanley, S.J., has shown in Mk 15:39, Mt 8:6, Lk 1:35, Jo 19:30, and Num 22:22-30.[37] *The "framework" of the earlier pericopes determines a structural and functional alteration* and in this respect has consequences with respect to the *history* of the form which must not be overlooked.

The example of the "ethical-paraenetical" interpretation [p. 89] of the christological and eschatological hymns, Phil 2:6-11 and 3:20f.[38] or I Peter 1:18-20, 3:18f., 22,[39] are well known, as well as: the application of Jesus' parables for the church's paraenesis,[40] the way they are connected

with the messianic secret motif in Mk 4:10-12,[41] the ecclesiological and paraenetic insertion of a miracle story in Mt 8:
23-27,[42] the ecclesiological and eschatological framing of the
parables in Mt 13:1-52,[43] the composition of the Lukan "travel
account" in Lk 9:52-19:27,[44] and finally the interpretation of
the passion, especially in Mk 15:20b-41, in terms of the Markan messianic secret theory.[45] The last-named cases of re-interpretation of a "pre-literary" unit by its "literary" framing are especially striking, since here by means of a certain
common sense one can grasp the redactional and compositional
and *theological* achievement of the evangelists, and therefore
the traditio-historical consequences of bringing the materials
into writing which they inaugurate.[45a]

The transition of a pericope from the "pre-literary" into the "literary" level of tradition can be understood almost
as a change in the *mode* of tradition, whose traditio-historical laws are in some cases very similar, in purely external
and formal ways, to the oral mode; however in actuality, and
especially with respect to hermeneutics, they have quite another function.[46] For the hermeneutics of a pericope it is
no longer sufficient in these cases [p. 90] simply to analyze
the pericope and its "sociological setting", but a comprehensive understanding must now also inquire about the structural
value of the pericope's place in the new, more complex form,
according to the structural and functional context of its
place within the whole composition, so that we start from
the pericope and move to the "framework", and then from the
"framework" back again to the original pericope.

In these cases the gospel "framework" is to be described
formally as a conglomerate of redactional insertions into the
traditional material and of compositional arrangement of the
pericopes, but we scarcely thereby explain its nature, that
is, we do not define exactly its function characterized by

the gospel form, or its "sociological setting".[47] Since the
principle unifying the redactional work on the "framework"
could always be conceived independently of theology stemming
from the pericope,[48] which imposes itself upon the collected
material, so that it may not be understood traditio-historically out of the material, but only in its own terms, and so
that for this reason it is by no means questionable *a priori*
whether "the oral origination of the tradition might be fundamentally different from the later fixation in writing".[49]
The "framework" is something quite different from being merely the written fixation of what has already had a long history
as oral material! That is even more the case when new written
genres can arise from the written level of tradition, genres
"that are more comprehensive, and whose formal characteristics
are not as clearly evident as those of the oral genres".[50]
For example, it seems that the "speeches" in Matthew in their
present form (cf. 5:1-7:28, 9:36-11:1, 13:1-52, 18:1-35, 23:
1-39, 24:1-25:46) are first certain in the written stratum
of the tradition, that is, when they have [p. 91] been for-
malized by Matthew and have become a characteristic marker
of Matthew's gospel-form.[51]

Some genres exist primarily or only in the written mode
of tradition.[52] Is that only accidental, or is it not essentially related to the earlier form-critical distinction which
differentiated the oral "sociological settings" from the
written "settings", i.e., the *form-critical* distinction between the oral and the written? To put it another way: In
spite of all the *conjectured* similarities of the traditio-
historical laws on the "pre-literary" and the "literary"
level, form criticism of the "literary" form has to take
into account particular aspects which are not present as
such in the "pre-literary" stage.[53] The alteration of the
mode of the tradition is not a subsidiary external for the

history of the form, but it is a constitutive dimension in the hermeneutics of the forms. Because such historical viewpoints were not treated as fundamental by form criticism it can be suggested that the observation of the framework itself appeared too quickly in form-critical studies.[54] To be sure it has not been sufficiently clarified *to what extent the "literary" framework is in tradition- and form-critical terms a dimension sui generis* that is essentially related to the ways the first evangelists conveyed the material into written form.

3. The Schematism of the "Constructive" Historical Picture in Martin Dibelius' Understanding of the Origination of the Gospel Form.

After the final demolishing of the thesis concerning the traditio-historical continuity of oral and written forms,[55] the question arose as to how this thesis could have become so widespread in form criticism in spite of the tensions with its beginnings that we have demonstrated. [p. 92] In my opinion the decisive factor was the considerable power of M. Dibelius' conceptual model, which we wish to analyze at this point.

(a) Martin Dibelius' Three "Principle Witnesses".

Dibelius begins his arguments concerning form-critical methodology[56] with what is to me a clear reference to F. Overbeck's thesis that if "a literature" should have a history "in its forms, form criticism would actually be literary history".[57] This judgment may not, according to Dibelius, "be applied indiscriminately to every type of written material", but is especially valid only with respect to litera-tures "in which the personality of the author recedes into the background". He is referring above all to folk-transmission, "where many anonymous persons are creatively active in the passing on of the material transmitted, in terms of altera- tion or expansion, and where the individual author has no literary goals" and "the personal uniqueness of the poet or narrator is insignificant". A. Olrik's "biology of the saga"[58] seemed appropriate to describe this anonymous mode of tradition.[59]

-1. This starting point of the "constructive" conceptual model encompasses many types of influences. There is first of all direct reference to F. Overbeck, who had proved, as Dibelius put it, "that for a part of the biblical writings, and especially for the writings of the first Christian de- cades, we do not have literature proper, created by authorial volition, but formulations that proceed of necessity from the existence and activity of circles in which literature is foreign".[60] A closer investigation of the foundations and consistency of Overbeck's statements would show that he had probed much more deeply the problem of the oral and the writ- ten character of "pre-literature"[61] than has been previously recognized, because the material has only recently been ac- cessible to a wider audience through M. Tetz' classification.[62] Without a doubt it is from Overbeck that Dibelius' description derives with respect to the claim that in the "literature" treated here the authorial personality recedes into the back- ground. But while Dibelius applied this thesis, as did earli- er folkloristics[63] to the anonymity of the [p. 93] folk-trans- mission, it is in Overbeck's work an element of his conception of "pre-literature", i.e., a paraphrase for the immediacy of the written medium and for the effective linguistic power of the unity of author and form in "pre-literature",[64] both ideas which at any rate could be brought together only very loosely with the earlier folkloristic conceptions by means of the conceptual medial term, the organism. *Whether or not form criticism agrees with F. Overbeck's conception without reservation is today a candid question.*

-2. Then Dibelius refers explicitly to earlier folkloristics since J. G. Herder, whose "investigation of folk Kleinliteratur, with which gospel form criticism is concerned...had already gained expertise in many areas and had developed methodologies".[65] To be sure it has been established within more recent folkloristics[66] that these methods are by no means only oriented to the empirical realities of folk "Kleinliteratur", but were themselves "constructively" drawn from a particular view of history. This view of history can be designated as a "romantic" variant of the philosophy of identity which is established by the metaphysical equation *actus purus* = life = orality = folk = lower classes of the nation.[67] *Whether or not form criticism agrees with earlier folkloristics without exception is today a candid question.* To be sure it also uses a botanical metaphor of the "organic connection" of the gospel-composition "with that of the history of the materials preceeding the gospels";[67a] but it ceases to use this metaphor in its romantic sense when it simultaneously accepts sociological conceptions.

-3. Finally, Dibelius' approach is explicitly related to H. Gunkel's suggestions, especially with respect to the category of the "sociological setting". Corresponding analyses of the O. T. have shown that "this collected material can only be analyzed if we reach back to the smallest perceptible forms of the transmission".[68] But a closer investigation of the foundations and consistency of Gunkel's suggestions will demonstrate that he too wrestled with the problem he recognized between the oral and the written more extensively than he would initially realize.[69] Furthermore particular theo-

logical and hermeneutical foundations of Gunkel's form-critical method have often been ignored in contemporary application
of form criticism.[70] *Therefore whether or not contemporary*
form criticism is to conform entirely to H. Gunkel's concep-
tion remains today a candid question.

[p. 94] (b) Martin Dibelius' Conceptual Model.

We can now treat further aspects of Dibelius' methodology, since we have pointed to certain uncertainties in the three
"principle witnesses" of his conceptual model. These aspects
are basically obtained by deduction and development of the
starting points already treated.

Dibelius turns, in even closer analogy to earlier folkloristics, to "Kleinliteratur", for which the anonymity, collectivity, and pre-literary character pointed out at the beginning are especially valid. Dibelius, in a sociological
reformulation of the "romantic" schema, situates the "Kleinliteratur" sociologically among the "lower classes",[71] "which
did not share in the artistic media and the movements of literary and artistic writing, and did not have to deal with its
public; the products of the Klein-Literatur found their readers in circles that had not been touched by literature
proper".[72] To be sure the primitive Christian literature
"developed from being private records until it neared the
bounds of literature proper", but the gospels "doubtless belong to Kleinliteratur; they do not desire to be, nor can they
be measured by, the standards of 'literary' works, but on the
other hand they are not just private records but are destined
for a public, no matter how small and modest".[73] The synoptic
writers preserve "collected material" [Sammelgut] to which the
evangelists in their roles as "collectors" and "reworkers"
contributed not their "original formation", but only their
"selection, framing, and final form":[74] "The form criticism

of the gospel, that is, of this material, does not begin somehow with the work of the evangelists, but it already attains
in the formation of the gospel-books a certain termination."[75]

Dibelius states explicitly in this thesis that he understands the gospel-form as being the final traditio-historical
consequence of the gospel-materials and that on the basis of
this premise the criteria of anonymity, collectivity, and the
"pre-literary" character of the tradition of the materials
must be *transferred* to the creation and formation of the gospel-form. We should always be aware that this is only a conceptual hypothesis, which as a "constructive" premise must
yield to the results of individual form-critical analyses.
Possibly this hypothesis has proved itself[76] but today we
should sooner refer to the uncertainties in the position
which can no longer be blinked, and it is my feeling that
they cause strong reservations against taking the "constructive" conceptual model as being all too certain. It should
be [p. 95] expressly noted that in the present work I have
no hostility to form criticism in general; on the contrary,
I am concerned with finding better methodological foundations
for the method by means of a long-overdue dismantling of
those premises that have impeded the method and which today
can be readily replaced by integrating sociological findings
in linguistics and literary criticism.[77] Therefore this book
works toward a more careful and more productive methodological
*development of form criticism by overcoming its stagnation and
its unnecessary isolation from the linguistic and sociological
disciplines.*

130

4.   The Foundation of the "Non-Literary" Character
     of Kleinliteratur in the Eschatological Charac-
     ter of Primitive Christianity.

     (a)   The Thesis.

     F. Overbeck was one of the first to discover the funda-
mentally-eschatological character of primitive Christianity.[78]
Overbeck's concept of "pre-literature" is closely related to
this discovery. Analogously form criticism sought repeatedly
to find the foundation of the "pre-literary" character of the
"Kleinliteratur" in primitive Christian eschatology. It is
interesting, and in the framework of this book necessary, to
look more closely at this foundation.
     As we have already shown above,[79] M. Dibelius connects
the primitive Christian eschatology with the sociological
structure of the primitive church, in order to derive from
this connection primitive Christianity's "distance toward the
world", and within this framework, its distance from the medium of literature proper.[79a] So a main argument in favor of
the "non-literary" or "pre-literary" character of the "Kleinliteratur", above all of the gospels, is the primitive Christian expectation of a temporally-near eschaton: "A community
of non-literary persons, awaiting the end of the world today
or tomorrow, has neither the capacity nor the inclination toward production of books, and hence we ought not to anticipate
real authorial activity on the part of the Christian churches
of the first two or three decades."[80] "The Christian sermon
was directed toward the end of the world; its hearers could
not create literature proper. The beginnings of the gospel-
'literature' therefore occurred without the intentions of the
participants being directed toward literary production."[81]
This "non-literary character [p. 96] of primitive Christianity" excludes an "immediate connection between life and ex-

pression".[82] In other words: Because the church was not sociologically oriented toward the world, nor eschatologically toward the representation of the past, in the gospel-form that leads into gospel-tradition we are confronted not with "literature proper", but with "Kleinliteratur", not that is with "literary" representation of Jesus' past and that of the church or its traditions, but with a "non-literary" phenomenon reflecting the "non-literary" character of the primitive Christian community. Even if Dibelius only sketches this chain of thought, it seems indisputable to me that it actually represents here a sociology-of-religion description of the milieu which produced the "Kleinliteratur". Dibelius' argument has been treated so often by others that no further evidence need be cited. However: is it possible to hold onto such a position without buying into its constituent discrepancies? Several reasons lead me to suspect that the argument still has more than just hypothetical value.

(b) Psychological or Historical Analogy?

The first question that arises is how the historian is in a position to know that a collective's eschatological attitude is the sociology-of-religions basis for a distancing from literary pursuits. It seems to me that this represents a quite general *psychological* conclusion from analogy, one which reduces primitive Christian eschatology, especially the presumed "apocalyptic" expectation, so completely to a psychological phenomenon,[83] that the primitive Christian distancing from the world and consequently also from the literary world appears to be a peculiarity needing psychological explanation. Certainly it is evident that at least the dialectics of the Pauline *hōs mē* (cf. I Cor 7:29-31)[84] has been psychologically misunderstood. But even this conclusion by psychological

analogy--which certainly makes one wonder that a community
living so ecstatically outside all "worldly" ties would even
give thought to so "worldly" a matter as daily bread--is anything but historically based. What do we actually know about
an "apocalyptic" collective's attitude toward literary matters?
Does not our entire historical knowledge speak against the recent thesis that the "apocalyptic" attitude of the primitive
church could not have led to the establishment of "literature
proper", but only to "Kleinliteratur"?

(c) The Missing Analogy in Jewish Apocalyptic.

Here the subject of apocalyptic literature as a historically analogous phenomenon is referred to especially,[85] namely
to that horizon in the history of religion from which already
H. v. Soden[86] and again more recently E. Käsemann[87] derive
the genre "gospel". The form of the apocalypses, the frequent reports of visions,[88] and even wisdom materials[89] are
traced back to the authorship of the righteous[90] and wise
persons[91] of the Israelite pre-history (Enoch, Noah, Abraham,
Moses, Elijah, Baruch, Daniel, Ezra), in contradiction to the
linkage of revelation to the new aeon asserted by D. Lührmann.[92] [p. 98] To be sure the anticipatory proleptics of
the "historical survey in future-form"[93] associated with
pseudonymity rests upon the literary fiction of the pre-
historicality of the revelation of these secrets;[94] but this
fictionality is intended to emphasize precisely by means of
its esoteric quality[95] that God will allow the elect righteous (cf. I Enoch 1:1) and wise persons (cf. I Enoch 100:6,
104:12) of the present day to participate already in his
revelation that has proceeded from the mouths of the righteous and wise ones of pre-history, *through the "literary"
medium of the book.*[96] Only at the end of all days will what

is now already a public secret known by the elect through
secret writings be made known to all humanity by agency of
the predicted events themselves.[97] So the "literary" anticipation of the eschatological revelation basically means
that the elect have been saved from the dualism of the two
aeons[98] by means of secret writings. By the plain fact of
the literary genre of apocalyptic, for the readers of this
literature, the dualism of the two aeons is disarmed, since
the righteous will already have been initiated into God's
secrets through the esoteric material, and so saved from the
general fallenness of the old aeon, so long as they trust the
guidance of the apocalyptic writer and regard history as the
circumscribed time for decision,[99] insofar as they learn from
the apocalyptic [p. 99] books "every sort of uprightness"
(cf. I Enoch 104:13) and are able to conceive and hold fast
(cf. IV Ezra 12:38) with their hearts to the secrets of these
books, since they are the wise ones of the chosen people[100]
after having scrutinized the sealed books in order to grow
in knowledge (cf. Dan 12:4). The eventual salvation of
humankind depends upon its obedience to the Law practiced
in this aeon, because the eschatological *jus talionis* is
valid (cf. Syr. Bar. 54:21f.)[101] and Deut 30:19 was warning-
ly recalled (cf. Syr. Bar. 18:1f., 19:1-4a).[102] The three
paraenetic farewell speeches of the seer Baruch (cf. Syr.
Bar. 31:3-32:7, 44:2-15, 45:1f., 77:1-10)[103] at the conclusion of the three parts of the apocalypse of Syr. Bar.[104] and
the paraenetic portions in the so-called Epistle of Baruch
(Syr. Bar. 78-87)[105] also repeatedly impress the eschatological significance of the law: The interest of the writer "consists without a doubt in addressing his own generation through
the mouth of the fictional figure Baruch and in making them
conscious of the only trustworthy path to salvation".[106] The
righteous ones are the addressees of the future aeon.[107]

However the law which the righteous uphold is not only that law which makes itself known in the O. T., but the law of Moses in the minatory instruction, that is, in the apocalyptic interpretation, of Baruch, who also appears as a second Moses: "for the Mighty One commanded me to instruct you: therefore I will give you some of the commandments of his judgment before I die" (Syr. Bar. 84:1).[108] The readers of the apocalyptic writings are to uphold the law (cf. Syr. Bar. 44:3),[109] i.e., not forget it (cf. Syr. Bar. 44:7).[110] They do that when they concern themselves with its literal words as well as with its apocalyptic commentary, learn from the latter "all sorts of righteousness" (cf. I Enoch 104:13) and comprehend from the example of Ezra what is the reward of studying the law (cf. IV Ezra 13:53-56).[111]

[p. 100] It can be seen in this historical analogue to the reconstructed apocalyptic of primitive Christianity[112] that the apocalyptic attitude of "near expectation"[113] is not absolutely in tension with the "literary" medium, but can be taken up into its service: The written character of the secret teaching for the elect is an indication of its character as revelation in a time approaching the end, a time without revelation, for this esoteric written character is the exegesis of the law which is to be studied. The written character of apocalyptic literature and authoritative study of scriptures are an inalienable element of Jewish apocalyptic. From the point of view of the sociology of religion the Jewish practitioners of apocalyptic are authors, users, and interpreters of literature, *who are primarily constituted as a sociological phenomenon by their "literary" behavior.* Here we see a crucial lack of clarity in Dibelius, which demands that we question the stringency of his argument, which seems to me insufficiently safeguarded against short circuits. Dibelius apparently did not differentiate sharply enough among

the relationships in the tradition of the gospels he suspected
from the point of view of the sociology of religion, treating
them as a case without analogy within the sociology of religion of apocalyptic and eschatological groups.

(d)   "Near-Expectation" is Not the Determinant
of the First Gospel.

Naturally Mark cannot be form-critically compared to the
esoteric character of apocalyptic literature,[114] although for
M. Dibelius it was indeed "a book of secret epiphanies".[115]
But precisely in the case of Mark [p. 101] we must inquire
whether at his time--about 40 years after the earliest church
--we may still presuppose[116] a tensive near-expectation, or
not.[117] After all this gospel already contains indications
of a "delay of the parousia" (cf. Mk 9:1, 13:7b, 8b, 10, 13b,
23, 29b, 30, 32-37),[118] which to be sure are at least in part
redactional, but which therefore inform us about the evangelist's eschatology.[119] If following J. Schreiber we regard
particular traits in Mk 15[120] as originally "apocalyptic"
and used redactionally[121] then there is the problem of how
Mark has conceived the relationship of the occurrence of the
eschatological world-judgment at Jesus' crucifixion[122] to the
proclamation of similar occurrences in Mk 13.[123], [124] [p.
102] Was Jesus' crucifixion the "prolepsis" of the occurrence of the world-judgment and hence a doubling of this occurrence, since in the eschaton the world-judgment is still
to be expected?[125] Or are the promises of Mk 13 completely
fulfilled by Mk 15, so that the Christian can hold fast to
the "Son of God" by believing in the cross as the occurrence
of salvation? (cf. Mk 15:39) We can only indicate this problem here in order to suggest that a simple carrying-over of
a relationship between apocalyptic near-expectation and distance from the "literary" medium which perhaps existed in the

primitive church, into Mark's changed situation, is not to be presumed without grave difficulties.[125a] Our contemporary interest is precisely Mark's attitude toward the "literary" medium; given the uncertainties indicated, it seems wisest to steer away from a "constructive" conceptual model concerning this attitude. Whether therefore apocalyptic and eschatology can be taken as the basis of the "non-literary" character of "Kleinliteratur" is precisely the question in contemporary research. *Today reference to the "non-literary" character of the "Kleinliteratur" has at most the value of a hypothesis about the gospel form, but not the force of an argument.* It occasions the objection that a reference to the apocalyptic "near-expectation" has, from the point of view of the sociology of religion, a historical [p. 103] analogy against it. That it could remain valid in reference to the history of the tradition prior to the gospel form, which to be sure is now only hypothetically to be reconstructed, is therefore expressly conceded.

(e) Minimalizing the Written Aspect of the Gospel-Form.

It seems to me that M. Dibelius was fully aware of the difficulties posed by the application to the written tradition of the categories of the anonymity, collectivity, and "pre-literary" character of the oral tradition described above. Under the presupposition that the oral elements of transmission "should cohere" "with gospels written a generation later", Dibelius inquires "in what ways these reminiscences were disseminated in the oldest communities, how they thereby obtained a certain stability, if not in the actual sequence of words, at least in the external and inner structure, and above all, which interests guided this process of dissemination and stabilization".[125b] He does not think it wise "simply to designate these procedures 'oral tradition' and then to be satisfied with this labeling. For it is not immediately evident what would have led these future-directed believers to have disseminated their reminiscences of the most recent past with singular zeal; that which was to come, of which they were confident and which they awaited as very near in time, was indeed much more splendiferous than all of the past! And to top that off it cannot be seen in advance in how such dissemination should have led to stabilization."[125c] "Stabilization is only to be assumed where transmission occurs either in the organized activities of teaching and learning, or when controlled by immanent laws. However stabilization must be presupposed in the process if we are to conceive of the gospels or their sources as having actually arisen from the community tradition." The "oral tradition" (the process of the dissemination of the tradition) in the general sense is therefore to be made more precise by the concept of the "stabilization" "at least in the external and inner structure, if not with respect to word-sequence", so that structural laws of dissemination, formation, and conservation can be assumed. "If this law were not at work, the writing-down of the gospel books would signify not an organic break with the process through collection, framing, and connecting, but rather the beginning of a new purely-literary development."[126] So on the sly Dibelius *confesses that we must reckon with a break in the tradition-history* [p. 104] *of the gospel form*, if we are not going to apply the same sociological laws that were used for the tradition of the materials.

The written character of the gospel-form must therefore be minimized. Actually it does not represent a written consciousness of its own consequences,[127] i.e., an individual act of composition,[128] but *clearly a surrogate for the mo-*

mentarily impossible oral character. Mark's taking up the
pen is therefore not a real act of composition but a variant
of the oral, to be conceded in its form of appearance, uniqueness, and consequences. G. Gillet, a pupil of M. Dibelius,
makes this especially clear: Mark "is indeed mostly only a
collector and framer of material in this respect. He desires
only to write down the gospel that is proclaimed by all missionaries, and that means the non-literary and impersonal aspects of the whole presentation--the author as such never
makes an appearance."[129] What keeps us in such a perspective
from drawing the final consequence, as Th. Boman has recently
done, in regarding the entire Gospel of Mark, in terms of its
oral and formal aspects, as having been written down for the
purpose of immediate transformation back into the oral mode
by being read aloud?[130] At any rate the written would then
be a genuine surrogate for the oral.

It seems evident to me that with this the "non-literary"
character of the "Kleinliteratur", especially of the gospel-
form, is more "constructively" deduced than it is demonstrated
from the pre-history of the materials, and that this is connected to the indirect *concession that in other instances the
gospel form as such would not be explicable in terms of pre-
history of the materials*. The aporia of this position is apparent: Either the gospel-form is genuine, that is, it derives from an individual who is conscious of the consequences
of fixed writing, in which case an immediate empiricism of the
collectively oral is no longer present--or what is written,
and with that also the literary individuality, has to be conceded, in which case we could assume a tradition without gaps.
However as soon as the newer redaction critics decided to
stress the individual achievement of the evangelists, form
criticism was obligated to reconsider its earlier premises.
Therefore it is at least an open question as to whether we

[p. 105] need to maintain the "constructive" conceptual model as conclusive and compelling, or in light of the manifold methodological and historical difficulties, we may not have to choose the possibility that Dibelius rejected, especially when the emphasis upon the proclamation also no longer comports with the findings of contemporary research.[131] The concept of "Kleinliteratur" is, for the gospel form, at most a heuristic concept, which however immediately encounters complications when it is too thetically tied to a particular conception of the tradition-history, which is certainly an attractive hypothesis, but is not an empirical and analytical proof that can be defended against falsification. *Today we once again recognize the thesis concerning "Kleinliteratur" for what it always was, namely a "constructive" hypothesis.*

Notes to #5

1. Discussion of the concept "sociological setting": see below, p. [167ff.].

2. See the evidence below, p. [155ff.].

3. On the multiple natures of the "sociological setting", see Marxsen, *op. cit.*, 8f.; Koch, *Formgeschichte*, 30ff.; Zimmermann, *Ntl. Methodenlehre*, 172ff.

4. Cf. Dibelius, *Formgesch.*, 8-34.

5. Cf. below, p. [190ff.].

6. Cf. Dibelius, *op. cit.*, 9: To answer the question, "which transmissions can have originated at that time", "the analytical method is insufficient in that it works backwards from the texts to their sources and individual transmissions. Rather the constructive method is necessary in that it attempts to encompass conditions and functions of living present within the early Christian congregations." The "sociological setting" becomes clear not through analysis, but only by means of construction" [i.e., through Dibelius' "constructive method"--W.G.D.].

7. Bultmann, *ThLZ* 50 (1925) 314.

8. K. Stendahl, *The School of St. Matthew and its Use of the Old Testament*, 1954, 13.

9. Cf. below, p. [226ff.].

10. This explanation is perhaps still possible for Mk 2:1-3, 6; 4:1-34; 4:35-5:43; 12:13-37, but not for the passion or for Q.

11. H. Conzelmann, *Die Mitte der Zeit*, 1957-2nd ed., 1. Accepted by Schreiber, *Theol. des Vertrauens*, 18.

12. *Ibid.*, 11.

13. *Ibid.*, 11f.

14. Cf. above, p. [44ff.].

15. Cf. W. Bauer, "Der Wortgottesdienst der ältesten Christen," in his *Aufsätze und kleine Schriften*, ed. G. Strecker, 1967, 155-209; O. Cullmann, *Urchristentum und Gottesdienst*, 1956-3rd ed.; H. Conzelmann, "Christus im Gottesdienst der neutestamentlichen Zeit," *Pastoraltheol.* 55 (1966) 355-65.

16. Cf. H. Lietzmann, *Messe und Herrenmahl*, 1926; J. Jeremias, *Die Abendmahlsworte Jesu*, 1960-3rd ed.

17. Cf. G. Schille, *Liturgisches Gut im Epheserbrief*, Diss., Göttingen, 1953; Schille, *Frühchristliche Hymnen*, 1962; R. Deichgräber, *Gotteshymnus und Christushymnus in der frühen Christenheit*, 1967; E. Güttgemanns, *Der leidende Apostel*, 240-47. *Ibid.*, 242 n. 17, further bibliography.

18. Cf. R. Bultmann, *Theol.*-3rd ed., 49; E. Käsemann, "Zum Verständnis von Röm. 3, 24-26," in his *Aufs.*, vol. 1, 96-100; E. Lohse, *Märtyrer und Gottesknecht*, 1955, 149ff.; K. Wegenast, *Das Verständnis der Tradition bei Paulus und in den Deuteropaulinen*, 1962, 76ff.

19. Cf. W. Kramer, *Christos. Kyrios. Gottessohn*, 1963; V. H. Neufeld, *The Earliest Christian Confessions*, 1963; K. Wengst, *Christologische Formeln und Lieder der Urchristentums*, Diss., Bonn, 1967.

20. On indications of the primitive Christian service of worship in 1 Cor 15, see W. Bauer, *op. cit.*, 168ff.

21. Cf. G. Schille, "Das Leiden des Herrn," *ZThK* 52 (1955) 161-205.

22. Koch, *Formgesch.*, 32.

23. Cf. *ibid.*, 27f., 31f.

24. Cf. E. Sellin and G. Fohrer, *Einleitung in das Alte Testament*, 1965-10th ed., 281ff., 302ff. Further bibliography there.

25. The German term "actuosen Subjekt", here translated as "active subject", has been customary in practical theology since the time of C. E. Nitzsch (1787-1868) to designate the church as the central theological function: the church is the subject which is the moving active, power of tradition. Cf. L. Fendt, *Grundriss der Praktischen Theologie*, vol. 1, 1949-2nd ed., 29f., 35, 40-49. It is just as suitable as a form-

142

critical concept. [Footnote altered for the E.T., 1978. W.G.D.]

26. Concerning change in the "sociological setting" or its transformation into another "sociological setting", and into multiple "sociological settings", see Koch, *op. cit.*, 42ff.; Zimmermann, *op. cit.*, 174f.

27. Koch, *op. cit.*, 42.

28. Cf. W. Bauer, *Das Leben Jesu im Zeitalter der neutestamentlichen Apokryphen*, 1967-new ed.; H. Köster, *Synoptische Ueberlieferung bei den apostolischen Vätern*, 1957.

29. See bibliography, etc. in J. Doresse (and T. Mina), "Nouveaux textes gnostiques coptes découverts en Haute-Egypte," *VigChr* 3 (1949) 129-41; H.-Ch. Puech, "Les nouveaux Ecrits gnostiques découverts en Haute-Egypte," in *Coptic Studies in Honor of Walter Ewing Crum*, 1950, 91-154; Puech, and G. Quispel, "Les écrits gnostiques du Codex Jung," *Vig Chr* 8 (1954) 1-51; Puech, "Gnostische Evangelien und verwandte Dokumente," in E. Hennecke and W. Schneemelcher, *Neutestamentliche Apokryphen in deutscher Uebersetzung*, vol. 1, 1959-3rd ed., 158-271; W. Foerster, "Neuere Literatur über die gnostischen Papyri von Chenoboskion," *ThLZ* 79 (1954) 377-84; A. D. Nock, "A Coptic Library of Gnostic Writings," *JThS* 9 (1958) 314-24; S. Schulz, "Die Bedeutung neuer Gnosisfunde für die neutestamentliche Wissenschaft," *ThR* 26 (1960) espec. 237-66; W. C. van Unnik, *Evangelien aus dem Nilsand*, 1960; E. Haenchen, "Literatur zum Thomasevangelium," *ThR* 27 (1961) 147-78, 306-38; Haenchen, *Die Botschaft des Thomas-Evangeliums*, 1961; Haenchen, "Literatur zum Codex Jung," *ThR* 30 (1964) 39-82.

30. Cf. A. Resch, *Agrapha*, 1967-new ed.; J. Jeremias, *Unbekannte Jesusworte*, 1963-3rd ed., with O. Hofius.

31. Cf. S. Schulz' report, *op. cit.*, 252-58.

32. Cf. W. Schrage, *Das Verhältnis des Thomas-Evangeliums zur synoptischen Tradition und zu den koptischen Evangelienübersetzungen*, 1964; Schrage, "Evangelienzitate in den Oxyrhynchus-Logien und im koptischen Thomas-Evangelium," in W. Eltester, ed., *Apophoreta*, 1964, 251-68. -- The use of a conditional sentence above represents a purely neutral description of the alternatives here, not at all reference to a decision of the author.

32a [+1978: Some exegetes misinterpret this clear sentence as being a total negation of an oral stage of tradition at all. I am only pointing to the non-directness of empiricity concerning oral processes. To be sarcastic, I might ask: Where are the phonograph records demonstrating oral processes in N. T. times?]

33. Cf. Koch, *op. cit.*, 43f. Cf. also below, p. [168ff.]. With reference to the pre-literary redaction, cf. U. Wilckens, *ThLZ* 86 (1961) 276: Dibelius did not recognize "that just the fact of the collection of the materials--especially initial collections such as Mark and Q--represents a striking novum in the history of the transmission as a whole".

34. The stylistic evidence of such alterations in individual cases is, by the way, quite hypothetical, since what lies before us directly is, in the last analysis, only the "literary" final form.

35. The term "preliterary" is not meant to indicate any sort of disqualification such as inferior-literary; it merely designates the levels prior to the actual literature. Cf. Koch, *op. cit.*, 85.

36. Emphasized correctly by Koch, *ibid.*, 43, 63, 97ff. Already Cullmann, *Vorträge*, 67, in the dispute with M. Albertz, mentioned the problematics of the transition from the oral tradition into the "literary" genre.

37. Cf. D. M. Stanley, S.J., "Balaam's Ass, or a Problem in New Testament Hermeneutics," *CBQ* 20 (1958) 50-56.

38. Cf. E. Käsemann, "Kritische Analyse von Phil. 2,5-11," in his *Aufs.*, vol. 1, 51-95; D. Georgi, "Der vorpaulinische Hymnus Phil 2,6-11," in E. Dinkler, ed., *Zeit und Geschichte*, 1964, 263-93; G. Strecker, "Redaktion und Tradition im Christus-hymnus Phil 2,6-11," *ZNW* 55 (1964), 63-78; Güttgemanns, *Der leidende Apostel*, 240-47. Further bibliography: *ibid.*, 241, n. 4.

39. Cf. R. Bultmann, "Bekenntnis- und Liedfragmente im ersten Petrusbrief," in E. Dinkler, ed., *Exegetica*, 1967, 285-97.

40. Cf. J. Jeremias, *Die Gleichnisse Jesu*, 1965-7th ed., 39-45.

41. Cf. W. Marxsen, "Redaktionsgeschichtliche Erklärung der sogenannten Parabeltheorie des Markus," in his *Der Exeget als Theologe*, 1968, 13-28; T. A. Burkill, "The Cryptology of the Parables in St. Mark's Gospel," *NovTest* 1 (1956) 246-62.

42. Cf. G. Bornkamm, "Die Sturmstillung im Matthäusevangelium," in Bornkamm, G. Barth, and H. J. Held, *Ueberlieferung und Auslegung im Matthäusevangelium*, 1960, 48-53; Held, in *ibid.*, 190f.

43. Cf. Bornkamm, "Enderwartung und Kirche im Matthäusevangelium," in *ibid.*, 13-47.

44. Cf. Conzelmann, *Mitte der Zeit*, 48-60.

45. Cf. J. Schreiber, *Der Kreuzigungsbericht des Markusevangeliums*, Diss., Bonn, 1959; Schreiber, "Die Christologie des Markusevangeliums," *ZThK* 58 (1961) 154-83; Schreiber, *Theologie des Vertrauens*, 1967, 22-49.

45a Naturally I do not deny the possibility of pre-Markan composition; but I consider it an unprovable hypothesis. Cf. below, p. [229f.].

46. Somewhat too schematically, Koch, *op. cit.*, 98, states: "Even if alterations in the oral transmission occurred primarily unintentionally and in passing, even the smallest *addition* to a writing is a conscious act." It *can* at least be that, i.e., in the oral and the written modes of tradition, understanding and intention are related in reverse relationship so that the individual moment has a greater weight in the written than in the oral mode of tradition.

47. It remains to ask further whether the "framework" always existed as a "form" in itself with its own "sociological setting". Cf. below, p. [201ff.]. If this question is answered in the negative, the problem confronting us here would become imperative, namely the extent to which we can refer, with respect to the "literary" work of the evangelists to the same sort of a "sociological setting" in the case of a "preliterary" level of tradition. The solution of this problem is given below, p. [167ff.]. Sociologically speaking, the relationships have altered themselves in the movement toward writing. This *possibility* has had to be radically denied by traditional form criticism, along with a minimalizing of the written, if it did not want to relinquish its premises. As soon as one begins to doubt the correctness of these premises, the question placed here arises.

48. Zimmermann, *op. cit.*, 137, expresses in this respect the usual opinion that the "framework" perhaps owes its structure to a prior "kerygma". Examination of this thesis: see below, p. [189ff.].

49. So G. Schille, *ThLZ* 88 (1963) 498, n. 34.

50. Koch, *op. cit.*, 98.

51. Cf. G. Bornkamm, *RGG*-3rd ed., vol. 2, 1958, 762.

52. H. Gunkel, *Die israelitische Literature*, 1963-new edition, 3, who means of course in antiquity: "Actual 'literary', i.e. written, genres are rare."

53. Hence it is thoroughly understandable why V. Taylor, for instance, in *Formation*, 10, primarily refers criticism of forms to the oral period, although precisely in this case the problem we have described intrudes itself.

54. Cf. Conzelmann, *Mitte*, 2. Similarly E. Haenchen, *Gn* 29 (1957) 626: The framework created by the redactors "are apparently without historical value, and therefore not of interest".

55. Cf. however the additional reasons in ##6-8, below.

56. Cf. Dibelius, *Formgesch.*, 1-8. Criticism: cf. Fascher, *op. cit.*, 52-57.

57. Cf. #6, n. 4, below.

58. Cf. A. Olrik, "Epische Gesetze der Volksdichtung," *Zeitschr. für dt. Altertum u. dt. Lit.*, 51 (1909) 1-12. [Translation of this article, which was so important to Bultmann in *The History of the Synoptic Tradition*, with introduction and notes relating the article to folklore studies, will be found in Alan Dundes, ed., *The Study of Folklore* (Englewood Cliffs: Prentice-Hall, 1965), pp. 129-41. W.G.D.] [+1978: Meanwhile it has been determined that the biological metaphors go back to the biological offspring of "Formengeschichte". Cf. R. Breymayer, *LingBibl* 15/16 (1972) 60ff., who points to Goethe's morphological-osteological researches, and to F. J. Schelver, *Lebens- und Formgeschichte der Pflanzenweld*, 1822. E. G.]

59. Dibelius, *op. cit.*, 1.

60. *Ibid.*, 5.

61. Cf. below, p. [109f.].

62. Bibliography is given in #6, n. 2, below.

63. Cf. below, p. [109ff.]. On Dibelius' relation to folkloristics, which is differentiated by the respective sociological concept, cf. below, p. [94].

64. Cf. below, p. [115ff.].

65. Dibelius, *op. cit.*, 4.

66. Bibliography: see below, #7, n. 65.

67. Cf. below, p. [129ff.].

67a Cf. above, #4, n. 12.

68. Dibelius, *op. cit.*, 5.

69. See below, p. [157ff.].

70. See below, p. [161ff.].

71. See below, p. [130], and above, p. [45f.].

72. Dibelius, *op. cit.*, 1.

73. *Ibid.*, 2.

74. Cf. *ibid.*, 2f. [+1978: That "selection" is a semantic, "framing" a syntactic operation, constituting a new *form* of text, seems never to have been considered.]

75. *Ibid.*, 3.

76. See however the criticism below, p. [190ff.].

77. See above, pp. [48ff., 57ff.].

78. See #6 below, n. 73.

79. See above, p. [45f.].

79a [+1978: I cannot agree with P. Vielhauer, *Geschichte der urchristlichen Literatur*, 1975, 287, n. 15, that I misinterpret Dibelius' thoughts. If this would indeed be the case, how could one explain the citations? It seems to me evident that Vielhauer's polemic against me is a clear sign of helplessness with respect to argumentation, which can be hidden only by emotions.]

80. Dibelius, *op. cit.*, 9.

81. Dibelius, *ThR* 1 (1929) 190.

82. *Ibid.*, 189.

83. See Güttgemanns, *VF* 12/2 (1967) 43.

84. Cf. Bultmann, *Theol.*-3rd ed., 186, 352f.; Bultmann, *Exegetica*, 220f., 227; W. Schrage, "Die Stellung zur Welt bei Paulus, Epiktet und in der Apokalyptic," *ZThK* 61 (1964) 125-54.

85. Cf. P. Vielhauer, "Apokalypsen und Verwandtes," in E. Hennecke and W. Schneemelcher, *Neutestamentliche Apokryphen in deutscher Uebersetzung*, vol. 2, 1964-3rd ed., 405-454. Further bibliography is cited there. The most recent study is: W. Harnisch, *Verhängnis und Verheissung der Geschichte*, 1969.

86. Cf. H. v. Soden, *Die Entstehung der christlichen Kirche*, 1919, 66ff.

87. Cf. Käsemann, *Aufs.*, vol. 2, 95: It is true "that it was apocalyptic that first made possible historical thinking within Christianity". "Here the necessity arises, not just to proclaim the kerygma about Jesus, but to narrate it. Such can only lead to the development of the incomparable literary form of the gospel...." Cf. also P. Stuhlmacher, *Das paulinische Evangelium*, vol. 1, 1968.

88. Cf. for example Dan 2:1, 4:2, 7:1ff.; I Enoch 83f., 85ff.; II Enoch 1:3ff.; 4 Ezra 11:1, 12:1, 13:1, 13; Syr. Baruch 13:1f., 22:1.

89. Cf. for example I Enoch 8, 72-79, 42; IV Ezra 5:9f.

90. Cf. I Enoch 1:2, 12:4, 15:1, 71:14; IV Ezra 6:32f.

91. Cf. Dan 1:3ff., 2:30, 48; I Enoch 32:2-4; IV Ezra 14:50.

92. Cf. D. Lührmann, *Das Offenbarungsverständnis bei Paulus und in paulinischen Gemeinden*, 1965, 98: "Revelation is in the apocalyptic literature...the final eschatological coming-into-appearance of the new aeon, which dissolves this aeon." *Ibid.*, 99: "'Revelation' demarcates...the border between this aeon and the coming one." "Revelation in this sense is a salvific acting of God, which closes off this aeon to the past and opens up the new aeon." With this, however, the occurrence of the revelation is too strongly

tied to the linear schema, although the apocalyptic esoterics
and the pre-temporality relegates the "revelation" to the
past--hence to the old aeon--which is transmitted to the wise-
men and the righteous ones of the present by means of the book.
Because of the literary esoterics Lührmann must immediately
hedge his thesis. Cf. *ibid.*, 104: "Revelation is...an eschatological act of God, which leads to the new aeon, but at
the same time it is the anticipated disclosure of this eschatological revelation in the signification of dreams and
visions, whose intent is to strengthen the hope of God's eschatological acting and obedience to the law." The vascil-
lating concept of "prolepsis" present here actually creates
a doubling of the eschatological event of revelation. Cf.
below, n. 125. However he does not conceal the fact that
revelation is not simply given in a linear future, but already in the historical past, which is transmitted to the
present by means of the literary medium of the book, so that
the "eschatological" is tied to that which from the beginning
is not linear in terms of what is communicated by the apocalyptic books. Lührmann has to deny the constituitive tension
between the two-aeon-schema and the "revelatory" function of
the literary medium, since he radicalizes the linear tendency
of the two-aeon-schema, and can only bring the fact of the
"apocalyptic" books into the linear schema by means of the
concept "anticipation". The main issue is the justification
of this schema. The past is precisely not only destiny, but
also has promise; the relationship to time and history is
much more developed in Jewish apocalyptic, as Harnisch, *op.
cit.*, has demonstrated in his very thorough and careful analysis.

93. Cf. Vielhauer, *op. cit.*, 410.

94. Cf. *ibid.*, 410f.

95. Cf. P. Volz, *Die Eschatologie der jüdischen Gemeinde
im neutestamentlichen Zeitalter*, 1934, 5; Vielhauer, *op. cit.*,
420.

96. Cf. I Enoch 104:12f.: "...I know another mystery,
that books will be given to the righteous and the wise to become a cause of joy and uprightness and much wisdom. And to
them shall the books be given, and they shall believe in them
and rejoice over them, and then shall all the righteous who
have learnt therefrom all the paths of uprightness be recom-
pensed." [English translations of the pseudepigrapha from
R. H. Charles, *The Apocrypha and Pseudepigrapha of the Old
Testament in English*, 1913.] Cf. IV Ezra 12:37f.: "...write
all these things that thou hast seen in a book, and put them

in a secret place; and thou shalt teach them to the wise of the people, whose hearts thou knowest are able to comprehend and keep these mysteries." Cf. Dan 12:4: "But you, Daniel, shut up the words, and seal the book, until the time of the end. Many shall run to and fro, and knowledge shall increase." [R.S.V. translation.]

97. Cf. Bornkamm, *ThW* 4 (1942) 822, 11-15: "the mysteries are those decrees of God intended for the final revelation, i.e., they are the final events and circumstances which already in heaven have a real, visible existence, but which will only be thrust out of their hiddenness at the End in order to be come public event." (Italics in original.)

98. Cf. Vielhauer, *op. cit.*, 412f.; Harnisch, *op. cit.*, 89ff.

99. Cf. the evidence presented by Harnisch, *op. cit.*, 142ff.

100. On predestination, see Volz, *op. cit.*, 109.

101. Cf. Harnisch, *op. cit.*, 198ff.; W. Bousset and H. Gressmann, 293ff., 298ff.

102. Evidence in Harnisch, *op. cit.*, 201ff.

103. Cf. *ibid.*, 208ff.

104. On the arrangement of the verses, cf. O. Plöger, *RGG*-3rd ed., vol. 1, 1957, 901f.

105. Cf. Harnisch, *op. cit.*, 215ff.

106. *Ibid.*, 222. On law in apocalyptic cf. also D. Rössler, *Gesetz und Geschichte*, 1960. Criticism: Vielhauer, *op. cit.*, 416f.; Harnisch, *op. cit.*, 12ff.

107. Cf. *ibid.*, 222ff.

108. Translation and interpretation according to Harnisch, *op. cit.*, 220.

109. Cf. Rössler, *op. cit.*, 85ff.

110. Cf. Harnisch, *op. cit.*, 210.

111. 4 Ezra 13:53-56: "Therefore has this been revealed to thee, and to thee alone, because thou hast forsaken the

things of thyself, and has applied thy diligence unto mine and
searched out my Law; Thy life thou hast ordered unto wisdom
and hast called understanding thy mother. Therefore have I
showed thee this; for there is a reward laid up with the Most
High." [E.T. from Charles, *APOT*.]

112. On the recent discussion about primitive Christian
apocalyptic, see E. Käsemann, "Die Anfänge christlicher Theologie," in his *Aufs.*, vol. 2, 82-104; Käsemann, "Zum Thema
der urchristlichen Apokalyptik," in *ibid.*, 105-31; E. Fuchs,
"Ueber die Aufgabe einer christlichen Theologie," *ZThK* 58
(1961) 245-67; G. Ebeling, "Der Grund christlicher Theologie,"
ibid., 227-44; A. Strobel, *Kerygma und Apokalyptik*, 1967.

113. Cf. Vielhauer, *op. cit.*, 414-17. The "near-expectation" had already been neutralized within Jewish apocalyptic.
Cf. Harnisch, *op. cit.*, 268ff. If we accept Harnisch's use
of the evidence, the apocalyptic literature is no longer
properly a historical analogy to the "avoidance of literature" by primitive Christian apocalyptic, since it would be
possible to speak of the "near-expectation" as being there
only *cum grano salis*.

114. Differently E. Sjöberg, *Der verborgene Menschensohn
in den Evangelien*, 1955, 1ff., 100ff., 122ff., according to
whom the Markan messianic secret is to be understood as a
general primitive Christian presentation coming from the
Jewish-apocalyptic association of secret and revelation.
Criticism: H. E. Tödt, *Der Menschensohn in der synoptischen
Ueberlieferung*, 1959, 268-73.

115. Dibelius, *Formgesch.*, 232. This thesis has found
almost universal agreement.

116. So Marxsen, *Evglist. Mk.*, 101ff., 112-28, 141-47;
Marxsen, *Einleitung*, 124-27; Suhl, *Funktion*, 16-25.

117. So W. G. Kümmel, *Einleitung*, 48f.; P. Vielhauer, *ThR*
31 (1965/66) 142f.; E. Grässer, review of A. Suhl, *op. cit.*;
ThLZ 91 (1966) 667-69; Schulz, *Stunde der Botschaft*, 94ff.;
Schreiber, *Theol. des Vertrauens*, 126ff.

118. Bornkamm, "Die Verzögerung der Parusie," in his
Aufs., vol. 3, 46-49; E. Grässer, *Das Problem der Parusieverzögerung in den synoptischen Evangelien und in der Apostelgeschichte*, 1957, 128ff., 152ff.; H. Conzelmann, "Geschichte
und Eschaton nach Mc 13," *ZNW* 50 (1959) 210-21. Cf. the
bibliography cited in #13, n. 331, below.

119. Cf. Schreiber, *op. cit.*, 83ff.

120. The issues are the motif of darkness (Mk 15:33), the
ninth hour (Mk. 15:34a), the tearing of the temple veil (Mk 15:
38), and the death cry of Jesus (Mk 15:37). Cf. Schreiber,
Diss., 121-31 (the voice of Jesus), 132-47 (darkness), 160-
69 (tearing of the veil); Schreiber, *Theol. des Vertrauens*,
33ff.

121. Schreiber, Diss., 44ff.; Schreiber, *ZThK* 58 (1961)
157, n. 5; Schreiber, *Theol. des Vertrauens*, 24ff., where he
distinguishes: a) an old historical report with personal and
theological-apologetical backgrounds (Mk 15:20b, 21, 22a, 24,
27); b) an O.T.-Jewish-apocalyptically influenced tradition
(Mk 15:25, 26, 29a, 33, 34a, 37, 38), and c) the redactional
addition of Mark, who combines both traditions (Mk 15:20b,
23, 29b-32b, 34b-36, 39-41). Whether or not this analysis
is successful cannot concern us here. However the thesis
tied to this analysis is refuted, namely that the Christology
of Mark was a hellenistic-gnostic transformation of apocalyptic motifs in the sense of a secret epiphany. So Schreiber, *ZThK* 58 (1961) 154-83. Against this: Vielhauer, *Aufs.*,
200.

122. Cf. Schreiber, Diss., 167f.: "At the moment that the
dying son of man by his cry of judgment annihilates the world
which has been entirely darkened by sins and therefore by the
assault of the powers of chaos in God's judgment of anger, the
temple veil is ripped. With Jesus' death cry and the subsequently fulfilled judgment of the world, the inner temple
veil, i.e., the temple itself, on whose continuance the world
is dependent, is destroyed. God no longer dwells in the Holy
of Holies. The chosen people, the Jews, drove the elect one
of God to the cross. Now God answers to these frightful sins
through the mouth of the crucified one who is apparently so
helpless: He destroys the temple of Israel, his house which
has been desecrated by the sins of the Jews. Thereby he also
simultaneously establishes the law, the belief of Judaism."
Ibid., 196: "Jesus' death cry signifies not only the judgment of this world, but simultaneously also the elevation of
Jesus as king of the new world and of the true Israel, i.e.,
of those who have believed in him." *Ibid.*, 215: "The actual
meaning of Mk 15:37, 39, lies in the fact that the death of
Jesus as judgment and salvation is the offer of deliverance
to the gentiles."

123. To be emphasized: the destruction of the temple (Mk
13:1f.), the darkness (Mk 13:24), and the knowledge of the
hour (Mk 13:4, 8b, 13b, 23, 29b, 32-37).

152

124. Cf. Schreiber, *Theol. des Vertrauens*, 127ff.: Mk 13 is directed "not in the final analysis to the Parousia, but beyond it 'to the new community independent of the temple', which is established by Jesus' death, and which will be gathered to him before the eyes of the unbelievers, in public majesty, at the Parousia of the crucified one, in a way yet more final and for eternity (13:26)" (127). "Death and resurrection of the son of man have pressed the Parousia of the son of man materially and temporally into the distance and out to the margins of concern as a contemporaneously effective act of salvation" (129). On the connection with the second crucifixion tradition, cf. *ibid.*, 130f. Cf. *ibid.*, 145: "The evangelist rejects the near-expectation from his kerygma of the passion insofar as this kerygma itself already promises and fulfills the eschaton in the time of this world, in that it establishes the distinction between belief and unbelief. The Parousia which lies temporally in the distance only further confirms this eschatological happening which is already now being fulfilled."

125. The doubling of the event by the concept "prolepsis" = *happening* before hand [Vorwegereignung] only indicated here is thought to be crucial by W. Pannenberg, *Grundzüge der Christologie*, 1964. Cf. for instance p. 56: In Jesus "the end is not only--as in apocalyptic--brought into view in advance, but has taken place as an event in advance." But if the end *has* already occurred in Jesus, how then is Jesus still referred to as the confirmation at the ultimate event (cf. *ibid.*, 59f.), that more or less brings forward the end as the doubling of the prolepsis once more? In my opinion it arrives at this doubling because the linear historical design and the premises of the translucence in terms of its *ultimate* conclusion, which lends it its character of pastness, forces it that way. In view of this error, the concept of "prolepsis" should be accepted into exegesis only with great caution.

125a Moreover in my opinion there are no direct sources for the theology of the *early* primitive community that demonstrate to us the *un*broken rapturous near-expectation. We are talking about a psychologistic construction.

125b Dibelius, *Formgesch.*, 9.

125c *Ibid.*, 9f.

126. *Ibid.*, 10.

127. See below, p. [113ff.].

128. What is meant here is the act "set up" by the intentional linguistic phenomenon, in Husserl's sense. Bibliography: see #12, n. 26, below.

129. G. Gillet, *Evangelium. Studien zur urchristlichen Missionssprache*, Diss., Heidelberg, 1924, 127.

130. Cf. Th. Boman, *Die Jesus-Ueberlieferung im Lichte der neueren Volkskunde*, 1967, 91, 94. Cf. also below, p.

131. See below, p. [190ff.].

[p. 106] *#6.* *Franz Overbeck's Understanding of the*
Written Character of the "Pre-Litera-
ture".[1]

1. The Roots of Form Criticism.

F. Overbeck (1837-1905)[2] is now correctly regarded as one
of the most influential originators of the form critical approach.[3] One of his statements has become almost classical:
"A literature has its history in its forms, and therefore
form criticism will actually be literary history [Literatur-
geschichte--otherwise translated here as "literary criticism".
W.G.D.]."[4] Along with that of F. Chr. Baur, Overbeck's program of a "profane description of church history"[5] aims at
"representing primitive Christianity purely historically,
that is, as it actually happened",[6] especially by means of
form criticism, which already in his lifetime was being for-
malistically misunderstood.[7] Contemporary form criticism
would do well to re-orient itself, given a similar formalism
today,[8] [p. 107] to Overbeck's methodological reflections. It
can be seen rather quickly that Overbeck's critical spirit
discovered or anticipated contents and connections which for
the most part have now been forgotten.

2. The Correspondence of "Pre-Literature"
and "Pre-History".

For N. T. form criticism the decisive concept in Overbeck's methodology is that of "pre-literature" [Urliteratur],
to which that of "pre-history" [Urgeschichte] corresponds.[9]

It is certainly correct that Overbeck did not arrive at either concept "on the basis of speculative deduction, but by means of historical observation".[10] Just such observation, however, led him to intensive reflection on the thematized categories "space" and "time" in I. Kant's transcendental aesthetics.[11] In my opinion the intention of the two concepts can only be grasped when we seek out these concepts in Overbeck's works and posthumous writings, where they are occasionally only mere suggestions, and seek to reconstruct their logic.

Overbeck's sharpened consciousness of the implications of historical method with reference to time-categories led him to the radical thesis that only something belonging radically to the past can be fully "historical",[12] that is, something wasted, dead.[13] For this reason the historical viewpoint treats "only those things which are completed"[14] and excludes the history of origination, the mysterious process by which things come to be and then pass on. Historical study occupies itself only with the past-character of history, which represents a process of being engulfed in degeneration and progress;[15] it relates not to the periods of pre-history ennucleated within history,[16] to the history of origination of what has actually been effective in history:[17] "The history [p. 108] of origination is without peer in the history of everything living, in life itself."[18] Similarly pre-history and history are oriented to the past, but to a "past in a special sense",[19] to a "past in a second degree of potency—more-than-past, overly-past: almost nothing of the present remains yet within it".[20]

This *stratification of history by means of categorial differentiations of temporality* finds its corroboration in its application to primitive Christian form and literary criticism: The N. T. literature is pre-literature, i.e., literature in which the past is ennucleated. "The past aspect of all pre-literature is not a simple pastness, but a qualified pastness",[21] which can be documented by the fragmented character of this pre-literature.[22] Overbeck defines the concept, Christian "pre-literature", in the following way: "It is a literature which Christianity created, as it were, by its own means, insofar as it grew up exclusively on the basis and unique inner interests of the Christian community before its admixture to the surrounding world."[23] What is primarily decisive in this definition is *the factor of the literary-historical isolation of the Christian pre-literature* both with respect to the forms of the environment and with respect to the literature of the patristic church.[24] Actually the primitive Christian literature is [p. 109] not even literature in the proper sense, that is, something written for the sake of the communicative possibilities of writing prevalent in the environment.[25] The oldest Christian literature is rather "occasional literature proceeding entirely from practical needs"; it "is completely derived from local or immediately-given purposes, and is not intended to be significant in its own right".[26]

3. The Written Character of the Forms of "Pre-Literature".

With this formula Overbeck reflects, as I see it, the old linguistic position that literature as a "written symbol" not only stands for the "oral symbol",[27] but also is effective "by means of itself".[28] However that may be, it seems certain to me that Overbeck has concerned himself more deeply than any other subsequent form critic with *the significance of the written for the literary-character of the Christian pre-literature*. To be sure the Christian pre-literature encompasses not only the N. T. canon,[29] but also contains quite

unique forms, such as the gospel form, "which is certainly
the single original form with which Christianity enriched
literature",[30] and the N. T. letters, which actually represent a "literary non-form".[31] If we attend more closely to
Overbeck's formulations concerning these two [p. 110] forms
of pre-literature, the series of problems surrounding the
concept of the written can easily be demonstrated.

(a) Franz Overbeck's Treatment of the
     N. T. Letters.

The N. T. letter represents an expediency of the apostolic period "for the maintenance of spiritual intercourse
among all the members of the young community".[32] The written
form of its letters is related "to the circumstance of the
spatial separation of the correspondents that appears in
retrospect to be only occasional to the expression of human
thoughts". "Here the written word is, without meaning as such
to signify anything, actually nothing other than a thoroughly
artless and chance surrogate for the spoken word."[33] "The
origination of a letter is due only to chance, since both
persons who desire to engage in discourse are spatially separated from one another. When the writer and the recipient
of the letter are once again together, the written communication becomes superfluous."[34]

In spite of this, however, this "expediency" has something
inevitable about it, for it became "more and more indispensible
for the most rapid spatial expansion of the preaching of the
gospel in the extensive area of the Roman empire".[35] In contrast to the surrogate-character of the written aspect of the
letter in the pre-literature, the written aspect was an essential characteristic of the Christian literature from the time
of the patristic apologists onward.[36] *What is decisive about
the written nature of the pre-literature is its nearness to*

its original public:[37] "The letter has both an entirely determinate, momentary occasion, and an entirely determinate
and momentary public"; in contrast, the author does not possess "the immediate [p. 111] and clear consciousness of a
letter-writer concerning the extent of his public".[38]

Overbeck defines the written nature of the literature in
contrast to that of the pre-literature as follows: "Literature is a characteristically *extended* and *intensified* written
form of spiritual intercourse in human society."[39] "*Intensified* insofar as the written aspect here is no longer either an
expediency or a surrogate, but the indispensible medium for
the purpose, the medium without whose application the intended
intercourse simply could not take place--*extended* insofar as
the spiritual intercourse produced by the literature no longer
has the immediacy of matters directly touching what the correspondence is all about."[40] In view of this quotation it is
clear that Overbeck's intention is directed toward the essential disposition of the written aspect of the primitive Christian letter: *Its written aspect is no "literary" phenomenon*;
it is not an actual aspect such as literature possesses, and
to that extent it is not to be considered as some sort of conditioned prior-stage of the later canonization.[41]

(b) The Contemporary Problematics of the Pauline Letters.

We can only ask whether Overbeck's conceptual model is
actually valid for the primitive Christian letter, or whether
it allies it too closely with the private letter. Naturally
Paul's letters are *real* letters,[42] but "by no means *purely*
occasional writings, but partly conceptualized from the beginning for reading aloud and proclamation among further
reading audiences, and destined for circulation and exchange
among the other congregations (cf. Gal 1:2, Col 4:15f.)".[43]

Especially the Pauline paraenesis has claims to universality.[44]
The apostle is also simultaneously an authoritative teacher
and prophet (cf. I Cor 14:6).[45] His prescripts--to be differentiated form-critically from the letter corpus, to be sure,
but not to be separated from it--clearly show Paul's intensified consciousness of being an authorized and commissioned
apostle (cf. Ro 1:1, 5; I Cor 1:1; II Cor 1:1; Gal 1:1f.).[45a]

[p. 112] The apostle is the bearer of the literal epiphany of the really-present earthly Jesus, which draws to its
service his entire existence.[46] As bearing the apostolic life-
for-the-sake-of-proclamation, the apostle fundamentally distinguishes himself, on the basis of the Pauline teaching about
charisma (I Cor 12-14)[47] from the addressees of his letters.[48]
God revealed himself to him when he called him to be an apostle
to the gentiles for his son (cf. Gal 1:15f.),[49] that is, impressed upon him the *stigmata tou Iēsou* (Gal 6:17),[50] the *sē-
meia tou apostolou* (II Cor 12:12). Certainly the apostle's
reference to his *kauchēsis* remains paradoxical.[51] The apostle
nowhere poses as a sort of "static" authority.[52] Because of
his apostolic existence determined by the proclamation, the
apostle exists in a double relatedness: As "agent" of the gospel he is related to Jesus as the Lord who constitutes the time
of the gospel;[53] as functionary of the kerygma (*diakonos*), he
is simultaneously related to the church.[54] And insofar as
salvation is only possible by means of the kerygma of the
church,[55] the church is bound to the bearer of the kerygma,
since without a bearer the kerygma is not effective (cf. Ro
10:14f.).[56]

All in all these theological connections are important
enough for Paul that we may reasonably question whether his
letters are only a surrogate for his oral sermons or speeches[57]
or whether they are indeed something else that is difficult to
describe more accurately, [p. 113] something like "letters of

the apostle in official capacity".[58] Already during Paul's life, at any rate, a difference between the important letters and the "non-pneumatic" oral appearances was recognized (cf. II Cor 10:10),[59] and at a somewhat later time the communicative value of these letters was measurably reduced (cf. II Peter 3:15f.), since the unity between writer and witness[60] had dissolved when Paul died, and the letters had already become "historic" by being preserved and collected.[61]

It is difficult to say whether or not Paul himself could have reckoned or would have been able to have reckoned with such an objectifying process, and hence whether the step toward the written form of the letter had within it from the beginning more imminent and logical consequences which more and more decisively escaped the consciousness of the person speaking by means of writing, and his intentions,[62] and so led to a self-deception about the implications of taking up pen to write when what was perhaps intended was the written's surrogate quality and its immediacy. However could Paul have so deceived himself if his letters (in terms of I Thess 5:27, Gal 1:2, II Cor 1:1; cf. Col 4:16) were tending "toward becoming literary texts with an official character",[63] and therefore something quite different from being a surrogate for something oral? Was Paul so very unclear about the special nature of the written aspects of a letter when he used the means of a letter after his second visit to Corinth (cf. II Cor 13:2),[64] after the so-called "painful event" [p. 114] which most likely conveyed to him by the ringleader of his Corinthian opponents (cf. II Cor 2:5, 7:12),[65] with the so-called "tearful letter" (cf. II Cor 2:4, 7:12a),[66] evidently because he yet hoped to achieve what had apparently not been possible by means of the oral alone? Are the opponents of this distinction between the oral and the written not to be granted that they are to some extent correct (cf. II Cor 10:10)? Independently of whether

Paul *wanted* (intention, intentional act of writing-down) to
have written in certain letters only occasional writings for
a small circle of readers ("Kleinliteratur"), the way these
letters were also preserved by the readers or other contemporaries involved, and therefore the (mis- ?) understanding reception of this intention by the other side of the epistolary
correspondence[66a] is essential to the linguistic and form-
critical phenomenon of the Pauline letter. Without there
having been from the beginning such a tendency toward preserving and collecting the apostle's letters we would now
have no "genuine" letters of Paul at all, but at the most
reports about lost or hypothetically-reconstructed letters
(cf. I Cor 5:9, 11; II Cor 2:4, 9; 7:8, 12). The apostle's
letters were never treated by the congregations to whom they
were written as occasional writings to be simply thrown away,
such as the congregation's letters to Paul through the apostle
clearly were (cf. for instance I Cor 7:1). We must not forget
the tension which may have existed between Paul's intention
with respect to the letters and their reception by the congregations that read them, so long as it is only the intentional act that is emphasized by the form-critical characteri-
zation; this is just as impossible as the elimination of the
heuristic linguistic analogy between that which is "composed"
in language and that which is to be understood in this "composition", although the possibility of misunderstanding is
built into such an analogy.[66b] Either Paul already had to
deal with this problem of the written, and did so success-
fully, or he was not (fully) aware of what he was doing, so
that his letters therefore in *any* case contain a trans-mental
and also trans-intentional factor precisely because of their
written nature and the possibility [p. 115] of objectification inherent in them.[66c] But here I am not interested in
pursuing further speculations about the history of the

Pauline correspondence, but only in pointing to difficulties
in Overbeck's theses as we go along.

> (c) Franz Overbeck's View of the Implica-
>   tions of the Written Nature of the
>   Gospel-Form.[66d]

That Overbeck was not the least naive in this respect is
shown by his reflections on the one genuine primitive Christian form within the pre-literature, the gospel. The gospels
are a phenomenon of pre-history in that we know absolutely
nothing about authors hidden behind a "wall of books": "The
gospels are pre-literature, i.e., a literature whose originators [Menschen] are more thoroughly hidden from us behind
their surviving books than is the case with any other literature."[67] "In this pre-historic [prae-historischen] time book
and author remain actually and immediately united, a situation
which ceases in the period of historical concern with books."
"In the pre-historic time the author virtually lives in the
book; the book's life is itself so complete that *next to it*
there is simultaneously no place left for the life of the author."[68] Again Overbeck emphasizes the *immediacy* of the medium of the written and the linguistic power of the *unity* between author and form in the pre-literature. These two factors explain why in pre-historic time books that are now "historically" effective were "taken entirely seriously as books":[69]
*The written nature of the gospels is not in opposition to their
immediacy*. An entirely different seriousness toward books came
to pass in the historical period, within the history of literature: "In historical time and in its product, the history of
literature, the book now has its life only *in itself*, it has
no life left over for its author."[70] The "historical" manner
in which books are taken seriously in the history of literature presupposes the dissociation of the unity and immediacy;

it is a qualitatively different manner of taking books seriously, "because history [p. 116] has come onto the scene in
the meantime, and so that which was once contemporary and
living is now dead and gone".[71] We might say that it is
therefore taking seriously the "historical" mediacy of the
Christian pre-literature, *whose written character is altered
by the dissociation of unity and immediacy*.

Overbeck, thanks to his methodological reflection, is
perfectly aware that this last sort of serious attitude is,
in spite of every inconvenience it may cause,[72] and in spite
of the disparateness of the concepts "Christianity" and "historic",[73] both the only possibility, and a compelling necessity for the "secular writing of church history";[74] and with
that Christianity is truly delivered over to irredeemable dissolution.[75] For if as a consequence of the "historic" dissolution of the unity and immediacy of the written, the character of the Christian pre-literature has been altered, then
from the standpoint of the "historic" a posteriori,[76] *the
canonization of the gospels is to be seen as a possible* a
priori *consequence of its written nature*, its provenance,
from writers:[77] "Such is the history of the origination of
the gospels, as it can be seen to have taken place from the
standpoint of its subsequent history, which occurred through
its canonization, or expressed differently: the pre-history
[p. 117] of the gospels can be considered the pre-history of
their canonization."[78]

Even if our interpretation of Overbeck's fragmentary observations should be doubtful or indeed contestable, we can
scarcely deny that the "self-canonization of the gospel"[79] we
have described should be shown to be a necessary consequence
of the written nature of the gospel *at that juncture where
history dissoves pre-history*. For if the gospel writers, as
a consequence of the dissolution of the pre-history by his-

tory, became "historic", then their works will be so comprehended paradoxically under the aspect of "historical witnesses", that their truer historical explanatory value as
pre-literature, previously emphasized, is precisely what is
lost. The *kata* of the (secondary) gospel-superscripts[80] emphasizes the secondary roles of the evangelists:[81] Thereby
the author is "represented expressly as only a circumscribed
borrower of an external form impressed upon materials given
to him and constraining him".[82] In such a perspective to be
sure the gospels are still not actually literature, but moving in that direction.[83]

Nonetheless such a conceptual penetration of the problem
of the written nature of the gospels suggests that the written
quality of the primitive Christian literature has ingredient
to it a possibly unintended, but actual, problematics which
along with the differentiation between "Kleinliteratur" and
"literature proper" has still not been resolved. Overbeck's
interest in the history of forms and literature and in the
transition from the surrogate-written to the "literary" written leads to the question about the relation of the *modus
tradendi* "to the respective *actus tradendi* and to the *tra-
ditum*".[84] [p. 118] In such a way Overbeck's conception of
the "pre-literature" can lead us to reflect once more on the
implications of the written nature of the forms. In order to
do that, we turn now to a more consciously detailed glance at
the disciplines related to form criticism.

Notes to #6

1. Cf. K. Barth, "Unerledigte Anfragen an die heutige
Theologie," in his *Die Theologie und die Kirche*, 1928, 1-25;
W. Nigg, *Franz Overbeck*, 1931; H. Schindler, *Barth und Over-
beck*, 1936; P. Vielhauer, "Franz Overbeck und die neutesta-
mentliche Wissenschaft," in his *Aufsätze*, 235-52; Vielhauer,
"Overbeck," *RGG*-3rd ed., vol. 4, 1960, 1750-52; M. Tetz,
"Ueber Formengeschichte in der Kirchengeschichte," *ThZ* 17
(1961) 413-31; Tetz, "Altchristliche Literaturgeschichte--
Patrologie," *ThR* 32 (1967) 1-42. -- Further bibliography in
Overbeckiana I, E. Staehelin, ed., with M. Gabathuler, 1962,
29-38.

2. One should consult especially F. Overbeck, *Ueber
Entstehung und Recht einer rein historischen Betrachtung der
Neutestamentlichn Schriften in der Theologie*, 1875-2nd ed.;
Ueber die Christlichkeit unserer heutigen Theologie, 1963-
new ed.; *Ueber die Anfänge der patristischen Literatur*, 1966-
2nd ed.; *Ueber die Anfänge der Kirchengeschichtsschreibung*,
1965-special ed.; *Manuskript A 105. Geschichte der Littera-
tur der alten Kirche. Patristik*, 1895 (not edited; I am
grateful to Dr. M. Tetz for a chance to examine this); *Christentum und Kultur*, C. A. Bernoulli, ed., 1963-new ed.; *Selbst-
bekenntnisse*, E. Vischer, ed., and intro., 1941; *Overbeckiana
II. Der wissenschaftliche Nachlass Franz Overbecks*, described
by M. Tetz, 1962.

3. Cf. Vielhauer, *Aufs.*, 246ff.; Vielhauer, *RGG*-3rd ed.,
vol. 4, 1960, 1751; W. Klatt, Diss., 2, n. 3; Tetz, *ThZ* 17
(1961) 416; Klatt, *ThR* 32 (1967) 11ff. [+1978: Cf. however
above, p. [55], n. 5.]

4. Overbeck, *Anf. patr. Lit.* 12. Cf. Vielhauer, *Aufs.*,
247; Tetz, *ThZ* 17 (1961) 424; Tetz, *ThR* 32 (1967) 11ff.

5. Cf. Overbeck, *Christlichkeit*, 7; *Christ. u. Kult.*,
10, 18f.; *A* 348: "The writing of church history is part of
the writing of world history, can be nothing else, and has
also never been anything else" (cited according to *Overbeckiana II*, 164). Cf. Nigg, *op. cit.*, 111-131; Vielhauer, *Aufs.*,
238f.

6. Overbeck, *Christlichkeit*, 4. Similarly already *Entstehung u. Recht*, 4.

7. Cf. Tetz, *ThR* 32 (1967) 16f., 19f., 35.

8. See above, #2, nn. 19, 27.

9. Cf. Nigg, *op. cit.*, 85ff., Vielhauer, *Aufs.*, 246ff.; Tetz, *op. cit.*, 16ff.

10. Vielhauer, *op. cit.*, 247.

11. Cf. Overbeck, *Christ. u. Kult.*, 1ff.

12. Cf. *ibid.*, 1: In reality the writing of history is "at present only acclimatized in a definitely circumscribed province of the past, and has nothing to do in and with the present and in the so-called primal-times only with certain reservations".

13. Cf. *ibid.*, 6: "In the entire sequence (*scil.* of a historical development) there is nothing other to be represented, according to the nature of the subject matter, than the *past-ness* of the whole, its ruin. That is true of every historical image that is actually and earnestly treated in a *historical* manner."

14. *Ibid.*, 21: "Insofar as historical observation takes up only things that are already finished, it can primarily be nothing other than the history of ruin."

15. Cf. *ibid.*, 6.

16. Cf. *ibid.*, 20: Pre-history lies "behind", i.e., behind the history that is conceivable through monuments that have been clarified and written records that are trustworthy.

17. Cf. *ibid.*, 24: "Pre-history has as its essential characteristic the fact that it treats the history of *origination.*" *Ibid.*, 21: "If it is possible therefore to distinguish things which possess historical life, historical actuality, in terms of their pre-historic and their historic times, then pre-history builds a pathway to the basis of their historical actuality."

18. *Ibid.*, 21.

19. *Ibid.*, 20. Cf. Vielhauer, *op. cit.*, 250.

20. Overbeck, *op. cit.*, 23, referring in the original to the Urliteratur. Cf. *A 105*, 137f.: "Such a history however is always another history as the history of another period of time, also as another *past* period of time. We call something primal [Uralt] when it is more than old, something whose orig-

ination is lost in antiquity that is no longer accessible, and of whose origination we also, given the lasting conditions of existence, are unable to represent clearly any more. Correspondingly we also speak of a primal time [Urzeit]. It is a past time, but more than past, a time in which what came about did so under conditions which no longer prevail, and when things came about that do so no longer."

21. Overbeck, *Christ. u. Kult.*, 23. Cf. Vielhauer, *op. cit.*, 248.

22. Overbeck, *Anf. patr. Lit.*, 36: The observation of the "ruins of this pre-literature" take "on all the difficulties of a palaeontology" (a summarization of Overbeck's point). Cf. Overbeck, *A* 196: "Actually the situation here, as with all primal history, is in an extraordinary sense that which prevails elsewhere, that we are concerned with literary ruins rather than with human beings, ruins which we have to resist combining arbitrarily, under the illusion that in the process we can re-substantiate the life that they once exhibited" (cited according to *Overbeckiana II*, 89). Cf. Nigg, *op. cit.*, 86f.

23. Overbeck, *Anf. patr. Lit.*, 36. Cf. *A 105*, 132: "The Christian pre-literature is the literature of the primitive church. Only that will express *either*: the preliterature is the literature of the period or of the time of the primitive church."

24. Overbeck, *Anf. patr. Lit.*, 16f., 18f. Cf. Vielhauer, *Aufs.*, 247; Vielhauer, *RGG*-3rd ed., vol. 4, 1960, 1751. Cf. also Overbeck's addition: "In N. T. ways, i.e., in the N. T. forms, the ecclesial literature was continued for a long time, but even so maintained itself outside literature proper (with letters, official publications, etc.) or turned away from further development of the unique, actual literary form of the N. T., or had to turn away from it (apocryphal literature). Hence it did not give to world literature any further new literary form and was in this sense (as an offshoot of the primitive Christian literature) virtually dead" (cited according to *Overbeckiana II*, 161).

25. Cf. Overbeck, *Anf. patr. Lit.*, 19: "the written form is essential for the content of every literary work." *Ibid.*, 38: The patristic literature demonstrates "that Christianity, only by relying upon the available world literature, created for itself an adequate literature". Cf. also Nigg, *op. cit.*, 88f.; Vielhauer, *Aufs.*, 24f.

26. Overbeck, *A*, 272 (cited according to *Overbeckiana II*, 130). It is probable that the quotation does not refer directly to the Christian pre-literature but to the Christian literature between it and the patristic literature, which existed during the period from the apostles until canonization. But perhaps it makes sense if applied to the pre-literature, since neither were actually "literature proper", but "expediencies to meet a need". Overbeck, *A 105*, 206, calls the N. T. letters "occasional pieces" (cf. also below, p. [110f.]); from that I consider my use of the analogy justified. Cf. also Overbeck, *Anf. patr. Lit.*, 21: "But it would not occur to anyone to derive such occasional writings of the ancient church from those of apostolic times, in the history of literature, any more than it could be said that one had thereby shifted oneself onto the very foundation of the actual literature."

27. Cf. above, #2, n. 46.

28. Cf. below, p. [137ff.].

29. Cf. Overbeck, *Anf. patr. Lit.*, 29, 32f.

30. *Ibid.*, 36.

31. Cf. *ibid.*, 21.

32. *Ibid.*

33. *Ibid.*, 19. Cf. Vielhauer, *op. cit.*, 247; Tetz, *op. cit.*, 12f. Cf. also A. Deissmann, *Licht vom Osten*, 1923-4th ed., 194: "The letter is something non-literary: it serves as a means of communication between persons who are separated." "It is not essentially different from the oral dialogue; it could be referred to as a promise of a long-distance call, and it is not incorrectly referred to as half a dialogue." Cf. A. N. Wilder, *The Language of the Gospel*, 1964, 39: "In short the letter as a written form is almost as flexible as oral speech itself, and like direct oral address has an implicit dialogue character." Differently R. W. Funk, *Language, Hermeneutic, and Word of God*, 1966, 238, 248f.; Funk, "Saying and Seeing: Phenomenology of Language and the New Testament," *JBR* 34 (1966) 197-213: The Pauline letter exists in the dialectic between immediacy and distance; it is intended to be an adequate substitute for the oral word, and therefore protects itself from the results of the objectification of the written word; at the same time as the mode of primary reflectivity it keeps its distance from the *presupposed* kerygmatic proclamation. -- On the linguistic form of the letter, cf. A. Deissmann, "Prolegomena zu den biblischen Briefen und Episteln," *Bibelstudien*, 1895,

187-252; Deissmann, *Licht*, 118f., 193ff. (cf. here #8, n. 18);
E. Fuchs, *Hermeneutik*, 1958-2nd ed., 181-91; Wilder, *op. cit.*,
39-43; Funk, *Language*, 124ff., 224ff., 250ff.

34. Nigg, *op. cit.*, 89.

35. Overbeck, *Anf. patr. Lit.*, 21.

36. Cf. *ibid.*, 45, 47, 67.

37. Cf. Overbeck, *Christ. u. Kult.*, 23f.

38. Overbeck, *Anf. patr. Lit.*, 20. Cf. Nigg, *op. cit.*,
89f.

39. Overbeck, *A 105*, 156f.

40. *Ibid.*, 158.

41. Cf. Overbeck, *Christ. u. Kult.*, 17: "The concept of
canonical books could only arise when they were completely
blind to the conditions of existence which historical tradition presupposes...." Cf. also below, p. [116f.].

42. Cf. W. Schrage, *Die konkreten Einzelgebote in der
paulinischen Paränese*, 1916, 38. -- We do not treat the non-
Pauline letters in the N. T. here since Overbeck was clear
about their transitional character to literature. Cf. Nigg,
op. cit., 90f.

43. Schrage, *op. cit.*, 41.

44. Cf. *ibid.*, 119; H. Schlier, "Die Eigenart der christlichen Mahnung nach dem Apostel Paulus," in his *Besinnung auf
das Neue Testament*, 1964, 340-57.

45. Cf. Schrage, *op. cit.*, 182f.

45a [+1978: It seems to be typical of his argument when
P. Vielhauer, *Geschichte der urchristlichen Literatur*, 1975,
63, n. 8, suggests that my argumentation above and below ignores two facts, namely that not all Pauline letters were preserved, and that the phenomenon of preserving them was not
something specific to Paul. *Ibid.*, 62, he agrees that the
letters as *apostolic* letters "bear a public, official, and
authoritative character". *Ibid.*, 64, he speaks of "getting
books against will" (transl. E. G.). *Ibid.*, 63f., the relation between the "public" character and the "publication" of
the letters remain unclear. A careful reader who compares

Vielhauer's argumentation with mine will soon detect how his main positive statements are indirect or even direct quotations without quotation marks. My questions as to how "non-literary letters" could *become* literature, and my stress upon the impossibility of letters (*litera*) without literature (*literatura*), are ignored by him in his very first sentence. Cf. *ibid.*, 58.]

46. Cf. the extensive proof in Güttgemanns, *Der leidende Apostel*, 112ff., 135ff., 142ff., 165ff.

47. Cf. Käsemann, "Amt und Gemeinde im Neuen Testament," in his *Aufs.*, vol. 1, 109-34.

48. Evidence in Güttgemanns, *op. cit.*, 170ff., 323ff.

49. For evidence concerning this understanding of *en emoi*, cf. *ibid.*, 117, n. 133.

50. Cf. *ibid.*, 126-35.

51. Cf. *ibid.*, 154-70.

52. Cf. H. Frhr. v. Campenhausen, *Kirchliches Amt und geistliche Vollmacht in den ersten drei Jahrhunderten*, 1963-2nd ed., 32ff.

53. Cf. Güttgemanns, *op. cit.*, 324-27.

54. Cf. J. Roloff, *Apostolat--Verkündigung--Kirche*, 1965, 104ff.

55. Also K. M. Fischer, *Die Bedeutung des Leidens in der Theologie des Paulus*, Diss., East Berlin, 1967, was not able nor did he desire to show that there was no Christ-immediacy of the Christian in the apostolic kerygma. B. Chr. Lategan, *Die aardse Jesus in die prediking van Paulus volgens sy briewe*, Diss., Kampen, 1967, did not contribute to this question because of a different approach. Otherwise he eliminates the differentiation from the "historical" and the "earthly" Jesus, and hence does not engage my thesis, in spite of a more comprehensive treatment.

56. On the theme, mission, proclamation, and apostolate, see Güttgemanns, *VF* 12/2 (1967) 61-79.

57. A direct identification between the letters and the oral sermons is difficult. Rather the letters refer back to the proclamation that has taken place and been accepted by the

church, and which is now reflected upon anew in the letters (cf. I Cor 15:1-3a). Cf. N. A. Dahl, "Anamnesis. Mémoire et Commémoration dans le christianisme primitif," *StTh* 1 (1947) 69-95; G. Eichholz, "Bewähren und Bewähren des Evangeliums," in his *Tradition und Interpretation*, 1965, 138-60; H. Conzelmann, *Grundriss der Theologie des Neuen Testaments*, 1968--2nd ed., 186f. Cf. also above, n. 33.

58. So P. Feine, J. Behm, W. G. Kümmel, *Einleitung in das Neue Testament*, 1963-12th ed., 174.

59. On the reproaches of Paul's opponents, see Güttgemanns, *Der leidende Apostel*, 94-97; further bibliography is cited there.

60. Cf. Overbeck, *Christ. u. Kult.*, 22: "The book had ceased, in this stratum where it had historic significance, to be completed organism of unity between author and witness that it had when it began to be effective." "The authors in particular are either simultaneously present along with their books or simply not there at all, at any rate not there as the only interpreters of their witness who can be trusted." *Ibid.*, 23: The effectiveness of the N. T. literature "rests precisely upon the immediate unity of origination and effectiveness present in the time of their beginning. Immediate conversation with their authors make the books themselves superfluous and cancels out their historical existence."

61. On the collection of the Pauline letters as the beginning of the process by which they become literature, cf. Deissmann, *Licht*, 200f., 205; Kümmel, *op. cit.*, 203-05, 254, 264, 283, 316, 350, 353f.

62. The intentions of the author (cf. Nigg, *op. cit.*, 90) can only have existed in tension with the choice of the media; perhaps the consciousness of these intentions was even in contradiction to the actual implications of the linguistic media chosen. But these questions touch upon the difficult complex of problems which we will not further discuss, whether and in how far the intention of linguistic media can be reduced to the phenomenon of consciousness. We can go no further without engaging E. Husserl. Bibliography: cf. #12, n. 26. An attempt will be made in the special publication, "Formgeschichte und Linguistik".

63. Kümmel, *op. cit.*, 175.

64. Cf. Güttgemanns, *op. cit.*, 142f. Further bibliography is given there.

65. Cf. W. Schmithals, *Die Gnosis in Korinth*, 1956, 27; Güttgemanns, *op. cit.*, 143, 178. Further bibliography is given there. For criticism of Schmithals, see G. Bornkamm, *Die Vorgeschichte des sogenannten Zweiten Korintherbriefes*, 1961, 23, n. 89.

66. Cf. Bornkamm, *op. cit.*, 9. [+1978: Note how Vielhauer, *op. cit.*, 147f., agrees *de facto* with my view although he polemicizes against it, *ibid.*, 63, n. 8. Even an unsuspicious reader gets the impression that there is something arbitrary here.]

66a Cf. Güttgemanns, *Der leidende Apostel*, 45f.

66b Especially W. Schmithals, *Die Gnosis in Korinth*, 1965-2nd ed., who deals very strongly with the possibility of a misunderstanding of the "opponents" by Paul. Less the thesis in itself so much as the manner of its execution and foundation have brought it into disrepute in introductions to the Pauline corpus. Criticism: Güttgemanns, *Der leidende Apostel*, 58, n. 25; 64, n. 59; 113, n. 109; 114, n. 111; 138, n. 20; 146f., n. 27; 156-58. In view of the many gaps in the "pre-literature", it is no longer scientifically possible to wager either to construct the position of the "opponents" from their epistolary struggle with Paul, or to identify more clearly the opponents or to desire to understand them as the immediately-encountered combatants.

66c Cf. however Güttgemanns, "Sprache des Glaubens--Sprache der Menschen," *VF* 14/2 (1969) 86-114; Güttgemanns, *LB* 8 (1970), 24-27.

66d [+1978: The reader should note that I am always speaking about the gospel-*form*, not about the content. Vielhauer, *op. cit.*, 335, n. 6, accuses me of "onesidedness" in that I have a preference for the oral nature of the pre-Markan tradition, and leave out the process by which tradition becomes scripture, and the foundation-process of the gospels. Both theses are clearly not mine, but those of a phantom antagonist. *Ibid.*, 349, he himself sees the problem that "the totality of the life of Christ" was never constructed as a written book *before* the gospel-*form* arises. That is precisely my position: the gospel-form is available only in a written stage, in the presence of which each regress is only hypothetical. Besides that it must be proved (and not presupposed) that the gospel-form is a result of a historical process. I do not have the feeling of being understood here at all.]

67. Overbeck, *A 105*, 196 (cited according to *Overbeckiana II*, 89.

68. *Ibid.*, 90. On this topic, cf. Barth, *op. cit.*, 10f.

69. Overbeck, *op. cit.*

70. *Ibid.*, 91.

71. *Ibid.*, 90.

72. The following should be kept in mind when looking at the background indicated (Overbeck, *Christ. u. Kult.*, 25): "Hence pre-history is an undertaking of the same precariousness as history of the present." Neither is encompassed within the category of "character of pastness".

73. Cf. *ibid.*, 7: "Thereby *Christianity* had begun to reject history in itself, and experienced such only against its own primally-expressed volition." "To present Christianity within the concept of the historical, that means to grant that it had developed historically, meant to grant that Christianity was of this world." *Ibid.*, 9: "History and Christianity, according to Christianity's own volition, would never be united." Cf. Barth, *op. cit.*, 9f. The foundations of such a view are to be found in the eschatological character of primitive Christianity. Cf. Vielhauer, *Aufs.*, 250; Vielhauer, *RGG*-3rd ed., vol. 4, 1960, 1751. Eschatology also establishes distance from literature. Cf. Nigg, *op. cit.*, 102f.

74. Overbeck, *A 105*, 140, solves the problem of a "historical" presentation of the pre-history by means of analogical concept: "Historical presentation of a pre-history can only stand in a relationship of analogy to the rest of history."

75. Cf. Overbeck, *Christ. u. Kult.*, 8.

76. We can only understand Overbeck's reflections, in my opinion, when we are careful to observe the temporal-category division between "prehistory" and the only "history" possible to us.

77. Cf. Overbeck, *A 105*, 196: "To what extent and in which forms are the authors of the canonical gospels present in the gospels represented in the canon? The canon is therefore a presupposition, i.e., of the gospels, since the latter are only transmitted in the canon, with the presuppositions of their conception given only in the canon itself. Appropriate to this presupposition, the gospels are all, collectively and individually with respect to their components, the historical witnesses of the evangelical history, of the his-

tory of Jesus gathered under the concept of the 'gospel'"
(cited according to *Overbeckiana II*, 87). Canonization makes
the four gospels equivalent as historical witnesses, "i.e.,
as that which they did not originally want to be at all, and
became continuously less so in the development which they
themselves founded. For in the final analysis the gospels
became history in which the writer himself came forward. The
result was that the authors of the gospels became authorial
individuals. Writers of materials transmitted to them, i.e.,
in spite of their anonymity, nothing less than identical individuals in the designation of this material, except that it
took a while until they were able to demonstrate unanimously
what they were from the beginning" (*ibid.*, 88). On the in-
clusion of the authorial personalities within the form-critical program, cf. H. Karpp, *ThR* 24 (1956/57) 254f.; Tetz, *op.
cit.*, 35f.

78. Overbeck, *A 105*, 196 (cited acc. to *Overbeckiana II*,
88). On canonization, cf. Nigg, *op. cit.*, 105ff.

79. Overbeck, *A 105*, 196 (cited acc. to *Overbeckiana II*,
86).

80. Cf. Overbeck, *Das Johannesevangelium*, ed. C. A. Bernoulli, 1911, 496: In literature proper the author covers up
his work and takes its place. "In the canon on the other hand
the gospels have no authors. It knows nothing of them and
only appends their names, with the so characteristic *kata*,
as a form of etiquette. Whoever therefore searches in the
canon for authors of the gospels should not complain when he
thereby destroys the gospels for the use for which they are
determined in the canon. He is warned by the canon."

81. Cf. Overbeck, *A 105*, 228f.

82. *Ibid.*, 229.

83. Cf. Nigg, *op. cit.*, 91ff.

84. Tetz, *op. cit.*, 13.

#7. *The Peculiarity of the Written Nature of Genres in Linguistic and Literary-Critical Perspective.*

Although in our presentation above the principle legitimacy of the question about the special quality of the written nature of genres has been shown to be an interior one within a form-critical orientation of N. T. theology, and we can proceed today only in terms of a modern modification of the older form-critical program by including new linguistic and literary-critical methods, we want--and are now able--to focus in a preliminary way upon purely hypothetical and leading questions addressed to the contemporary state of research in N. T. form criticism by the disciplines that are oriented to language. Even if, in the course of the present work, consequences for N. T. form criticism may be drawn from the research that has been carried out in these disciplines, their real confirmation can first be discovered when they have been practically tested by more extended application in teamwork among N. T. scholars whose interests include form criticism and literary criticism as well as linguistics. Dependence of such a program upon the co-work of others, and upon an extended period of data-collection, is by no means an objection to its fundamental justification, for the development of the "form-critical school" from its first faint-hearted beginnings up to its fundamental consolidation in Germany occurred with the crucial co-operation of both factors. It is probably necessary to appeal to scientific fairness in asking that the new program be allowed the same conditions that are acknowledged with respect to traditional form-critical conceptions. Only in such a manner can

we justifiably anticipate a new breakthrough in the history
of research.

[p. 120] 1. The Written Nature of the Genres:
Johann Gottfried Herder and Wilhelm
von Humboldt.

(a) The Oral and the Written: Johann Gottfried
Herder.[1]

Decisive roots of the form-critical method were available
for application by Gunkel in the works of J. G. Herder (1744-
1803).[2] Since exact knowledge of Herder's thought[3] has often
been blocked, a more intensive observation of his linguistic
and literary-critical concepts is always rewarding.

Herder developed two intersecting lines of thought about
the oral and written nature of the genres. On the one hand
the written is to him a depotencing of the oral, and on the
other, an almost divine gift and a pillar of reason. How can
we understand this apparent antinomy?

"Already as an animal the human has language," Herder begins his *Treatise Concerning the Origin of Language* (1771).[4]
Language as natural sound is an expression of sensitiveness.[5]
Each, genre of nature has its own language.[6] Language is immediately related to the liveliness of nature;[7] it is itself
a style of the natural liveliness, as it were, *actus purus*.[8]
Therefore [p. 121] it is impossible to maintain in writing the
liveliness of language. "No single lively-resounding language
can be completely brought into letters of the alphabet, and
even less into twenty letters." "What living language allows
its tones to be learned from the letters of a book, and which
dead language can be so re-awakened? The more lively a language is, the less anyone has thought that it could be expressed in letters; the more original it rises up into the

manifold, non-selective sounds of nature, the less it can also be written, even less so with twenty letters, and indeed to strangers it often remains entirely inexpressible."[9]

Every writing-down, because of the selective character of the letters,[10] represents an abstraction of the living sound-gestalt of language, as the writing-down of Hebrew strikingly demonstrates.[11] Writing only incompletely replaces living orality.[12] According to the linguistic theory of signs, semiotics,[13] the written sign stands for the oral sign:[14] writing is *signum signi*.

Since for Herder, because of his orientation to the *actus purus*, the liveliness of the oral quality of language possesses priority over the written, hearing is for him "a degree of mediacy in the middle" of the human senses (hearing, feeling, vision).[15] Within an ontological speculation concerning the three conceivable variants of perceiving creatures (creatures that hear, that feel, that see), we hearing-creatures are situated "in the middle: we see, we feel; and the descried, felt nature sounds forth. She becomes the teaching mistress leading to language by means of sounds. We become at the same time an audience through all our senses." "The meaning of language has become the meaning of our media and associations: we are creatures of language."[16] In such a way the priority of the oral is also ontologically secured.

The *depotencing of the written* in Herder's usage is understandable against this background. In the presence of letters what gets lost "gradually" are "the [p. 122] living accents and shapes";[17] "and as well human thought and its living spiritual power weaken in the presence of this artificial guide to pre-designed forms of thought".[18] "Enchained in letters, the understanding creeps in at the end, and with difficulty; our best thoughts become dumb in dead written tongues."[19] In this manner the living language of the people gradually dies and be-

comes the language of books.[20] The *actus purus* coagulates into the created. As in the human organism, so also in language
do several stages occur, from the youthful liveliness of the
purely oral to the senile torpidity of the purely written.[21]
The oral is a medium of the education of the people, the written a medium of the education of the learned.[22] So there develops a sociological stratification of the nation in the linguistic media.

In spite of this depotencing of the written oriented to
the thought of the living national organism as the locus of
the *actus purus*, Herder was a realist with enough psychological sensitivity not to give pride of place to the written
rather than to the spirit. The written as a mode of tradition
of the national traditions is a medium of the "eternalizing
of reason": "Mortals who came to this means of capturing the
fleeting spirit not only in words but also in letters, discovered that it may be regarded as a god among men."[23] The
tradition of writing is "to be regarded as the most persist-
ing, most tranquil, most effective institution of God, through
which nations upon nations, centuries upon centuries are effective, and the entire human race perhaps finds itself over
time tied into a chain of fraternal tradition."[24]

So the written also plays *a positive role with reference
to linguistic reason*: "One thing especially evident is...the
advance of language through reason and of reason through language,...after writing is found, when one genre of the manner
of writing after another takes shape. Hence no progress can
be made, no new entrée, wherein there has not already been an
impression of the human soul."[25] Therefore the written nature
of the genres exists, to be sure, in a certain tension with
the living folk spirit, but it can also always develop further
toward meeting the needs of both. The *actus purus* can then
itself utilize the written as an appropriate working tool.

When the appropriateness of the written nature of literature
contrasts with the genres,[26] language becomes the "working
tool of literature",[27] that is, the oral liveliness of language coincides with the written nature [p. 123] of literature, as in the case of the written nature of folk-poetry,
which therefore is not an actual written, that is, something
separated from an *actus purus*, but a surrogate for liveliness.[28] *In the case of "folk-poetry" the written, because
of its coincidence with and its adequation to the* actus
purus, *is solely a surrogate phenomenon, not however an
objectification.*[28a]

(b) Language as *Energeia* and *Ergon*:
Wilhelm von Humboldt.[29]

W. v. Humboldt (1767-1835) built upon Herder's observations and systematized them.[30] Here we need discuss only
briefly the dialectic of language as *energeia* and as *ergon*[31]
and its relation to the oral and written nature of language,
for these thoughts find renewed expression in the so-called
Neo-Humboldtianism,[32] although they have parallels also in
B. L. Whorf's metalinguistics in cultural anthropology,[33] and
have been especially influential in America.[34] We must be
satisfied here with the following suggestions.

Language "itself is not a work (*ergon*), but an activity
(*energeia*)";[35] that is, what is essential in the phenomenon of
language is not the finished and therefore fixable linguistic
shape, but the unique inner creative *linguistic power*,[36] which
corresponds to the power of thinking and with it utilizes the
dialectic of analogy and differentiation from spiritual culture.[37] [p. 124] Language and spirit mutually influence one
another.[38] Although contrasted with objects, the word is something subjective, it has effects upon the spirit as a linguistic objectification of the spirit.[39] Language is effective as

a linguistic power in the circle of speech-act and linguistic-law and thereby demonstrates its liveliness which is never to be permanently fixed:[40] "To that extent language is precisely an object and independent, as it is a subject and dependent. For it never has, even in writing, a permanent standing, but must always be evinced anew in thought, and consequently entirely devolves into the subject."[41] Language is simultaneously *actus purus*.

With that *the problem of the written* is already indicated. Formally it is to be described—as is the problem of the linguistic as a whole—[42] as a problem of adequation: The question concerns the true writing which is singularly appropriate to language, which is related to the living *energeia* neither by opposition nor tension.[43]

Each language emits the sound of the essential.[44] Each language exists for a long time without writing; writing, as a *signum signi*, is a secondary phenomenon:[45] "writing, which is taken only as a sign of the sign, becomes simultaneously a sign of the object, and becomes weaker, in that it introduces its immediate appearance into thought; the effect which the word thus exercises is only intended as a sign."[46] The linguistic *energeia* "for the most part is transformed only in weakened and impoverished form into writing and books". "The structure of a literature resembles the structure of the ossifying joints of the aging human body." "For the letter of the alphabet has a chilling effect upon spoken speech which yet lives on in its manifoldness next to it [p. 125] ...and it soon tolerates nothing near itself except what is like itself."[47]

Since Humboldt situated *energeia*, "the source of this power, freshness, and liveliness of languages", within the nation, in the folk, i.e., in the uneducated classes,[48] it is understandable why he followed Herder in attributing writing to the educated classes: the language of writing "simultaneously becomes the everyday language of the educated classes".[49] "Between this and the folk language there obtains a distinction found in every nation possessing a literature."[50] So the written effects a sociologically understandable stratification of language. *The assignment of linguistic phenomena to the oral and popular character is a consequence of the* energeia-*principle*, which is therefore a postulate of a particular metaphysics. At the same time the written causes the *energeia* to be paralyzed into *ergon*,[51] since it serves that drive toward eternalization and fixation immanent in every language.[52] Writing lends to linguistic forms yet more stability and uniformity, and effects a generalizing of language, "which bit by bit makes the transition into education as a unique dialect".[53]

But precisely this new linguistic phenomenon caused by writing now also demonstrates the positive *value of the written*. The use of writing is the beginning point of a more precise processing of language.[54] In writing, language is elevated to a higher level: "While social and authorial education is not to be denied, on the one hand it weakens the power of the folk language, but on the other it creates in language something new, higher, more noble, and worthier, something which belongs to it alone."[55] The spirit is not lost, but "attains through writing a lasting body".[56] Writing "fastens together" the living and transitory language[57] and so with literature [brings] "more and more life and activity into the spiritual activity, produces more attempts to validate the language and its form".[58] Although here writing is not only externally a means of thought for the "inner language", but also a means of representation,[59] there is present in this case such a great [p. 126] *adequation of energeia and the written* that the latter is made to serve the former.

184

2. The Relationship of the Bases of Form Criticism
    to Johann Gottfried Herder and Wilhelm von Hum-
    boldt's Thought and the Crisis of Recent Folk-
    loristics.[59a]

(a) The Extent of the Crisis in Recent
     Folkloristics.

It can be seen in H. Gunkel's work how greatly form criticism's methodological foundations developed in analogy to the
linguistic ideas of J. G. Herder and W. v. Humboldt, which were
applied to the biblical material.[60] However W. Klatt's judgment is also valid in this connection: "We utilize today in
theology an exegetical method without fully sharing the theological presuppositions which have always accompanied this
method but were never clearly brought into view."[61] In presenting Herder's and Humboldt's thoughts it may have become
evident to any expert in contemporary form criticism what
separates our contemporary form-critical consciousness from
earlier considerations, as well as what is common to them,
without however necessarily assuming the metaphysical postulative character of many of the theses of Herder and his followers for contemporary form criticism.

Here we must point to a much more important factor in the
history of research, namely the critical attack upon Herder's
theses in folkloristics and literary criticism. Since this
crisis is of a fundamental nature, and concerns the interests
of both gospel form criticism and folkloristics in "collective
art", form criticism is also involved in this foundational
crisis, so that it has every reason to concern itself about
them.[62]

[p. 127] K.-E. Gass has summarized the scepticism of
contemporary literary criticism in this manner: "Specialists
in both Germanic and Romance language studies agree...on the
fact that the validity of the idea of a folk poetry has to be

rescinded quite a bit; this fact, gained by means of a more stringent application of historical criticism and aesthetic formal analysis, can be supported by results that no one can dispense with."[63] After progress by others,[64] H. Bausinger has recently summarized the foundational crisis of folkloristics in the following antithesis: While traditional folk research considered "folk poetry" to be the oldest and most original in the entire field of poetry, on the basis of more recent research on the "romantic school", *"folk poetry"* must be designated *as the invention and construction of romantic science.*[65] "Folk poetry" is "from its beginnings a mixed product stemming from the objective fundament of folk-transmission, a product of ingenious and productive interests".[66] Because of its significance we will sketch briefly the establishment of this thesis in recent folkloristics.

(b) The Aporia of the Concept "Folk Poetry".

The simultaneously fruitful and vague concepts, "folk poetry", "folk poesy", and "folk song" [Volksdichtung, Volkpoesie, Volkslied] are Herder's coinages.[67] As their most characteristic aspect the Grimm brothers emphasized their non-individual origination:[68] vegetal metaphors (growing, blooming, dying, becoming, bearing seed, springing forth) characterize "the lack of an individual generation and the presence of a vegetative origination".[69] With the help of these metaphors Herder's theses gradually became metaphysically mystified, and established as leading premises of the folklorists' work as collectors. The development from Herder to the Grimm brothers transpired approximately as follows.[69a]

[p. 128] As signs of nature poetry Herder considered: "the inner truth in the poetic conception, the liveliness of the historical givenness in the immediate sensible fancy, the natural form of the inversion and the foundation of the saying."[70] The Grimm brothers took over these characteristics as premises of their researches, expanding them and transforming the concept of "nature poetry" from the more ethnological into the more metaphysical.[71]

To the feeling-moment of nature poetry belong: "innocence, sensible nearness, immediacy and presence of the object, in which only the significant is apparent, and that one-sidedly, founded in experience".[72] The romantics felt themselves related to these feeling-moments and developed their research as, we might say, representatives of the "folk", entirely from this perspective,[73] which also did not shirk dealing with stylistic transformation such as is found in fairy tales. They "wanted to share consciously in the unconscious naiveté, freshness of youth, and originality of the folk as in its poetic transmission, which was produced from a primal creative fountain that bubbled up before their very eyes".[74]

A. W. Schlegel (1767-1845) was not convinced of the collective character of folk poetry because of the peculiar relationship of the Grimm brothers to the materials they collected.[75] In fact W. Grimm (1786-1859) had, "in that he brought all these ideas into the concrete process of transmission, stylized fairy tales into the contexts of his conception of nature poetry",[76] so that a decisive individual factor came into play in their formation. For this reason F. Nicolai (1733-1811) correctly took exception to "the striving for the folksy, connected to great sentimentality, and he exposed the originality of a second authorial hand"; "what apparently stems immediately from nature and is plainly anti-modish, was here characterized as expressing a mode of time, i.e., the 'à la mode'".[77] That justifies the claim that: "The concept of nature poetry of Jakob (*scil.* Grimm; 1785-1863) did not have the character of a result. It is already so much an attitude and a heuristic presupposition that it can be presupposed as an unquestionable fact."[78]

[p. 129] (c) "Nature Poetry" as a Rous-
seauean Fiction.

The perspective of the Grimm brothers is weighted down
by a particular philosophy-of-culture metaphysics. The association of folk (lower classes) and primordiality or nature
and naturalness, was criticized already by F. Nicolai as being a Rousseauean fiction.[79] J. G. Herder, J. G. Hamann (1730-
88), and G. A. Bürger (1747-94), did actually conceive "nature"
"in Rousseau's sense as the most original, genuine, innocent,
as the opposite of the developed social order, of culture, of
reason".[80] In this philosophy of culture, history becomes a
"style of nature".[81] "Nature poetry and ancient history are
one; they are streams of one and the same river".[82] Poetry is
immediately related to nature.[83] It is life's reflection in
deeply affected temperament.[84] By the equivalizing of pro-
miscuous application of folk, nature, and nation, the equation
arises: folk poetry = nature poetry = national poetry; and beyond this equation the thought "that the entirety of the folk
is engaged in nature poetry".[85] By a scientific trick nature
poetry is therefore "simultaneously rendered independent as a
primal phenomenon".[86]

In specific instances we can demonstrate an identity between concepts from Herder to the Grimm brothers. Herder still
principally distinguished what became a differentiated unity
for J. Grimm: "National poetry (the characteristic, the aspect determined by climate and temporal conditions), folk
poetry (the sensual and emotional, the genuine), nature poetry
(the given, the exemplary and concrete beautiful) were differentiated categories--historical, psychological, aesthetic; they
were occasions for literary-historical analysis, but were not
simultaneously taken together as explanation of a *single* sub-

ject at hand."[87] The connection between folk (lower classes) and nature now became a conscious methodological identification.

If today we examine the later metaphysicalizing and mystifying of Herder's concepts, the appeal to nature demonstrates "precisely not only the natural expressions of people, arising from the folk and natural ethnic occasions, but in the first degree from fantasy and the experience of poetry". "All this makes clear that 'folk poetry' here is not something like a factor of the oral transmission, but a creative fiction which brings together folk and art."[88]

[p. 130] (d) The Lack of Clarity in the "Folk" Concept.

The vague concept of "folk", which already led in Herder's work to the confusing concept of "folk poetry",[89] is especially critical in this connection, and was criticized already by Herder's contemporaries.[90] "Folk" meant to Herder "an ethnic and social dimension, *populus* or *natio*, and at the same time, a stratum thereof, the *vulgus*".[91] In this conceptual unclarity of "folk", there were manifold problems from the beginning.

H. Moser criticizes Herder's concept of "folk" with respect to its sociologically primary layer, "in that he differentiated too sharply between the educated and the elementary layers, between high- and folk-culture. Like the romantics, he did not recognize that both are in many ways mutually influential, that there are intermediate strata..., and that what is produced by the various strata are constantly exchanged, a process wherein without a doubt the upper strata are primarily, but by no means exclusively, the givers".[92] Also H. Bausinger determines, on the basis of more recent research in folkloristics (H. Naumann),[93] *that the "folk material" is frequently material that has sunk down from*

the upper strata:[94] "What appears to us...as folk-culture is
in general not the flowering that grows directly out of this
soil, but is the result of an elipse: pronounced individual-
culture draws its powers from the 'mother earth' and then
transmits its materials to the lower strata."[95]

(e) The Metaphysical Conception of History in Earlier Folkloristics.

With this we have an image of the tradition-history of
folk poetry opposed to that of Herder. His view can be represented this way: "While in early times the totality of a folk
is the carrier of myth and folk poetry, after the division of
culture where one must distinguish educated persons from the
folk (Herder sees this as a sign of its senescence), myth and
folk poetry withdraw into the basic social level, which was
further maintained and transmitted in the form of sagas, tales,
and folk songs."[96] This conception of history is determined by
a controversy concerning the temporal relation of nature poetry
and artistic poetry;[97] it is a consequence of a metaphysic [p.
131] which, as "a penetration of a historical doctrine of
epochs and a psychological typology",[98] perceives in poetry
"spellbound life itself", the unendingly manifold and inex-
haustibly flowing *actus purus.*[99] Life, folk, and epic are for
W. Grimm the forms in which this *actus purus* appear: "The
epic is a representation and a perishing of a metaphysical
life. What corresponds to its carrier, the folk, is not the
commercial *demos,* 'but the greatest essence of the spiritual
life', which is only represented."[100] Herder's aporia between
the folk spirit as unchangeable,[101] and its development, is
also related to this:[102] *Life remains, in spite of all development, identical with itself.* So little as the individual
is all of life, so little can folk poetry be "invention and
fabrication of an individual, but only living tradition, life

itself".[103]   For J. Grimm the origination of folk poetry remains inexplicable, "since it knows no single poet, but is
"a sum of the whole', it is pure, innocent, simple, its form
develops from within itself and from eternal validity".[104]
Only the unintentional has to do with God, and consequently
with the *actus purus*; the intentional passes away.[105] So
finally the thesis of the collective origin of folk poetry is
for J. Grimm a circumlocution for its divine origin; "nature
poetry is pre-human; it is of divine origin, simultaneously
given through revelation to youthful humanity and inexperi-
enceable to humans today; 'nothing is held on to more per-
versely than the presumption that one can write epic poems
or even poetry at all, when it is only they that can enable
themselves to become poetry'".[106]

The logic postulated therefore runs: Since on the one
hand language is *actus purus* and poetry consequently the
greatest liveliness; since on the other hand the "folk" is
the locus of the *actus purus*, folk poetry *can* not have an
individual, but only a collective origin, that is, an origin
in the most absolute *actus purus*, in God. *The thesis concerning the collective origin of folk poetry is the consequence
of a particular metaphysic.*

The metaphysical conception of history of the Grimm
brothers also forms the background to the postulate of a historical sequence from nature poetry to artistic poetry. "Humans are not at all the same at all times, [p. 132] but in
origin the divine has revealed itself immediately in them."
"The course of history is a descent from those primordial
origins, which came about necessarily and therefore are not
subject to arbitrary valuation."[107] "For the Grimms, what
takes place in history is an irreversible process in which
God reveals himself: out of a condition of the nearness of
God and creative innocence, the development leads necessarily

into an always-greater distance from God."[108] May we not so
interpret: From God as from the original locus of the *actus
purus* the history of language runs on toward a complete distancing from life? The "metaphysics of history"[109] is at any
rate clear.

Result: Insofar as form criticism rests upon the earlier
folkloristics (even if in a more recent sociological transformation of concepts), it cannot be inconsequential that more
recent folkloristics no longer stresses as a metaphysical
postulate the connection between liveliness, the oral, the
folk, and folk poetry. Form criticism should attempt to develop a conceptuality for its description which proves itself
more resistant to attack.

(f) The Purely-Gradual Distinction between
"Folk Poetry" and "Artistic Poetry".

H. Moser summarizes the criticism of the absolute distinction between folk poetry and artistic poetry.[110] The
sharp distinction cannot be valid any longer,[111] since folk
poetry and artistic poetry, in contrast to the position of
the Grimm brothers, exist not only sequentially in history,
but also in a process of continual intercourse. Much that
was previously considered folk poetry has shown itself to be
artistic poetry or as artistic poetic transformation of folk
materials.[112] Doubtless the romantics overvalued the creative
power of the elementary social level, the folk. To be sure,
folk poetry = community poetry, "above all in the sense that
the community which took it up is more immediately present
and responsive than with respect to artistic poetry". But
the anonymity of folk poetry "is at the same time only present conditionally"; often artistically gifted persons belonging to the elementary level are the originators,[113] whose
creations are not naive and completely unrecognized, "but

are further recognized".[114] To be sure folk poetry is "an
expression of a pronounced community life and a strong group
feeling, which is much stronger than in the upper classes".[115]
But behind it there is a particular anthropology, namely "the
'healthy' attitude of the unbroken, nonproblematic, whole humanity",[116] in short, of the humanity [p. 133] which still
feels itself at home in its surroundings. So the distinctions
between folk poetry and artistic poetry are "not so much essential as gradual. Not different forms of poetry, but different classes of poetry are involved, and they are differentiated according to the various situations from which they
arise, and according to different inner attitudes; they stem
not only from different social classes, but also from different spiritual classes."[117]

H. Kuhn considers that folklore no longer remains for
contemporary folkloristics an "original" cultural artifact
since the conceptual model of the continuity of the total
"folk" culture has been replaced by fragmentation into different subject areas of cultural artifacts that have penetrated into a high culture.[118] What relates the individual
subject areas of contemporary folkloristics to one another
"is only one thing: their collectivity, the more restricted
division of work because of a tighter typology, a more meager
historical consciousness because of the firmer hold of tradition, and so forth. Folkloristics is the science of the collective elements in high cultures."[119] No one can any longer
speak in the old sense of a "folk originality" of folklore.

Result: Form criticism needs to re-examine and clarify
anew its sociological premises to see what empirical proof
there may actually be for the homogeneousness between the
"small units" and the lower classes. Today, in view of the
crisis in older folkloristics, form criticism should clarify
especially in what sense the traditio-historical uniqueness

of the "Kleinliteratur" it affirms is a "sociological" phenomenon that permits a conclusion by analogy with the structures of the collective that passes along the material. A *proven* collective mode of tradition of a genre is, according to the contemporary position of folkloristics, still not an index for the sociological structure of the group that transmits the genres or collectively "creates" them. In this context a whole string of candid questions remains to be resolved by form criticism.

(g) The Oral and the Written as What
Distinguishes Genres.

The revision in recent folkloristics also touches the conceptual model having to do with the unbroken oral character of the folk traditions. [p. 134] Herder's postulate was: The poetic souls, the youthful ones in the childhood of the world, are "untainted by a book culture".[120] Over against the assumption of thorough-going orality of folk poetry, recent results of narrative research apparently "call in the least for great caution".[121] In this connection P. (Grigorevitch) Bogatyrev and R. Jakobson have taken up the attempt to make principle delineations between oral poetry or folklore and literature.[122] H. Bausinger formulates these results as follows.

"The distinction is especially constituted by the fact that a work of folklore is actualized only as a social act, that in general it is communicated to others--is shared with others." "Since folklore has this social function, it is oriented to collective persuasion, to the dominant taste of the respective group."[123] From this Bausinger correctly draws consequences with respect to the nature of folklore and literature: "In contrast to folklore, literature has in each case individual existence." "It is in principle inde-

pendent from the transmission, since it is deposited in determinate form. On the other hand folklore exists *only* in
its functioning, in the performance [in der jeweiligen Ak-
tualisierung], as part of the transmission."[124] "The outer
form corresponds to this nature of folklore: not the determinate gestalt, but *variability* is constitutive to it. For
literature on the other hand uniqueness and commitment characterize the authenticity of the text."[125]

P. Bogatyrev and R. Jakobson draw wide-ranging consequences for the traditional conditions of both areas from
the differentiated natures of oral material (folklore) and
written material (literature).[126] The very "concept of
literary transmission is itself an indication of a quite
different one than those used in folklore. In the realm of
folklore the possibility of re-actualization of the poetic
data is significantly less. If the carriers of a particular
poetic tradition have died out, they can no longer be revived,
while in literature phenomena a century or indeed even several
centuries old may appear anew and be made productive once
more."[127] [p. 135] *While in the written the possibility of
the tradition of the objectification, even that of the written itself, can be abandoned, for the tradition of folklore
the necessary condition is the milieu that bears it.* The
existence of a folkloristic work must "presuppose a group
which accepts and sanctions it".[128] "The milieu trims...the
created work to shape, and again everything rejected from the
milieu simply does not exist as a fact of folklore; it falls
out of use and dies away." In folklore "only those forms
maintain themselves that prove themselves functional for the
given community. In the process one function of the form can
naturally be replaced by another. But as soon as a form becomes functionless, it dies away in folklore, while in a literary work it maintains its potential existence."[129] In its

ultimate consequences this leads to a modified re-acceptance of the romantic affirmation of a principal differentiation between oral poetry and literature, although a certain intermeshing between them cannot be denied.[130]

Bausinger draws from this concession the following conclusion: The principles of folklore are valid to a certain degree in the written transmission; and likewise the opposite: "in the oral realm of transmission, phenomena and principles of literature have attained entry to such an extent that some have correctly noted the contraction of the independent field of folklore." Folklore and literature are no longer to be separated strictly, but mutually influence each other: "The literarizing of folklore expands in a counter movement that we could almost designate the folklorizing of literature."[131] "The dictate of the actual research object eliminates the systematic borders of the scientific optics: folklore and literature touch back to back."[132]

These divergences in the theses of folklore research may be taken merely to indicate the need for the greatest caution in using a one-sided conceptual model. Probably the historical development is much more complicated than the model of a gradual dissolution of the oral by the written will demonstrate. However recent research on epics has emphasized the empirical difference between the oral and the written.[133] The last word on this difficult complex of problems, at any rate, has not yet been spoken.

Result: Again form criticism ought to be conscious of the hypothetical character of its fundamental premises [p. 136] and protect itself from over-confidence concerning the affirmation of a one-sided historical pattern with regard to the tradition of the "small units". In light of folklorists' recognition of a decisive difference in the nature of oral and written genres, contemporary form criticism must earnestly re-examine its premises concerning the lack of differentiation between "oral" form criticism and "literary" redaction criticism (see #4, section 2.a.).

3.   The Oral and the Written in Contemporary Linguistics.

M. Taube has correctly described the linguistic principle of "common sense" as follows: "Many scientific linguists represent the viewpoint that the written language gives only an incomplete representation of the actual, precise linguistic facts of the spoken language. For these linguists a written sign has significance in the linguistic realm only as a symbol for a sound or a sound-category."[134] The final consequence of this is expressed in the theses: "There is a spoken language and a written language, and they are not identical with one another."[135] Contemporary linguistics, therefore, lends a certain amount of support to some of Herder's and Humboldt's theses. However in the process the question about the oral and the written character of the *genres* is stressed less than the uniqueness of both modes for language as a whole.

(a)   The Oral and the Written: Different Styles or Different Languages?[135a]

Already F. de Saussure, in his foundational work, set out the essential factors of the written aspect of language. Writing replaces *l'image acoustique* with *l'image visuelle*, and thereby stabilizes the linguistic contents.[136] Although writing is not an absolute condition of linguistic stability,[137] the written sign alters itself more slowly than the oral sounds.[138] Although the written aspect represents, as *signum signi*, the oral *signum*,[139] [p. 137] language (*langue*) and

writing create "deux systèmes de signes distincts":[140] The
written becomes *langue littéraire.*[141]

Does this distinction between *langue parlée* and *langue
écrite*[142] concern another language (*langue*) or only another
style?[143] Today the tendency is to see *stylistic distinctions as genuine linguistic distinctions.* Since language
is always the medium and mode of communication,[144] the oral
(speech) and the written (writing) are "two modes of linguistic communication".[145] "The relationship between these two
forms of language is not uniform"; in some cases there is a
total contrast: "Some written styles are virtually unintel-
ligible if read aloud or if used as a spoken medium, for example the formal language of legal contracts and legislative
enactments."[146] Stylistic differentiations can be differentiations in the linguistic medium and in the linguistic forms.
If medium and form are regarded as the decisive "gestalt" of
language, then media- and form-distinctions can be understood
as differences of various languages. These problems have not,
so far as I am aware, been completely or unanimously resolved
in linguistics,[146a] but the suggestions made above seem to me
to justify H.-D. Bastian's demand: "A form criticism of ecclesial speech will...not be spared having to concern itself
seriously with a 'knowledge of media'."[147]

(b) The Special Qualities of the Written.

Contemporary linguistics considers that between the oral
and the written there are *differences on all structural levels,*[148] and that means on the [p. 138] levels of phonology,[149]
morphology,[150] syntax, vocabulary, and style.[151]

On the phonological level the written can no longer profit
from the semantic and significative possibilities of the phonetic signal element.[152, 153] In order to recognize the whole

expressional richness of language especially in terms of emotional contents,[154] it is necessary to move from the observation of writing to that of phonemics,[155] that is, the rever-
sal of the written into the phonetic:[156] The written "is
only understandable in terms of the inner language".[157] This
necessity shows that there is a system of the oral and a system of the written intonation.[158]

The written "simultaneously objectifies the information",[159] and makes it more easily communicable,[160] in that
it takes advantage of the permanent and transportable.[161]
Writing, in contrast to language, contains within it ambition
that reaches toward expansion.[162] It has the advantage of the
definitive,[163] which at the same time can be a disadvantage if
the words, because of the suppression of the continuous correlation between speaker and hearer, take on independent existence.[164] The consolidation of the written into an almost
"independent" dimension in the consciousness of the linguistic community can be so marked that the written [p. 139]
"takes away the dispositional power of its creator".[165] The
written is the "transition of the 'objective' (alive in a community) form of language to the 'objectified' (deposited in
the community in permanent form) status".[166] What is written
[Schriftliches] becomes, by means of the written [die Schrift-
lichkeit], independent of the present time of the author and
hence also largely from his volitional influence and so from
his intentional act; it makes itself understandable as a
spiritual child like a physical child and has its own--often
surprising--history.

In spite of the abstraction and objectification of the
written in contrast with the oral, writing also has its ad-
vantages in terms of its capacity to be effective.[167] It develops language into a greater consistency,[168] it has its
special possibilities of expression,[169] its relative abun-

dance of homonyms and synonyms.[170] *Writing spatially fixates the linguistic*, and thereby permits the reader access to things which seem less important: inversion of previous sequences, turning-back to earlier pages, repetition which is both favored and arbitrary each time, etc.,[171] all those phenomena which are not possible in this form to the immediate *temporal* correlation of speaker and hearer in the oral state: "Along with the spatial fixation, entirely new possibilities for mastering spiritual contents appear, which the merely-spoken word was not able to offer."[172] We face here the phenomenon of the "special, spatially-bound and time-free manner of being, which language assumes by means of writing".[173]

Also related to this *time-free nature of the written* is the freeing of what is written from the cultural "context-situation"[174] of the oral: "written statements are set down with the purpose of being self-contained and self-explanatory."[175] They do not automatically deliver their "sociological setting", as do the oral linguistic forms, but at best allow it to be reconstructed by someone for whom the milieu is foreign only after critical analysis. While the [p. 140] "sociological setting" belongs to the oral as its hermeneutical context, inseparably with the linguistic "meaning" of, the linguistic work, such an aid to understanding disappears in the case of the written: "The book by itself is sufficient to direct the reader's mind to its meaning; and we might be tempted to say metaphorically that the meaning is wholly contained in or carried by the book."[176] The immediacy of the unity of "sociological setting", language-event, language-form, and understanding communication has developed in the written mediacy of the fundamental possibility of the disintegration of the unity (see #6, Sect. 3), which has the potential possibility of misunderstanding, if written medium and intentional expression are in tension

with one another. Every writer must reckon with these implications when he takes up pen and exercises this reaching toward the written as a conscious act. Thereby we have arrived
at the hermeneutical questions of every serious literary criticism.

4. The Nature of Oral and Written Genres in Literary Criticism.[177]

We will not treat here the entire complex of the nature
of linguistic products, but only those aspects of the nature
of oral and written genres that will help us demonstrate the
literary-critical problem of the process of writing.

(a) The Consequence and Implications of the Different Types of Objectification.

W. Porzig emphasized the connections and transitions in
the movement from the oral to the written in language. Only
in its manner of being is the written text to be distinguished
from oral speech; within the flow of linguistic expression
there are "certain determinate forms..., which can be recorded, repeated, and even expressed in concrete form". However apart from this special manner of being "the written text
has all the unique qualities of speech: it is directed toward
a partner and speaks to him about something, and the partner
reacts in particular ways".[178] It seems to me that this under-
values the chief importance of distinguishing [p. 141] the nature of the thing. In each of the three relationships of the
written linguistic product (author, addressee, object)[179] there
is a decisive distinctiveness of the written in contrast to the
oral.

By means of the written the *author* establishes the linguistic form's fundamental separateness and independence from

his acts of consciousness.[180] It is the inclination of the form objectified in the written, "to render itself independent from its creator, to develop its own manifold laws, and finally to procure recognition for itself as a constituting power".[181] In many respects the form of language objectified in the writing develops an independent life:[182] Although writing "is a conscious human addition to language, it escapes the continuation of its influence. Certainly it is the human being who suffers here, but it does so because of the persistent power of the objectified form, and it almost appears as if we trust ourselves the less, the more the distance between sound and letter develops".[183] "Objectified spirit presupposes even more the conscious operation of the knower: The language of writing can be manipulated; the spirit embodied in it can control the striving for power."[184] *The form of existence of the energeia becomes the dispositional form of the ergon.*[185]

The *addressee* has an entirely different relationship to the written language-form than to its oral counterpart.[186] The distinction between listener and reader "consists in the entirely different opposition in which the author finds himself related to his reader because of the dialectics in the conversation between speaker and partner, and in the reading of a text".[186] The oral mostly presupposes the opposition of the dialogue. The listener can eventually request clarification and repetition from the speaker. On the other hand the written [p. 142] *eo ipso* and according to its own nature, is repeatable at any time, at any place, and to any group, in each instance, of course, in terms of the addressees the writing implies. The reader lacks not only the immediacy of the oral and the contribution to comprehension which the unity of "sociological setting" and linguistic form provide,[188] but also the living contrapuntal otherness of the author, who

can always give him new information: The written is objectified for the addressee in place of the speaker; it is replaced
with language forms with all their consequences. The "written
work is silent and without a will of its own; it can neither
answer nor defend itself. That is all of the more consequence
insofar as it may as easily fall into the hands of someone who
engages it competently as of someone who does not. The actual
securing of the spiritual content is only a given in oral
speech: it guarantees the appropriate transmission of the
thought to the pupil, it permits immediate explication and
correction; the written version basically has only the value
of jogging the memory."[189] With reference to the addressees,
every author has to consider the dangers of writing, as already Plato recognized: "to one person it is given to create
the elements of an art, to another to judge the extent of harm
and usefulness it [scil., in the context, writing] will have
for those who are going to employ it."[190] Like painting,
writing harbors the danger that that which is represented
will be mistaken for the living thing itself, and will be
seen therefore as a doubling of it,[191] although it is silent
before questioning. "Once a thing is put in writing, it rolls
about all over the place, falling into the hands of those who
have no concern with it just as easily as under the notice of
those who comprehend it; it has no notion of whom to address
or whom to avoid. And when it is ill-treated or abused as
illegitimate, it always needs its father to help it, being
quite unable to protect or help itself."[192]

Therefore the author by utilizing the medium of the written as opposed to that of the oral especially has to consider
the altered situation of understanding on the part of the addressee: "The content is no longer spoken..., but taken up
into life. Thereby new challenges and possibilities appear
in the inverbalizing, especially with respect to understand-

ing."[193] "In the case of what is read the meaning must [p.
143] ...be expressed by means of the style, so that the voice
carries clearly and with the true soul in an accessible manner. A 'deciphering' ['Erlesen'] of the meaning is expected
of the reader [dem Leser] as an achievement of resonant understanding."[194] A group of readers is something other than a
group of hearers, which was situated, in antiquity at least,
and until lately in modern times, at *one* given time at *one*
given location. If the written does not serve only as a
"remembrance on paper", the group of readers can indeed be
quite dispersed in time. The time of the reading is no longer
established by the author, but is entrusted to the spatial connection with the writing, which is left up to the time of the
reader.

At any rate the *objectivity* of the object differentiates
between the oral and the written. P. Bogatyrev and R. Jakobson have described this differential nature thus: "In folklore the relation between the work of art on the one hand and
on the other its objectification, i.e., the so-called variants
of this work as it is carried forward through various persons,
is completely analogous to the relation between *langue* and
parole.[195] The folkloristic work is, like the *langue*, impersonal, and leads only a potential existence, it is only a complex of determined norms and impulses, a canvas of topical tradition which enlivens that which is transmitted by the ornamentation of the individual creation, just as do the producers of
the *parole* in contrast to those of the *langue*."[196] The case
with the work of literature is entirely different; it "is objectified, it exists concretely in independence of the reader
and every successive reader applies himself immediately to the
work. As such it does not follow the course of the folkloristic work, from speaker to speaker, but a course from the work
to the speaker." "Observed from the standpoint of the speaker

of a folkloristic work, these works represent a matter of
langue, i.e., an impersonal given, independent of this speaker, as well as the de-formation and insertion of a new poetic
object that also makes everyday materials accessible."[197]
Here the differential manner of objectification of the oral
and the written is precisely comprehended.

(b) Albert B. Lord's Empirical Findings
Concerning Tradition History in the
Oral and the Written.

While with the oral the uniqueness of a particular performance in a particular genre is an aspect of the multiplicity [p. 144] of the creative forming of the relevant thematic
in oral genres, such uniqueness is "total, in contrast, in
the written literary tradition".[198]   A. B. Lord, the American
Homer specialist, relying on the preliminary work of the pioneer M. Parry, concerned himself with this distinction, using
empirical analysis (for example phonograph recordings, folkloristic milieu-comparisons) of Balkan epic poets, and thereby set into motion an intensive methodological discussion especially in Germanic studies.[199]   Lord's empirically-based
theses concerning the oral nature of so-called folk-transmis-
sions have since been confirmed with respect to the oral transmission of the Nibelungenlied,[200] and have been extended somewhat with respect to study of the so-called "minstrel's
epic".[201]   By and large Lord's work has become the standard
work of comparative literature (comparative studies); it is
fundamentally significant for any research that is concerned
with the transition from the oral into the written tradition.
For this reason it is directly relevant to our subject. Lord,
and relying on his work, F. H. Bäuml, came to the following
results:

1. *The single performance of a work of art*, for example a poem, *is not the work of art itself.*[202] Rather it is the process within which the oral genre is each time a new occurrence, so that the "editions" found in various performances are not related genetically to one another or to a postulated "original edition", but they represent expressions of the oral multiplicity. Each performance "is an invention in itself, which the performer does not merely repeat, but always creates anew".[203] The oral, such as the epic, does not signify just "oral repetition" alone. "What is important here is less the oral performance itself than the origination of the epic *during* the performance."[204] The epic poet does not proceed on the basis "of a presentation of a pre-determined model text".[205]

2. *The oral poet does not know of the fixation of word and form*, in short, of the "text". "It is not a case...of verbal repetition, but of the 'correct' assembling of the component units of the epic. These components are the husks of the narrative that reappear from epic to epic, whose detailed exposition [p. 145] varies from poet to poet and performance to performance--variations which can be perceived and named only in the sense of written, fixed, transmission as such. For the oral poet these are not alterations, since for him the idea of a normative-text, a normative-performance by which all others can be measured as the same or as deviating, does not exist."[206] "The expression 'oral literature' is obviously a contradiction in itself."[207] It transfers phenomena of the written and the 'ur-text', as a conceptual model, onto the oral, under the premise that the tradition process is similar in both oral and written genres, namely that it is the continuing tradition of an oral "original edition" transmitted through the modified editions of the oral transmitters. The term "oral" is implicitly utilized

in this conceptual model in quite different ways, and especially in heteronomous analogy to the written.[208] However it leads
to misconceptions, "if we use the formulation that the oral
poet learns his songs 'orally', causes them to come about
'orally', and passes them on 'orally' to others";[209] "'oral
transmission', 'oral construction', 'oral creative act', and
'oral performance' are only various aspects of the same process",[210] that is, *the phenomenon of the oral nature of the
genres must be understood exclusively in terms of the creative processes of continually new performances*, since only in
such a manner do we respect the particular nature of the oral.
What we might call the "ur-form" is only the first performance;
it "consists of the transfer of traditional narrative husks, by
means of narrative formulae, to the elements of the 'new' material".[211] It is "of extraordinary significance, that concepts such as 'author' and 'ur-text' in the oral tradition are
either wholly meaningless or take on a meaning that differs
entirely from our usual use of language". "A performance is
something unique, it is not an imitation, but a creative act,
and therefore can have only one author."[212] Out of the dis-
appearance of the "ur-text" as a *fata morgana* [mirage] it follows "that we may not correctly speak about 'variants', either,
since there is no 'original' which could be varied"! "Our
greatest error lies in having sought to determine 'scientifically' a phenomenon that has a flexible gestalt."[212a] The
consequence of this for Lord is the rejection of the anonymity of the "folk epic", indeed of the theory of "folk epic"
as a whole: "a poet is never a type, but an individual".[212b]

[p. 146] 3. These are judgments of a scholar who has
concerned himself intensively with the so-called folkloristic
forms, especially in order to understand the epics of Balkan
bards, as a means of clarifying the problem of the oral and
the written in the Homeric epics.[213] His work proves experi-

mentally and empirically *what great difficulties accrue to the bards from the pressure of writing*, insofar as many circumstances of the oral (e.g., music, tempo, etc.) do not survive. With their reserve toward writing, the bards know "that an epic cannot be reduced to writing".[214] Even requests to repeat the performance do not advance the process of writing, since repetitions are never the same,[215] and they themselves demonstrate that *the "normative edition" is a phantom*. This edition first makes its appearance in a written version, since now unintentionally a "determinate text" appears, on the basis of which alterations of the oral editions are measured.[216] This beginning of literary technology signifies the rejection of the processes of the oral, in order to learn the technology of the construction of written verse.[217] This radical transition from the oral to the written has its effects upon epic-collections, since now only the "correct" text will be cited,[218] a phenomenon that simply did not exist in the oral stage: "If we read a printed text to an experienced epic poet, he reacts to it in the same way as if he were listening to another bard. Epic collections first cause the deterioration of the oral character of the transmission at the point where the singer is convinced that a song may only be performed in this one particular form."[218a]

4. *This radical transition from the oral to the written* can be demonstrated in particular instances in the comportment of the Balkan bards described earlier. In the oral period the bards were compelled to think in formulae and formal models,[219] since otherwise their songs would not have been produced with such astonishing rapidity.[220] However in the moment of writing, the tempo of the production is slowed down,[221] the singer becomes more uncertain in the process of dictation,[222] the [p. 147] verse structure is thrown into confusion,[223] and a single reading of what has been dictated constricts the bard from then

on.[224] If writing penetrates far enough into the creative
process so that the bard "consciously breaks with the old
models, intentionally modifies them, and considers this
'proper', then in such a step writing has become a matter
of 'literary' technology";[225] thematic variations are introduced into the genres,[226] and "the audience context is also
changed" with respect to its taste and the length of the
epic.[227] "The written, determinate text...was written down
in order to be *read*. With this we have a whole new approach."[228] "The idea of the fixed text now determines the
further transmission, whether or not it takes place orally
or in writing."[229] For all these reasons there is little
support for the idea "that any written text we now possess
has been copied down during the performance".[230]

    5. Lord also considered the problem of so-called "*tran-
sitional texts*":[231] "Can a text be located between the oral
and the written literary traditions?"[232] Such a question
arises especially in view of the fact that a performance
which has come to be a "text" has "the same markers as any
other performance, since even though now it is available to
us in written form, its origins were oral".[233] But these
performances, dictated, composed in writing, or "oral-auto-
graphs", are not "transitional texts", "but form a class unto
themselves".[234] On the basis of the different technologies
of the oral and the written which Lord conceived empirically,
he considered it impossible that a poet can at the same time
be an oral and a literary poet: "If the oral technology of
transmission has once been suppressed, it is not possible
ever to awaken it to new life. On the other hand the technology of writing cannot be united with oral transmission,
and it would be impossible to combine the two and create a
third, a 'transitional technology'."[235] Hence three levels
are to be distinguished culturally and structurally from one

another: the level of the purely oral, the first transformation of the "performance" into the "text", and the level of
written technology. The continuity in the sociology of tradition between these levels is a broken one: At most there
is a certain continuity of individual structures; but [p. 148]
functionally these structures are entirely differently arranged, since the total structure has changed. In specific
linguistic terminology we could therefore express it this
way: The continuity of certain micro-structures remains, but
the macro-structure, i.e., that structure that has "framed"
the micro-structure from time to time, has changed.

6. *Result:* It is my conviction that these analyses not
only can, but must lead every earnest form critic to ask
whether he can actually line up empirical proof for his premises or hypotheses if the traditio-historical laws of the
oral are almost completely identical with or similar to the
laws of the written. If it be conceded *tout à fait* that the
problem of historical analogy must be faced one way or the
other by the form critic, the question is whether Lord's results are to be accepted by N. T. form criticism without
reservation; for we might be dealing with a phenomenon that
is based in a particular form-critical uniqueness of the
relevant genres. To be sure, Lord himself faced this question, since he sought to clarify the developed tradition history of the Homeric epic by means of an analogy which is today still empirically conceivable, namely that of the Balkan
bards. Lord's methodology therefore represents a conscious
process of conclusion by analogy on the basis of empirical
material which is still relatively conceivable; he applied
it to the hypothetically-reconstructed history of materials
from antiquity, so that the scientific construction of hypotheses was tested and normalized by an empiricism of
"original" materials that is still possible in isolated

cases today. This conclusion by analogy is an essential component of comparative literary criticism, which helped earlier
form critics attain more exact description of the gospels, considered as unique and without analogy. The newer trend toward
empirical experiments must concern N. T. form criticism, if it
is to be a "historical and empirical" methodology, reaching
conclusions by means of analogies. If scientific honesty is
to be fully respected, the form critic must not be afraid to
relinquish a few precious concepts if literary criticism--
which from its own point of view includes both the oral and
the folkloristic genres--[236] has reached well-supported results [p. 149] that contradict form criticism's own findings.
Even if methodological modifications are necessary with respect to individual details, in taking over literary-critical
findings into N. T. form criticism, we simply cannot overlook
the whole movement in research represented by contemporary
literary criticism. However if the form critic ignores analogies offered him by folkloristics and literary criticism concerning the traditio-historical oral materials, it would be
even more pressing to determine whether something other than
the *immediate* empiricism for materials yet accessible can be
offered in its place in order to give form-critical construction of hypotheses critical controls. The biblical texts are
in their present state always "literary", and can only be
taken back to a "pre-literary" state by means of reconstruction using historical conclusions from analogy (therefore by
means of a *mediated* empiricism), so that the problem of form-
critical foundations which is apparent here is unavoidable.
Much would be gained if the new horizon of inquiry in recent
literary criticism sketched above would be recognized for its
fundamental worth to biblical exegesis. Its concrete investigation across the entire field of biblical exegesis can only
be tackled as a communal endeavor.[237]

Let me briefly indicate here the directions wherein the value of these comparative results for gospel research appear to reside. If the structural-functional dissimilarity of "oral" and [p. 150] "literary" technology is valid not only for Lord's material, but can also be shown to be valid for other material, then for gospel form criticism there remain only two possibilities: Either it must consider the gospels as a "special class" of "oral-autograph" "texts", representing the first stage of writing--with the inevitable consequence of approaching Th. Boman's conception[238]--or it must revise the standard combination of J. C. L. Gieseler's traditions-hypothesis with the utilization-hypothesis of C. Lachmann, C. G. Wilke, Chrs. H. Weisse, and H. J. Holtzmann. Since according to the utilization-hypothesis at least Matthew and Luke utilized at least one written "source" (Mark), then they have availed themselves of a "literary technology" in A. B. Lord's sense; they cannot also simultaneously have used an "oral technology", although it is not disputed that they incorporate "oral tradition". With reference to technology, however, this assumption is structurally and functionally a completely different phenomenon from that of the "oral tradition" itself, because next to it there is already a written form. For Mark the question is similar except that no "sources" have been demonstrated convincingly.[239] So the pioneer work of the American Homer scholar [Lord] leads us to question whether in form criticism the unbroken continuity of the gospel-tradition up to the point of the gospel-form should be considered an unquestionable fact.

5. Oral and Written Tradition in the Rabbinate.

One objection to be expected is reference to the Jewish-rabbinical tradition with its emphasis upon accuracy and uni-

formity regarding the scriptural wording, so that Lord's research on oral tradition would not be relevant as a parallel
or analogy for the folkloristic synoptic tradition. M. Dibelius refers to rabbinical Halakah and Haggadah in explaining the different transmissions of Jesus' words and deeds,[240]
considering both as phenomena at least analogous or comparable
to the oral Jesus-tradition. In this connection we are close
to Th. Boman's reminder of the mode of tradition for religious
materials in Palestine,[241] which he thinks was maintained in
the "Jewish" concern for transmissional veracity in the synoptic writers [p. 151] in their attitude toward their sources,[242]
which can be studied in detail in B. Gerhardsson's work.[243]
This conception can be somewhat supported by the fact: "that
early Christianity was born within a historical sphere in
which tradition and transmission had already to some extent
become conscious ideas and distinct activities".[244] But the
postulate that the methods respecting tradition in primitive
Christianity "must for the most part have resembled those used
by other teachers in the same milieu",[245] is certainly doubtful in methodological terms, since here one must operate with
general conceptual possibilities rather than with incontest-
able empirical proof. Since fantasy recognizes no boundaries,
Boman can depend upon such questionable foundations, suggest-
ing that the tradition of the gospels concerns "reminiscences
of a striking historical person, about whom eyewitnesses speak,
reminiscences which were transmitted orally for decades".[246]
On the basis of Jewish mnemotechnology, that would hardly be
astonishing.[247] The primitive Christian situation of speakers
situated within the lower classes of the people, and coming
from the minor office-bearers of the primitive Christian communities, is thought to have made possible the passing-on of
the oral narrative tradition by means of this technology,[248]
until finally Mark was charged by Peter and other leaders of

the earliest church to prepare an official presentation of the
public deeds of Jesus, which then supposedly had to be memo-
rized by other gospel narrators in the apostolic congregations.[249]

Apart from the completely unprovable nature of such
products of fantasy, in view of the meagre sources at hand,
its foundations in B. Gerhardsson's presentation have drawn
such annihilating criticism[250] that Gerhardsson himself has
recently conceded empirical flaws in his work.[251] The arbitrary misrepresentations of form criticism may be noted in
the same manner.[252] On the whole the form critic will have
strong reservations about referring to these studies.

[p. 152] However the decisive counterargument against
the utilization of the Jewish-rabbinical modes of tradition,
is *their relation as scriptural exegesis to the scripture's
revelation.* Both the Halakah and the Haggadah are to be understood as scriptural exegesis, and perhaps because of their
recourse to the scripture (*hk(t)wb*) were originally only orally formulated, in order as exegesis not to be mistaken for
that which was being exegeted. While Halakah as the normative
religious statute, as the precept valid without regard to its
derivation from holy scriptures, unequivocally serves the exegesis and safe-guarding of the Moses-Torah, and as such is
designated as *hl(k)h lmšh msnî* (cf. Pea II,6; Edujoth VIII,7;
Jadajim IV,3),[253] the Haggadah is the non-Halakic scriptural
explication, the "designation of that realm of scriptural exegesis whose object is not explanation and development of the
pentateuchal laws, but the exposition of the non-legal biblical texts."[254] That the Jesus-tradition as a whole does not
represent scriptural exposition--nor haggadic scriptural exe-
gesis--hardly need to be demonstrated. To be sure, H. Riesenfeld[255] and B. Gerhardsson[256] have sought to prove that the
tradition of the gospels represents the "holy" texts of Jesus'

words and deeds, which would have been utilized as liturgical
readings in the meetings of the churches either as amplifica-
tion of, or replacements for, the Old Testament texts. However this construction is not demonstrable from the texts
themselves.[257] Moreover it is necessary to distinguish between the tradition history of Jesus' words, which may perhaps be comparable to the rabbinic tradition, and the tradition history of the materials which are not composed of
logia.[258]

   Result: The circumstances of the rabbinic traditional
technology cannot be applied to the tradition of the Jesus-
material since the latter does not represent scriptural exposition of the same type. We do not have any sort of immediately empirical knowledge concerning the *procedure* of the oral
tradition of the Jesus-material, but merely about the *state* of
this tradition which is solidified into writing in the synoptic gospels, in John, the Apostolic Fathers, and the apocryphal gospels; naturally this occasionally allows conclusions
concerning the pre-literary process, but [p. 153] not the
specific details of a regular process that can be applied
form-*critically* [i.e., with respect to the *historical* developments of forms, form*geschichtlichen*] in every case. Especially because here more judgment should have been exercised, in
our future traditio-historical work we should attempt to include in our considerations the results of the disciplines
discussed above, and continue to be guided by total methodological meticulousness. Exegetical theology can never rest
satisfied or unconcerned when related disciplines attain such
completely divergent methods and results.

   At this conclusion of an admittedly elementary presentation, it must be emphasized once again that the present work
is only intended to bring to shared awareness the hypothetical
character of many form-critical theses by confronting them

with aspects of general linguistics and literary criticism.
Here we have merely worked out "candid questions concerning
gospel form criticism" in high relief, i.e. bringing into
the open some of its hypotheses which are apparently war-
ranted but are often hidden from the sort of candid examination they deserve. Our purpose has been to indicate the importance of methodologically securing the concepts that gov-
ern its work. We have purposively not gone into the much-
discussed questions of the so-called Uppsala-school in Old
Testament studies,[259] because that would have necessitated
extensive analysis of its own. We turn now to a further
example in the history of research in order to clarify the
ways both O. T. and N. T. form criticism after H. Gunkel's
work are subject to candid questions and re-evaluation.

Notes to #7

1. Cf. J. G. Herder, *Sprachphilosophische Schriften*, E.
Heintel, ed., 1964-2nd ed. On research on Herder: H. D.
Irmscher, "Probleme der Herderforschung I," *DVjs* 37 (1963)
266-317; D. Gutzen, *Poesie der Bibel: Beobachtungen zu ihrer
Entdeckung und ihrer Interpretation im 18. Jahrhundert*, Diss.,
Bonn, 1968. Further bibliography there. Cf. also R. Haym,
Herder nach seinem Leben und seinen Werken, two vols., 1880-
85; M. Kronenberg, *Herders Philosophie nach ihrem Entwick-
lungsgang und ihrer historischen Stellung*, 1889; M. Redeker,
"Wort Gottes und Sprache. Im Anschluss an die Sprachphiloso-
phie des jungen Herder," *ZThK* 37 (1929) 348-56; Redeker,
"Herder," *RGG*-3rd ed., vol. 3, 1959, 235-39; Th. Litt, *Kant
und Herder als Denker der geistigen Welt*, 1930; B. v. Wiese,
Herder: Grundzüge seines Weltbildes, 1939; H.-G. Gadamer,
Volk und Geschichte im Denken Herders, 1942; D. W. Jöns, *Begriff und Problem der historischen Zeit bei J. G. Herder*,
1956. -- For some essential reference to bibliography I am
grateful to my colleagues Dr. M. Beller, Dr. E. Nellmann, Dr.
D. Guzen, all of the philosophical faculty at Bonn. -- On the
problem "speaking and writing", cf. Alonso Schökel, *Sprache
Gottes*, 160ff.

2. Cf. H.-J. Kraus, *Geschichte der historisch-kritischen
Erforschung des Alten Testaments von der Reformation bis zur
Gegenwart*, 1956, 309ff.; Redeker, *RGG*-3rd ed., vol. 3, 1959,
237; Klatt, *Gunkel*, 106ff.

3. Cf. K. Barth, *Die protestantische Theologie im 19.
Jahrhundert*, 1960-3rd ed., 279-302; E. Hirsch, *Geschichte der
neuern evangelischen Theologie im Zusammenhang mit den allgemeinen Bewegungen des europäischen Denkens*, vol. 4, 1952, 207-
47; Kraus, *op. cit.*, 103-119. On Herder's language-philosophy,
cf. E. Heintel, "Herder und die Sprache," in Herder, *op. cit.*,
xv-lxvii; further bibliography there.

4. *Ibid.*, 3, cursive in original.

5. Cf. *ibid.*, 3f.

6. Cf. *ibid.*, 5.

7. Cf. *ibid.*, 11: The origin of language "is not trans-
human, but clearly related to the animals: the natural law of
a sensitive machine" (in italics in original).

8. Cf. Redeker, *RGG*-3rd ed., vol. 3, 1959, 238, and below, espec. p. [131].

9. Herder, *op. cit.*, 8.

10. Contemporary linguistics has greatly developed this trait. Cf. for instance L. Weisgerger, *Grundzüge der inhalt-bezogenen Grammatik*, 1962-3rd ed., 280: The difficulty of the evidence of the vocal-formal elements "occurs insofar as our writing is not understood as the sensible form of the means of speaking, and correspondingly the role that the written fixation plays in making language conscious, is not completely made evident". Cf. also below, p. [138].

11. Cf. Herder, *op. cit.*, 9: The Hebraic manner of writing "runs against the course of sound reason: to write the non-essential and to leave out the essential, so that it would be inconceivable to grammarians, if grammarians were so accustomed to conceive it".

12. The formulation depends upon the scholastic designation of the *signum-res* schema: *aliquid stat pro aliquo*. Cf. above, p. [42].

13. In Herder, *op. cit.*, 95, 134.

14. Cf. above, #2, n. 46.

15. Herder, *op. cit.*, 41.

16. *Ibid.*, 42.

17. *Ibid.*, 177.

18. *Ibid.*, 177f.

19. *Ibid.*, 178.

20. Cf. *ibid.*, 141.

21. Cf. *ibid.*, 132f.

22. Cf. *ibid.*, 177.

23. *Ibid.*

24. *Ibid.*, 178.

25. *Ibid.*, 54.

26. Cf. *ibid.*, 104f.

27. *Ibid.*, 91, 93.

28. These last sentences draw out the conceptual consequence of von Humboldt (cf. below, p. [123ff.]) and apply it
to Herder's contributions. Cf. also the modern thesis of
Betti, *Allg. Auslegungslehre* [cf. #3, n. 39], 102: "Writing,
and reading, toward which writing is directed, are actually
only a surrogate for spoken speaking and the experienced conversation."

28a Cf. also above, p. [110f.].

29. Cf. W. v. Humboldt, *Schriften zur Sprachphilosophie*,
1963, ed. A. Flitner and K. Giel, *Werke*, vol. 3.

30. Cf. for instance E. Heintel, "Sprachphilosophie," in
W. Stammler, ed., *Deutsche Philologie im Aufriss*, vol. 1,
1956-2nd ed., 563ff.; H. G. Gadamer, *RGG*-3rd ed., vol. 6,
1962, 267f.; B. Liebrucks, *Sprache und Bewusstsein*, vol. 1,
1964, 215ff., 345ff.

31. Cf. the bibliography given in #9, n. 38, as well as
L. Weisgerber, "Das Problem der inneren Sprachform und seine
Bedeutung für die deutsche Sprache," *GRM* 14 (1926) 241-56;
"Die Sprache als wirkende Kraft," *Studium Generale* 4 (1951)
127-35; "Zum Energeia-Begriff in Humboldts Sprachbetrachtung,"
WW 4 (1954) 374-77; and "Innere Sprachform als Stil sprach-
licher Anverwandlung der Welt," *Studium Generale* 7 (1957)
571-59.

32. Cf. the bibliography in #2, n. 51.

33. B. L. Whorf, *Sprache, Denken, Wirklichkeit*, 1968-4th
ed., P. Krausser, ed.

34. Cf. Krausser, *ibid.*, 140-47; H. Hoijer, "The Sapir-
Whorf Hypothesis," in H. Hoijer, ed., *Language in Culture*,
American Anthropologist, Memoir No. 79, 1954, 82-91; Neubert,
Semantischer Positivismus, 91-116.

35. Humboldt, *op. cit.*, 418.

36. Cf. *ibid.*, 34: "Not what may be expressed in a language, but that which it incites and inspires from out of its
own inner power, is decisive with respect to its superiority
or its insufficiency." [+1978: It should be noted that I am
alluding here to N. Chomsky's theory of grammar, even though
I do not quote it because of the self-restrictions mentioned

earlier. Critics should have in mind that our German situation in 1967/68 was not prepared for Chomsky, whom I always
understood as being a rationalist and idealist, not a positi-
vist. Against H. Thyen, "Positivismus in der Theologie und
ein Weg zu seiner Ueberwindung?", *EvTh* 31 (1971) 472-95.]

37. Cf. *ibid.*, 217: "The power of thought needs something like to itself, and yet different. By the alike it is
set going, by what is different it receives a touchstone of
the essential nature of its inner generation." "So language
is a necessary requirement to the first generation of thought,
and to the continuing expansion of the spirit." *Ibid.*, 201:
"Between the power of thought and the ability to think, the
only transmitter is language."

38. Cf. *ibid.*, 58f.

39. Cf. *ibid.*, 201.

40. Cf. *ibid.*, 226: "Language belongs to me because I
bring it forth. It does not belong to me, because I can bring
nothing else to it than I do."

41. *Ibid.*

42. Cf. *ibid.*, 56f.: "If language is to be appropriate
to thinking it must correspond as much as possible to its
organic construction. Otherwise since it is to be in all a
symbol, it is precisely something incomplete of that where
with it is immediately related." Doubtless the following
comes from this, *ibid.*, 32f.: "Every language is, in spite
of its powerful and living influence on the spirit, still at
the same time an inanimate and passive tool."

43. Cf. *ibid.*, 111f.

44. Cf. *ibid.*, 199: "In its determined creativeness, as
such and no other, every oral style and language speaks only
itself by means of its sounds."

45. Cf. *ibid.*, 84, 88.

46. *Ibid.*, 86.

47. *Ibid.*, 28.

48. *Ibid.*, 285. Cf. *ibid.*, 145.

49. *Ibid.*, 260.

220

50. *Ibid.*, 259.

51. Cf. Porzig, *Wunder der Sprache*, 98: The written expression "is no longer act, but the result of such, namely
object". Similarly L. Weisgerber, *Die Grenzen der Schrift*,
1955, 10: "It becomes possible (*scil.*, with writing) to make
conscious something that exists unconsciously in a community,
to 'determine', to record, to overview, to organize, to do
all that is what leads Humboldt from the famous formulation
concerning the form of *existence* of an *energeia*, of a 'reality', to the form of *availability* of an *ergon*, of an 'image'."

52. Cf. Humboldt, *op. cit.*, 157.

53. *Ibid.*, 104.

54. Cf. *ibid.*, 85.

55. *Ibid.*, 287.

56. *Ibid.*, 191.

57. Cf. *ibid.*, 28f.

58. *Ibid.*, 338.

59. Cf. *ibid.*, 110f.

59a The following discussion consciously omits (up to p.
[150ff.]) the theses of Th. Boman, *Die Jesus-Ueberlieferung im
Lichte der neueren Volkskunde*, 1967, which are not-discussable,
in part because of their reckless fantasy. A comparison of
the literature used in this work and in Boman's will demonstrate what of his approach is to be maintained, in order to
represent "the contemporary position of folkloristics...cor-
rectly in every essential point". (*Ibid.*, 6.)

60. Cf. below, p. [154ff.].

61. Klatt, *op. cit.*, 13.

62. On my disagreement with Boman's view of the revision
of folkloristics cf. below p. [150ff.]. On folkloristics, cf.
also K. Krohn, *Die folkloristische Arbeitsmethode*, 1926 [cf.
Krohn, *Folklore Methodology*, transl. R. L. Welsch, 1971]; A.
H. Krappe, *The Science of Folklore*, 1965; W.-E. Peuckert and
O. Lauffer, *Volkskunde*, 1951; A. Bach, *Deutsche Volkskunde*,
1960-3rd ed. (further bibliography there). -- To a certain
extent this literature has been made out of date by H. Bausinger.

63. K.-E. Gass, *Die Idee der Volksdichtung und die Geschichtsphilosophie der Romantik*, 1940, 8.

64. Cf. for instance E. Lichtenstein, "Die Idee der Naturpoesie bei den Brüdern Grimm und ihr Verhältnes zu Herder," *DVjs* 6 (1928) 513-47; R. Schmitz, *Das Problem "Voklstum und Dichtung" bei Herder*, 1937; H. Moser, "Volks- und Kunstdichtung in der Auffassung der Romantiker," *RhJbfVk* 4 (1953) 69-89; Moser, "Volk, Volksgeist, Volkskultur," *ZfVk* 53 (1956/57) 127-40; Gass, *op. cit.*

65. Cf. H. Bausinger, *Formen der "Volkspoesie,"* 1968, 9f. On Romanticism see R. Haym, *Die romantische Schule*, 1961-new ed., orig. 1870; R. Wellek, *A History of Modern Criticism*, vol. 2, 1955.

66. Bausinger, *op. cit.*, 10.

67. Cf. *ibid.*, 12.

68. Cf. *ibid.*, 18.

69. *Ibid.*, 21.

69a Cf. K. Ulmer, "Die Wandlung des Sprachbildes von Herder zu Jakob Grimm," *Lexis* 2 (1949) 263-86.

70. Lichtenstein, *op. cit.*, 520.

71. Cf. Gass, *op. cit.*, 34.

72. Lichtenstein, *op. cit.*, 544. Cf. Gass, *op. cit.*, 39.

73. Cf. Moser, *RhJbfVk* 4 (1954) 71: "One no longer condescends...as did the followers of the *Sturm und Drang* school, to the folk (a residue of enlightenment temperament), but wants himself to be like it."

74. *Ibid.*

75. Cf. Bausinger, *op. cit.*, 26.

76. *Ibid.*, 24. See the rich store of details concerning the intensity of this restylization in F. Panzer, in his ed. of *Die Kinder- und Hausmärchen der Brüder Grimm*, 1947, 5-51.

77. Bausinger, *op. cit.*, 15.

78. Lichtenstein, *op. cit.*, 516f.

79. Cf. Bausinger, *op. cit.*, 15, 17.

80. H. Moser, *RhJbfVk* 4 (1953) 70.

81. Bausinger, *op. cit.*, 22.

82. Lichtenstein, *op. cit.*, 523.

83. Cf. Bausinger, *op. cit.*, 33.

84. Cf. Gass, *op. cit.*, 37.

85. Bausinger, *op. cit.*, 20.

86. Lichtenstein, *op. cit.*, 529.

87. *Ibid.*, 523.

88. Bausinger, *op. cit.*, 14.

89. Cf. Moser, *RhJbfVk* 4 (1953) 69; Moser, *ZfVk* 53 (1956/ 1957) 135.

90. Cf. *ibid.*, 128.

91. *Ibid.*

92. *Ibid.*, 134f.

93. Cf. H. Haumann, *Primitive Gemeinschaftskultur*, 1921; Naumann, *Grundzüge der deutschen Volkskunde*, 1922.

94. Cf. Bausinger, *op. cit.*, 41.

95. *Ibid.*, 41f.

96. Moser, *ZfVk* 53 (1956/57) 134; *RhJbfVk* 4 (1953) 70.

97. Cf. *ibid.*, 74f.

98. Lichtenstein, *op. cit.*, 525.

99. *Ibid.*, 526.

100. *Ibid.*, 542.

101. Cf. H. Moser, *RhJbfVk* 4 (1953) 69: "The folk, in the sense of the nation, possesses for Herder an unchangeable character, a national character, corresponding to the theory of Voltaire and Montesquieu."

102. Cf. Moser, *ZfVk* 53 (1956/57) 136.

103. Lichtenstein, *op. cit.*, 520.

104. Gass, *op. cit.*, 20.

105. *Ibid.*, 22.

106. Panzer, *op. cit.* [in n. 76], 34.

107. Gass, *op. cit.*, 19f.

108. *Ibid.*, 30.

109. *Ibid.*, 42.

110. Cf. Moser, *RhJbfVk* 4 (1953) 82-89.

111. Cf. *ibid.*, 88.

112. Cf. *ibid.*, 82f.

113. *Ibid.*, 83.

114. *Ibid.*, 84.

115. *Ibid.*, 85.

116. *Ibid.*, 84.

117. *Ibid.*, 87. Here I think we can see the influences of B. Croce's aesthetics (cf. *ibid.*, 88). Cf. Gass, *op. cit.*, 10f.

118. Cf. H. Kuhn, *Zur Typologie mündlicher Sprachdenkmäler*, 1960, 7f.

119. *Ibid.*, 8.

120. Cf. the quotation in Lichtenstein, *op. cit.*, 513.

121. Bausinger, *op. cit.*, 40.

122. Cf. P. (Grigorevitch) Bogatyrev and R. Jakobson, "Die Folklore als eine besondere Form des Schaffens," in *Donum Natalicum Schrijnen*, 1929, 900-13. [+1978: P. Vielhauer, *Geschichte der urchristlichen Literatur*, 1975, 286, n. 14, judges my line of thought as a "circumstantial expenditure in the history of spirit and research" (transl.

E.G.) with a tendency to do my utmost to "puff up" the difference between the oral and scripture. "But in the literature
on the subject there is no agreement", because Wellek-Warren
stress against Bogatyrev and Jakobson an unbroken continuity
between the oral and scripture. This sort of argumentation
is typical, and effective only for readers not so well in-
formed. Wellek and Warren suggested this in 1942, eighteen
years before Lord published his *empirical* results. Besides
that, are we somehow forbidden to search for *theological*
foundations once more? If this "expenditure" proves *philosophical* presuppositions and thereby disabuses a departure
"without an *a priori*" as impossible, how is it itself to be
blamed? Today no important scholar of "oral literature" rejects Bogatyrev and Jakobson. Cf. Heda Jason, *Ethnopoetry*,
1977; Heda Jason and Dimitri Segal, eds., *Patterns in Oral
Literature*, 1977. Great courage is needed to degrade one of
the most famous scholars, Roman Jakobson, in the way quoted.
[Already since 1910 what the experimental "field-work"
of P. N. Rybnikow (*Pesui sobranye P. N. Rybnikovym*, ed. A. E.
Gruziuskij) had established could have been known: "Make him
(*scil.* the narrator) repeat (the tale), he will render much
(of it) in different words....It will be narrated not only in
other words, in another style, but even in a different tone....
Telling a tale means putting it together." Translation of a
Russian letter by H. Jason, *PTL* 3 (1977) 475. Cf. *ibid.*,
475f.: "it is not a fixed text which is transmitted by memory, but a living improvised creation."

123. Bausinger, *op. cit.*, 44.

124. *Ibid.* Cf. Bogatyrev and Jakobson, *op. cit.*, 901:
"The first existence of a folklore form as such is when it
has been taken up by a particular community, and before that
it exists only as that which is unique to that community."

125. Bausinger, *op. cit.*, 45.

126. Cf. also below, p. [143ff.].

127. Bogatyrev and Jakobson, *op. cit.*, 903.

128. *Ibid.*

129. *Ibid.*, 902.

130. Cf. *ibid.*, 908.

131. Bausinger, *op. cit.*, 49.

132. *Ibid.*, 50.

133. Cf. below, p. [143ff.].

134. M. Taube, *Der Mythos der Denkmaschine*, 1966, 28.

135. *Ibid.*, 56. Cf. L. Lavelle, *La parole et l'écriture*, 1947. On the hermeneutics of the written, cf. H.-G. Gadamer, *Wahrheit und Methode*, 1960, 367ff.

135a [+1978: A survey of recent philosophical and linguistic investigations would underline the difference. Cf. J. Derrida, *De la grammatologie*, 1967; *L'Écriture et la différence*, 1967; "La Différance," in Ph. Sollers, ed., *Théorie d'ensemble*, 1968; W. J. Ong, S.J., *Interfaces of the Word*, 1977, 17ff., 82ff.]

136. Cf. F. de Saussure, *Cours de linguistique générale*, Ch. Bally, A. Sechehaye, and A. Riedlinger, eds., 1967-new ed., 32.

137. Cf. *ibid.*, 45.

138. Cf. *ibid.*, 48f.

139. Cf. also H. A. Gleason, Jr., *An Introduction to Descriptive Linguistics*, 1966-rev. ed., 425; R. H. Robins, *General Linguistics*, 1967-4th ed., 122.

140. Saussure, *op. cit.*, 45.

141. Cf. *ibid.*, 47.

142. Cf. A. Martinet, *Eléments de linguistique générale* 1967, 158f.

143. Cf. *ibid.*, 159f.

144. This is strongly emphasized in information- or communication-theory. A presentation of this theory will have to wait for the intended later publication. Cf. at this time only M. McLuhan, *Understanding Media*, 1968-rev. ed.

145. Robins, *op. cit.*, 121.

146. *Ibid.*, 122.

146a "Textual linguistics" (cf. #8, n. 92) seemingly represents here a deviating standpoint. Cf. I. T. Piirainen, "Zur Linguistisierung der Literaturforschung," *Linguistische Berichte* 1 (1969) 70-73.

147. H.-D. Bastian, *Verfremdung und Verkündigung*, 1967-2nd ed., 24, applied in the original context primarily to matters of practical theology, but expressly thinking of form-critical exegesis (cf. *ibid.*, 34ff.). The demand for a media-science for N. T. form criticism is made in R. W. Funk, *Language, Hermeneutic, and Word of God*, 1966.

148. Cf. above, pp. [49ff., 54ff.].

149. While *phonetics* investigates the physical and accoustic aspect of a language sound within the framework of the linguistics of the *parole, phonology* observes the psychophysical and significative aspects of the sound as part of the linguistics of the *langue*; the latter studies what it is that lends the sound a *differentiating* function with respect to meaning. Cf. N. S. Trubetzkoy, *Grundzüge der Phonologie* 1967-4th ed.

150. Morphology investigates the structural formation laws of linguistic phenomena. Cf. St. Ullmann, *Semantics*, 1964-2nd ed., 23ff.

151. Cf. Gleason, *op. cit.*, 425.

152. What is intended is that which is constituted and carried *within* the sound's "meaning" and "sense".

153. Cf. K. Bühler, *Sprachtheorie*, 1964-2nd ed., 277f. Similarly but earlier: H. Paul, *Principien der Sprachgeschichte*, 1960-new ed. (orig. 1920-5th ed.), 376.

154. Cf. K. Ammer, *Einführung in die Sprachwissenschaft*, vol. 1, 1958, 69: "a fixed written version does not give us any clarification of the emotional contents of a text, which is mostly found in intonation, the strength of the sound, and its tempo."

155. Cf. L. Weisgerber, *Grundzüge der inhaltbezogenen Grammatik*, 1962-3rd ed., 281.

156. Cf. Paul, *op. cit.*, 373; O. Jespersen, *The Philosophy of Grammar*, 1963-9th ed., 18.

157. Porzig, *Wunder der Sprache*, 4th ed., 97.

158. Cf. E. Albrecht, *Sprache und Erkenntnis*, 1967, 35f.

159. Cf. F. v. Weizsäcker, in *Die Sprache*, ed. Der Bayer. Akad. der schönen Künste, 1959, 36.

160. Cf. Gleason, *op. cit.*, 426.

161. Cf. L. Bloomfield, *Language*, 1967-rev. ed., 283.

162. Cf. H. Ammann, *Die menschliche Rede*, 1962-new ed., 25.

163. Cf. Martinet, *op. cit.*, 7.

164. Cf. Jespersen, *op. cit.*, 17.

165. L. Weisgerber, *Die vier Stufen in der Erforschung der Sprachen*, 1963, 141.

166. *Ibid.*; cf. Weisgerber, *Die Grenzen der Schrift*, 1955, 8f.

167. Cf. Paul, *op. cit.*, 373.

168. Cf. *ibid.*, 382.

169. Cf. Ammann, *op. cit.*, 28f.

170. Cf. Gleason, *op. cit.*, 435ff.

171. Cf. W. Flemming, in W. Krauss, *Grundprobleme der Literaturwissenschaft*, 1968, 197: In the written the new basic situation is that "the reader can stop and start when he wishes, that he can break off reading and reflect upon what he has read, turn the pages forwards or backwards, and set his own pace at reading".

172. Ammann, *op. cit.*, 31.

173. *Ibid.*, 145.

174. Cf. below, p. [174ff.].

175. B. Malinowski, in C. K. Ogden and I. A. Richards, *The Meaning of Meaning*, 1966-rev. ed., 306.

176. *Ibid.*, 307.

177. Cf. G. Müller, "Ueber die Seinsweise von Dichtung," *DVjs* 17 (1939) 137-52; R. Ingarden, *Das literarische Kunstwerk*, 1960-2nd ed., 6ff.; H. Brinkmann, "Zur Daseinsweise der Dichtung," *WW SB* 3 (1963) 70-75; R. Wellek and A. Warren, *Theorie der Literatur*, 1966 [in German transl.], 121-36. *Ibid.*, 294f.: further bibliography.

178. Porzig, *Wunder der Sprache*, 4th ed., 98.

179. On the referents of the linguistic sign, cf. the planned publication I have mentioned as well as Bühler, *Sprachtheorie*, 28; Ogden and Richards, *op. cit.*, 11; and H. Hörmann, *Psychologie der Sprache*, 1967, 168f.

180. Cf. G. Müller, *DVjs* 17 (1939) 145: "the significative articulation of poetry constituted by the act of consciousness becomes disengaged by means of the written or memorative determination of the expressions which carry it from the consciousness of the author, the poet, and independent of their acts of consciousness."

181. L. Weisgerber, *Der Buchstabe und der Geist*, 1961, 18. Cf. *ibid.*, 25: "it is the utterance of the independence of the objectifying image that always threatens to de-rail the distributive power of its creator."

182. Cf. *ibid.*, 21ff.

183. *Ibid.*, 21.

184. *Ibid.*, 18. Cf. Weisgerber, *Grenzen der Schrift*, 19f.

185. Cf. above, n. 51.

186. Cf. Brinkmann, *WW SB* 3 (1963) 73: "orally transmitted and writing-determined poetry are to be distinguished not only by their means of continuation, but tied to that in each case there is a different relationship to the persons who receive the materials, and a different sort of articulation."

187. Betti, *Allg. Auslegungslehre*, 267.

188. Cf. above, p. [134f.]; below, p. [174ff.].

189. Weisgerber, *op. cit.*, 16.

190. Weisgerber, *op. cit.*, 15; Weisgerber, *Grenzen der Schrift*, 7ff. [The quotation, originally given in Greek, is from Plato, *Phaedrus* 274E, following W. C. Helmbold and W. G. Rabinowitz, transl. (Indianapolis: Bobbs-Merrill, 1956; Library of Liberal Arts 40).]

191. The connection of the Platonic *mimēsis* doctrine and the danger of a doubling of reality by means of the linguistic sign (cf. Plato, *Craylus* 432D) cannot be further dis-

cussed here. But see E. Haag, *Platons Kratylos*, 1933, 17f., 42ff.

192. For interpretation and translation, see Betti, *op. cit.*, 104. On this subject: H. Gundert, *Der Platonische Dialog*, 1968. [Quotation is from *Phaedrus* 275DE; see note 190.]

193. Flemming, *op. cit.* [see n. 171], 196.

194. *Ibid.*, 197; applied to printed matter in the original context, but fundamentally valid for the written in general.

195. Cf. above, p. [49ff.].

196. *Op. cit.* [n. 122], 904f.

197. *Ibid.*, 905.

198. A. B. Lord, *Der Sänger erzählt*, 1965, 197. [It has not been possible to follow the author's wishes that I track down every quotation from the original version of *The Singer of Tales*, 1960; that work is readily available in a College Edition paperback published by Atheneum. Of interest in this general context: *Semeia* 5 (1976): *Oral Tradition and Old Testament Studies*, ed. Robert C. Culley, where the Parry-Lord findings are discussed, and Lord himself contributes a critical response. - W.G.D.]

199. Bibliography: F. H. Bäuml (and D. J. Ward), *DVjs* 41 (1967) 352f., n. 3; 356f., n. 20.

200. Bäuml (and Ward), "Zur mündlichen Ueberlieferung des Nibelungenliedes," *DVjs* 41 (1967) 351-90.

202. Cf. Wellek and Warren, *op. cit.*, 123f.

203. Bäuml, *op. cit.*, 358.

204. Lord, *op. cit.*, 24.

205. *Ibid.*, 47. Cf. *ibid.*, 31.

206. Bäuml, *op. cit.*, 355.

207. H. Levin in Lord, *op. cit.*, 11.

208. Cf. *ibid.*, 24f.

209. *Ibid.*, 24.

210. *Ibid.*, 151. Cf. *ibid.*, 25.

211. Bäuml, *op. cit.*, 358, n. 21.

212. Lord, *op. cit.*, 152.

212a *Ibid.*, 151.

212b *Ibid.*, 59. Cf. *ibid.*, 25f., 152.

213. Cf. *ibid.*, 184-205: Oral Transmission and Writing.

214. *Ibid.*, 184.

215. Cf. *ibid.*, 186.

216. Cf. *ibid.*, 185.

217. Cf. *ibid.*, 192f.

218. Cf. *ibid.*, 202f.

218a *Ibid.*, 122.

219. Hence formulaic analysis is a criterion to determine "whether or not a particular text is oral or 'literary'" (*ibid.*, 193). On "formulae" see *ibid.*, 58ff.; on "theme" cf. *ibid.*, 107ff. Otherwise the significance of "formulae" and "husks" has been demonstrated for other genres. Bibliography: see M. Curschmann, *DVjs* 40 (1966) 605, n. 256; Bäuml, *op. cit.*, 355, n. 13. -- Formulaic analysis of the N. T. needs to be brought into dialogue with such results.

220. Cf. Lord, *op. cit.*, 193.

221. Cf. *ibid.*, 184, 185f.

222. Cf. *ibid.*, 187f.

223. Cf. *ibid.*, 189.

224. Cf. *ibid.*, 189f.

225. *Ibid.*, 193.

226. Cf. *ibid.*, 194f.

227. *Ibid.*, 195.

228. Bäuml, *op. cit.*, 359.

229. *Ibid.*, 360.

230. Lord, *op. cit.*, 187.

231. Cf. *ibid.*, 190f.

232. *Ibid.*, 190.

233. *Ibid.*, 185. With qualifications, *ibid.*, 189: It
appears "that a dictated text, even when it has been recorded
under favorable circumstances and with the best of transcrib-
ers, is never exactly the same with respect to the verse-
structure as the performed text".

234. *Ibid.*, 190.

235. *Ibid.*, 191.

236. See for instance H. M. and N. K. Chadwick, *The
Growth of Literature*, vols. 1-3, 1932-40; see espec. vol. 3,
701ff.; Wellek and Warren, *op. cit.*, 39f.; H. Kuhn, *Zur Typologie mündlicher Sprachdenkmäler*, 1960. -- G. Iber (*ThR*
24 [1957/58] 322, n. 5) asks critically whether the works
analyzed in Germanic studies are in any way comparable with
the synoptic gospels, for in the last analysis the folkloristic methods to which form criticism is related (cf. above,
p. [93]), were developed from these works. And whether or
not the existence of "folkloristic" genres is "to be denied
absolutely" (*op. cit.*, 322) is precisely the problem, since
the "folkloristic" itself has become so controversial. When
the "existence" of these genres is designated as being supported "by the life of a community and not by the will of a
creative personality" (*ibid.*), it will be apparent that at
least for Lord's material this represents a false alternative, since to be sure the characteristic nature of these
genres is only vaguely indicated, but the "literary" conceptual model prohibits the acceptance of an oral "ur-text" created once for all times and then only varied and passed along
by the collective, so that the sequence of the words originates in each case from a "creative personality" belonging to
the collective, which actualizes in the *parole* the merely potential *langue*. What is "supported", therefore, is merely
the characteristic nature of the folklore, but not of the
"text" (cf. above, p. [143]), since the latter is a category
of the written (cf. above, p. [146]). Naturally Lord's are
epic analogies, and because of the special nature of their
rhythmic qualities and so far as I am aware, the lack of a
composition from "small units" comparable to that of the
gospels, are only applicable with reference to the "oral

literature" type of tradition, but with reference to the content. However N. T. (and also O. T.) form criticism now faces the question concerning how justified it is in regarding the different variants transmitted only by "literary" means, such as a credo, the doublets of a miracle story, etc., as form-*historical* variations of a *primal-edition* [*Urfassung*], which is repeatedly regarded by literary critics, from a methodological point of view, as a scientific phantom. However here we face one of those major tasks of research which cannot be resolved at this point. In light of the quotation from G. Iber, however, we can only remember to be on the guard against too quickly treating customary hypotheses as certain facts.

237. D. O. Via, Jr. (cf. Introductory Remarks, above, n. 10) has made a promising beginning in this respect within American exegesis. On functional stylistics, cf. also W. Richter, *Traditionsgeschichtliche Untersuchungen zum Richterbuch*, 1963, 344-99; Richter, *Recht und Ethos*, 1966. Cf. the bibliography given above, p. [15].

238. Cf. below, p. [150f.].

239. Cf. below, p. [223ff.].

240. Cf. Dibelius, *Formgesch.*, 26f. Also J. Schniewind, *ThR* 2 (1930) 135f.; P. Benoit, *RB* 53 (1946) 490f.

241. Cf. Th. Boman, *Die Jesus-Ueberlieferung im Lichte der neueren Volkskunde*, 1967, 13.

242. Cf. *ibid.*, 50.

243. So *ibid.*, 13. Cf. B. Gerhardsson, *Memory and Manuscript*, 1961, and *Tradition and Transmission in Early Christianity*, 1964.

244. Gerhardsson, *Tradition*, 7.

245. *Ibid.*, 22.

246. Boman, *op. cit.*, 9.

247. Cf. *ibid.*, 14f.

248. Cf. *ibid.*, 42f.

249. Cf. *ibid.*, 40, 47.

250. Cf. especially E. Käsemann, *VF* 10 (1960/62, 1963/65)

85-87; G. Widengren, "Tradition and Literature in Early Judaism and in the Early Church," *Numen* 10 (1963) 42-83; P. Benoit, *RB* 70 (1963) 269-73; M. Smith, "A Comparison of Early Christianity and Early Rabbinic Tradition," *JBL* 82 (1963) 169-76. On Gerhardsson, "Die Boten Gottes und die Apostel Christi," *SEÅ* 27 (1962) 89-131, see my brief remarks in *VF* 12/2 (1967) 67, 70f.

251. Cf. for instance Gerhardsson, *Tradition*, 9; 12, n. 20; 15, n. 25; 19, n. 34.

252. Cf. for instance *ibid.*, 5: "One of the basic assumptions of the form-critical school is that the early Christian Church was not interested in tradition or its transmission." "From this viewpoint the formation of tradition in early Christianity was a process, whose character was largely hidden from those who were concerned in it--i.e., the early Christians themselves."

253. Cf. W. Bacher, *Die exegetische Terminologie der jüdischen Traditionsliteratur*, vol. 1, 1899; 1965-new ed., 42f.

254. *Ibid.*, 34.

255. Cf. H. Riesenfeld, *The Gospel Tradition and its Beginnings*, 1961-2nd ed., espec. 17ff.

256. Cf. Gerhardsson, *Memory*, 225ff., 280ff.

257. Cf. G. Iber, *ThR* 24 (1957/58) 315f.

258. Cf. H. Schürmann, *Traditionsgeschichtliche Untersuchungen zu den synoptischen Evangelien*, 1968, 40.

259. Cf. however E. Nielsen, *Oral Tradition*, 1955-2nd ed.; A. H. J. Gunneweg, *Mündliche und schriftliche Tradition der vorexilischen Prophetenbücher als Problem der neueren Prophetenforschung*, 1959; R. C. Culley, "An Approach to the Problem of Oral Tradition," *VetTest* 13 (1963) 113-25; E. Sellin and G. Fohrer, *Einleitung in das Alte Testament*, 1965-10th ed., 36ff. Further bibliography is given there.

#8. *"Setting in Folk-Life" and the Written: Hermann Gunkel.*

1. The Present Research Situation with Regard to Gunkel's Work.

Several times H. Gunkel (1862-1932) has been correctly named as one of the most important founders of the form-critical method.[1] Gunkel's work was especially influenced by J. G. Herder, and brought his influence into the methodological foundations of the form-critical method.[2] We have already seen that there were in Herder's conception of the modes of tradition of the genres essential preliminary-decisions that are questioned today both in studies of Herder and in folkloristics.[3] H. Gunkel is also indirectly involved in this crisis. Hence it seems advisable to seek out the problem of the transition of the genres from the oral to the written in Gunkel's work; then we can easily enough see whether Gunkel himself was aware of this problem and how he resolved it. In my opinion it can be shown that the form-critical method, with reference to the oral nature of the folkloristic genres, followed H. Gunkel's basic observations from the start, and hence was betrayed into tensions or difficulties that now have finally come to a head in the thesis of the discontinuity between form and redaction criticism. First, however, we must look at W. Klatt's comprehensive work, for without its contributions, Gunkel's life and work can no longer be appropriately judged.[4] Klatt has not only edited and reworked previously unknown documents, especially from the correspondence and unpublished materials of Gunkel and the history of religions school, but has also given us so thorough an introduction to the origins of the form-critical approach in Gunkel's lifetime,[5] to the origin of Gunkel's method,[6] to the connection between the history of religions and literary criticism,[7] [p. 155] to the "sociological setting", the history of transmission and genres,[8] and to the problem of the individual narrative and composition,[9] that my observations, which arose independently of Klatt, can be related by and large to his findings.

2. The "Setting in Folk-Life" and the Oral.

In order to be able to appraise the full extent of Gunkel's methodological foundations of the form-critical method, we need to remind readers of the original sense of the form-critical *terminus technicus* [technical term] "sociological setting". It has been recognized that Gunkel brought[10] this expression into form criticism as one of its central concepts;[11] and it has been used recently in folkloristics concerned with so-called "folk poetry" as a means of expanding research on genres, as in the field of Germanic studies.[12]

Gunkel understood the task of form-critical research to be that "of making clear that portion of the folk life belonging to the respective genre, and hence to understand the one in terms of the other. Precisely because these oldest genres originated not on paper but in the course of life, the original units were so short, corresponding to the meager receptivity of listeners, and especially of listeners in antiquity."[13] In this quotation we find all the threads that will explain the way Gunkel utilized the concept "sociological setting", as well as subsequent developments in form criticism.

The "sociological setting" is more precisely expressed as "setting in *folk*-life": "One has to be aware of Israel's quite colorful and temperamental folk-life in order to know how Hebraic poetry developed from this life, and how it has its 'setting' in particular segments."[14] The oldest genres[15] originally[16] "possessed a quite specific place in Israelite folk-life, [p. 156] of which they represent an important part precisely because they originated not on paper, but in life; hence their oldest units are so brief, corresponding to the meagre receptivity on the part of the ancient listeners".[17]

Here the life of the folk is represented entirely in Herder's sense, in its primordiality and liveliness over against paper and literature, considered as distanced from life:[18] "A specific 'sociological setting' belongs to the concept of the antique genre. The literature of the pri-mordial times did not come about almost exclusively on paper, as ours has, but it was the expression of particular occa-sions of actual life."[19] In other words: paper, literature, in short: *The written for Gunkel as for Herder does not belong to the actual life of a primordial folk:* "We must con-ceive of these poetries not as written, but sung, not as on paper, but in life."[20]

According to Gunkel, even the brevity of the original units is a consequence of the oral nature of the "setting in the folk-life", and what distinguishes it from writing; for this reason the transition to writing indicates an expansion in what was included.[21] In this context, W. Klatt has at-tempted to prove that Gunkel supports the unity of form and redaction criticism,[22] finding [p. 157] that Gunkel has "so thoroughly anticipated the history-of-transmission approach that it merges without a break into redaction criticism".[23] Klatt suggests that Gunkel was thoroughly aware of the con-temporary question concerning the composition of the bibli-cal books;[24] and that he never took as an absolute any *one* stage in the transmission-*process*, according to his under-standing of the history of religions and transmission his-

238

tory,[25] and therefore did not give pride of place to the redactor.[26] Klatt suggests: "It seems to me that his partiality for the individual narrative unit is a relic from the
period of confrontation between Gunkel and source criticism,
against which he had passionately emphasized the original independence of the individual saga"; "even where a larger organic literary work has come about, the individual unit remained the germinal unit, standing at the beginning of the
development."[27]

In fact Gunkel conceived *form criticism as a criticism of
an overused source criticism.* * While in the period of source
criticism there was little interest in folk transmission, and
focus was upon the literary,[28] Gunkel emphasized the distinction between form criticism and the earlier source criticism.[29]
Since the latter ignored the oral tradition,[30] form criticism
emphasized the oral.[31] "The background here is a conception
of literature and life that represents a new component in the
horizon of the history of ideas at the turn of the century."[32]

3. The Written and Redactional Framing.

To be sure, it is a question whether there is not something more to Gunkel's antithesis between folk-life and the
written, whether Gunkel's reliance upon Herder did not imply

*The reader who may not be familiar with the development of
exegetical methodologies such as source or "literary" criticism, the history of religions school in biblical criticism,
etc., may be referred to Chapter 3, "The Search for Proper
Methods", in the translator's *Contemporary New Testament Interpretation* (Englewood Cliffs: Prentice-Hall, 1972), or to
a more recent work, Richard N. Soulen's *Handbook of Biblical
Criticism* (Atlanta: Knox, 1976). I will not otherwise call
attention to problems such as translating Religionsgeschichte
with "history of religions". W.G.D.

something that led him into difficulties with respect to the continuity of form and redaction criticism. In contrast to Klatt, I think that Gunkel had some idea of these difficulties. As we have demonstrated, the "setting in folk-life" represents Gunkel's aestheticism,[33] [p. 158] in contrast to the emphasis in modern literature upon the written and the author,[34] which to a certain extent is an element of distance from real life. In terms of these premises the transition of a "form" from "setting in folk-life" to the author[35] or the written must also have consequences in terms of the *history* of forms: Genres have a pure style only in the oral "sociological setting".[36] "Under the influence of writing the genres experienced manifold alterations."[37] The growth of what could be included belongs to these alterations,[38] as well as the manipulations and admixtures of the pure style:[39] The genres "simultaneously lost their sociological setting and purity of style."[40] "The conceptions and forms of expression of the genres were produced from out of the oral 'sociological setting' and are to be understood from there..., so later when writing came to dominate the life of the spirit, these oldest loci of the genres were more or less given up in favor of the written book."[41]

Therefore in its original meaning the *terminus technicus* "sociological setting" is completely opposed to the written nature of the form, so that it cannot be transferred *a priori* or without methodological reflection to a phenomenon within the "literary" mode of traditions. Gunkel's understanding of folk poetry—following Herder—is that it is so distant from the written *that with the act of writing a* metabasis eis allo genos [*transformation into another mode*] *occurs.*[41a] One consequence of this connection between "sociological setting" and the oral, with its simultaneous antithesis to the written, is the minimalizing of the written nature of the "Kleinliteratur".[42] For if one [p. 159] must accede that this is already a "genuine" act of writing, it would already represent a fundamental movement away from the level of the folk, with the consequence that it would only be possible--or possible only in a very difficult way--to draw any direct applications to the folk level from the extant written situation. However it it clear to me that Gunkel and, following him, form critics, deceived themselves with respect to the consequences of writing, when they minimalized the written nature of the "Kleinliteratur", although Gunkel was aware of the difference between the oral and the written and, for that reason, stumbled over certain methodological aporias with respect to the immanent and logical premises of form criticism.

Of course it is possible to object against such a limitation of the expression "sociological setting" in terms of the oral that it is too greatly oriented to the modern production of books.[43] But the danger is that of losing Gunkel's feeling for the special quality of the written. For Gunkel writing is not only the presupposition for particular genres, e.g., the writing of history; rather "the process of writing [serves] a tradition by stabilizing it; oral transmission cannot keep itself pure over a long period, and hence it is not in a position to become the sufficient vessel for history".[44] The oral transmission "in its very nature never [maintains] that security that is possible only in writing: *littera scripta manet* [the written word remains]".[45] As did earlier folkloristics, Gunkel therefore rejected the written, not as a completely negative phenomenon, but recognizing its specific qualities. However this proves that on closer consideration he did not regard the transition from the oral to the written as something happening without a break and nonproblematically, as occurred in later form criticism. Moreover K. Koch's objection is mistaken in that the transition from the oral mode of tradition into the written *may* simultaneously represent the transition from the sociological to the individual,[46] i.e., that relationship of the sociological pressure of the "sociological setting"[47] to the freedom of the individual formation made problematic by the author [i.e., by the fact that in "writing" the personal role of the "author" has to be taken into account - W.G.D.]. We can continue our reflections in #5 at this point.

[p. 160] Then to what extent and in which sense is it only the "framework" that represents the independent achievement of the redactor?[48] The framework can be understood in theological aspects as an independent creation of the evangelists,[49] so that the evangelists "in their work as redactors must also be seen to a certain extent as *authorial personalities*, who by means of their methodological operation, especially by grouping the material within particular contexts, sought to express their own theology, or beyond that, the theology of a particular group and direction in primitive Christianity".[50] However precisely the question about the degree of independence of the evangelist's theology in the framework of the theology of his group gains a particular emphasis by means of this description: Is not the "framework" thus ascribed an even greater independence, since it, in contrast to the individual elements brought together in it, can be *materialiter* presupposed only in quite rare instances,[51] and hence designates that distinction between an original oral "sociological setting" and a form primarily extant in writing? Furthermore is not the concept of the "tradition" unduly restricted to the individual units fixed *materialiter* in their sequence, although the *materialiter* cannot be determined in advance by the fixed "frameworks" of prior theological aspects, which would have precedence in any case, as the "tradition" of the theological independence of the redactors?[52] In other words: Also in the

"form" that existed originally or only in the written, tradition is often effective--effective, to be sure, in other ways
and also partly according to other [p. 161] rules than in the
redacted individual units. All these reflections indicate
that in the transition from the "sociological setting" to the
"framework", there are inherent form- and tradition-critical
tensions which have not been sufficiently taken into account.

4. Gunkel's Methodological Unity of Form Criticism
   and the History of Religions as a Task for Contemporary Methodology.

W. Klatt has correctly emphasized the connection between
form and redaction criticism in Gunkel's work.[53] For Gunkel
form criticism has a close relationship to the history of
religions "in that both disciplines must interact with one
another in many ways, since there is no form without content
or content without form".[54] Form criticism and the history
of religions are therefore related as form and content are.
Their fundamental inseparability is thereby illuminated as
well; the two methods focus upon different aspects of *one* set
of circumstances, which today is understood as a linguistic
phenomenon.[55] In my opinion Klatt rightly notes the preponderance, in the mutual relationship of form criticism and the
history of religions, of the latter,[56] although his consequent
movement toward a new theology of the history of religions in
the sense of the group around W. Pannenberg[57] is not relevant
to the present discussion. According to Klatt, Gunkel reached
the conclusion "that he could not get any further in questions
concerning the history of religions, if he did not take into
account literary-critical elements".[58] Hence Gunkel was fundamentally clear that the form and content of a work of art
cannot be entirely separated, "no matter what the dear Philis-
tine may believe; rather they belong as closely together as

possible; for the correct form is the *necessary* expression of the content".[59] Hence he expressly emphasized "that a literary-critical treatment does not *only* concern the form, but *also the content* of the poem".[60] For these reasons, Gunkel was a long way from the distinction between [p. 162] the history of religions and form criticism which today has become standard, especially in studies of the [hellenistic] environment.[61] According to Gunkel, "there can be no penetration into the world of religious thought without an understanding of the materials and forms".[62] "There can be no history of religions without literary criticism; for how can anyone hope to understand the contents of something if he does not concern himself with its form?"[63] This avoidance of methodological atomism permits Gunkel to inquire to what extent the division of genres is something inherent to the particular nature of the materials,[64] to ask in which forms something like the eschatological contents of the Psalms can be expressed,[65] to what extent a common store of concepts and articulations was available for formally-related elements from their "sociological setting",[66] and which forms of expression are tied to these concepts.[67] Similarly R. Bultmann emphasizes "that a genre is tied more or less definitely to one type of contents".[68]

In the light of such quotations, W. Klatt rightly emphasizes the way a body of concepts and articulations is tied to distinct formal expressions and a certain "sociological setting".[69] Gunkel apparently knew that every linguistic utterance "walks hand in hand with its manner of expression in characteristic forms",[70] i.e., that it represents a connection between linguistic form and conceptual and spiritual contents, in short: a linguistic "gestalt".[71] From the preponderance of the conceptual and spiritual it can be seen that for Gunkel form criticism was not *just* a matter of formal,

aesthetic observation,[72] even though the aesthetic approach
had largely become the new hermeneutical principle of literary criticism.[73] But what is "primary is not the linguistic
work of art, but the contents of the linguistic expression,
which can first be correctly understood when it is employed
in its original sociological setting. That signifies...the
theological precedence of the history of religions over literary criticism".[74]

Simultaneously this means that co-ordination is a task
for the contemporary methodology of form-critically influenced
treatment of texts, since awareness about the partial unity of
form criticism and the history of religions gets lost to view,
and its connections with a linguistic perspective oriented
specifically to the so-called "motifs" [p. 163] has scarcely
been established.[174a] In the framework of the restrictions
explained in the introduction to this book, I must be satisfied with the following suggestions concerning the inner *connection*, oriented to the linguistic phenomenon, *between the
history of religions, form criticism, and linguistics*.[75]

Traditional *history of religions* (as well as tradition
history) asks about "motifs" in the texts of the bible and
within its religious environment,[76] mostly therefore about
religious "presentations". To be sure such inquiry is aimed
at a particular aspect of the linguistic phenomenon which encounters us in the texts, but it is immediately misused when
it is used for genealogical explanation of the act of thought
on the basis of the mostly-unknown background of an evolutionary world view,[77] for something like an "alchemy of
ideas".[78] In another publication I have demonstrated extensively that this current procedure is "pre-Bultmannian" and
hermeneutically inadequate, if it is used to explain the *act*
of thought.[79] Furthermore that interest is dominated by the
visible "presentations" of associative psychology, as it is

still present in linguistics in F. de Saussure's work,[80] and
as it has long ruled thinking in the humanities by means of a
combination of the naturalism of Th. Hobbes, the empiricism
of J. Locke and D. Hume, the transcendental realism of B. de
Spinoza, and the critical realism of J. F. Herbart.[81] This
associative psychology is so thoroughly refuted by cognitive
psychology,[82] [p. 164] that today no one ought to rely on it
any longer. It has been unequivocally proved by means of
empirical experiments that in our experiences of thought the
"presentations" come into consciousness quite fragmentarily,
sporadically, and entirely by chance, and therefore cannot be
regarded as the *carriers* of the strictly structured and continuous contents of thought.[83] "Every researcher seriously
regarded in our subject has recognized that the occurrence of
a thought cannot be conceived as a simple sum of presentations."[84] The way "presentations" are currently added to the
explanation of the origination of a new cognitive image is too
dependent upon that associative psychology which has been replaced by cognitive psychology. I cannot treat further here
the details of the proofs of cognitive psychology, but only
want to ask: What is the source of our experience of consciousness that is foreign to us, and of the "presentations"
found within it? Only through the extrinsic linguistic utterance, which is concretized by conclusion by analogy, on the
basis of relationships of our own consciousness, can something
be "understood".[85] *We never encounter "presentations" directly in texts*, but only in each case by means of the medium of
a linguistic phenomenon, in the gestalt of the words shaped
by the linguistic structure (*langue*) of the genres.

There we touch upon *form criticism* (#3, sections 3 & 4),
which enquires about the linguistic form, the linguistic-
sociological-structural "gestalt" of the presentations or
the act of thought. Since the "presentations" are never di-

rectly, nor in the act of thought ever immediately, "given" to us, the methodologically primary question is therefore that concerning the form, and after that we may then place the methodologically secondary question which is inseparably bound up with this form, namely the question as to cognitive contents, so that form criticism in Gunkel's sense entirely precedes the history of religions. But is this pride of place sufficient?

In order to be able to discover the inner structure (*langue*) of the forms as linguistic "gestalts", we need a clarified linguistic method,[86] which inquires about the "motifs" impressed structurally in the "gestalts", [p. 165] which however are no longer motifs of "presentation", but *linguistic* motifs, the linguistic "signs". Hence *linguistics* is recognized and accepted as the mode of inquiry that takes precedence over form criticism. Naturally H. Gunkel was unable to see this connection so clearly, but his approach to the transcending of methodological atomism is helpful to us yet today. In traditional history of religions discourse it is mostly the "presentations" found in the texts that is meant, in terms of particular words (terms). But the latter are not now being investigated by means of actual linguistic methods, or only by referring to their contents understood as being form-critically conditioned in some instances, and hence with reference to the structural *valeur* of the terms within the linguistic gestalts;[87] but they are set forth almost absolutely as "visible" presentations possible at any time and without reference to a particular linguistic form, i.e., as independent, or as contents which can be treated apart from the given linguistic form, as images at the level of the psyche shaped and bound to a particular worldview, somewhat similarly to the [procedure in the] psychology of J. F. Herbart. As the relationship of this level of the visual and presentational experience to the level of the linguistic phenomenon of the circumstances is formed, it is mostly left unreflectively open or omitted, or at any rate so conceived that the presentations are deposited in the linguistic form, whereby it seemingly becomes, in the history of religions approach, a neglected, somewhat "external" wrapper. That it can also happen the other way around, in that the structure of the linguistic form (*langue*), the system of rules of the "mother tongue", can also determine the extent of the presentations, or better: the extent of the linguistic creation of world,[88] of the unconscious understanding and ordering of world which is expressed in "naming",[89] in brief: that the linguistic "gestalt" could definitely and with many consequences determine all psychic processes manifesting themselves linguistically,[90] [p. 166] is not even taken into account in traditional history of religions or even tradition history, something that seems to me, especially in the case of tradition history, to lead to a caricature of the actual primitive Christian history of theology.[91] It is no longer understood to what extent "presentations" are *only* accessible to us as linguistic phenomena with all the implications that implies. This separation of "form" and "content" is a consequence of the atomistic co-existence of the history of religions (tradition history), form criticism, and philology, although the linguistic phenomenon itself so pressingly demands a universal methodology which will do it justice, something like a methodology which as a general science of linguistics would be able to unite all the aspects we have named, without the difficulties present in contemporary research. Has fragmented exegesis (here in the history of religions, there in form criticism) actually already recognized in the forms, i.e., in the analytically inseparable union of "contents" and "form", the linguistic phenomenon we have been considering? It is to

H. Gunkel's merit that he suspected and named this phenomenon by means of his co-ordination of form criticism and the history of religions. *It is our task to re-integrate the atomistically-splintered methodologies again into a unity which will do justice to the unity of the linguistic phenomenon, "text".*[92] The present work is to be seen as a first step in that direction.

Notes to #8

1. Cf. Dibelius, *Formgesch.* 5; Dibelius, *ThR* 1 (1929) 186; Bultmann, *Syn. Trad.*, 4f.; Schniewind, *ThR* 2 (1930) 162.

2. Cf. W. Klatt, *Hermann Gunkel*, 1969, 106ff.

3. Cf. above, pp. [120ff., 126ff.].

4. Cf. n. 2, as well as W. Klatt, "Die 'Eigentümlichkeit' der israelitischen Religion in der Sicht von Hermann Gunkel," *EvTh* 28 (1968) 153-60.

5. Cf. Klatt, *Gunkel*, 46ff.

6. Cf. *ibid.*, 106ff.

7. Cf. *ibid.*, 104f. Cf. also K.-H. Bernhardt, *Die gattungsgeschichtliche Forschung am Alten Testament als exegetische Methode*, 1959, 31-33.

8. Cf. Klatt, *op. cit.*, 144ff.

9. Cf. *ibid.*, 156ff.

10. Cf. W. G. Kümmel, *Das Neue Testament*, 1959, 550, n. 388.

11. Cf. K. Koch, *Was ist Formgeschichte?*, 1964, 30-44.

12. Cf. Bausinger, *op. cit.*, 62f., 159, 203.

13. H. Gunkel, *RGG*, vol. 1, 1909, 1193.

14. Gunkel, *RGG*-2nd ed., vol. 3, 1929, 1644. -- We might well ask whether today we could still speak of an immediate empiricism with respect to Israelite folk-life.

15. This restriction must be taken to indicate that later genres could well have arisen of a purely literary type, and from the influence of a literary milieu.

16. That seems to indicate that the non-literary "setting in folk-life" can be entirely lost in the course of the process by which literature arises. Cf. below, p. [157ff.].

17. Gunkel, *op. cit.*, 1679.

18. Cf. Gunkel, in *Fünfter Weltkongress für Freies Christentum und Religiösen Fortschritt*, ed. M. Fischer and F. M. Schiele, 1910, 175: "Such folkoristic forms...are distinguished...according to the various genres of popular literature, which have had at one time in their life a setting in particular places." -- The antithesis of life (nature, folk, etc.) and culture (art) is--one last reflection of J. J. Rousseau (cf. above, p. [129])--also characteristic for the differentiation of letters from epistles. Cf. Deissmann, *Licht vom Osten*, 118f., 193ff. (cf. the quotation above, #6, n. 33). In an uncritical reception of this foundation the differentiation remains unclear with respect to the ways "art" does not belong to "life", when in *both* cases the factual reality of sociological regularities is constitutive for the linguistic form, and the sociological realms are not to be seen as unrelated. Everything is basically reduced to the postulate of the antithesis: "In the beginning was not the written book, but the living word, not the gospels but the gospel, not the letter, but the spirit, in the beginning was Jesus" (*ibid.*, 212). The way Deissmann distinguishes letters and epistles is justified, but its basis dogmatic. [Cf. the translator's discussion of Deissmann's distinctions: "The Classification of Epistolary Literature," *Catholic Biblical Quarterly* 31/2 (1969) 183-99. - W.G.D.]

19. Gunkel, *ThR* 20 (1917) 269. Cf. Gunkel and J. Begrich, *Einleitung in die Psalmen*, 1933, 10: It should be remembered that the literary witnesses of primordial folk are not only conceivable on paper, "but derive from the actual life of persons and have their setting there". (Partly italicized in the original.)

20. Gunkel, *Reden und Aufsätze*, 1913, 100. Cf. Gunkel, *SAT* I/1, 6: "The origination of all literature of antiquity was first something that happened not in written, but in oral form."

21. Cf. Gunkel, *Reden*, 33f.; and *RGG*-2nd ed., vol. 3, 1929, 1679.

22. Cf. Klatt, *Gunkel*, 156ff.

23. *Ibid.*, 159.

24. Cf. *ibid.*, 157.

25. Klatt, *ibid.*, 13f., 271, relates Gunkel's theses to the modern reflections of the circle around W. Pannenberg, having in mind a new theology of the history of religions. Cf. also above, #2, n. 25.

26. Cf. Klatt, *op. cit.*, 160.

27. *Ibid.*, 156f.

28. Cf. G. Bertram, *ThBl* 2 (1923) 28.

29. Cf. Gunkel, *RGG*-2nd ed., vol. 3, 1929, 1678. Similarly K. L. Schmidt, *RGG*-2nd ed., vol. 2, 1928, 638f.

30. Cf. R. Bultmann, *ThLZ* 50 (1925) 313.

31. Cf. Klatt, *op. cit.*, 139.

32. *Ibid.*

33. It is recognizable in the confession of impressionism. Cf. Gunkel, in *5. Weltkongress*, 174, 176: "Aesthetic experience should lend us strength for religious experiencing even of that which lies far distant from the present and which would otherwise remain closed to us."

34. Cf. Gunkel, *SAT* II/2, XXXV: We must "recognize that the genres play a much greater role in the literature of an ancient folk than is true today, and that the individual authorial personalities which seem in modern literature to be the be-all and end-all, retreat in antiquity in a manner that initially estranges us".

35. Indications of this problematics are found in Gunkel, *Reden*, 35. Cf. *ZAW* 42 (1924) 183: The genres are to be understood from the "sociological setting", even when they "have, to be sure, in recent times more or less given up the oldest circumstances where writing rules the spiritual life".

36. Gunkel, *RGG*, vol. 1, 1909, 1193: "On the basis of the...'sociological setting' we can see further that these oldest genres possess entirely pure style: they were intended for a particular situation, and thoroughly correspond to it."

37. *Ibid.*

38. Cf. above, n. 21.

39. Gunkel, *Reden*, 36; *Die israelitische Literatur*, 1963-new ed., 4; *RGG*-2nd ed., vol. 3, 1929, 1679.

40. Gunkel, *RGG*, vol. 1, 1909, 1193. On the postulative character of this thesis, see E. Schick, *Formgeschichte und Synoptikerexegese*, 1940, 79.

41. Gunkel, *ZAW* 42 (1924) 183.

41a [+1978: Meanwhile I have discovered that the idea of "transformation", i.e., the central idea of my "Generative Poetics", was already present in W. v. Goethe's morphology, with its motto: "A theory of gestalts is a theory of transformation." Insofar as Gunkel is a pupil of Goethe's morphology, the idea of transformation is a point of continuity between original form criticism and Generative Poetics. Besides that it is clear now that the term "form history" was first used by a biologist (Franz Joseph Schelver, 1822) within the sphere of Goethe's influence. Cf. R. Breymayer, *Ling Bibl* 15/16 (1972) 64.]

42. Cf. above, p. [103ff.].

43. So Koch, *op. cit.*, 31f., n. 2.

44. Gunkel, *SAT* I/1, 14.

45. Gunkel, *Das Märchen im Alten Testament*, 1921-2nd ed., 4.

46. Gunkel proposes, without argumentation, *ibid.*, 3: "Of course there were individual narrators who first established [the folkloristic genres]." Cf. *5. Weltkongress*, 175: "For such authors utilize forms that have developed over a long period of time." Apparently the problem of the relation between individual and sociological has not yet been solved in folk-poetry.

47. Cf. the quotation in #3, n. 10. A spontaneous creation by an "author" is almost totally excluded here. However this antithesis between folkloristic and spontaneity is questionable. Cf. below, p. [179ff.].

48. Cf. J. Rohde, *Die redaktionsgeschichtliche Methode*, 1965, 21: Redaction criticism conceives "the concept of the framework much more extendedly, and regards it as the *actual* achievement of the writers of the gospels".

49. Cf. *ibid.*, 17.

50. *Ibid.*, 13.

51. I am presenting here only a general consideration of vague possibilities; I am thinking for instance of Mark 1:32-34, which Bultmann, *Syn. Trad.* [Germ. ed.], 366, treats as a redactional creation, but E. Lohmeyer, *Das Evangelium des Markus*, 1963, 41, and W. Grundmann, *Das Evangelium nach*

Markus, 1965-3rd ed., 46, treat as traditional material (except perhaps 1:34b). The decision is partly dependent upon whether we take *hote edusen ho hēlios* (Mk 1:32) as a secondary addition to *opsias de genomenēs* (cf. Mt 8:16). Cf. Schmidt, *Rahmen*, 47f. However these stylistic questions are still too dependent upon the personal taste of the exegete for us to speak of certain results. Even conjectures here remain much too subjective.

52. On the expansion of the kerygma, cf. below, p. [104f.] -- Zimmermann, *Ntl. Methodenlehre*, 222f., wants to take the concept "framework" more narrowly than redaction critics, who use it further to encompass the selection and arrangement of the materials. The concept is best used only to designate the framework-portions of the pericopes. But in my opinion such a position conceals the problem discussed above. Moreover such a narrow conceptual range is not the original one Schmidt, *Rahmen*, 1ff., 317, developed just for the sketch of the Jesus-story--and hence having to do with the disposition of the materials--although he remained too completely within the question about the *historical* value of this disposition.

53. Cf. Klatt, *op. cit.*, 13, 104f.

54. Gunkel, *RGG*, vol. 1, 1909, 1190.

55. Further reasons given below, p. [164ff.].

56. Cf. Klatt, *op. cit.*, 104: "What ever may be devised can only be put to use for the purposes of the history of religions inquiry. This is also the case with literary criticism."

57. Cf. *ibid.*, 13f., 271.

58. *Ibid.*, 104.

59. Gunkel, *Reden*, 23, my emphasis. On the relationship between form and content, see also Bernhardt, *op. cit.*, 34-38.

60. Gunkel and Begrich, *Einl. Ps.*, 23. Now similarly again: A. N. Wilder, *The Language of the Gospel* [in a later ed., entitled *Early Christian Rhetoric*], 1964, 32: "We should not confuse form proper with externals, or style with ornamentation." *Ibid.*, 33: "In all genuine artifacts, including language-forms, shape and substance are inseparable and mutually determinative."

61. A noted exception: J. Becker, *Das Heil Gottes*, 1964. Cf. Güttgemanns, *VF* 12/2 (1967) 82-87.

62. Gunkel, *Reden*, VII.

63. Gunkel, *5. Weltkongress*, 175.

64. Cf. Gunkel and Begrich, *op. cit.*, 9f.

65. Cf. *ibid.*, 344-47.

66. Cf. *ibid.*, 22. Cf. Gunkel, *RGG*, vol. 4, 1913, 1934.

67. Cf. Gunkel, *ThR* 20 (1917) 271.

68. Bultmann *ThLZ* 50 (1925) 317.

69. Cf. Klatt, *op. cit.*, 128.

70. *Ibid.*, 143.

71. Cf. below, p. [184ff.].

72. Cf. Klatt, *op. cit.*, 171f. At any rate interest in sociology soon followed emphasis upon aesthetics. Cf. above, p. [44ff.].

73. *Op. cit.*, 118.

74. *Ibid.*, 172.

74a [+1978: Meanwhile Generative Poetics developed a linguistic method of correlating "motifs" to "motifemes", i.e., to motif classes. Cf. *Semeia* 6 (1976).]

75. Cf. also H. Ringgren, "Literarkritik, Formgeschichte, Ueberlieferungsgeschichte," *ThLZ* 91 (1966) 641-50; R. Rendtorff, "Literarkritik und Traditionsgeschichte," *EvTh* 27 (1967) 138-53.

76. Cf. H. Jonas, *Gnosis und spätantiker Geist*, vol. 1, 1954-2nd ed., 9f.

77. Cf. G. Widengren, "Evolutionism and the Problem of the Origin of Religion," *Ethnos* 10 (1945) 57-96. On the boundaries of the history of religions method, cf. also A. Bea, "'Religionswissenschaftliche' oder 'theologische' Exegese?", *Bibl* 40 (1959) 322-41; S. Sandmel, "Parallelomania," *JBL* 81 (1962) 1-13; C. Westermann, "Sinn und Grenze religionsgeschichtlicher Parallelen," *ThLZ* 90 (1965) 489-96.

78. Cf. Jonas, *op. cit.*, 32: "Somehow in this as in similar derivations there seems to be an idea reflected that an

ideal process 'unexpectedly' overshoots its goal and could demonstrate something quite different from what would make sense in its own field. An alchemy of ideas!"

79. Cf. Güttgemanns, *Der leidende Apostel*, 46ff., 347ff., 393ff.

80. Cf. de Saussure, *Cours*, 27ff.

81. Individual proofs must be left again for a future publication; but see J. F. Herbart, *Allgemeine Pädagogik*, 1806; *Lehrbuch der Psychologie*, 1834-2nd ed.; *Ueber die Möglichkeit und Notwendigkeit, Mathematik auf Psychologie anzuwenden*, 1822; *De attentionis mensura*, 1822; and *Psychologie, neu gegründet auf Erfahrung, Metaphysik und Mathematik*, 1824/25.

82. Cf. for instance K. Bühler, "Tatsachen und Probleme zu einer Psychologie der Denkvorgänge, I.," *Archiv für die ges. Psychol.* 9 (1907) 297-365; part II, *ibid.*, 12 (1908) 1-23; part III, *ibid.*, 24-92; Bühler, "Antwort auf die von W. Wundt erhobenen Einwände gegen die Methode der Selbstbeobachtung an experimentell erzeugten Erlebnisse," *ibid.*, 12 (1908) 93-122; Ch. Bühler, "Ueber Gedankenentstehung," *ZfPs* 80 (1918) 129-200; R. Hönigswald, *Prinzipienfragen der Denkpsychologie*, 1913; Ch. Bühler, *Die Grundlagen der Denkpsychologie*, 1925-2nd ed.; K. Duncker, *Zur Psychologie des produktiven Denkens*, 1963-new ed.; J. Segal, "Ueber den Reproduktionstypus und das Reproduzieren von Vorstellungen," *Archiv f. die ges. Psychol.* 12 (1908) 124-235; O. Selz, *Ueber die Gesetze des geordneten Denkverlaufs*, 1913; Selz, *Zur Psychologie des produktiven Denkens und des Irrtums*, 1922; M. Wertheimer, *Produktives Denken*, transl. [into German, from 1945 English ed.] W. Metzger, 1957; R. Meili, "Denkpsychologie," in D. and R. Katz, eds., *Handbuch der Psychologie*, 1960-2nd ed., 172-94.

83. Cf. K. Bühler, *Archiv für die ges. Psychol.* 9 (1907) 317. [+1978: New aspects of the psychological process of thinking, e.g., in children, are developed by J. Piaget, *La genèse du temps chez l'enfant*, 1955, and *Genetic Epistemology*, 1970.]

84. *Ibid.*, 324.

85. On the linguistic principle of analogy, cf. above, p. [43]. [+1978: Cf. the new exposition of the problem in E. Güttgemanns, "Sensus historicus und sensus plenior," *LingBibl* 43 (1978) 75ff.]

86. Cf. above, p. [43].

256

87. Cf. above, p. [49ff.].

88. The following brief suggestions will have to be developed later in planned publications. Hence they must be taken here as yet hypothetical candid questions. See however L. Weisgerber, *Die sprachliche Gestaltung der Welt*, 1962-3rd ed.

89. That is especially emphasized by the metalinguistics of cultural anthropology (B. L. Whorf and others) and by neo-Humboldtianism (L. Weisgerber and others). Cf. bibliog. in #2, n. 51; #7, n. 31; #9, n. 39. Weisgerber, *Grundzüge*, 37 ff., and *Menschheitsgesetz*, 59ff., speaks in this connection of the "intermediate world of the mother tongue" ["mutter-sprachlichen Zwischenwelt"] which is what initially makes the world as world visible to us. Language is a power (*energeia*) of spiritual creation, a power that lets the world "speak". Cf. Weisgerber, *Gestaltung*, 79ff., 205ff., 242ff.; *Stufen*, 104ff.; and *Menschheitsgesetz*, 74ff.; H. Gipper, *Bausteine zur Sprachinhaltsforschung*, 1969-2nd ed.

90. Cf. E. Sapir, *Language* 5 (1929) 209f.: The basic error of a naive linguistics is the illusion "that one adjusts to reality essentially without the use of language and that language is merely an incidental means of solving specific problems of communication or reflection. The fact of the matter is that the 'real world' is to a large extent unconsciously built up upon the language habits of the group." Cf. also the "linguistic principle of relativity" (cf. Whorf, *op. cit.*, 12f.): "Persons who utilize languages with very different grammars are led by these grammars to typically different observations and evaluations of externally similar observations." (*Ibid.*, 20.)

91. Cf. below, pp. [195ff., 198ff.].

92. The program of "textual linguistics" is extensively concerned with the program noted here. Cf. V. Skalicka, "Text, Kontext, Subtext," *Slavica Pragensia* 3 (1961) 73-78; M. Bense, *Theorie der Texte*, 1962; Bense, *Einführung in die informations-theoretische Aesthetik*, 1969; K. E. Heidolph, *Grundprobleme einer Texttheorie*, 1964; K. Hausenblas, "Ueber die Bedeutung sprachlicher Einheiten und Texte," *TLP* 2 (1966) 59-69; P. Hartmann, "Text, Texte, Klassen von Texten," *Bogawus* 2 (1964) 15-25; Hartmann, "Textlinguistik als neue linguistische Teildisziplin," *Replik* 1/2 (1968) 207; Hartmann, "Zum Begriff des sprachlichen Zeichens," *Zeitschr. für Phonetik* 21 (1968) 205-22; R. Harweg, *Pronomina und Textkonstitution*, 1968; W. A. Koch, *Vom Morphem zum Textem*, 1969; E. Leibfried, *Kritische*

Wissenschaft vom Text, 1970. [+1978: My text-linguistic approach in "Generative Poetics" is guided by the question: What *makes* (constitutes) a text into a text? Answer: A set of grammatical rules constituting "form" and "content" as well.]

Examination of the traditional form-critical conceptual model concerning the traditio-historical continuity between the oral and the written nature of the genres led essentially to a negative result. At the same time, starting points for a positive alternative have become visible. It should be recalled once more that transgressing the traditional boundaries of the disciplines for the sake of the subject treated appears to be necessary and may offer a contribution to an alternative construct that will in turn perhaps occasionally remain hypothetical and also have the nature of a conceptual model. Our concern here therefore is not just negative destruction but finding positive alternatives for a form-critical method that is appropriate to its subject matter. In the following section we develop some of the new perspectives that were sighted in Part II, cautiously developing them further by constant reference to the candid questions and unresolved aporia we found there.

#9. *The Expansion of the Concept "Sociological Setting".*

1. Historicizing the Sociological Laws of the "Sociological Setting".[1]

Following the proceedings of M. Albertz[2] and E. Fascher,[3] a sort of "historicizing" of the concept "sociological setting" can be sighted today even within the redaction-critical approach, something that is in tension with its sociological posture. Now the concept, within the framework of inquiry about the "historical Jesus", no longer primarily designates a *general* sociological situation of a particular genre, but a *specific* historical situation of a specific linguistic creation in the life of the historical Jesus. In the process, as for instance [p. 168] in the case of C. H. Dodd[4] and J. Jeremias,[5] a primary "setting in Jesus' life" is distinguished from a secondary "community setting", to which W. Marxsen's[6] "third sociological setting" can be added--that of the redaction of the gospels: A traditional unit can, in the course of its history, have had a three-fold "sociological setting", namely a historical application-situation.[7]

Already R. Bultmann rejected such a reduction of the concept (from a sociological cultural-model-typology to a historical specification-of-contingency): What is meant by the concept "sociological setting" is "not the origin of a single account (as a report *about* something) within a *single* historic situation or person, but the relation of a literary segment (as literary) to a *general* historic situation (such as war, cult, commerce, etc.) out of which the genre that belongs to that segment developed".[8] "Sociological setting" is a concept belonging to a cultural-model-*typology*, which generalizes by means of the analogy principle, and thereby is solely restricted to the sociological posture of form criticism,[9] and is not to be transferred without further reflection in the same sense as a posture, which, as does redaction criticism, concedes greater latitude to the individual, to the contingents, or which is interested in individual specification, as is history. Is it incorrect, therefore, with respect to the framing of the "small units" and their application in the gospel form, to speak of their "sociological setting"?

2. The Different Natures of the Oral "Setting in
    Folk-Life" and the Literary Application of the
    "Small Units".

We might expect such an objection to be raised against
the comments in #5 above, which we want to expand upon here.
Are not the sociological laws of the oral "sociological setting" a linguistic phenomenon entirely different from the
literary framing of a "small unit", so that we may not in
both cases utilize the concept "sociological setting"? Affirmation of this question would, at any rate, [p. 169] confirm the thesis in #8 above, that the concept can only be
transferred to the facts of the literary level with difficulty, that in other words there already was from the beginnings
of the form-critical and analytical terminology an essential
distinction between the oral and the written. But with what
type of distinction are we involved? We can take up once
more the issues discussed above in #7, sections 2.g. and 4,
and refer again to the different natures of the oral and the
written.

While in the oral there is an immediate unity of genre
and "sociological setting", *the written delivers its "sociological setting" at most mediately alongside itself*, so that
it can be made accessible as a horizon of understanding.[10]
Naturally this distinction does not automatically determine
an antithesis between sociological laws with respect to the
oral and individuality with respect to the written. Even an
exclusively-written genre (for example an advertising circular)[11] is subject, to a greater or lesser degree, to sociological laws: "The person who wants to attain something with
what he/she writes must make use of a conventional genre."[12]
But the decisive distinction in the nature of the oral and
the written also conditions the transformation of the concept "sociological setting" we have discussed:[13] While the

nature of an oral genre is an *esse in potentia, esse in actu, esse in functione*, which is actualized when the time of the "sociological setting" has arrived (when the sociological application-situation occurs), the nature of a written genre is an *esse in objectivatione scripturae* and *hence fundamentally not unconditionally dependent upon a particular time of application*. While the oral folklore work must "presuppose a group which takes it up and sanctions it",[14] and hence in its nature, analogously to *langue*, is as a whole dependent upon an actualization that transmits it further in a particular "sociological setting",[15] *the written genre can "exist" as that which is present to itself*, even when it no longer has a "sociological setting"; in that case it has become a "text".[16]

This differentiated nature is also related to the *transformation of the concept "sociological setting" in its transference to the written* discussed in #5 above. A genre is dependent upon a "sociological setting" in the oral, because it only exists potentially as a creation at the level of *langue*, needing to be actualized in the *parole*.[17] [p. 170] As soon as the genre enters writing, and especially when it enters into the literary "framework", the unconditioned nature of its dependence upon a "sociological setting" changes: To the extent to which it may have a "sociological setting" as a portion of a written "framework genre", and furthermore can indeed maintain its old "sociological setting" in simultaneous oral existence,[18] so it will be integrated into a different sort of linguistic structure by its literary framework;[19] to the linguistic peculiarity of the structure belongs the integration of the parts in its texture by *simultaneous* application to the "sociological setting" determined by the "framework genre". Therefore the concept "sociological setting" implies, with respect to the components of the "frame-

work genre", their *structural insertion into the new genre,*[19a]
so that the conceptual expansion anticipated in #5 is thoroughly legitimate and corresponds to the alteration of the linguistic contexts. Both *sociological* laws appropriate to the application-situation, and *linguistic* laws indicated by the linguistic structure of the "framework genre", those of the *langue
écrite,* belong to the "sociological setting".[20] The dependence
of the oral genre on the situation of the *parole* (cf. #7, section 2.g.) has become that which is textually circumscribed by
the "framework genre", which is a linguistic context. If the
"sociological setting" were previously a phenomenon of the
esse in potentia, now it has become a phenomenon of the *esse
in objectivatione scripturae* (cf. #7, sections 3.b. and 4.a.),
so that the linguistic manner of appearance of the genre (and
with it, of the "sociological setting") has been fundamentally
altered: If it appeared in the oral *on the basis of* the
parole, it *exists* in the "literary" framework as *langue.* This
alteration provokes the guess that the "setting" determining
or surrounding the manner of appearance is by no means something like a "pre-linguistic" phenomenon prior to language.[20a]
In the long run, is the "sociological setting" a "linguistic"
phenomenon in itself? This question will be positively answered in #10.

3. The Sociological Continuity of the Tradition
   of the Gospels.

   (a) The Continuity of Faith as a Socio-
       logical Continuity.

Some time ago, H. Schürmann made a proposal that could be
used as a counter-argument against the thesis represented in
this book.[21] [p. 171] Fundamentally agreeing with form criticism, and especially emphasizing the sociological character

of the "sociological setting", Schürmann aims at overcoming a
false restriction of the form-critical method: Is it proper
to limit the analysis of [socio-economic] classes to the post-
Easter tradition in the thesis of the deep cleft between the
post- and the pre-Easter Jesus-community, between the primitive church and Jesus?[22] *With what propriety can we exclusively identify the sociological "community" which transmitted
the oral Jesus-tradition with the "post-Easter community of
faith"?* Did "'Christian faith' really first come into existence after Easter"?[23] "At any rate, no form critic will be
able to deny that there was already in the pre-Easter group of
disciples the creation of a community which represents a sociological phenomenon."[24] The presence of "genuine" words of
Jesus is explained by Schürmann by means of a continuity connecting this pre-Easter community and the post-Easter community, in spite of all discontinuity: "Only if there was a cul-
tivated continuum of tradition between the pre-Easter group of
disciples and the post-Easter community of faith are we able
to trust the transmitted words of the Lord."[25] This *sociological* continuity and this continuum of *tradition* also represent at the same time a *confessional* continuity: "the fact
of discipleship and the occurrence of a pre-Easter group of
disciples, testifies to some kind of disciples' confession
to Jesus' words and thereby to himself."[26] For the expansion
of form-critical class analysis, it is enough, "that the disciples who followed Jesus created a community very clearly
separated from the environment by the fact of that discipleship and the confession to Jesus it entailed, a community
which as such had certain clearly recognizable 'typical situations and types of behavior' exerting pressure toward the
creation of tradition".[27] In this manner it is possible to
distinguish a "setting in the inner life" of the pre-Easter

group of disciples[28] and a "setting in the outer life" of this group.[29]

(b) The "Setting in the Inner Life".

The first term--perhaps an echo of W. Herrmann--indicates the immediacy of the relationship of the obedient disciples to Jesus' words and the confession to these words arising from this relationship, which became the enabling foundation of the first creation of tradition.[30] [p. 172] Schürmann concedes that he thereby theologically oversteps the sociological components of form criticism,[31] since the tradition actually required no further "setting in the outer life", i.e., no further sociological situation,[32] although the various "confessional situations" can also be understood as quasi-sociological dimensions.[33] Just here lies the critical point of this conception, which is to be further investigated! But the "setting in the inner life" actually concerns only the "inner form" of the logia, i.e., the content, not the form.[34]

(c) The "Setting in the Outer Life".

Rather the "outer form", i.e., the linguistic formation, is conditioned by the "setting in the outer life": "at first a typical *outer* situation and an outer type of behavior sets in motion an extensive tradition-process and keeps it alive."[35] The *ratio essendi* of the tradition given with the "setting in the inner life" is not sufficient; it only creates something like the un-vivified *materia*; sociological laws must enter in and lend life to the *materia*. Hence we may (and must?) assume that Jesus mnemotechnically impressed upon his disciples the logia material for proclamation.[36] Deduction therefore suggests: "that the beginnings of the logia-tradition must lie in the pre-Easter group of disciples and hence with Jesus

himself. But in this manner we will have attained form-critical access to the 'historical Jesus', since the 'historical
Jesus' is now himself a component of the occurrence of tradition (as its initiator)."[37]

(d) Separation of "Form" and "Content"?

Schürmann's conception only indirectly touches our study,
since first of all he concerns himself only with the logia-
tradition and not with that of the gospels as a whole, and
secondly because he does not consider the sociological continuity of the oral and the written, but only that between the
pre- and the post-Easter Jesus-community. But in this sociological continuity lies the whole problematics of his basically "historicizing" expansion of the concept "sociological setting". What is initially striking here is the hardly sensible
separation of "form" and "content", "inner" and "outer".[38] Of
what is the "setting in the inner life" actually the *ratio essendi*? Hardly of the linguistic form, if this is dependent
upon the "setting in the outer life". [p. 173] If not that,
then perhaps of a somewhat formless "content"? But what would
that be, if precisely the confession to Jesus' word is a linguistic phenomenon? What then is actually constitutive for
the linguistic phenomenon both of the confession and of the
transmission that belongs inseparably to it: the *linguistic*
phenomenon of the "setting in the inner life", or the *sociological* phenomenon of the "setting in the outer life"? The
antithesis leads Schürmann's intended differentiation *ad ab-
surdum*. The differentiation, that evokes W. v. Humboldt, between "inner" linguistic form and "outer" linguistic form
succumbs to the same dilemma, since by the "inner linguistic
form" is meant precisely the "content" *conditioned by* the
"gestalt",[39] so that sociological laws are no longer necessary. What concrete manner does the continuity finally have,

if on the one hand "we must assume a strict discontinuity between the pre- and post-Easter confession and hence also between the pre- and post-Easter proclamation",[40] and if on the
other hand it is the *kyrios* and the *pneuma* that initially makes
the "Christian tradition what it actually is"?[41] Are supra-
natural interventions really necessary if the sociological
continuity is sufficient? To what extent then is there a
linguistic continuity between the word event of the "setting
in the inner life" determined by Jesus' immediacy *before*
Easter, and that "setting in the outer life" determined by
Jesus' mediacy in the spirit, and by ties to the Jesus-tradition, *after* Easter? As a whole these are questions which must
remain unresolved, so that Schürmann's conception cannot be
considered a serious objection to the theses of this work. I
think that Schürmann suspected that the "sociological setting"
itself could be a linguistic phenomenon, but immediately can-
celed this out with sociological concepts, which better suit
the traditional sociological posture of form criticism and the
precedence it gives to "non-linguistic" or "pre-linguistic"
phenomena rather than to linguistic phenomena.[42] At this
point we can move on to one final consideration of the concept of the "sociological setting".[42a]

268

Notes to #9

1. Cf. Rohde, *Redakt. Methode*, 23ff.

2. Cf. M. Albertz, *Die synoptischen Streitgespräche*, 1921, 59ff.

3. Cf. Fascher, *Formgesch. Methode*, 213f., 221.

4. Cf. C. H. Dodd, *The Parables of the Kingdom*, 1961-new ed., 85: "The original 'setting in life' of any authentic saying of Jesus was of course provided by the actual conditions of His ministry."

5. Cf. J. Jeremias, *Die Gleichnisse Jesu*, 1965-7th ed., 17: "the parables must be situated within the situation of Jesus' life!"

6. Cf. Marxsen, *Evglist Mk.*, 12.

7. Cf. A. Vögtle, *ZKTh* 86 (1964) 394f.

8. Bultmann, *ThLZ* 50 (1925) 316. Cf. Bultmann, *Syn. Trad.* [Germ. ed.], 4, 40; H. Schürmann, *Traditionsgeschichtliche Untersuchungen zu den synoptischen Evangelien*, 1968, 47f.

9. Cf. indeed Taylor, *Formation*, 36: "All the Form-Critics rightly emphasize the social aspects of the formative process."

10. Cf. above, p. [139f.].

11. Cf. Koch, *op. cit.*, 3f.

12. *Ibid.*, 5.

13. Cf. above, pp. [134f., 143].

14. Cf. #7, n. 128, above.

15. Cf. above, p. [143].

16. On the hermeneutical phenomenon of the "text", cf. Fuchs, *Hermeneutik*, 27ff., 47ff.; Fuchs, *Aufs.*, vol. 1, 93ff., 97ff.; vol. 3, 420ff.; Betti, *Allg. Auslegungslehre*, 265ff.

17. Cf. above, p. [51].

18. Cf. above, p. [86f.].

19. Cf. above, p. [89f.].

19a [+1978: Insofar as "insertion" is one of a set of linguistic transformations, it is a text-syntactical operation constituting contexts. This is the reason why "Generative Poetics" analyzed text-syntactical operations in its initial research.]

20. Cf. above, p. [136f.].

20a [+1978: Today I stress more expressly that every exegete has to clarify his position towards a Leninist icon-theory by which a "pre-linguistic" *materia* is the basis prior to *spiritus*. My position is clearly the reverse: Mental processes determine *what* can be seen as a "material object".]

21. H. Schürmann, "Die vorösterlichen Zusammenhänge der Logiontradition," now in his *Traditionsgeschichtliche Untersuchungen zu den synoptischen Evangelien*, 1968, 39-65.

22. Cf. *ibid.*, 41f.

23. *Ibid.*, 42.

24. *Ibid.*, 47.

25. *Ibid.*, 45.

26. *Ibid.*, 48.

27. *Ibid.*, 50.

28. Cf. *ibid.*, 51-55.

29. Cf. *ibid.*, 56-63.

30. Cf. *ibid.*, 51f.

31. So Jüngel, *Pls u. Jesus*, 299.

32. *Op. cit.*, 53.

33. Cf. *ibid.*, 55.

34. Cf. *ibid.*, 54, 55, n. 72.

35. *Ibid.*, 56.

36. Cf. *ibid.*, 56ff.

37. *Ibid.*, 63.

38. Cf. above, pp. [65ff., 161f.].

39. Cf. W. Porzig, "Der Begriff der inneren Sprachform,"
IF 41 (1923) 150-69; O. Funke, *Innere Sprachform*, 1924; L.
Weisgerber, *Grunzüge der inhaltbezogenen Grammatik*, 1962-
3rd ed., 14ff. Cf. also the bibliography given in #7, n. 31.

40. Schürmann, *op. cit.*, 49.

41. *Ibid.*, 64.

42. Cf. below, p. [174ff.].

42a [+1978: Vielhauer, *Literaturgeschichte*, 289, n. 22,
remonstrates against my ignorance of Schürmann's proof that
Luke 1:1-4 is a "historical" source. What if this "proof"
is dependent upon his untenable language-philosophy analyzed
above?]

#10. *The Cultural Context-Situation of Speech-*
Events in General Linguistics.

Here we might draw together some of the manifold lines of
connection between linguistics, especially research concerning
functions and fields,[1] and form-critical theory concerning the
"sociological setting". However we must be satisfied in this
brief excursus with the important linguistic reflections of
C. K. Ogden, I. A. Richards,[2] and the findings of the ethnolo-
gist B. Malinowski,[3] which should be given more attention within theology.[3a]

    1. "Sociological Setting" as a Psycholinguistic
       Context.

Ogden and Richards analyze the psychological and hermeneutical processes occurring in language when signs are exchanged. An appropriate theory of signs (semiotics) must take
into account the "sign-situations".[4] They can be described in
the following way, using the terminology of linguistic behaviorism.[5]

The key to the understanding of the "sign-situation" is
the observation of the process of interpreting experience as a
"sign", which is always present to some extent:[6] "In all
thinking we are interpreting signs."[7] The sign is the stimulus to which we react [p. 175] by means of interpretation.
"Our interpretation of any sign is our psychological reaction
to it, as determined by our past experience in similar situations, and by our present experience."[8] Every earlier stimulus has, as a type of adaptation, left behind in the organism

272

an engram, according to which we control interpretation of every subsequent stimulus:[9] "A sign is always a stimulus and sufficient to call up the engram formed by that stimulus."[10] *In this way a kind of psychological "context" occurs*, according to which we interpret every new experience by application of the analogy principle;[11] "experience has the character of recurrence, that is, comes to us in more or less uniform contexts", thanks to which alone interpretation is at all possible.[12] So "observable correlations or contextual uniformities among events"[13] arise, as it were, chains of "sign-situations".[14] We are confronting once more, in behavioristic reformulation, the old Platonic theory of knowledge: *knowledge is the re-cognition of earlier experience*; "without such recurrence or partial uniformity no prediction, no inference, no recognition, no inductive generalization, no knowledge or probable opinion as to what is not immediately given, would be possible".[15]

Ogden and Richards then investigate the psychological and external "contexts" in detail,[16] proceeding from the following definition: "A context is a set of entities (things or events) related in a certain way; these entities have each a character such that other sets or entities occur having the same characters and related by the same relation; and these occur 'nearly uniformly'."[17] With that, in the abstract terminology of linguistics, we have a definition of what is known to form criticism as the "sociological setting": The form-critical "sociological setting" may not be described in the sense of a "sociological" phenomenon, since its psycholinguistic components are thereby left out. Rather psycholinguistics leads to precision for those cultural types of relation only vaguely described as "sociological" during the period when form criticism was being established, since the sociological model of referents was never delineated *in extenso*.[17a] It would be interesting now to compare in detail the form-critical theory with the psycholinguistic explanation of the "symbol situations",[18] but the following will have to suffice.

[p. 176] Ogden and Richards develop a detailed picture of the psychological and hermeneutical processes in listener and speaker, and their interlacing in the laws of the "context-situations". These are not only something quasi-"external", something added to the "signs". Rather since the "situations" result from the summation and re-interpretation of the engrams resulting from earlier sign-stimuli, all of history and culture belongs to the *linguistic* context of a "sign": *The "sociological setting" is itself of a "linguistic" nature.*[19] Culture is a somewhat circular arrangement of "linguistic contexts",[20] of linguistic graspings toward the world,[21] which is constantly expanding (drawing all previous experiences contributing linguistically to "contexts" into larger "contexts".)

2. The "Context-Situation" in Cultural Anthropology.

B. Malinowski, on the basis of concrete philological and grammatical materials from Melanesia, comes to these same results independently. The "significance" of words and the "meaning" of sentences is clarified, in the analysis of totally foreign cultures, only on the basis of their concrete speech-situation.[22] Both ethnology and social psychology, as linguistics in the widest sense, as well as linguistics in the narrower sense, are parts of this analysis.[23] The concept "context of situation" must therefore be expanded so that the entire culture of a people is encompassed as the "linguistic" context:[24] *"The whole situation consists in what happens linguistically."*[25]

With that it becomes clear that previous form-critical theory of the "sociological setting" has focused only upon a portion of a much larger complex. The "sociological setting" belongs much more immediately to the forms or genres than has previously been recognized, since as a "linguistic" phenomenon it belongs to culture as the spiritual and linguistic horizon of understanding of all contextual "situations". Not only are the forms or genres linguistic phenomena, but also the "settings" belonging to them, and the entire culture, the culture-model as the linguistic horizon of understanding and creation of a culture area. Therefore it is methodologically improper to separate the speech-events as linguistic phenomena from the apparently "non-linguistic" "situations" considered to exist objectively in themselves. The "sociological setting" has [p. 177] a much greater significance in linguistics than previously has been expressly emphasized. *The linguistic theory of the "contextual situation of the signs" is the methodological framework for the form-critical theory of the "sociological setting".*

With that the problem of the extent to which the "sociological setting" is a sociological dimension which ontologically constitutes the form of language resurfaces. E. Jüngel has attempted to resolve this problem by giving precedence to the eschatological language-event over the sociological phenomena.[26] We have already indicated the methodological problems that result from such an enterprise. However we are dealing here with questions whose treatment has not been finally concluded and can only be further resolved in connection with more extensive linguistic studies. For now it is enough that the problem presented here has been recognized clearly and identified as a candid question.

Notes to #10

1. The theory of linguistic functions is treated in linguistics as the functional and structural effect of linguistic
phenomena. Cf. K. Bühler, *Sprachtheorie*, 1965-2nd ed.; F.
Kainz, *Psychologie der Sprache*, vol. 1, 1967-4th ed., 172-
266; W. Porzig, *Das Wunder der Sprache*, 1957-2nd ed., 344-75;
Schökel, *Sprache Gottes*, 91ff. -- Linguistic field-theory
treats the structural value of the position and significance
of individual words in its contextual (especially spiritual
and cultural) relationship to related or connected words.
Cf. J. Trier, *Der deutsche Wortschatz im Sinnbezirk des Ver-
standes*, 1931; Trier, "Das sprachliche Feld," *Neue Jahrb. für
Wiss. u. Jugendbildung* 10 (1934) 428-49; L. Weisgerber, "Die
Sprachfelder in der geistigen Erschliessung der Welt," *Festschrift J. Trier*, 1954, 34-49.

2. Cf. C. K. Ogden and I. A. Richards, *The Meaning of
Meaning*, 1966-new ed., 48-76, 209-42.

3. B. Malinowski, "The Problem of Meaning in Primitive
Languages," in *ibid.*, 296-36.

3a [+1978: Today I would also refer to speech-act
theory and the theory of the complex presupposition-situation
of communication. Cf. Güttgemanns, *Einleitung in die Linguistik für Textwissenschaftler* 1, 1978, 94ff.]

4. Cf. *ibid.*, 48ff. Cf. also C. Lévi-Strauss, *Struk-
turale Anthropologie* [Germ. transl.], 1969.

5. Cf. above, #3, n. 134.

6. Cf. *op. cit.*, 50f.

7. *Ibid.*, 244.

8. *Ibid.*

9. The practitioner of hermeneutics would speak in this
instance of the clarification of the preunderstanding by means
of an event which has to be newly integrated.

10. *Ibid.*, 53.

11. Cf. *ibid.*, 53f.

12. *Ibid.*, 55.

13. *Ibid.*, 52.

14. Cf. *ibid.*, 245.

15. *Ibid.*, 57.

16. Cf. *ibid.*, 54ff.

17. *Ibid.*, 58, italicized in original.

17a On psycholinguistics, cf. Hörmann, *op. cit.*, 359-80; further bibliography there. [+1978: The critique given to my book if incorrect if it is a criticism of a lack of sociology: The interference between language and "social" phenomena is much more complex. Cf. Güttgemanns, *Einführung in die Linguistik*, 52ff.]

18. Cf. *ibid.*, 209ff.

19. Cf. *ibid.*, 223ff.

20. Cf. *ibid.*, 220.

21. Cf. L. Weisgerber, *Die Muttersprache im Aufbau unserer Kultur*, 1957-2nd ed.

22. Malinowski, *op. cit.*, 300ff.

23. Cf. *ibid.*, 301f., 305.

24. Cf. *ibid.*, 306.

25. *Ibid.*, 315, my emphasis.

26. Cf. above, p. [65ff.].

#11. *The Disintegration of Gospel Form Criticism: Willi Marxsen.*

1. The Disintegration of the Concept "Synoptic Authors": Willi Marxsen.

We saw in #4 how W. Marxsen argued for a methodological distinction between form and redaction criticism by strongly emphasizing the individual achievement of the evangelists. By applying himself to the synoptic authors' various expressions of the gospel form, Marxsen established sharp differences in their theological meaning, attaining thereby to a theological disintegration of the concept of the "synoptic authors": "From the fact that the works of the 'synoptic authors' (and that of John) bear the same name, are called 'gospels', we may not conclude that they represent the same genre. In terms of *this* viewpoint we have simply to recognize that: There are no 'synoptic' gospels."[1] Marxsen considers it dangerous "to speak in more than a very external sense of synoptic authors. Theologically utilized, this concept is an inadmissible harmonization; indeed, theologically regarded, Mark and John are more closely related to each other than Mark is to Luke or to Matthew."[2] What is decisive with respect to the gospel form is not the undeniable number of parallels between their materials,[3] but their theological intentions accentuated in each case by the different "frameworks". According to Marxsen's pupil A. Suhl, closer examination demonstrates "that the concept 'synoptic author' can only signify in a very attenuated sense what is common to certain transmissional complexes and that in the case of the redactors of the first three gospels, we meet three very different and thoroughly indepen-

dent theologians, whose intention in each case we try to comprehend. To be sure they utilize the same material to a great
extent, but they apply it for quite different messages."[4]

[p. 179] Since the content of the theological messages
of the three synoptic writers differs greatly, in spite of
their relatedness in material and composition, in these circumstances the question arises whether the acceptance of a
gospel form common to the synoptic writers can be maintained
at all: "Can we refer to a gospel 'genre'? Could it not have
been that each church, or each period in which the evangelists
lived, developed a 'form' quite particularly corresponding to
its own problems and for its own purposes?"[5] A. N. Wilder
also considers it a mistake "to think of the four Gospels as
all of a type, and even to think of the Synoptic Gospels as
similar. They are very different and thus evidence the new
enlargement of literary means."[6] Alterations of pericopes
which occur between the different gospels are, according to
Marxsen, "not in the long run alterations of the pericopes
themselves, but the evangelists' alterations with respect to
the total work".[7] A final consequence of this would be that
the three synoptic authors because of their marked theological differences can be compared, in part, with respect to the
material they share, but not with respect to their common
form, since there was no common form. Accordingly, the gospel of Mark would be the single exemplar of the gospel form.[8]
The "synoptic gospels" only provide information about the
tradition history of the "synoptic" *materials*, but not about
the tradition history of the *form* of the gospels.

2. Form Criticism as a Problem of Literary
    Criticism.

In my opinion the problem Marxsen has raised is not just
a random and isolated exaggeration of the gospel form, which

can be ignored, but a foundational problem of any genuine *form-history* that, however astonishing it may be, has never been thoroughly treated in biblical exegesis, although it must have been a problem whenever a literary-*historical* presentation has been attempted. We must find our bearings here by means of a new and unavoidable [p. 180] overstepping of the boundaries in terms of "profane" literary criticism, treating the issue here as a brief excursus. Assistance is at hand in the writings of K. Viëtor and R. Wellek and A. Warren.[9]

What actually is the nature of the literary genres? Is the genre-type an "abstraction, i.e., a conceptual and schematic determination of that which so to speak is only in a particular instance the actual foundational structure, the 'general nature' of the genre"?[10] Is the literary classification of genres merely yet another artistic arrangement-principle,[11] a quasi-static naming, which is insufficient for the dynamics of historical evolution,[12] and the imperceptible graduated transformation of the genres?[13] Are there in linguistic works any "pure" genres having a sort of trans-temporal unchangeability (linguistic idealism),[14] or are they in view of the predominating "mixed genres" a purely scientific ennumeration (linguistic nominalism)?[15] Marxsen, at any rate, appears to have struggled with such questions unawares.

Wellek and Warren reject nominalism in that they coordinate the genre as a sociological "institution" with a historical dialectics,[16] so that both the changeability of the genres[17] as well as their historical continuity is assimilated to the dialectics[18] and the dilemma of a genre-*history* is resolved.[19] The structure of a genre contains the elements of identity and dynamics in identical ways, so that *the historical process of genre-history implicates structural laws and individuality*:[20] Literature is a whole system of works, "which, with the growth of new works, constantly changes its

relationships and develops as a self-altering whole".[21]   Therefore literary criticism ought to describe the quasi-"gestaltist", historical, and dialectical interaction of the individual
genres with one another: "History individualizes not simply
general values..., but the historical process always brings
about new and previously unknown [p. 181] value forms which
cannot be determined in advance."[22]   The problem of genre-
history is therefore to be resolved the way the historical
relationship between *langue* and *parole* is:[23]   A concrete
example of a genre is a dialectical and dynamic relationship
between regulative structural elements (*langue*)[24] and individual actualization (*parole*).[25]   Thereby a neo-Darwinian concept of evolution is avoided by form-*history*,[26] even though in
individual instances it can be more difficult to specify the
precise proportions of regulative structure and individual
actualization in a particular literary work.   What has to be
avoided above all is a simple "division" [Teilung--i.e., between the two elements; W.G.D.].

It is now clear how the problem raised by Marxsen could
be resolved.   It seems to me that with Marxsen's question we
also have to deal with the question *whether literary "gestalts"
can have a history*.   For example when Marxsen affirms that the
alterations of the parts within the synoptic gospels ultimately
represent an alteration of the total work, he thereby *de facto*
introduces a gestaltist argument.[27]   Does the gospel form as
"literary gestalt" have neither a traditio-historical genesis
nor a history of variations, since it must be understood consistently in terms of the individual compositions of the evangelists?   At any event, such a question would have to be addressed in one way or another not only with respect to the
gospel form, but fundamentally with respect to the form criticism of any language form.   The present work intends to treat
this as a meaningful and candid question with reference to the

gospel form, working toward a renewed treatment once more.

3. Is the Gospel Form a Redactional Act or a
   Result of the Collective-Tradition?

Marxsen's answer to the alternative suggested here clearly excludes the first possibility. But with his answer there
is a danger of a disintegration of the dialectics between the
collective and sociological laws of the *langue* and the individual originality of the *parole*, or in traditional terminology and a somewhat altered [p. 182] way of asking the question: it threatens the disintegration of the dialectical relationship between tradition and redaction.

This relationship has been extensively elucidated with
respect to the Lukan writings,[28] with the result that the tradition comprised by the form of "sources" becomes even more
inaccessible,[29] and the independent theology of Luke acquires
even sharper contours.[30] Luke appears in such a perspective
to deal so freely with his materials that the question must be
placed as to "whether the tradition that has become the material has any theological significance at all. Accordingly
once the weight of Luke's contribution itself is explained by
means of his writings, the danger arises that the question
about the tradition retreats behind that concerning his own
contribution."[31]

A similar danger arises also in Marxsen's conception of
the role of the individuality of the evangelists constituting
the gospel form. Even if the intentions of his work could be
clearly and sufficiently described theologically in every instance, it would still remain uncertain: *first*, to what extent the evangelist is merely the most prominent representative
of a "school",[32] or how far in his work the necessities of an
influence deriving from a "sociological setting" that stands

in tension to his own theological intentions have gained an upper hand;[33] and *second*, whether in this manner the relationship of the evangelist to his tradition is insufficiently reflected. Even if the "framework" of the form of the gospels has been conceived entirely independently of the individual materials, [p. 183] it does not remain entirely untouched by the insertion of the "material" even if we assume with Marxsen an interrelation of *all* elements within the linguistic "gestalt" of the gospel form, and do not now absolutize the "framework" in redaction criticism, rather than the absolute composition of the "material" in form criticism. *In the gestaltist perspective, "framework" and "material", in a dialectic interaction, commonly create the linguistic "gestalt" of the gospel form*, so that the description of this form as a simple addition of "material" and "framework" is inappropriate in every respect, and rules out an antithetical opposition between the two dimensions as non-dialectical. The theological motifs of the "material" can no longer be utilized only as a means for the expression of the theological intention of the "framework", but have also been influential in causing alteration precisely with respect to this intention,[34] especially when larger complexes of material may have been available to the evangelists[35] which could be less flexibly inserted into a different "framework" than could pericopes. In other words: The relationship between "framework" and individual units of material is much more differentiated than is normally recognized. We will return to this issue once more in #12. Future analysis should be aware of the dialectics specified here and guard itself from simple alternatives. *To what extent and in what sense is the gospel form a linguistic "gestalt"?* For orientation we can best turn to the disciplines related to linguistics.

Notes to #11

1. Marxsen, *Evglist Mk*, 144; the last sentence is italicized in the original.

2. Marxsen, *Exegese und Verkündigung*, 1957, 40. Cf.
also Bultmann, *Syn. Trad.* [Germ. ed.], 397: "But as a whole
they (*scil.* Matthew and Luke) have not further developed the
type created by Mark." "The gospel of John first actually
represents further development of the type created by Mark;
in John *mythos* has certainly completely conquered the historical tradition."

3. Cf. Marxsen, *ZThK* 52 (1955) 257f.

4. A. Suhl, *Die Funktion der alttestamentlichen Zitate
und Anspielungen im Markusevangelium*, 1965, 9f.

5. Marxsen, *Evglist Mk.*, 13. Cf. already Bultmann, *Syn.
Trad.*, 400: The gospel form is hardly to be designated as a
literary genre. "In the synoptic gospels the literary form
as such has attained no life of its own." The canonization
of the four gospels hindered a literary history of the gospel.
"To speak of the gospel as a literary genre, therefore, is
scarcely possible; the gospel is a dimension of the history
of dogma and cult." The mode of inquiry here, however, is
clearly different.

6. A. N. Wilder, *The Language of the Gospel*, 1964, 37.

7. Marxsen, *Exegese u. Verk.*, 41. [+1978: It is to be
stressed once more that such "alterations" are text-syntactical operations, so that only a text-syntactical grammar can be
the basis of resolving the problem.]

8. Cf. Marxsen, *Evglist Mk.*, 145: "If Mark is also the
creator of this literary work, his followers are so far from
him that there may be no exaggeration in speaking of a total
difference between them."

9. Cf. K. Viëtor, "Probleme der literarischen Gattung-
geschichte," *DVjs* 9 (1931) 425-45; Wellek and Warren, *op.
cit.*, 202-14, 227-45.

10. Viëtor, *op. cit.*, italicized in original.

11. Cf. Cl. Vincent, *Théorie des genres littéraires*, 1951-21st ed., 15.

12. Cf. F. Brunetiere, *L'évolution des genres dans l'histoire de la littérature*, 1849; Vincent, *op. cit.*, 4ff. [+1978: Today I would refer also to J. Mukařovský, *Kapitel aus der Poetik*, 1967, and *Kapitel aus der Aesthetik*, 1970, and to J. Tynjanov, "Ueber die literarische Evolution," in J. Striedter, ed., *Russischer Formalismus*, 1969, 433-61. Cf. also the brilliant sketch of the problematics in K. Hempfer, *Gattungstheorie*, 1973.]

13. Cf. Vincent, *op. cit.*, 10ff.; J. Petersen, "Zur Lehre von den Dichtungsgattungen," in *Festschrift für August Sauer*, 1925, 72-116.

14. Cf. Wellek and Warren, *op. cit.*, 203, 210.

15. So B. Croce, *Aesthetik als Wissenschaft vom Ausdruck und allgemeine Sprachwissenschaft*, transl. K. Federn, 1905, 35ff., 109ff.

16. Wellek and Warren, *op. cit.*, 203.

17. *Ibid.*, 203f.

18. Cf. *ibid.*, 213.

19. Cf. *ibid.*, 236f.

20. Cf. *ibid.*, 230f.

21. *Ibid.*, 231.

22. *Ibid.*, 233.

23. Cf. above, p. [51].

24. Cf. Wellek and Warren, *op. cit.*, 237.

25. Cf. also above, pp. [53f., 143].

26. Cf. Wellek and Warren, *op. cit.*, 231f.; K. Riezler, "Ueber den Begriff der historischen Entwicklung," *DVjs* 4 (1926) 193-225.

27. Cf. below, p. [185].

28. Cf. K. L. Schmidt, "Der geschichtliche Wert des lukanischen Aufrisses der Geschichte Jesu," *ThStKr* 91 (1918) 277-92; M. Dibelius, "Stilkritisches zur Apostelgeschichte," in his *Aufsätze zur Apostelgeschichte*, ed. H. Greeven, 1953, 9-28; E. Haenchen, "Tradition und Komposition in der Apostelgeschichte," *ZThK* 52 (1955) 205-25, as well as E. Grässer's report in *ThR* 26 (1960) 131ff.

29. The assumption of sources in Acts is confronted with growing scepticism today. Cf. for instance G. Schille, "Die Fragwürdigkeit eines Itinerars der Paulusreisen," *ThLZ* 84 (1959) 165-74; E. Haenchen, *Die Apostelgeschichte*, 1959, 14*, 72ff.; Haenchen, "Das 'Wir' in der Apostelgeschichte und das Itinerar," *ZThK* 58 (1961) 329-66; H. Conzelmann, *Die Apostelgeschichte*, 1963, 4-6. Cf. on the other hand R. Bultmann, "Zur Frage nach den Quellen der Apostelgeschichte," in his *Exegetica*, ed. E. Dinkler, 1967, 412-23; P. Vielhauer, *GGA* 221 (1969) 4-12.

30. Cf. the sketch of the history of research in M. Rese, *Alttestamentliche Motive in der Christologie des Lukas*, 1969, 11ff.

31. H. Flender, *Heil und Geschichte in der Theologie des Lukas*, 1965, 9f.

32. Cf. K. Stendahl, *The School of St. Matthew*, 1954; Koch, *op. cit.*, 63: "Most of the biblical writings are not the work of individual persons, but originate in teaching institutions, in *schools*, whether from prophets, priests, or evangelists."

33. The evangelist creates his work in a particular situation, his work is simultaneously intended for a specific "sociological setting", which has a decisive influence not only on the creation, but also on the further passing-on of the form. With this a trans-individual element entered the form-critical process from the beginning, which was made stronger by the objectification of the written (cf. above, p. [138f.]).

34. H. Meyer, "Geplante und gewordene Formen eines Schriftstellers," *Studium Generale* 8 (1955) 41-50, makes clear the tension between literary plan and final work in his biography of Goethe. His observations there are valid in general for literary criticism.

35. Cf. the analysis below, p. [223ff.].

#12. *Gestaltist Insights Concerning the*
          Gospel Form.

One of the most important and fruitful theories in the
humanities is the so-called *gestalt-theory*.[1] It has proved
itself so reliable in psychology,[2] linguistics,[3] and literary
criticism,[4] that it must now be considered one of the central
methods in these disciplines. Because of the limitations of
this work I cannot present details of its founding and scope;
for our context the following suggestions will have to be sufficient.

1. The So-Called "Trans-Summativity" of the
      "Gestalt"-Idea.

Chr. v. Ehrenfels, in his foundational work for all of
gestalt theory,[5] lays down several "gestalt-criteria", among
which the most important is the so-called "trans-summativity"
[Uebersummitivität, E.'s neologism]. The "gestalts" are not
"just a collection of elements, but...something (in contrast
to the elements they touch upon) new, and up to a certain extent, independent".[6] For example, a melody is more than the
sum of all its notes, since it can be transposed into another
pitch without losing its gestaltist effect (the Ehrenfels-
criterion of "transposability").[7] As a "gestalt" it possesses
a so-called "trans-logical plus", i.e., a sense or an aesthetic effect which does not arise from the [p. 185] aggregate
of the elements.[8] The "gestalt"-sense is not an association
of elements,[9] but of complexes.[10] It arises not out of the
disposition of a simple co-existence of presentations, but

from the disposition of the consciousness of subject relations, from dispositional knowledge and its actualization.[11] Cognitive psychology[12] has investigated such processes experimentally and made them understandable as associations of complexes.[13] From this the principle is produced, "that the simple sequence of presentations without conscious relationships between them does not allow the conclusion that reproductions are determined by the immediate contacts between them".[14] Not the elements, but only the complexes are associated.[15] "The whole perceptions are not simply aggregates of elements, but complexes."[16] Insofar as the "gestalt"-sense intended thereby with respect to linguistic phenomena is a thought, it can be stated, with K. Bühler, "that the thought is a whole, which only contains dependent components, not independent ones".[17]

Hence linguistic "gestalts", according to the Ehrenfels-criterion of "trans-summativity", possess a unique unity which must, in G. Ipsen's terms, "be considered an effective unity".[18] This unity, named the "innerness" of the "gestalt" by Ipsen,[19] is the opposite of a summation, since it as a whole, precisely as a "gestalt", causes its individual "components" or "traits" to appear in a *correlation that alters the "components" qualitatively:*[20] "The sum is indifferent to its parts; the same sum can be created out of whatever parts in whatever sequence, its parts are exchangeable for others and among themselves.[20a] Innerness, on the other hand, represents a different type of a unified product. Within an inner diversity the parts can neither be exchanged nor substituted; the components here relinquish their for-them-selves quality, they are altered, and they alter everything else."[21] The reader who has followed this exposition will already be struck by the connection between such thinking and the remarks in ## 4 and 5 above, which we can now advance further.

[p. 186] 2. The Gestaltist Dialectics between
             "Form" and "Material" in the Gos-
             pel Genre.

If we may conceive the linguistic forms in a semiotics
(which cannot be further discussed here) as linguistic "super-
signs",[22] then much as in the linguistic theory of signs (semiotics) they require supplementation by means of a theory of
functions which will explicate their linguistic means of function and effect.[23] Referring to the remarks in #5 above, and
given the greater precision which is now possible in this context, we might ask: How does the structured unity of the semantic function of the super-sign (and hence of the gospel
form) arise by means of the combination of the quite different
types of linguistic functions of the signs (hence of the "small
units")? Obviously nothing other than the unity of that linguistic "gestalt", namely as a gestaltist intention of the
articulated whole, which subordinates the individual functions
of the "components". The linguistic super-function of the
super-sign is not the simple sum of the functions of the signs;
rather here too the Ehrenfels-criterion of the "trans-summativity" prevails: The super-function of the super-sign is a
gestaltist and intentional "given", which integrates the functions of the signs first and foremost into a "sense"-context.

The value of such arguments for gospel form criticism
seems evident to me. For if we conceive of the "small units"
with their special linguistic functions as "signs", then their
framing in the gospel form represents their functional insertion into the intentional context of a "super-sign". In this
way it would be easy to explain *why in spite of all disparateness of the materials there is yet a wholeness of the form of
the gospels, namely that of their gestaltist unity*, which has
its own super-functions, to which the individual functions
are subordinated. Then no one could derive the gospel form

in a gestaltist manner because of its "trans-totality" *simply* genetically out of the tradition history of its material, which did indeed occur on the basis of the immanent criticism in the traditional model of form criticism.[24]   Rather the evangelist, in his selection, insertion, and expansion of the materials, would be guided by the viewpoint of the "gestalt"-*affiliation*, i.e., the "material" being so shaped in the production of the form of the gospels that *it accords with* the linguistic "gestalt" he intends.[24a]   The gospel form would then [p. 187] in gestaltist terms be seen as an intentional, individual compositional act, which dissolves the collective tradition of the "material" by the creation of a new form, in which he freely and at the same time dialectically "takes up" ["aufhebt"] the "material" into the "framework" in the truest sense of the word:[24b]   By means of the gestaltist and intentional circumscription of the "material" in selection, insertion, and redactional framing following the principle of affiliation with the intended gospel form, the "material" is raised onto another linguistic level; *it now serves a linguistic effect which is not produced solely by means of its sum, but also, by means of the intentional composition of the form of the gospels, bestows the contextual sense-horizon upon the "material"*. This would also accord well with the position that the written nature of this form cannot be correctly understood as a *collective* act of composition.

The analytical methods of literary criticism, source criticism, and form criticism lead—or at least incline toward—misunderstanding of the subject matter they describe. Traditional form criticism, as we have seen in #5 above, conceives the gospel form within its mosaic-theory as a sum or aggregation of "framework" and "small units", and so misunderstands the "trans-summativity" of the linguistic gestalt, although today it has become customary at the same time to ascribe to the form of the gospels a christological relevance, i.e., a particular linguistic function with reference to christology. Is this function the effect of an addition, an aggregative circumstance resulting from a collective process of tradition? A uniformly functioning linguistic effect, in the case of the form of the gospels in E. Käsemann's and others' view, the effect of a particular christological understanding of time and reality, can never be understood linguistically as a collective sum, if otherwise the form of the gospels is to be thought of as a new linguistic form with its own purposive intention. *Is the form of the gospels actually only a linguistically effective unity*--only then would talk about its christological relevance be at all meaningful!--*or is it merely a collective potpourri of various elements to be explained by means of a collective process of tradition?* In the latter case at any rate we may speak of the *sensus litteralis* in the sense of something "intended" by a speaker or a writer, i.e., intentional significance may be rather senseless, since a collective can scarcely attain to a uniform conception by means of what is "intended" in the result of a collective process of collection.[25] Therefore the first alternative remains the only one that makes sense, indeed it is the almost generally accepted possibility. How we are to avoid, in connection with the [p. 188] gestaltist unity of the gospel form, dependence upon E. Husserl's "intentional act" and R. Ingarden's associated literary analysis of classes is, to be sure, not clear.[26] Marxsen has conceded in his own way this dependence in his pronounced emphasis upon the literary individuality of Mark, and at the same time indicated that in this respect there remain within an un-reflective form criticism, inner tensions that have not been faced as candid questions.

Basically traditional form criticism is a type of "source"-theory in the sense of the Diegesen-hypothesis [i.e., the evan-

gelists' reliance upon fragments as sources; W.G.D.J. The
"small units" were, gradually and over a lengthy tradition
history, "brought together" into the unity of the form of the
gospels. In this relationship the mosaic-theory is an analogue to something like the Pauline theology, which indeed
has often been described as a unity comprised out of individual presentational building blocks, as a summative aggregate
of presentations.[27] *An "alchemy of linguistic form" corresponds to the "alchemy of ideas".*[28] The only difference is
that in this case instead of presentations, "small units" were
thought to have been available to the evangelist with whose
help he then expressed his theology. In the one case we have
before us a traditio-historical genesis of a theological act
of thought, in the other a traditio-historical genesis of a
speech act. Even in historical terms this is no real understanding of the existing linguistic form, since the linguistic
and gestaltist unity of effect of the form of the gospels is
indeed descried and affirmed, but *has* to be misunderstood, because of its analytical method, as an evolutionary and genetic
process.

For these reasons the present work does not follow traditional redaction-critical analysis, since that conceives only
insufficiently, because of its methodological foundations, the
gestaltist and linguistic-functional unity of the form of the
gospels. The recognized difficulties of redaction criticism
in the case of Mark[29] are less surprising, given these circumstances. They are rather an indication of the need to modify
the form-critical method, so that it is appropriate to the
existing linguistic phenomenon. *For these material reasons,
the acceptance of specifically linguistic methods and insights
within form criticism is in my opinion unavoidable.*

Notes to # 12

1. Again for comprehensive presentation I will have to refer to planned publications.

2. Cf. for instance G. Ipsen, "Ueber Gestaltauffassung," *Neue psychol. Studien* 1 (1926) 171-278; Ipsen, "Zur Theorie des Erkennens," *ibid.*, 279-471; D. Katz, *Gestaltpsychologie*, 1948-2nd ed.; B. Petermann, *Die Wertheimer-Koffka-Köhlersche Gestalttheorie und das Gestaltproblem*, 1929; further bibliography there.

3. Cf. for instance F. Kainz, *Psychol. der Sprache*, vol. 1, 115ff.; F. Tschirsch, *Weltbild, Denkform und Sprachgestalt*, 1954; L. Weisgerber, *Die vier Stufen in der Erforschung der Sprachen*, 1963, 38-61; M. Wegner, *Wort und Wesen*, n.d.; H. Brinkmann, *Die sprachliche Gestalt. Muttersprache*, vol. 1, 1949, 1-25; Brinkmann, "Der deutsche Satz als sprachliche Gestalt," *WW SH* 1952, 12-26; Brinkmann, *Die deutsche Sprache: Gestalt und Leistung*, 1962.

4. Cf. for instance O. Walzel, *Gehalt und Gestalt im Kunstwerk des Dichters*, 1957-2nd ed.; W. Weidle, "Das Kunstwerk: Sprache und Gestalt," in *Wort und Wirklichkeit*, ed. der Bayer. Ak. der schönen Künste, 1960, 129-63; G. Müller, *Die Gestaltfrage in der Literaturwissenschaft*, 1944; H. Seidler, *Die Dichtung*, 1965-2nd ed., 134-341.

5. Chr. v. Ehrenfels, "Ueber 'Gestaltqualitäten'," *Vierteljahrschr. für wiss. Phil.* 14 (1890) 249-92.

6. *Ibid.*, 250.

7. Cf. *ibid.*, 252, 259.

8. Cf. further the quotation from G. Ipsen, below.

9. Cf. *op. cit.*, 253f.: "How can...the mere circumstance that several presentations or experiences appear combined in one consciousness provide sufficient basis for the fact that there is always something new that is added to that sum that was not present in the elements being combined?"

10. Cf. *ibid.*, 252, 256, 258f., 262f.

11. Cf. O. Selz, *Ueber die Gesetze des geordneten Denkverlaufs*, 1913, 84.

12. Cf. bibliography given in #8, n. 82, above.

13. Cf. Selz, *op. cit.*, 89ff.

14. *Ibid.*, 84f., italicized in original.

15. Cf. *ibid.*, 93.

16. *Ibid.*, 97.

17. Bühler, *Arch. für die ges. Psychol.* 9 (1907) 329.

18. Ipsen, *op. cit.*, 452, italicized in original.

19. Cf. *ibid.*, 441.

20. Cf. *ibid.*, 440.

20a [+1978: In mathematical set-theory, this phenomenon is called "cummutativity" (Kommutativität).]

21. *Ibid.*, 441.

22. Again for presentation of semiotics I must refer to "Formgeschichte und Linguistik." -- H. Frank, *Kybernetische Grundlagen der Pädagogik*, 1962, 54ff., differentiates first-level super-signs (for example letters of the alphabet), from second-level super-signs (e.g., words). This sequence can be continued. On *langue* as superstructure, cf. Kainz, *Psychol. der Sprache*, vol. 1, 274ff.

23. Bibliography: See #10, n. 1, above.

24. Cf. above, pp. [78ff., 82ff.].

24a [+1978: Today I would make much more use of L. Hjelmslev's categories: The materials are as "substances of expression" functionally dependent upon the frame as the "form of content".]

24b [+1978: The German term "aufheben" has a Hegelian touch: something is invalidated or suspended and at the same time preserved, so that it is "in good hands".]

25. It is questionable whether the sociological conceptual model of form criticism and the history of religions is not too greatly oriented to the undifferentiated "masses" (G. LeBon). Collectives (or better: groups) at most have a tolerable "individual" organizational center, which correlates the roles in the organizing and integrating system of roles. Cf. P. R. Hof-

stätter, *Gruppendynamik*, 1968-9th ed. Differently: G. Mensch-ing, *Soziologie der Religion*, 1968-2nd ed., 166ff.

26. Cf. E. Husserl, *Logische Untersuchungen*, II/1, 1968-5th ed., 37ff., 61ff., 99ff., 343ff.; R. Ingarden, *Das literarische Kunstwerk*, 1960-2nd ed.

27. Güttgemanns, *Der leidende Apostel*, 330ff.

28. Cf. above, p. [163].

29. Cf. Vielhauer, *Aufs.*, 199; Schreiber, *Theol. des Vertrauens*, 9ff.

PART IV. THE GOSPEL FORM: EXTENSION OF
THE KERYGMA, OR AUTO-SEMANTIC
LANGUAGE FORM?

We attempted in Part III to bring into contrast to the
destruction of the form-critical conceptual model of the traditio-historical genesis of the gospel form, the construction
of a form-critical alternative within the framework of gestalt-theory. Thereby gospel form-*history* turned out to be
a dialectical interlacing of collectively transmitted "material" and individual and intentional "act", whereby the "material" was simultaneously raised to a new linguistic and
gestaltist level by the compositional act embodied in the
"framework": *By means of functional and structural insertion into a new linguistic horizon of "sense", the "material" serves at this stage as a means of presentation of the
structure of meaning of the gospel form established in the
new "sense"-horizon.*

In Part IV we will begin in a destructive manner once
more, in that we initially analyze the hypothesis that the
gospel form is in some way the further development of the
primitive Christian kerygma. After this hypothesis has been
shown to be a thesis inappropriate to a form-*history*, and
hence has reconfirmed our earlier results, we will turn in
#15 to development of guidelines for an alternative to that
rejected conceptual model, which must be developed in the
future. As a whole, however, even this Part concludes with
candid questions.

#13. *The Fragmentary Character of the "Pre-literature"*
      with Respect to the Primitive Christian Kerygma
      and the Pre-Markan Redactional Complexes.

We have already had several occasions to question whether
M. Dibelius' "constructive" conceptual model is any longer
serviceable.[1] One of the main supports of this model was provided by the preaching-theory,* which [p. 190] is even more
disputed today than it was when it was first proposed.[2] H.
Clavier suggested that the crystallization or the process of
the formation of the gospels was to be sure elegantly para-
phrased by means of this theory, but not precisely described
[elegant *um*schrieben...nicht genau *be*schrieben].[3] Hence the
situation with respect to this form-critical conceptual model
is similar to that which prevails with the conceptual model of
older folkloristics that influenced form criticism, concerning
which H. Bausinger recently noted that the collective creative
process of "nature poetry" had "never been characteristically
described".[4] Can the preaching-theory incorporated in Dibelius' form-critical conceptual model, which at first seems so
promising, still be maintained today, or are there not now so
many counterarguments against it that we may speak of it only

---

*The section referred to (here and in the notes) in Dibelius'
Die Formgeschichte des Evangeliums is entitled "Die Predigt",
and is translated as "Sermons" in the translation by B. L.
Woolf, with Dibelius (*From Tradition to Gospel*, New York:
Scribner's, n.d.). I have translated variously with preaching (as here), sermon/ic, homiletic, or even proclamation
(normally: Verkündigung), as the context has demanded.
"Preaching-theory" (die Predigt-Theorie) is awkward in English, but condenses something like "Dibelius' theory about
the extent to which preaching was the determinative impetus
in the formation of the primitive Christian literature",
which is obviously completely unwieldy. - W.G.D.

as having had a certain historical justification in the history
of research? To answer this question we turn to the counter-
arguments.

1. The "Constructive" Implications of Dibelius'
Preaching-Theory.

(a) The Preaching-Theory as Hypothesis
and Conceptual Model.

Dibelius begins his remarks on the "sermon"[5] by establishing the necessity of the "constructive" method, which the "analytical" method encounters unsatisfactorily in referring to the
possibility and necessity of the formation of the gospel tradition.[6] *Thereby it is fundamentally conceded that the preaching-theory cannot be analytically derived*, but serves as a hypothetical conceptual model for the [p. 191] reconstruction of
the traditio-historical process of the beginnings of the oral
transmission up to the literary fixation of the tradition in
the gospel form. As a hypothesis, the preaching-theory has to
meet the same conditions as any other hypothesis: First, it
must reasonably and simply explain the peculiarities of the
material; second, it may not contradict or be in tension with
analytical data; and third, it must be relinquishable at any
point without simultaneously causing the collapse of a whole
series of hypotheses. A hypothesis is always an isolated ex-
pedient for the explication of particular historical phenomena, and should avoid historical speculations dependent upon
the personal taste of the person making them; if at all possible, it should not be tied to additional hypotheses or incorporated within a network of hypotheses. Historical probability, which E. Troeltsch regards as one of the three primary
pillars of the historical method,[7] should not be misued to
create an atmosphere of scientific confidence,[8] since that

300

leads to a restorative tendency and a rejection of contingency by the applicable dominant scientific orientation.[9] Can we, therefore, still regard Dibelius' conceptual model as a possible hypothesis for us today? We have reason to answer in the negative.

(b) The Value of Luke 1:1-4 as a Source.

We have already seen that historical analogy broke down in attempting to establish the "non-literary" character of the "Kleinliteratur",[10] and that the thesis of the traditio-historical continuity between the collective oral and the more individual written nature of the gospel is more a postulate than a proof.[11] Hence [p. 192] two important premises of the preaching-theory are inapplicable. Dibelius draws from the prologue of Luke (1:1-4)[12] both the occasion and the rule of the tradition of the gospels: The *autoptai* [eyewitnesses] were at the same time *huprētai tou logou* [ministers of the word], and must so have served the primitive Christian missionary work:[13] "the missionary work offered the occasion, the preaching the means, of dissemination, of that which the followers of Jesus had preserved as reminiscence."[14]

It is very doubtful whether such a historical inference is still possible today. Of course Dibelius also knew about the authorial character of the Lukan prologue.[15] But it was G. Klein who only recently showed us how greatly the prologue is specifically Lukan in *every* detail.[16] While Dibelius left unclear the relationship of the *hoi ap' archēs autoptai* [the eyewitnesses from the beginning] to the *hupēretai tou logou*,[17] Klein has shown that the eyewitnesses *ap' archēs*, i.e., from the time of the baptism of John (cf. Acts 1:22), through the entire *historia* of Jesus up to his appearance as the resurrected one from among the witnesses chosen beforehand (cf.

Acts 10:37-41), after the forty days (cf. Acts 1:8), have *become (genomenoi) hupēretai tou logou.*[18] This can only mean, in terms of the Lukan concept of apostolicity,[19] that here the twelve apostles are intended.[20] Since the motif of the twelve apostles is certainly non-historical,[21] there is no possibility of drawing from the Lukan prologue a likely inference concerning a pre-Lukan historical situation with respect to the missionary occasion and dissemination of the gospel materials. *The Lukan prologue is not a historical source, but a wholly dogmatic program*, namely [a program intended to establish - W.G.D.] the trustworthiness (*asphaleia*) of the apostolic tradition and succession, by means of "historical" research answerable only to itself (cf. Lk 1:3: *edoxe kamoi parēkolouthēkoti anōthen pasin akripōs kathexēs soi grapsai* [it seemed fitting to me as well, having investigated everything carefully from the beginning, to write it out for you in consecutive order]).[22] Klein also made it clear that Luke considered the written fixation of the oral *diēgēsis* [narrative] handed down to the *polloi* [many] by the apostolic *hupēretai tou logou*,[23] [p. 193] inaccessible,[24] because it had not independently penetrated the traditio-historical gap between the *diēgēsis* and the facts preserved in it.[25] Just writing down the oral materials, therefore, Luke considered insufficient for *dogmatic* reasons. As a whole, the image of the pre-literary tradition of the gospels in Lk 1:1-4 disappears behind such a dense dogmatic haze that we are left only with mere guesses. Could they still carry the heavy weight of the preaching-theory today?

(c) The Concept of the "Preaching" as
Idealistic and Typological.

A further critical point of this theory is that of the basically idealistic and typological concept of the "preaching",[26] to which that of the "kerygma" corresponds.[27] It encompasses "every possibility of Christian proclamation": "missionary preaching, cultic and catechetical preaching".[28] Therefore it does not refer to the reconstruction of a particular type of preaching, "within which the whole tradition would find a place", the less so since actually "preached primitive Christian sermons...at least from the initial decades [have] not come down to us".[29] In other words it concerns a "constructive" quantity, a conceptual model. What justified us in coming to the conclusion today that what the Christian missionaries related, "was subordinated to this proclamation, had to confirm it and ground it"; or: "The oldest transmitted segments must have corresponded in their formation to this connection with preaching"?[30] It seems to me that Dibelius came to this conclusion less by means of a concomitant analysis of primitive-Christian-kerygmatic passages than by means of a conceptual model relying on modern homiletical practice,[31] which structures the sermon around a "text",[32] or a "paradigm",[33] that which then transforms or illustrates the non-concrete kerygma.[34] [p. 194] But is there an analytical proof for this hypothesis nonetheless, to be established on the basis of the passages Dibelius referred to only briefly (Acts 2:14-39, 3:12-26, 4:9-12, 5:30-32, 10:34-43, 13:16-38, I Cor 15:3-5)?[35]

(d) The Speeches in Acts as a Lukan Construction.

Our question has been firmly denied by U. Wilckens: The speeches in Acts are "entirely a Lukan composition" and not related to the kerygmatic formulae in Paul. "But if the apostolic sermons addressed to the Jews in Acts are therefore excluded with reference to the sermon, as the sociological setting for the origination of the earliest Jesus-narratives, neither can such be certainly derived from I Cor 15:3f., and similar passages. And so the decisive supports of Dibelius' concept show themselves to be thoroughly incapable of bearing any weight."[36]

Simultaneously Wilckens presents a very thorough analysis of the texts listed above, and his arguments are so convincing that it is only possible to accept them.[37] To be sure, the speeches in Acts, as Dibelius noted,[38] have a symmetrical schema (kerygma/proof from scripture/admonition to repent),[39] but they are neither formally[40] nor traditio-historically to be removed from their present theological context in Acts.[41] Traditio-historically, I Cor 15:3-8, I Thess 1:9f., and Hebrews 5:11-6:2 are not related to the speeches to the Jews in Acts, already mentioned, but to the gentile-Christian missionary preaching (cf. Acts 14:15-17, 17:22-31).[42] What we know at all about the Jewish-Christian mission to the Jews more resembles a continuation of Jesus' proclamation than the speeches in Acts.[43] The result of the traditio-historical analysis is a *non liquet* [unclear case]: "The traditional character of this preaching-schema cannot be demonstrated."[44] On the other hand the schema of the speeches makes such good sense and has such an appropriate function within the theological conception of Acts,[45] that it is probable "that the schema of this Jewish-Christian missionary preaching was shaped by Luke himself".[46] If a motif-critical analysis of the materials in the speeches of Acts demonstrates their Lukan character,[47] then the speeches are "to be evaluated not as witnesses of an old, or even the oldest primitive Christian theology, but [p. 195] as Lukan theology toward the end of the first century".[48]

Actually this result of the evidence is "at first embarrassingly disappointing; it appears to retroject the traditio-critical work with all its theologically-seductive aspects back to the raw state of its beginnings".[49] "Certainly, look-

ing at the matter purely in systematic terms, and beginning
with the speeches in Acts, a thoroughly comprehensible picture
of the development can be hypothetically reconstructed." "But
while such a purely systematic reconstruction can indeed be
set forth as a presupposition of a developmental presentation,
it does not *result* from the completed analysis of the individual traditions themselves and their interrelationships."[50]   In
these sentences Wilckens has elegantly described the analytically unproved, indeed even refuted, hypothetical character of
the preaching-theory. Should we today, in view of the advanced
destruction of the situation with respect to primitive Christian sources, nevertheless abide by the thesis of the preaching-theory, namely that the gospel form was a sermonic development of the primitive Christian kerygma? That would depend
primarily upon whether we can demonstrate that there was Christian kerygma in passages other than those Dibelius cited.

2.   The "Pre-historical" Obscurity Surrounding
     the Primitive Christian Kerygma.

In Part III we treated the gospel form in terms of gestalt-theory. Here we can vary this inquiry: Of what is the
gospel a literary "gestalt"? Or expressed differently: *What
was the structural and organizational principle of the gospel
"gestalt"? Perhaps the kerygma?* Following U. Wilcken's exposition of the miscarriage of Dibelius' "constructive" conceptual model, this question presses toward an answer all the
more in that the gospel form is regarded today almost universally as in one way or another an "extension of the kerygma".

          (a) Which Came First: Kerygma or the
               Tradition of the Gospels?

Others besides M. Dibelius, among them R. Bultmann, relying upon J. Schiewind's work, have held to the thesis that the literary task of the evangelists consisted "in giving shape to the 'kerygma of a particular situation and task'".[51] According to Schniewind the primitive Christian kerygma in its uniqueness "also created its own [p. 196] literary form, which corresponds neither to the biography [bios], nor to the cultic legend, nor to the encomium (the 'aretalogy') of antiquity"[52] so that the synoptic gospels are "even in their completed shape still a form of primitive Christian kerygma",[53] and research must be directed toward deriving the "synoptic kerygma",[54] indeed "cannot result in anything more fundamental than reproduction of the kerygma".[55] According to Bultmann the intention of Mark "is the unification of the hellenistic Christ kerygma, whose essential content is the Christ myth, as we know it from Paul (especially Phil 2:6ff., and Rom 3:24), with the tradition of the history of Jesus".[56] Although Mark's choice of material "cannot have been determined by the mythical foundation of the kerygma",[57] the Christ myth gives "to his book, the book of secret epiphanies, not a biographical unity, but a unity based on the myth of the kerygma".[58] In this aporia between the redactional choice of material not guided by the mythical kerygma, i.e., the individual redactional *act*, and the gestaltist unity of the form of the gospels based on myth, i.e., the collective *convention* of the structural and functional construct of signification resulting from the background of the worldview, lies the whole form-critical problem: Is the description of the gospels as "extension of the kerygma" in any way a form-*historical* thesis, i.e., is it correct to describe the form-critical relationship between the primitive-Christian/Jewish-Christian or hellenistic kerygma, and the form of the gospels, as one in which first "small units", then pre-Markan complexes, and finally the present redactional endproduct developed *gradually, but with traditio-historical consistency*, out of the kerygma, as a consequence of the needs and alterations of the sociological relationships of the churches? Was it then Mark's *intention* to "extend" the kerygma of his church by the creation of a new language form? Or have we thereby only described *from our own perspective* the actual relationship between kerygma and the form of the gospels, which however may not be confused with the literary *intentions*? Hence is the form-*historical* [p. 197] development of the terse, formalistic kerygma into the form of the gospels actually an evolution of the various language forms which can be established in the sense of an intentional act of the collective or individual who created or sanctioned, interpretively formulated, and passed on the language forms? Or is it also a form-critical evolution of a clear-cut causal and genetic sequence of various "sociological settings" and sociological needs determined by them with reference to the language form? Or can we determine in any case that there was a simple historical sequence, or even only a co-existence of language forms and "sociological settings", so that it is impossible to speak fundamentally about a form-*historical* relationship of the various language forms, *since already the right of the evolutionary interpretation of the co-existence which has been found is a doubtful premise of historical reconstruction?*[59] In the first case we have to assume the historical priority of the kerygma, which is then somehow "illustrated" by the tradition of the gospels (cf. #14). But is it at all certain which comes first historically, the kerygma or the tradition of the gospels?[60] Could not both have come about at the same time, since between them there is no form-*historical* relationship at all, but merely the commonality of a horizon of presentation, i.e., a history-of-*religions* relationship, to whose description contemporary form-critical analysis has mostly *de facto* restricted itself? In this case, the relationship between kerygma and the

form of the gospels would only come into focus for us *a posteriori*, but not in the sense of a language-*historical* intention to be assigned to the tradents and redactors of the tradition of the gospels. The gospel form would no longer be
"derivable", or, in the sense of a historical evolution, "re-
ducible", to its earliest beginnings; rather it would be *an
autosemantic language form*, i.e., a language form which in
its "sense" can only be explained through and by means of itself, since it has its linguistic "sense" through and in itself and does not "derive" or borrow it synsemantically.[61]
With that the question already placed in #12 undergoes a variation; [p. 198] [now we ask:] to what extent is linguistic
"sense" an individual and intentional act in the language form.
If the gospel form is actually a language form first *created*
by Mark, then we cannot simultaneously assume an immanent tendency within the tradition history of the material,[62] which
leads logically, consistently, causally, and genetically to
the gospel form, and which therefore makes it traditio-historically "derivable", since then the individual linguistic
and intentional act of creation becomes basically superfluous,
or de-individualized, as a behavioristically-explained "reaction" to the "stimulus" given by the collective tradition as
a component of a collective process itself. In the present
work we incline to an emphasis upon the intentional act on the
part of the evangelist, since neither can we clearly prove the
form-critical "development" of the language forms, nor can we
assume a causal and genetic "derivation" of language forms as
a linguistically sensible inquiry. Naturally historical analysis may, given certain premises, develop hypotheses concerning the historical course of events, but it must always be
ready to relinquish these hypotheses and premises when they
conflict with the fundamental methodological considerations
of other disciplines of the humanities that have not been re-

futed previously by form criticism, considerations whose methodological connection with form criticism is not to be denied.
Again we are confronted by a series of candid questions whose
methodological clarification is fundamental for form criticism.

    (b) Methodological Considerations with Respect
         to Tradition History.[63]

    The reconstruction of the primitive Christian history of
theology is heavily weighted down with one-sided features and
short-circuits of the traditio-historical method. Here we engage further the thoughts expressed in #8; for the sake of
brevity, we will restrict ourselves to a few fundamental considerations.[64]

    A traditio-historical method (motif-history) applied in
an atomistic manner, i.e., without continuous reference to
form criticism [p. 199] leads, in my opinion, to quite questionable results, not only because it is mostly tied to an
actual separation of "form" and "content",[65] but especially
because it does not consistently maintain the unique form-
critical premises. These include, for instance, the sociological law of the "sociological setting", which according to
form-critical theory is thought to have determined normatively
the shaping of all the linguistic details of a genre.[66] Accordingly it would be possible to differentiate style, the extent and choice of words, and also the so-called "synsemantic
field" of the individual words of this linguistic gestalt,[67]
each according to its "sociological setting", and therefore
it would be possible *to recognize the linguistic details of
a language form in their form-critical relativity*. However
experience with traditio-historical analyses demonstrates that
they very frequently replace linguistic sociology with its regard for the cultural models constituted by various "sociological settings" with a history-of-religions and/or motif-

critical model disassociated from form criticism and focused
upon the quasi-free-floating "presentations". Hence on the
basis of trifling linguistic distinctions which have not even
been tested with respect to the basis of their structural *valeur* for the particular language form, tradition history
reaches much too sweeping conclusions, especially by over-
utilizing the *argumentum e silentio* [argument from silence].
In this way one forgets not only H. Gunkel's co-ordination
of form criticism and the history of religions, but also A.
Harnack's warning that the history of religions should not be
practiced in isolation:[68] "Language is not only the scabbard
wherein the sword of the spirit is sheathed; it is much more
than the scabbard where religion is concerned. Religion has
partly created language, and the history of religions is mir-
rored in the history of language." If the whole area of linguistics and history is not studied by a faculty of theology,
but "only the history of religions cut loose from language and
history..., this will be judged an incredible dilettantism".[69]
Tradition history ought first of all to treat the sociology-
of-language diversity of the "sociological setting" for all
the linguistic phenomena linguistically analyzed by it, to
take more fully into account the sociological co-existence of
various language worlds within any *one* cultural area.[70] But
how then can tradition history assume--as we observe frequent-
ly-- [p. 200] the commensurability of the various genres in
the recognized multiplicity of the "sociological settings",
when factually, in the traditio-historical *argumentum e silentio* with respect to one of the "sociological settings", it
fails to see something that can only be linguistically possible
and permissible with respect to another "sociological setting",
and when it makes a traditio-*historical sequence* out of the
co-existence of different "sociological settings", which process "derives" step by step the observed linguistic differ-

ences? This procedure is to be explained only on the basis
of the evolutionism long customary within the history of religions, as for example H. Spencer sketched for the entire
range of beings,[71] and others, for sociology[72] and linguistics[73] as well, and as it extensively dominated ethnology and
comparative religion until it was finally rejected.[74] One
example of Spencer's evolutionary laws is that of the historical priority of simpler, briefer, and more isolated elements
as opposed to the more complex, longer, and aggregative elements;[75] such a principle has found frequent application in
the traditio-historical analysis of synoptic form criticism,
although abridgement can also happen for redaction-critical
reasons.[76] As soon as this "law", which in my opinion cannot
be empirically observed in culture, is applied schematically
and in the undifferentiated manner typical of [p. 201] tradition history (it often possesses no other criterion of age for
the various "levels"), a caricature of the real primitive
Christian history of theology threatens; the unilateral,
causal, and genetic sequence of the course of history, by no
means thoroughly clear and transparent, and in its co-existence and simultaneity, is logically rationalized—something
that contemporary history of religions takes into account by
replacing the concept of "development" by the concept of
"change", which cannot serve as a criterion of time.[77] It
is an essential premise of the traditio-historical way of
working with levels that the various versions of something
like a logion may be brought into traditio-*historical* relationship, with the intention of approaching an ur-formulation
that has been varied in the different versions[78]—indeed a
surrogate for the search for the *ipsissima verba* [the very
words...i.e., of Jesus] which has been relinquished.

In view of this danger of logically rationalizing the
course of history and especially in view of the fragmentary

character of the "pre-literature" which will be justified shortly, we must seriously inquire whether it would not be more discerning, and especially more responsible for the historian, to follow I. Engnell in holding out for the present circumstances of the biblical books[79] since their oral tradition history cannot be elucidated with respect to details, and to refer with F. Overbeck to the "ur-historical" problems which are in constant danger "of being driven into that light in which all cats are grey. Hence they are only accessible to researchers who are able to see in this light--researchers with 'cats' eyes' that can find their way in the dark."[80] The "ur-historical" territory seems to be a pretty shaky terrain, because of the often considerable differences in the traditio-historical results in each case, and it is necessary to persuade oneself of its safety, since the evolutionary implications of the method produce only false hopes and scientific phantoms--whereas in the "ur-historical" darkness nothing else is to be seen than what a person is prepared to see by particular premises.

(c) The Framework of the Gospel Narrative: Charles Harold Dodd.

(i) Dodd's Conception.

C. H. Dodd's proposal concerning the form-critical development of the kerygma of the primitive church [p. 202] into the Gospel form, which he has developed in various publications, has found a ready audience, especially in Anglo-Saxon language areas.[81] He begins with the question whether Mark's "framework" gives us a chronological sequence of events of the life of Jesus,[82] hence the question which recurs repeatedly in Anglo-Saxon areas concerning the historical value of the gospels as witnesses.[83] Can we say that the destruction of this

historical value and the demonstration of the redactional and
Markan character of the "framework" which were the contributions of K. L. Schmidt have therefore been successful? Indeed it is possible to ask "whether the order in which the
units appear is indeed quite arbitrary, and the framework
nothing more than an artificial construction of the Evangelist".[84] Even Schmidt concedes that there are pre-Markan
fragments of an itinerary[85] and of pre-Markan compositions
(blocks),[86] so that the thesis concerning entirely independent "small units" and concerning the redaction according to
topological aspects must be modified.[87] In many cases we can
ask why the arrangement of complexes according to thematic aspects is without fail artificial and arbitrary, and not arranged according to the actual historical sequence.[88] If we
take the summaries Schmidt named (Mk 1:14f., 21f., 39; 2:13;
3:7b-19; 4:33f.; 6:7, 12f., 30) except for 4:33f., as a connected account, then we obtain a connected narrative, " a per-
spicuous outline of the Galilaean Ministry, forming a framework into which the separate pictures are set".[89] Such a
sketch (outline) is more likely traditional than a specifically Markan creation.[90] In fact we can suspect, relying on M.
Dibelius, that in I Cor 15:3-7, [p. 203] 11:23-25, Acts 10:
37-42, 13:23-31, "some kind of outline formed a regular part
of the kerygma everywhere".[91] The editing of Mark's gospel
took place as a compromise between the chronological order
passed on in the kerygma and the topological order offered,
to some extent, by the material.[92] That this framework actually belonged to the kerygma of the primitive church can be
proved by means of an anlaysis of the primitive Christian
preaching. Although Paul's letters are not themselves kerygma, but as exegesis presuppose the preaching,[93] it is possible
to draw from passages such as I Cor 15:1ff.; Gal 1:4; Rom 10:
8f., 14, 9f., 2:26; I Thess 1:9f., a kerygma which is "a proc-

lamation of the facts of the death and resurrection of Christ in an eschatological setting which adds significance to the facts".[94] According to I Cor 15:1-3a, 11, Paul had to draw on those facts that were common contents of the primitive Christian kerygma.[95] The great age of this kerygma which Paul took over about 33/34 C.E.,[96] and his agreement with the speeches in Acts going back to the Aramaic tradition,[97] demonstrates that: We have here "the kerygma of the church at Jerusalem at an early period".[98] The summary in Mk 1:14f. "provides the framework within which the Jerusalem kerygma is set":[99] The kerygma of the primitive church had, to be sure, "an eschatological setting",[100] but the framework mentioned above, "the historical section of the kerygma", also gives Mark his theme. "It is the theme of the kerygma as a whole",[101] so that Mark is "a commentary on the kerygma".[102] "The kerygma is primary, and it acted in such a way as to preserve the tradition which conveyed the facts. The nearer we are in the Gospels to the stuff of the kerygma, the nearer we are to the fountain-head of the tradition",[103] for the gospels "represent the testimony of those who stood nearest to the facts, and whose life and outlook had been molded by them".[104] *The "gospel pattern", on the basis of which the gospels fashion a special literary genre*, is not a product of Mark's literary art and therefore an *ad hoc* improvisation, but *has its "sociological setting" in the apostolic proclamation about Jesus*, which worked against the centrifugal tendency of the primitive church.[105] So the historical value of the gospels as witnesses is as a whole secure.

Dodd's compact proposal, to be sure, does not argue in favor of the substantial historical exactness of the Markan "framework" [p. 204] on the basis of the eyewitness accounts of Peter and others,[106] but it is interested in the unity of the N. T., in the skeleton of the apostolic kerygma which re-

appears throughout,[107] and is "a genuinely chronological starting point for the history of Christian thought".[108] Such a
model is not only able to support a seemingly widespread consensus,[109] but may also be tied to a similar, dogmatically-
engaged Roman Catholic exegesis.[110] But a number of well-
grounded criticisms[111] cause us to reject this model.

(ii) The Miscarriage of the Conception
in Luke's Works.

Initially Dodd is also struck by U. Wilcken's convincing
destruction of the traditional character of the speeches in
Acts. Their character is essentially Lukan,[112] and their assessment cannot be separated from that of the whole book of
Acts.[113] Since there is a literary unity between the gospel
of Luke and the Acts, it is necessary to ask what this unity
means for the relationships between kerygma and the tradition
of the gospels in Luke's eyes,[114] so that Dodd's thesis may be
examined in terms of the proper object: "is it likely that St
Luke, having just completed a detailed account of the Lord's
ministry in the gospel, would then, in his second volume, ascribe to the original Apostles accounts of that ministry in-
consistent with the one he had just given", indeed because
Luke rejects the Markan "framework"?[115] However that is only
the case if Luke himself knew nothing of the fact that the
gospel form should be a "commentary on the apostolic kerygma".
Rather from his standpoint the "correct" sequence, the only
one dogmatically permissible, would indeed be just the opposite: the apostolic kerygma has [p. 205] no historical priority over the *vita Jesu*, rather the *vita Jesu* "historically"
authorizes the authenticity and legitimacy of the apostolic
proclamation. The eyewitnesses of the *vita Jesu ap' archēs*,
who at Pentecost became *hupēretai tou logou*, as twelve apostles and bearers of the sole legitimated authority, pass on

with their *logos* the *pragmata* which were to be attained in the
time of the church (Lk 1:1f.).[116] For the Lukan design of the
salvation history,[117] this "historical" founding is likewise
the dogmatic sequence, since only in such a way is the *asphaleia* [certainty] of the Christian *logoi* guaranteed (Lk 1:4).[118]
So the *logoi* of the apostle offer, to be sure, "historical" access to the *vita Jesu* and along with that, also dogmatic le-
getimacy and noetic certainty about the *vita Jesu*, but that can
never mean for the consciousness of Luke himself that he or the
polloi he names (1:1) would have created the gospel form according to the standard of the speeches in Acts in a conscious
literary act. From this we can only conclude *that Luke himself
knew nothing (more?) about the historical and form-critical relationship between apostolic kerygma and the form of the gospels*, but just the opposite, that he let the data of the *vita
Jesu* be the norm for the apostolic kerygma.

(iii) The Form of an Apostolic Kerygma-
Schema as Sheer Hypothesis.

Hence we can only doubt the form-critical existence of an
"outline" of the apostolic kerygma. Since the apostles themselves were certainly not dependent upon it, but could speak
spontaneously and from memory,[119] and since further no "sociological setting" for the repetition and maintenance of the authentic apostolic speaking or its schema is to be imagined, it
seems more likely that Luke will have oriented himself to contemporary sermons, "which he undoubtedly considered apostolic".[120] If we do not follow Wilckens in taking the speeches
as *only* a literary and Lukan phenomenon, therefore, but understand them as also somehow "traditional", then perhaps contemporary forms come into the picture as a hypothetical prototype while the present version at any rate is arbitrarily ar-
chaized not in Aramaic stylizations,[121] but in Lukan [p. 206]

language,[122] and hence is pretty certainly Luke's own literary product. Every reconstruction of a pre-literary version here must already depend upon several hypotheses, so that there is the danger of mutually-supportive hypotheses.

(iv) The Postulate of the "Outline".

Similar form-critical questions confront the hypothetically-deduced "framework". Apart from the completely unproved justification of adding "framework"-elements to a presumably connected account,[123] which "sociological setting" and which circle of tradents should be assumed for the framework?[124] It would scarcely have been an essential component of the apostolic and obligatory kerygma: *a*) since the variations in Matthew and Luke exhibit no interest in the exact ordering of the events of salvation;[125] *b*) since the kerygma cannot be designated in the traditional sociological sense as a "sociological setting" for the framework; *c*) since the speeches in Acts cannot be used as sources for the kerygma;[126] and *d*) since I Cor 11:23-25 and 15:3-7 concern not the reconstructed Markan "outline" but the passion narrative.[127] The continuity of the reconstructed framework does not permit anything to be derived concerning their continuity as an account,[128] and even less with respect to the "Galilaean period". The impression of the continuous "framework"-elements is proof neither for nor against their historicity.[129] In fact this becomes even more doubtful:[130] Since on the one hand the supposed "outline" must have been rather brief, and since on the other very few pericopes offer support for their exact place in the "outline", the evangelist was dependent in his composition upon vague conjectures.[131] But the framework was for him by no means a binding, controlling factor, since Mark never submits himself to the material, for example the topological complexes, without reservation.[132] So we cannot rule out that Mark is himself responsible for the composition. If the literary intention of Mark actually was to be a "commentary on the kerygma", why did he not more clearly indicate that to his uninitiated [p. 207] circle of readers, for instance by reciting this kerygma briefly in a prologue, and commenting in conclusion on the material of the gospels? It is at this point that we see the danger of a phantasy-laden eisegesis of a construction into the present text.

(v) The Postulated Unity of the Primitive Christian Kerygma.

Moreover Dodd presupposes a unity of the primitive Christian kerygma that is otherwise controversial:[133] "it would be better to speak of 'kerygmata' than, too confidently, of 'the kerygma'."[134] Because of the theological contradictions existing between, for instance, Luke and Paul,[135] we should no longer affirm that the Acts repeats the kerygma of the primitive and the apostolic church that was obligatory even to Paul. The theological unity of the N. T. has today been so completely demolished,[136] that the hypothesis of one apostolic kerygma that was everywhere normative can no longer even be meaningfully discussed.

(vi) The Imprecise Form-critical Character of the Conception.

Finally Dodd's conception is developed in the absence of a strict form-critical methodology,[137] so that it cannot be valid as a form-critical thesis in the strict sense. Instead of being directed to the form-critical process of the evolution of various language forms, it is mostly oriented to the content of the kerygma,[138] so that *the term "kerygma"* is no longer used in a precise form-critical manner, but *as a cipher for the theological importance of the content.* The form-crit-

318

ical process is at most hypothetically deduced, but not concretely demonstrated. So it remains entirely questionable
whether the passages named by Dodd contain "kerygma" in the
precise sense at all, i.e., as evidence for a language form
serving the missionary proclamation of Jesus with *one* "sociological setting" that can be determined, or only something
like "kerygmatic elements".[139] In the latter case it would
be only a quite vague designation [p. 208] of "presentations"
not tied to a particular language form with a particular language function in a particular "sociological setting", or of
terminologically manifested motifs, and hence the description
of a phenomenon of the history of *religion*, namely of the linguistic background of a world view which would be common to
these "kerygmatic elements" and the gospel form. But that
would imply a form-*historical* relationship between "kerygma"
and the form of the gospels in the sense that one language
form, because of the soteriological needs of its "sociological setting", replaces the other language form; or can we
speak in any case of the linguistic character of the understanding manifesting itself in the form of the gospels which
does not permit itself to be "derived" from other language
forms, since not only the "kerygma", but also the sociological
laws in the "ur-historical" obscurity remain hidden? In other
words: A form-*historical* proof following Dodd's conception is
an unprovable construction with form-critically imprecise con-
ceptualities.

(d) The Invariable Primitive Christian
     Credo-Formula: Alfred Seeberg.

(i) The Thesis.

C. H. Dodd's conception has certain parallels with that
of A. Seeberg,[140] which in turn has a few echoes in M. Dibe-

lius' preaching-theory and in H. Conzelmann's work.[141] Seeberg assumes, as did Dodd later, a unity of doctrine in primitive Christianity up to the beginning of the second century;
he finds this unity demonstrated by the central place of a
"faith formula" that remains essentially the same. Beginning
from an analysis of I Cor 15:3-5,[142] Seeberg reconstructs the
full contours of the "faith formula" he postulates:[143] I Cor
15:3-5 was expanded at the end by the theme of the creator's
sending the Son of God (cf. Gal 4:4 and Rom 8:3),[144] as well
as at the beginning: by the bestowal of the title *huios tou*
theou as Son of David in connection with the [p. 209] resurrection (cf. Rom 1:3f., II Tim 2:8);[145] by the *sessio ad dex-*
teram Dei [seat at the right hand of God] (cf. Rom 8:34, Col
3:1, Eph 1:20);[146] by the subordination of the angels (cf.
Eph 1:20, Col 2:10, Eph 4:8, Phil 2:11, Mk 12:36f., Polyc. ad
Phil. 2:1);[147] and by the last judgment (cf. II Tim 2:8 with
Rom 2:16 and I Thess 1:10).[148] Seeberg finds evidence for
this "faith formula" remaining the same up to the end of the
first century in spite of all variations: in I Peter,[149] in
the Pastoral Letters,[150] in the Lukan corpus, especially in
the speeches in Acts,[151] in Hebrews,[152] in the Ascension of
Isaiah,[153] in Mark and Matthew.[154] Since the "formula" must
have arisen between 30 and 35 C.E., because of its use by
Paul,[155] and most of its elements "have their basis in Jesus'
sayings",[156] and since Paul's gospel stems from Christ himself as *euangelion tou christou* (subjective genitive; cf. Rom
15:19, I Cor 9:12, II Cor 2:12, 9:13, 10:14, Gal 1:7, Phil
1:27, I Thess 3:2),[157] the "formula" goes back to Christ himself,[158] who confessed it already before Pilate (cf. I Tim
6:13 with Mk 14:61).[159] This "faith formula" then served the
primitive Christian preaching which it "expanded", as a preaching formula,[160] but was also used in missionary work as a formula for instruction and confession,[161] in the baptismal litur-

gy,[162] in which the person baptized responded with the hom-
ology *kurios Iēsous* (cf. Rom 10:9, Phil 2:11) in response to
the "faith formula" recited by the baptizer.[163] It also
stands behind the term *euangelion* in Mk 1:14f., 8:35, 10:29,
13:10, 14:9[164]--all passages which Mark took over from an apostolic source[165]--so that it is understandable how the historical work of Luke (and Mark) "can be considered an implementa-
tion of the *euangelion*", and "that the synoptic historical
works can be considered as the *one* gospel according to the
presentation of various persons".[166]

(ii) The Traditio-historical Lack of Unity in Primitive Christianity.

What is decisive in our context is not the uncritical
derivation of the "formula" from Jesus (or even from "Christ")
in this conception, which is self-contained and interested in
historicity,[167] [p. 210] but its mixture of form-criticism and
tradition history, which lacks a clear form-critical methodology. In a similar "constructive" manner to that used by M. Dibelius,[168] A. Seeberg postulates a "faith formula" as an *a
priori* model for the reconstruction,[169] naturally not without
connection to the primacy of the "faith formula" in G. E. Lessing and the nineteenth century controversy over the apostolate.[170] In the remarkable observation of the expressions today regarded as "traditional", "imprinted" ["geprägt"], "kerygmatic", *et al.*, the development of the "formulas"[171] was essentially more complicated than the assumption of the *a priori* and
lasting unity of the credo would admit.[172] This traditio-historical unity is no longer recoverable today since the assumption of various "primitive communities" of similar origins and
independent of one another, confuses considerably the lines of
the "development".[173] However the main basis of the criticism
remains the postulate which is a form-critically completely un-

provable postulate of an ancient, *all-encompassing* credo, in which all the expressions which were "imprinted" somehow must have been somewhat integrated according to the model of the apostolic office, in which process a history-of-*religions presentational* construct, but not a *form*-critical *language* field is normative.[174] The form-critical unity of the language field of the "imprinted" expressions is today unequivocably rejected. So today it is no longer to be discussed earnestly whether the "confessional formula" underlies the so-called "confessional words" such as Mk 8:31, 9:31, 10:33f., 14:61, Mt 16:16, or Mk 1:15, 12:6, 16:6f., or the term *euangelion*;[175] now the discussion concerns only whether somehow behind the passion summaries there is an "imprinted", somehow-"kerygmatic" tradition which, in its "expansion" and as a structural means, founds and carries the gospel form. For that it is better to stand by such studies as possess a developed form-critical approach.

[p. 211]   (e)   The Summaries of the Passion
(Mk 8:31, 9:31, 10:33f.) as a
Structural Factor in the Form
of the Gospels.

(i)   The Structural Function of the Summaries of the Passion in Mark 8:27-10:52.

There is almost unanimous agreement about the structural function of the summaries of the passion with respect to the arrangement of Mark from 8:27 onward.[176] The triple repetition of the summaries within 8:27-10:52 which clearly subdivide this section,[177] demonstrates the compositional uniformity of the complex:[178] The section is defined "by the three-fold announcement of the suffering of the Son of Man (8:31, 9:31, 10:32-34), thrice followed by a complete misunderstanding on the part of the disciples (8:32f., 9:32-34, 10:35-37), and thrice eventuating in the call to discipleship (8:34ff., 9:35f., 10:38ff.)".[179] Since the misunderstanding-motif belongs to the Markan messianic-secret theory,[180] the complex 8:27-10:52 (or to 10:45)[181] in its present state is certainly a Markan composition. Hence it appears that the functional role of the passion summaries--otherwise something new in the form criticism of the Son of Man words in general[182] --certainly go back to Mark.[183] The summaries "show themselves to be typical for the gospel of Mark and they serve the broadening understanding of the event of the passion",[184] but they are also "indispensible carriers of the message of the Lord's resurrection".[185] They belong to the words of the suffering Son of Man primarily occurring only in 8:27-10:45, 14:1-42 (cf. further 9:9, 12; 10:45; 14:21, 41),[186] with the problematics of whose contents we will not concern ourselves here.[187] Our concern here is only with their form-critical and traditio-historical aspects.

> [p. 212] (ii) Linguistic and Form-critical Precision with Respect to the "Kerygma" Concept.

It has been questioned whether the summaries are independent Markan formulations or, following a modification of A. Seeberg's thesis, ultimately rest in some manner upon an already pre-formed kerygma. Partly the discussion stems from an imprecise application of form-critical terms. By "kerygma"--a modern form-critical *terminus technicus*[188] --we understand here a quotation-like language form consisting of traditional formulations taken over in blocks by Mark, which primarily serve missionary proclamation,[189] and which possess a relatively closed, imprinted "word sequence",[190] better: a stereotypical word field associated with a specific language

form, a so-called "synsemantic field".[191] It is less the theological dignity of the content, which is given its potency by
the secretive ceremonial "kerygma",[192] than *this linguistic and
form-critical aspect that gives to the term the necessary form-
critical precision*, while the usual term "kerygmatic", avoided
here, indicates the soteriological and theological significance
of the content, more or less its language-functional manner of
effect, and hence not unconditionally tied to form-critical
facts in the traditional sense.[193] Is the complex Mk 8:27-
10:52 in this precise form-critical sense an "expansion of the
kerygma", as it is cited in 8:31, 9:31, 10:33f., and deployed
throughout the composition of this segment?[194] This question,
with its important restriction to the given complex,[195] must
be affirmed, with very crucial qualifications to be sure.

[p. 213] (iii) Traditio-historical Constraint and Redactional
Freedom.

G. Strecker has clearly recognized the problem at hand:[196]
To what extent is the redactor slavishly tied to an earlier
pattern,[197] or free in his compositional work, so that it is
improper to draw "far-reaching traditio-historical consequences from minor differences which can indeed be clarified
in terms of redactional re-working"?[198] In fact customary
traditio-historical analysis, on the basis of terminological
differences--certainly without actual linguistic methodology--
seeks various stages of the tradition, tacitly applying premises that have never been proved and in my opinion are also
not provable: on the one hand following the evolutionary
premise that the simpler, shorter, more isolated formulation
or language form is older, than the more complex, longer, and
more aggregative,[199] on the other following the premise of a
development that began with a primal version, and proceded

rather gradually and without stops and starts,[200] a development which can be reconstructed with the aid of quasi-logical
laws. That the evangelist could compose the summaries unique
in form-*historical* formation, but terminologically quite within a customary "Christian" *langue*, has not been sufficiently
considered and differentiated,[201] indeed because the consequences of the redaction-critical manner of approach have not
been thoroughly enough thought through with respect to the
gestaltist individuality of the evangelist. The following
analysis attempts to show in detail that methodologically non-
reflective tradition history fails to meet linguistic objections, and that results are only to be awaited from a more
materially careful and painstaking investigation. Likewise
the following reflections are an example for the ways--ini-
tially [p. 214] very cautious ways--specific linguistic findings can be made fruitful for form-critical, traditio-historical, and redaction-critical analyses as they are now practiced.

(iv) The Failure of the Traditio-historical Reconstruction.

Considerable methodological uncertainty is also demonstrated in G. Strecker's own attempt at a solution. We will
discuss his arguments briefly here, while referring to other
research at the same time.

Strecker suggests the thesis "that the ur-form of the predictions of the passion is present in 8:31; it has been tripled
by Mark and progressively made to suit the account of the passion".[202] I think that is true for the Markan redaction, but
not for the quotational character of 8:31 introduced in its
support. Strecker discusses the interrelations of the individual summaries,[203] especially those of 9:31 and 10:33f. to 8:
31.[204] He accepts the possibility of the traditio-historical
dependency of 9:31 and 10:33 upon 8:31 because of its isola-

tion in the context.[205] Thereby it is recognized in principle
that isolated logia can be later than those that are tied to
contexts, in which case the evolutionary premise of the priority of the briefer language forms has been at least partial-
ly penetrated.[206] But Strecker's argument does not work,
*since all three summaries have to be evaluated as isolated
logia, because of redactional phrases.*[207] Are they therefore
pre-Markan? At any rate Strecker must, following the same argument, consider 8:31 as also belonging to an earlier level.

According to Strecker, *9:31* is a redactional and Markan
expansion of 8:31, assuming the passion tradition of Mk
14f.,[208] whereas H. Grass, E. Schweizer, and W. Popkes, on
account of certain deletions in later additions, consider it
the oldest form of the kerygmatic summary,[209] and F. Hahn takes
it together [p. 215] with 14:41b, which over against the passion tradition represents a more recent type to be contrasted
with that which is related to the holy scripture (cf. 8:31,
9:12b, 14:21), as an older type of the words of the suffering
Son of Man.[210] The existence of these varying judgments can
be explained, it seems to me, only by means of the pronounced
uncertainty of the method. While the argument for the priority
of the word play also present in the Greek text,[212] *ho huios
tou anthrōpou paradidotai eis cheiras anthrōpōn,*[213] which essentially rests on a hypothetical Aramaic basis,[211] Hahn and
Strecker more correctly trace the *paradidotai* back to a terminological reminiscence of 14:11; 18:21, 41f., 44; 15:10, 15,[214]
noting that *14:21, 41b* likewise contain the expression *ho huios
tou anthrōpou paradidotai*, even if with a different synsemantic
field. Mark certainly relied on a compositional reference to
what was recounted later, so that the *redactional* function of
9:31 (and 10:33f.) is obvious; a suspected traditio-historical
variant entirely disappears behind it, to my way of thinking.
At any rate, since the "brief formulas" of 14:21, 41b, are the

traditio-historically older version as opposed to 9:31,[215] the only thing in its favor is the evolutionary premise of the priority of what is briefer, since form-critically these passages are not summaries and do not concern, in the same precise sense as is possible in 9:31, an isolated quotation of the kerygma.[216] The paratactic style of the individual members (*kai*!)[217] common to all the summaries [p. 216] is lacking in the "brief formulas"; and besides it would be senseless from a compositional point of view to quote the "more developed" version such as 9:31 in 14:21, 41b, so that the "brief formulas" may be a redactional allusion to the more comprehensive and anticipatory summaries. *A striking example of the way tradition history is actually being practiced without regard to redaction criticism!* The *argumentum e silentio* is redaction-critically meaningless, since the context permits no "more developed" version. Mark is degraded to being a mechanical and seemingly thoughtless redactor who merely puts onto paper what the tradition offers him, without effacing the traditio-historical levels, so that traditio-historical conclusions can be drawn from the present text without regard to the redactional "sense" of the formulations. This is then a striking instance of the atomistic co-existence of tradition history and form criticism, since the pre-history of the form of the summaries is viewed merely as a gradual addition of originally independent expressions, i.e., not belonging to the form of the summaries, and are not named at all as a basis for the development of this language form except as a gradual aggregation of expressions. If we pay attention to the redactional function of 14:21, 41b, it is no longer possible to speak of a "formula", but only of reminiscence of a traditional expression, of a redactional reference back to the summaries, so that a traditio-historical value as a source vanishes. There would then remain only *Lk 9:44* as a reference to a "brief formula", which is said to have been connected after the fact with the traditio-historically different *apokteinein* / *anistēmi*, which belongs more to 8:31.[218] But the change of subject from *paradidotai* to *apoktenousin* and the participial use of *apoktantheis* in 9:31 do not establish the pre-Markan traditional connection of the "brief formula" (Lk 9:44) with secondary expansions,[219] but at most a materially necessary grammatical *constructio ad sensum*, by which the material subject, *anthrōpōn*, is named for [the verb] *apoktenousin*. Therefore Lk 9:44 belongs to the features peculiar to Luke,[220] which can be evaluated only as being a slavish relationship to his pattern on the part of the redactor, favoring a "special source".[221] [p. 217] Its hypothetical possibility[222] can never be used as an argument in favor of the wider traditio-historical hypothesis.

Result: The quotation-character in the precise sense of Mk 9:31 is not provable; form-*historically* the summary is not derivable, since there are no demonstrable traditio-historically prior levels. The objection, "that...the existence of such formulaic, isolated predictions of the passion is difficult to verify",[223] refers to the lack of a conceivable "sociological setting". The summary is rather a purely "literary" redactional phenomenon, in which the choice of words and style throughout can have been taken from the traditional "Christian" language-*usage*; but it is not possible to prove unequivocably that a block-like self-contained language-*form* was adopted.

According to F. Hahn, *Mk 10:33f.* is a Markan development of 9:31;[224] according to G. Strecker, the same, but of 8:31;[225] but according to H. E. Tödt,[226] U. Wilckens,[227] and (with qualifications) W. Popkes,[228] it is pre-Markan. Here again the judgment is entirely dependent upon the evaluation of Mark's redactional freedom, but also upon the observance of the form-critical and structural *valeur* of individual terms. *Must* we conclude on the basis of the minor differences between 10:33f. and chs. 14f. that there was an independent tradition,[229] an "old

formula" utilized by Mark,[230] a recapitulation of the passion
narrative, "as it perhaps [would have been] used in liturgy or
catechism",[231] [p. 218] or "doesn't this argument carry all too
much weight"?[232] When on the one hand Tödt leaves open the
possibility "that the third prediction of the passion as a
whole has been created by Mark on the basis of available elements",[233] but concludes from the lack of *stauroun* and the an-
tagonism toward the gentiles at an earlier level, "that is not
yet determined by views belonging to the hellenistic church",[23]
and when on the other hand W. Popkes, referring to the specifically Lukan problematics of the anti-Jewish and pro-Roman polemic, deduces a secondary level,[235] then we see the methodological uncertainty of traditio-historical judgments. When today we reckon more extensively with the redactional freedom of
the evangelists, only the linguistic argument of the mutual
lack of *stauroun* or *apoktenein* is given any weight. But in its
usual version it is by no means actually a form-critical and
linguistic argument, since the possibility of the form-critical
and structural *valeur* of a term is not considered; but by sep-
arating the form-critical inquiry from that respecting the content and the tradition history, an arbitrary applicability of
the terms dependent upon the language form is brought into the
picture *sub rosa*.[236] A structural and linguistic form criticism could at any rate only recognize a terminologically based
analysis, which on the one hand attends to the dialectical
sense-procurement[237] of *apoktenousin / anastēsetai* (cf. Mk 9:
31, 10:33f.) or *apoktanthēnai / anastēnai* (cf. 8:31), and on
the other of *apothnēskein / egeiresthai* (cf. Rom 6:9, 8:34, I
Cor 15:3f., II Cor 5:15),[238] which has been secondarily altered
into *apokteinein / egeigesthai* (cf. Mt 16:21, 17:23 [20:19],
Lk 9:22, Acts 3:15)[239] and *apothnēskein / anistēmi* (cf. I Thess
4:14, Rom 14:9 *G lat Or*).[240] What is *form-critically* produced
by this is a connection between *apokteinein / anistēmi*, in the

Markan summaries of the passion, and [p. 219] the Son of Man title,[241] and between *apothnēskein / egeiresthai*, in christological applications and the *christos*-title,[242] i.e., a form-critically *linguistic dissimilarity*, determined by the different "sociological setting", of the "synsemantic field", but not yet a traditio-*historical series*, whose genealogical sequence could be established without an *a priori* historical model. Even the lack of *stauroun* in the Markan summaries can be explained by the stereotyped synsemantic connection between Son of Man and *apokteinein*, while *stauroun* in Mk 14f. never forms a synsemantic connection with the Son of Man.[243] Before traditio-historical conclusions are drawn from these two different synsemantic fields, it is first necessary to take into account the possibility of a form-critical establishment of the linguistic dissimilarity: Following linguistic rules, terms cannot be arbitrarily joined into a unified "gestalt"-sense, into a specific language form with an impressed synsemantic field, but only according to those structural laws that constitute the language form (*langue*). Only if this fact were acknowledged fully by tradition history could we speak of a *sociology*-of-language methodology in form criticism.

Result: A pre-Markan form-*history* of the summary is not clearly discernible, but indeed an inner-Markan one is, which can be explained most easily as a redactional expansion of Mk 9:31 with the purpose of preparing for chs. 14f. The terminological distinctions which will be used in the isolated traditio-historical analysis can perhaps be explained in terms of a form-critically determined nature of the "synsemantic field", concerning whose traditio-historical stages nothing direct can be stated. The "kerygma"-character in the precise form-critical sense cannot be elicited.

Mk 8:31, according to H. E. Tödt, on the basis of Mark's reference to scripture (Ps 117:22f.; LXX) in *apodokimasthēnai*,

related to *ēxoudenēthē* (cf. 9:12b with Acts 4:11),[244] has been
shown by 12:10f. to be pre-Markan, and is therefore considered
"certainly pre-Markan";[245] and also [p. 220] G. Strecker considers it, in terms of a search for reasonable redactional additions,[246] an original component of the pre-Markan unity of
the tradition in 8:27*, 29:31*, 32b-33 [Asterisks in Strecker's
text. - W.G.D.].[247] But the mere *apodokimasthēnai*, which here
possesses a "synsemantic field" entirely different from the
symbolic imagery of Ps 117:22f. (LXX), can in any case awaken
ancillary associations to this verse of scripture[248] and could
just as well have been utilized by Mark himself as a "usual"
term in the summary, which is certainly redactional in its
function; that Mark does not himself have to experience his
langue is of course evident.[249] Further, Strecker's analysis
is by no means convincing, since [p. 221] it does not ignore
a redactional framing of v. 31 by vv. 30, 21aα, 32a, and even
affirms considerable interference with v. 31 itself,[250] according to which deletion of the remaining residuum hardly permits
further judgments concerning its original form-critical gestalt. However that also means that 8:31 as well as 9:31,
10:33f., is a logion that can be readily dissolved from its
content,[251] and according to Strecker's analysis, indeed only
a fragment of such, no longer recognizable with respect to its
pre-Markan context. If redactional freedom holds with respect
to 9:31, 10:33f.,[252] than it is not evident why such cannot
also be the case with respect to 8:31. Supporting this would
be Strecker's reference to the thoroughly Markan language
style, not only in v. 31, but in the entire pericope, which
paradoxically cannot support Strecker's thesis of a thorough-
going *pre*-Markan tradition,[253] but only the thesis of a Markan
shaping as a whole, *which has disappeared behind the suspected
prior-levels in the "ur-historical" obscurity*. In that case
we are faced with a redactional confessional statement, "which

would be easily imaged on the basis of firmly shaped community formulation",[254] since Strecker's reference to the uncertainty of a "sociological setting" for a pre-Markan summary is valid for 8:31 as well as for 9:31, 10:33f., as is his objection "that...the existence of such a formulaic, isolated prediction of the passion is difficult to verify".[255] Evidently because Strecker wants to reach a pre-Markan stage, he argues that 8:31* belongs to the suspected pre-Markan unity of the tradition,[256] although according to the exclusion of the redactional insertions in vv. 27a, 30, 31aα, 32a, it is not an uninterrupted transmission,[257] but "at any rate [there is] no longer any relation between 8:29 and 31aβ".[258] Even the paratactic style (three-fold *kai*), otherwise considered redactional,[259] which allows the summary to function as a specification [p. 222] of the stages of the passion in chs. 14f., is more suitable to the similar style of the other Markan summaries,[260] so that v. 31 is entirely a Markan stylized insertion. Against this there seem to be purely emotional reasons based on contents and types of presentation; so the Son of Man title, which A. Strobel suggests "speaks fittingly of a Son-of-Man/passion-secret-theory",[261] and the phrase *meta treis hemēras*,[263] which is frequently seen in presentational terms as being in tension with *tē hēmera tē tritē* (cf. I Cor 15:4, Mt 16:21, 17:23, 20:19, 27:64, Lk 9:22, 13:32, 18:33, 24:7, 21:46, Acts 10:40) or with *dia triōn hēmerōn* (Mk 14:58) / *en trisin hēmerais* (15:29);[262] *meta treis hēmeras* (except for the contextually different passages Lk 2:46, Acts 25:1, 27:17) is *only* evidenced in the Markan summaries. However these findings do not definitely speak for a pre-Markan formulation, for which otherwise there is no evidence,[264] the less so since there is here no trace of a different temporal fixing of Jesus' resurrection, and scarcely a material distinction from *tē tritē hēmera*,[265] if the Jewish counting of the days is be-

hind this.[266] The assumption of traditio-historical distinc-
tions--it would be better to speak more neutrally of the linguistic and form-critical differences--is in any case not a
criterion for the temporal sequence of the traditio-historical
layering.[267] Hence basically there remains only the vague
suspicion of pre-Markan expressions, which probably were first
combined by Mark into the present summary-form. That would
mean, however, that a block-like transmitted "kerygma" cannot
be proved, but at most we can assume a conventional theological language whose form-critical character disappears entirely
behind its present function as a summary.

There remains only a traditio-historical reconstruction
of a prior stage to 8:31 in the "brief formula" *Lk 17:25*,
which has been filled out and embellished later.[268] But
against this: first, the same linguistic objections are to
be raised as against the priority of the other "brief formulas"; second the possibility of a Lukan expansion of the
probably redactional condensation in Lk 9:22,[269] hence of a
Lukan insertion into the otherwise "apocalyptic" [p. 223] context;[270] and third but most important, the introductory *prō-
ton*, which demands some sort of supplementary context, even if
such did not refer to the promise of the parousia and hence to
a period of time between the passion and the parousia in historical Jesus-words.[271] Whether this context is a prior stage
leading to the Markan summary can no longer be supposed.

*Result: It is not possible to get behind the primary re-
dactional function of Mk 8:31*, since the validity of Strecker's
arguments regarding 9:31 and 10:33f., can also be applied to
8:31. A transmitted "kerygma" in the precise form-critical
sense is not at all what we have here, but rather a theologically and materially significant summary, which does not shape
the gospel as a whole, but only the portion from 8:27 on, in
a form-critical and structural manner. Since the analysis of

the primitive Christian "kerygma" presented in Sect. 2 of this chapter almost completely disappears in the "ur-historical" obscurity, it seems best to relinquish the form-*historical* thesis that the gospel form is an "expansion of the kerygma". Consequently the most that can be stated is that in it a theologically important content has attained a gestalt. A historical and evolutionary relation between two language forms is not provable in any case, since there is no provable primitive-community kerygma in this precise sense, concerning what is available in the passages examined by means of the various conceptions (#13, Sects. 1 & 2). Thereby U. Wilcken's traditio-historically destructive criticism has been sustained once more and indeed sharpened.

3. The Purely Hypothetical Character of the Pre-Markan Redactional Complex.

The thesis of the traditio-historical contingency of the gospel form (#5) appears to have a weighty counter-argument against it, namely the form-critical evidence of a *gradual* redaction of the material of the tradition, advanced by R. Bultmann and others.[272] But is this evidence to be regarded as certain, or does it concern a hypothesis which might be revised according to the changed situation of research which has occurred because of redaction criticism? We will examine the carrying capacity of the argument here in detail by asking: Is it possible definitely to prove a *continuous* redactional process for the tradition history [p. 224] of the synoptic material, at whose termination the gospel form *inevitably* stands as the evolutionary consequence of the collective tradition history of the material?

(a) Bultmann's Premises and Concessions.

That the way we have expressed the question is not a dis-
tortion of the circumstances Bultmann has in mind, is shown by
Bultmann's thesis that the connected presentation of the life
of Jesus first appearing in Mark is the only natural consequence of a need at the time of the gradual victory of the
realm of the oral tradition: "We may say that it simply *had*
to arrive at a connected presentation of the life of Jesus on
the basis of the available tradition consisting of individual
elements and small collections."[273] But is this what we may
call a causal and genetic derivation of the form of the gospels from out of the collective history of the material? To
be sure, Bultmann concedes at once that the peculiar character of the form of the gospels, created by Mark, can only be
understood "on the basis of the character of the Christian
kerygma, whose expansion and visualization the gospel had to
serve".[274] Apparently this "expansion and visualization of
the kerygma" went back to the creative act of Mark,[275] who
was entangled dialectically with the immanent tendency of the
materials for the gospel form, emphasizing the literary act
of creation:[276] The gospel needs no form-critical analogy.
"It grew up out of the immanent drive toward development which
lay in the tradition that grew up from various motifs, and out
of the Christ-cult and Christ-myth of hellenistic Christianity."[277] It seems to me that in this opinion we have an indirect concession *that the gospel form, in the absence of a*
form-critical analogy, is not only explicable on the basis of
the immanent development of the collective material, but that
a genuine Christian literary act of creation must be assumed,
an act which indeed essentially lives in tension between the
more individual and the immanent tendency of the material.
Looking back at Chapters ##4, 5, 11, and 12, it appears that

our reflections there are therefore justified *a posteriori* in
that they were already put forward indirectly by R. Bultmann.

In what ways do the immanent tendencies of the material
serve as "preparation" for the form of the gospels? According to Bultmann the collection of the traditional material began in the Palestinian primitive community, [p. 255] which
created no new literary genres, but took over those long developed within Judaism: "With all of that however the type
of the gospel was not created, but only prepared for."[278] By
means of the isolation of the words of Jesus from other au-
thorities, in distinction to the cumulation of various au-
thorities in the rabbinic tradition, "the gospel was without
a doubt prepared for, but still not yet created".[279] But in
what sense can we speak of a "preparation", if we first encounter the type of the gospel in Mark's creative act?[280]
Bultmann seems to have perceived this aporia as an unresolved
question [offene Frage], and we will be well advised to watch
for other signs of methodological uncertainty.

Although Bultmann considered various pre-Markan redactional complexes probable, and indeed as written sources, he refused "to consider such sources as having *fixed* dimensions,
since basically it does not much matter whether one or another
redactional process, inherent in the written transmission, took
place already *before* or only first *within* our gospels, if the
subject is of any consequence at all".[281] *Therefore Bultmann
refused consciously the exact determination of the time of a
redactional operation*, because it only mattered in terms "of
clarifying and illustrating the main viewpoints".[282] A presupposition for this disclaimer is the concession that the
analysis lacked certainty:[283] It is uncertain "which redactional connections were created by Mark himself and which belong to an earlier level of the redaction. We must deal with
the latter, as is quite clear in a few instances. But mostly

the decision is not of fundamental significance; the main
thing is to recognize how the redaction works as a whole."[284]
So it also remains unresolved [offen] whether the authorial
and dogmatic motifs in the redactional work described stem
from Mark or from his predecessors.[285] In the long run this
disclaimer means a disclaimer with respect to a *precise* description of the *gradual* process of redaction at whose end
Mark stands as the final redactor *without a break*, immanently,
and consistently.[286] However in my opinion it is quite clear
that in this manner the creative act is lost to the collective
process of tradition, and remains in problematic tension with
the form-critical and *sociological* conceptual model: In what
sense is the material of the speeches "made one with a connected presentation" by means of the pre-Markan redactional
activity [p. 226] and in what sense does the redactional activity lead "to work executed...hand in hand with the connection of the material as a whole into a summarizing presentation",[287] if the "aptitude" for this presentation as a whole
has not been created by the intentional act of a self-conscious creative [gestaltenden] evangelist who chose the material to belong to the intended form (Ch. #12)? In what
sense is only this act "to be derived" from the sociological
and form-critical laws of the materials? This question remains unresolved in Bultmann's work since the sociological
conceptual model with its prior-judgment "that a literary history is not possible except in the sense of an explanation of
an original subject matter by means of some other kind of human activity",[288] leads him into un-resolvable methodological
aporias. Is any sort of certainty possible with reference to
the exact form-*historical* process of the pre-Markan redaction?

(b) Examination of the Hypothesis of
   Pre-Markan Redaction.

For the sake of brevity I will restrict the discussion
here to the question of the pre-Markan complexes accepted by
early form criticism, passing over the discussion of special-
ized source-theories such as those proposed by A. T. Cadoux,
J. M. C. Crum, R. Thiel, E. Hirsch, D. F. Robinson, B. P. W.
Stather Hunt, H. Helmbold, W. L. Knox, L. Vaganay, and E.
Trocmé,[289] which for the most part are not of a form-critical
nature.

1.   *Mark and Q.*   The question whether or not Mark knew
Q, and hence whether there was a literary and form-critical
dependency, is sooner to be negatively than positively answered.[290] Apart from the uncertainty of the exact extent of
the text and word order of Q,[291] and apart from whether Q was
oral or written,[292] the form of the gospels cannot be [p. 227]
a simple consequence of the immanent tendencies of this level
(something that Bultmann did not affirm, either), whether
these be only of purely paraenetic[293] or more christological
nature.[294] *A gradual, consecutive process of redaction is not
observable.*

2.   *Mark and the Pre-Markan Passion Narrative.*   The passion narrative is given a primary position in our context not
only because M. Kähler, "somewhat defiantly", called the gospels "passion narratives with extensive introduction",[295] but
also because of the newly introduced thesis that Mark incorporated the principles of composition already effective in the
passion narrative transmitted to him, and so expanded the kerygma "backwards" by surrounding the passion narrative with
the other materials by means of the summaries of the passion
(Mk 8:31, 9:31, 10:33f.), so that the forward-directed *history* of Jesus corresponded "to the backwards expansion of the

kerygma proceding from the passion narrative".[296] According to
W. Marxsen the Markan theory of the messianic secret also corresponds to this compositional principle, with whose help Mark
corrected an image of a historical sequence and a history of
Jesus arising inevitably from the parataxis of the single pericopes, one "which presented a permanent, historically demonstrable epiphany of his messiahship".[297] Mark wanted by means
of his principle of composition to take up the sayings of the
pre-Markan passion narrative and simultaneously to specify
them by means of the motif of the *repraesentatio Christi* in the
euangelion: "The resurrected one becomes--in the contemporary
proclamation--an epiphany in the narratives of his earthly
life."[298] However can the redaction-*historical* process affirmed here be unequivocably proved?

J. Schreiber has recognized the problem whether the presumed pre-Markan passion narrative was from the beginning conceived as a whole, or gradually composed, like the rest of the
tradition.[299] Only in the latter case could the gospel of
Mark be the final consequence of redactional tendencies immanent in it. While *on the one hand* only for K. L. Schmidt is
it "clear without further ado" "that here a consecutive narration was intended from the beginning", which has "almost entirely vanished" from the analytical process, so that thereby
"another [p. 228] literary appraisal" is demanded;[300] and
while further for M. Dibelius "its relative compactness", except for Mk 14:3-9, is striking[301]--it is the only portion of
the transmission "that in the earlier period presented events
in a larger context"[302]--*on the other hand* R. Bultmann and G.
Bertram seek a mediating position: To be sure "very early a
context was created; indeed we might almost say that the context here was the primary thing";[303] certainly the passion
narrative is "evidently...the oldest firmly shaped portion of
Christian transmission";[304] but in spite of that it is not

possible to affirm here any organic whole, but only a mosaic
comprised of individual elements.[305] The analysis makes it
clear "that the passion narrative also is comprised of individual pericopes, which only gradually grew together into
a whole".[306]

In my opinion these differences of judgment are an indication of a considerable uncertainty in the exact description
of the gradual process of redaction. The composition here is
so condensed that every tradition- or redaction-*historical*
analysis must assume far too many hypothetical combinations
in order to be able to demonstrate exactly the probably
rather complicated process of origination. [A situation in
which, as here] the one finds [a set of data] "probable" or
"illuminating", the other "improbable", is too greatly dependent upon the personal taste of the one making the judgment,
[so much so] that we can no longer confidently propose a historical image of the process of redaction. We may and can be
able here to break through the *circulus vitiosus* of the inner
conviction of the "coherence" of one's own network of hypotheses in view of the difficulty of the material. The "analytical process" is betrayed here unforseen into a methodological
aporia: If a concededly special instance of gospel tradition
is present here, we are lacking an analogy which would permit
the exact description of the pre-Markan (pre-literary) tradition *process*; at any rate we can guess such as a prior-stage
of the present "literary" *state* of the tradition, but we can
no longer reach further than the present strongly compressed
Markan composition and its structural and compositional function in the entire gospel, unless we must accept in the same
bargain a whole network of hypotheses with many uncertainties.
Therefore we should be satisfied with inner-Markan structural
analysis (that of the "literary" level). As interesting for
historical reasons as the reconstruction of hypothetical

prior-stages may be, the [p. 229] functional structural-analy-
sis of the "literary gestalt" at hand is much more urgent for
the understanding of the form of the gospels.[306a] *A gradual,
consecutive process of redaction cannot be unequivocably observed here.*

3.   According to R. Bultmann *Mk 1:16-39* is to be regarded
as a small pre-Markan collection.[307] But the passage is heavily permeated by Markan redaction, such as the expansion of the
choral conclusion in 1:28,[308] 1:32-34, indeed a Markan creation
that has the nature of a summary account,[309] the summary 1:
39,[310] 1:22, which is perhaps an insertion,[311] which would
prove that the *didachē*-motif (1:21f., 27a) is Markan,[312] the
redactional expansion of 1:29, which connects 1:16-20 with 1:
21-28,[313] the affiliation of 1:38 to the redactional creation
1:35-39,[314] and so forth. *The redactional network is so im-
penetrable that the assumption of a pre-Markan collection must
remain an unprovable guess.*

4.   Mark 2:1-3:6 is considered a pre-Markan collection of
controversy discourses or miracle stories,[315] indeed by W.
Marxsen, a "source of controversy discourses".[316] Nonetheless K. L. Schmidt considers the pre-Markan redaction only the
more probable assumption--without further reasons[317]--while
the section in its present form has been shaped by Mark,[318] as
a result of 3:6.[319] Perhaps 2:1f., 13, et al., may be added
to it.[320] The uncertainty of the interpreters shows that the
decision for pre-Markan or Markan redaction essentially depends upon one's premises. *A gradual, consecutive process of
redaction cannot be observed here, either.*

5.   According to R. Bultmann *Mk 4:1-32* likewise appears to
have been a small collection,[321] W. Marxsen indeed taking it
as a "parable source", which encompassed 4:3-8, 9, 10, 13-20,
30-32.[322] P. Vielhauer states [p. 230] in a more lapidary

manner, that the existence of such collections is "possible, but completely unprovable". We should "not represent as facts what are only hypotheses".[323] Even if here we were to wager reconstruction with greater certainty, we would only be able to establish, as in 2:1-3:6, the collection of similar genres. *It is not evident how the immanent tendencies of this redaction should have developed further as a gradual continuation of the gospel form.*

6.   *Mark 4:35-5:43* is seen as a pre-Markan cycle of miracle stories by Bultmann, Dibelius, and Marxsen.[324] But here too there is an uncertainty similar to what we found in the previous instances, because the time of the redactional operations cannot be determined exactly. Neither does the immanent tendency of this redaction provide a consistent path to the gospel form. Indeed here the theological motif of the *theios anēr* is present;[325] but this motif concerns at most a particular stratum of the Jesus-tradition.[326] If, following U. Luz, we understand the Markan christology as the attempt "to make understandable the *theios anēr*-christology and the epiphany-idea of the hellenistic church...from the point of view of the kerygma of the cross",[327] this is a history-of-*religions* description of the phenomenon, not a *form*-historical one. *Again we cannot determine how the immanent tendencies may have further developed a possible pre-Markan redaction as a gradual continuation of the gospel form.*

7.   According to M. Albertz and W. Marxsen, *Mk 11:27-12:37* represents a pre-Markan complex of teaching and controversy discourses.[328] But here the situation is similar to that obtaining in 2:2-3:6. What *compels* us to question the "final redactor" of such complexes? Clearly an unexpressed premise resonates, namely that such an expanded compositon could have arisen from a redactor with such meagre ability only by means

of linking together small compositions. But this premise is precisely what has to be proved. *A gradual process of redaction is again not something that can be demonstrated.*

8.   *Mark 13* is considered a Jewish-apocalyptic source,[329] an apocalyptic circular.[330] But even if that were something that were free of doubt, the present composition is so very Markan,[331] that a *gradual* process of redaction can no longer be determined.

Result: The assumption of pre-Markan redaction is to a large extent an assumption and cannot be unequivocably demonstrated. A gradual process of redaction with an immanent tendency toward the gospel form is therefore not observable. Naturally we do not deny that it occurred; redaction-*historically* the gospel form remains uniquely contingent. The traditio-historical attempts outmaneuver that by their history-of-*religions* description, which bypasses the *form*-historical aspect. The formal powers of the "kerygma" were never proved and free from objection in the *process* of transmission and redaction, but are merely quasi "form-free presentations". We are still a long way from an actual form and redaction *history* of the gospel. Our concern here is especially with the candid question whether the collective tradition of the "small units", and perhaps also of collections, has prepared for the evangelists' intentional act of selection and formation genealogically and immanently, in the sense of its traditio-historical "derivation", or whether this act, as well as each genuine linguistic act of creation, and finally as life itself, is underivable, even if it has sociological "conditions" which however do not work causally and coercively. Form criticism faces today the candid question as to how far evolutionary and genealogical premises are able to explain the phenomenon of form *history* in a manner that is appropriate to the subject.

Notes to #13

1. See above, pp. [46, 70, 83, 91ff., 95ff.].

2. See for instance Fascher, *formgesch. Methode*, 54ff., 62ff.; Dibelius, *ThR* 1 (1929) 191; Dibelius, *Formgesch.*-3rd ed., 307ff. (G. Iber); Iber, *ThR* 24 (1957/58) 308ff.; G. Schille, *NTS* 4 (1957/58) 11ff.; U. Wilckens, *ThLZ* 86 (1961) 274f. -- Many find Bultmann's differentiated categories more usuable here. Cf. Iber, *op. cit.*, 288. Alongside the *kerygma*, the apostolic catechism (cf. J. A. Ubieta, "El Kerygma apostólico y los Evangelios," *EstBib* 18 [1959] 21-61), or the Didache, has been supposed to have been effective upon the formation of the evangelical tradition (cf. C. H. Dodd, *The Apostolic Preaching and Its Developments*, 1966-rev. ed., 7ff., 36ff., Dodd, *History and the Gospel*, 1960-rev. ed., 51ff., 84ff.; Dodd, *Gospel and Law*, 1952-3rd ed., 3ff., 9f.), or the personal witness of the apostle, so that Mark would be something situated between *kerygma* and *didache* (cf. C. C. Cowling, "The Involvement of the Community in the Apostolic Tradition," *ChQR* 164 [1963] 6-18), or the gospels a continuum between *kerygma* and *martyrion* (cf. W. Trilling, "Jesusüberlieferung und apostolische Vollmacht," *TThZ* 71 [1962] 352-68). All these theses are thoroughly hypothetical, since we have no *direct* sources about the forms presupposed, to which the gospel tradition could be form-critically reduced. Furthermore, it is precisely the problem, to what extent the form of the gospel may at all be reduced form-*historically*. [+1978: Seen linguistically, the presupposed forms would be "kernel-texts" to which the final gospels would have a relation of "extension-projection". But such relations have to be proved by explicit grammatical laws, constituting the relation between "kernel" and "extension".]

3. Cf. H. Clavier, *EThR* 9 (1934) 278.

4. H. Bausinger, *Formen der "Volkspoesie"*, 1968, 18.

5. Cf. Dibelius, *Formgesch.*, 8-34.

6. Cf. *ibid.*, 9.

7. Cf. E. Troeltsch, "Ueber historische und dogmatische Methode in der Theologie," in his *Zur religiösen Lage, Religions-philosophie und Ethik*, 1913 (*Ges. Schr.*, vol. 2), 731: The "principal habituation to historical criticism" means, "that in the area of history there can only be judgements of

probability, of very different degrees of probability, from the greatest to the least, and that every tradition therefore must be measured against the degree of probability that it is granted".

8. Differently, Troeltsch, *Die Bedeutung der Geschichtlichkeit Jesu für den Glauben*, 1911, 34f.: There is a general "feeling of historical admissibility which is produced by the impression of scientific research". Agreement in W. Pannenberg, *Grundfragen systematischer Theologie*, 1967, 59f. Cf. against this, G. Klein, *Theologie des Wortes Gottes und die Hypothese der Universalgeschichte*, 1964, 61.

9. Cf. for instance T. Rendtorff, *ThLZ* 90 (1963) 98: Confidence in the confirmation of the historical conception by the course of history is simultaneously scientifically-applied confidence.

10. Cf. above, p. [95ff.].

11. Cf. above, p. [103ff.].

12. Cf. E. Lohse, "Lukas als Theologe der Heilsgeschichte," *EvTh* 14 (1954) 256-74; G. Klein, "Lukas 1, 1-4 als theologisches Programm," in E. Dinkler, ed., *Zeit und Geschichte*, 1964, 193-216.

13. Cf. Dibelius, *op. cit.*, 11f.

14. *Ibid.*, 12, partly italicized in the original.

15. Cf. Dibelius, *Aufsätze zur Apg.*, 79, 108, 127f.

16. Cf. bibliography in n. 12. Cf. also E. Norden, *Die antike Kunstprosa*, vol. 2, 1958-5th ed., 483.

17. Cf. Dibelius, *Formgesch.*, 11.

18. Cf. Klein, *op. cit.*, 201ff.

19. Cf. Klein, *Die zwölf Apostel*, 1961. Agreement and criticism: Güttgemanns, *VF* 12/2 (1967) 70-76.

20. Cf. Klein, *Zeit u. Gesch.*, 205.

21. Cf. Klein, *zwölf Apostel*, 44-49; W. Schmithals, *Das kirchliche Apostelamt*, 1961, 56-77, 217ff. Cf. on this Güttgemanns, *op. cit.*, 67.

22. Cf. Klein, *Zeit u. Gesch.*, 212ff. On the legitimation of apostolic tradition and succession, cf. Güttgemanns, *op. cit.*, 75f.

23. On the foundations for this understanding, cf. Klein, *op. cit.*, 199f.

24. *epicheirein* has a negative undertone. Cf. *ibid.*, 195f.

25. Cf. *ibid.*, 205ff.

26. Cf. Wilckens, *ThLZ* 86 (1961) 274: "Apparently [Dibelius] did not want to designate a definite phenomenon with the concept proclamation."

27. Cf. K. Stendahl, "Kerygma und kerygmatisch," *ThLZ* 77 (1952) 715-20; K. Goldammer, "Der Kerygma-Begriff in der ältesten christlichen Literatur," *ZNW* 48 (1957) 77-101.

28. Dibelius, *op. cit.*, 13.

29. *Ibid.*, 14.

30. *Ibid.*

31. Wilckens, *op. cit.*, 275, also raises the question "whether the analogy of modern times was not much closer to Dibelius' concept of proclamation than to the primitive Christian material itself".

32. Cf. Dibelius, *op. cit.*, 21: "We must therefore presuppose the early existence of a self-contained passion narrative, since the proclamation, both missionary- and church-proclamation, used such a text."

33. Cf. *ibid.*, 34-66.

34. Cf. #14, below.

35. Cf. Dibelius, *op. cit.*, 15ff.

36. Wilckens, *op. cit.*, 274.

37. Cf. Wilckens, *Die Missionsreden der Apostelgeschichte*, 1961.

38. Cf. Dibelius, "Die Reden der Apostelgeschichte und die antike Geschichtsschreibung," in his *Aufs. zur Apg.*, 120-62.

346

. Cf. Wilckens, *op. cit.*, 32-55.

40. Cf. *ibid.*, 56-71.

41. Cf. *ibid.*, 72-91.

42. Cf. *ibid.*, 86ff.

43. Cf. *ibid.*, 89f.

44. Cf. *ibid.*, 91.

45. Cf. *ibid.*, 91-99.

46. *Ibid.*, 99, italcized in the original.

47. Cf. *ibid.*, 100-86.

48. *Ibid.*, 186.

49. *Ibid.*, 188.

50. *Ibid.*, 191.

51. Bultmann, *Syn. Trad.* [Germ. ed.], 362.

52. J. Schniewind, *ThR* 2 (1930) 140. Cf. also K. L. Schmidt, "Die Stellung der Evangelien in der allgemeinen Literaturgeschichte," in *Eucharisterion*, vol. 2, 1923, 50-134.

53. Schniewind, *op. cit.*, 152, italicized in the original.

54. Cf. *ibid.*, 153. So now once more H. Conzelmann, *Grundriss der Theologie des Neuen Testaments*, 1968-2nd ed., 115ff.

55. Schniewind, *op. cit.*, 180.

56. Bultmann, *op. cit.*, 372f., partly italicized in the original. Similarly J. Schreiber, *ZThK* 58 (1961) 155ff. Cf. on the other hand P. Vielhauer, *Aufs.*, 199f.; E. Best, *The Temptation and the Passion*, 1965, 125-33.

57. Bultmann, *op. cit.*, 374.

58. *Ibid.*, 397.

59. It originates from an evolutionary premise of the history of *philosophy*, making a causal and genetic dependency

out of a merely ascertainable co-existence and sequence. D. Hume, *Philosophische Versuche über die Menschliche Erkenntniss*, 1755 (*Enquiry concerning Human Understanding*, 1748), 45ff., 149ff., 191ff., first showed that the necessary connection between origin and effect is neither to be rationally established nor empirically ascertained. Sequence, which alone is ascertainable, says nothing about the causal relationship.

60. Cf. R. A. Bartels, *Kerygma or Gospel Tradition... Which Came First?*, 1961.

61. The distinction between autosemantics and synsemantics is not represented in these terms in Aristotle, but substantively; it has been developed by A. Marty and O. Funke. Cf. H. Kronasser, *Handbuch der Semasiologie*, 1968-2nd ed., 47; St. Ullmann, *Semantics*, 1964-2nd ed., 44.

62. Cf. below, p. [224ff.].

63. Cf. I. Engnell, "Methological Aspects of Old Testament Study," *SupplVetTest* 7 (1960) 13-30; R. Rendtorff, "Hermeneutik des Alten Testaments als Frage nach der Geschichte," *ZThK* 57 (1960) 27-40; "Geschichte und Ueberlieferung," in R. Rendtorff and K. Koch, eds., *Studien zur Theologie der alttestamentlichen Ueberlieferung*, 1961, 81-94; and "Literarkritik und Traditionsgeschichte," *EvTh* 27 (1967) 138-53; W. Pannenberg, "Kerygma und Geschichte," in Rendtorff and Koch, eds., *Studien*, 129-40; T. Rendtorff, "Ueberlieferungsgeschichte als Problem der systematischen Theologie," *ThLZ* 90 (1965) 81-98; E. Käsemann, "Konsequente Traditionsgeschichte?", *ZThK* 62 (1965) 137-52; H. Ringgren, "Literarkritik, Formgeschichte, Ueberlieferungsgeschichte," *ThLZ* 91 (1966) 641-50.

64. Cf. however the criticism of the traditio-historical analysis of the summaries of the passion, in which linguistic methods are also used in an initial way. Below, p. [211ff.].

65. Cf. above, p. [161ff.].

66. Cf. above, p. [44ff.].

67. Cf. below, p. [212].

68. Cf. A. Harnack, *Die Aufgabe der theologischen Fakultäten und die allgemeine Religionsgeschichte*, 1901, 9f.

69. *Ibid.*, 10. It is astonishing how many of Harnack's fears have come true today.

70. The example of Egyptian religion, in which popular religion and priestly theology became widely separated, is well known (cf. *Wörterbuch der Religionen*, A. Bertholet and H. Frhr. v. Campenhausen, ed., K. Goldammer, 1962-2nd ed., 9 b), and further the construction of a thoroughgoing "magical worldview of the primitive" most recently revived by L. Levy-Bruhl. See A. E. Jensen, *Mythos und Kult bei Naturvölkern*, 1951, 16ff.; C. Lévi-Strauss, *Das Ende des Totemismus* [Germ. transl.], 1968-2nd ed.; and *Das Wilde Denken* [Germ. transl.], 1968. In either case an undifferentiated orientation on the presentational and linguistic distinctions of the "language worlds" could lead to the complete separation of their cultural localization if we are not conscious enough by other criteria that these different "language worlds" have arisen alongside another within *one* culture. [+1978: Meanwhile, I have developed more clearly a theory of "several worlds" in continuity with ideas of Leibniz. Cf. Güttgemanns, *Einführung*, 119ff.]

71. H. Spencer, *First Principles*, 1966-rev. ed., 222ff. Cf. Chr. v. Ferber, "Herbert Spencer," *RGG*-3rd ed., vol. 6, 1962, 237f.; G. Mensching, *RGG*-3rd ed., vol. 5, 1961, 966f.; W. Holsten, *ibid.*, 990. -- H. Spencer, *op. cit.*, 321, after several preliminary definitions, finally gives the following definition: "Evolution is an integration of matter and a concomitant dissipation of motion; during which the matter passes from an indefinite, incoherent homogeneity to a definite, coherent heterogeneity; and during which the retained motion undergoes a parallel transformation." (Italics in the original.)

72. Cf. Spencer, *The Study of Sociology*, 1966-rev. ed.; *The Principles of Sociology*, vols. 1-3, 1966-rev. ed.

73. Cf. Spencer, *First Principles*, 256ff., 279ff.

74. Cf. G. Widengren, "Evolutionism and the Problem of the Origin of Religion," *Ethnos* 10 (1945) 57-96, with reference to A. Lang, *The Making of Religion*, 1898; F. Boas, *Primitive Art*, 1927; Boas, *The Mind of Primitive Man*, 1929; A. Goldenweiser, *Anthropology*, 1937.

75. Cf. for example H. Spencer, *First Principles*, 229: "the process of evolving, though it implies increase of a concrete aggregate, and in so far an expansion of it, implies that its component matter has passed from a more diffused to a more concentrated state--has contracted."

76. Cf. below, pp. [216ff., 222f.].

77. Cf. G. Mensching, *Die Religion*, n.d., 266-88.

78. Cf. above, #7, n. 236.

79. Cf. I. Engnell, *Gamla Testamentet: en traditions-historisk inledning*, vol. 1, 1945.

80. E. Overbeck, *Christentum und Kultur*, ed. C. A. Bernoulli, 1963-new ed., 20.

81. Cf. C. H. Dodd, "The Framework of the Gospel Narrative," in his *New Testament Studies*, 1953, 1-11; and his *The Apostolic Preaching and Its Developments*, 1966-2nd ed. Agreement in F. B. Clogg, *ET* 46 (1933/34) 536f.; V. T. O'Keefe, *CBQ* 21 (1959) 183f.; A. Jones, *Script* 12 (1960) 67f. Further bibliography: J. A. Allan, *Interpretation* 9 (1955) 134. Cf. also below, n. 109.

82. Dodd, *Studies*, 1.

83. Cf. V. H. Stanton, *The Gospels as Historical Documents*, 3 vols., 1903/20; Dodd, *History and the Gospel*, 1960-rev. ed.; R. O. P. Taylor, *The Groundwork of the Gospels*, 1946; R. Dunkerley, "The Principle of Coherence in the Gospel Story," *ET* 58 (1946/47) 133-36, 161-64; Dunkerley, "The Context of the Gospel Story," *ET* 59 (1947/48) 4-7; B. P. W. Stather Hunt, *Primitive Gospel Sources*, 1951, viiiff.; D. M. Stanley, S.J., "The Conception of Our Gospels as Salvation-History," *ThSt* 20 (1959) 561-89; A. M. Ramsey, "The Gospel and the Gospels," in *TU* 73 (1957) 35-42; V. T. O'Keefe, S.J., "Towards Understanding the Gospels," *CBQ* 21 (1959) 171-89; I. T. Ramsey, "History and the Gospels," in *TU* 88 (1961) 201-17; Ch. W. F. Smith, "Is Jesus Dispensable?", *AnglThR* 44 (1962) 263-80; H. E. Turner, *Historicity and the Gospels*, 1963.

84. Dodd, *Studies*, 3.

85. Cf. Schmidt, *Rahmen*, 127, for the stories of Capernaum and the lake (Mk 1:16ff.); 146 for Mk 5:21; 150ff. for Mk 4:35-5:43; 181 for Mk 6:31-8:26; 274 for Mk 10:46-13:37. Recently doubts have been expressed about the form-critical existence of itineraries. Cf. the bibliography, #11, n. 29.

86. Cf. below, p. [5f.].

87. Cf. Dodd, *op. cit.*, 4.

88. Cf. *ibid.*, 5f.

89. *Ibid.*, 8.

90. Cf. *ibid.*, 8f.

91. *Ibid.*, 9.

92. Cf. *ibid.*, 10f.

93. Cf. Dodd, *Preaching*, 9f. Cf. also above, #6, n. 57.

94. Dodd, *Preaching*, 13.

95. Cf. *ibid.*, 13f.

96. Cf. *ibid.*, 16.

97. Cf. *ibid.*, 19f.

98. *Ibid.*, 21. On the comparison of Paul and Acts, cf. *ibid.*, 25ff.

99. *Ibid.*, 24. Cf. *ibid.*, 48.

100. *Ibid.*, 36.

101. *Ibid.*, 47.

102. *Ibid.*, 48.

103. *Ibid.*, 55.

104. *Ibid.*, 56.

105. So O. A. Piper, "The Origins of the Gospel Pattern," *JBL* 78 (1959) 115-24.

106. Cf. D. E. Nineham, in Nineham, ed., *Studies in the Gospels*, 1957-2nd ed., 224. Cf. also #14, n. 63.

107. Cf. C. F. Evans, *JThS* 7 (1956) 25; Wilckens, *Missionsreden*, 17, 19.

108. C. H. Dodd, *According to the Scriptures*, 1952, 11.

109. Cf. the bibliography in Wilckens, *op. cit.*, 20, n. 2 and 25, n. 306.

110. Cf. J. Gewiess, *Die urapostolische Heilsverkündigung nach der Apostelgeschichte*, 1939; E. Schick, *Formgeschichte und Synoptikerexegese*, 1940, 60ff.; J. Schmitt, *Jésus ressuscité dans la prédication apostolique*, 1949, 3ff.; J. R. Gei-

selmann, *Jesus der Christus*, 1951; L. Cerfaux, *Le Christ dans la theologie de Saint Paul*, 1954-2nd ed.

111. Cf. F. C. Grant, *The Earliest Gospel*, 1943, 46ff.; D. E. Nineham, "The Order of Events in St Mark's Gospel," in Nineham, ed., *Studies in the Gospels*, 1957-2nd ed., 223-39; C. F. Evans, "The Kerygma," *JThS* 7 (1956) 25-41; Wilckens, *op. cit.*; R. A. Bartels, *Kerygma or Gospel Tradition*.

112. Cf. Evans, *op. cit.*, 27, 30ff.

113. Cf. *ibid.*, 32.

114. Cf. Bartels, *op. cit.*, 13ff., 77ff.

115. Nineham, *op. cit.*, 229. Cf. Bartels, *op. cit.*, 37: "The order of Mark, the gist of Mark, and the conception of Jesus in Mark's Gospel remain in the Third Gospel what they originally were." On the Markan framework in Luke, cf. Kümmel, *Einleitung*, 20, 27f., 78ff.

116. Evidence in Klein, *op. cit.* (in n. 12), 196ff., and above, p. [192].

117. Cf. H. Conzelmann, *Die Mitte der Zeit*, 1964-5th ed.; H.-W. Bartsch, *Wachet aber zu jeder Zeit!*, 1963; W. C. Robinson, *Der Weg des Herrn*, 1964; M. Rese, *Alttestamentliche Motive in der Christologie des Lukas*, 1969; H. Flender, *Heil und Geschichte in der Theologie des Lukas*, 1965.

118. Cf. above, p. [192f.].

119. Cf. Nineham, *op. cit.*, 229.

120. Evans, *op. cit.*, 28. Cf. *ibid.*, 40.

121. Differently, C. C. Torrey, *The Composition and Date of Acts*, 1916, and others. Cf. the bibliography in Wilckens, *op. cit.*, 10f., n. 4. Against this: Evans, *op. cit.*, 37f.; H. F. D. Sparks, "The Semitism of Acts," *JThS* 1 (1950) 16-28; E. Haenchen, *Die Apostelgeschichte*, 1956, 69ff.

122. Cf. Evans, *op. cit.*, 40.

123. It is unfortunate that Mk 4:33f. was overlooked. Also the choice of the summaries or of the redactional passages was seemingly arbitrary. Why were, for example, Mk 1:32-34 (cf. above, #8, n. 49), 1:45, 4:1-2a, and other verses not treated? Absolutely nothing in the text itself suggests

that the "framework", to which not only the summaries belonged, was ever present in connected form.

124. Cf. Nineham, *op. cit.*, 230f.

125. Cf. *ibid.*, 231.

126. Cf. *ibid.*, 229: "they afford no clear evidence for the currency in the early church of a formal outline account of the progress of the Lord's earthly ministry"; "they are so slight in content that they could afford only the most limited support to the historicity of Mark's order."

127. Cf. *ibid.*, 229f., for the most recent argument.

128. Cf. *ibid.*, 231f.

129. Cf. *ibid.*, 236f.

130. Cf. *ibid.*, 228.

131. Cf. *ibid.*, 226.

132. Cf. *ibid.*, 226f., 237.

133. Cf. Wilckens, *op. cit.*, 20ff.; N. B. Stonehouse, *Origins of the Synoptic Gospels*, 1963, 136.

134. Evans, *op. cit.*, 41.

135. Cf. P. Vielhauer, "Zum 'Paulinismus' der Apostelge-schichte," in his *Aufs.*, 9-27; Klein, *zwölf Apostel*, 114ff. Cf. also O. Bauernfeind, "Vom historischen zum lukanischen Paulus," *EvTh* 13 (1953) 347-53.

136. Cf. E. Käsemann, "Begründet der neutestamentliche Kanon die Einheit der Kirche?", in his *Aufs.*, vol. 1, 214-23; H. Braun, "Hebt die heutige neutestamentliche Forschung den Kanon auf?", in his *Gesammelte Studien zum Neuen Testament und seiner Umwelt*, 1962, 310-24; Braun, "Die Problematik einer Theologie des Neuen Testaments", in his *Aufs.*, 325-41; H. Schlier, "Ueber Sinn und Aufgabe einer Theologie des Neuen Testaments," in his *Besinnung auf das Neue Testament*, 1964, 7-24.

137. Cf. Wilckens, *op. cit.*, 18, n. 1.

138. Cf. *ibid.*, 19.

139. So Bartels, *op. cit.*, 96.

140. Cf. A. Seeberg, *Der Katechismus der Urchristenheit*,
1966-new ed.; *Das Evangelium Christi*, 1905.

141. Cf. H. Conzelmann, "Was glaubte die frühe Christenheit?", *Schweizer. Theol. Umschau* 25 (1955) 61-74, espec. on
the approach to Rom 10:9, whose traditio-historical consequences are drawn out in his *Theol.*, 81ff.; Kramer, *Christos*,
16ff., 28f., 61ff., 68f. Therefore in the fact that theology
is understood "as exegesis of the original *texts* of faith,
and therefore of the oldest formulations of the credo" (Conzelmann, *Theol.*, 13), one can see a relationship to A. Seeberg.
Cf. on the other hand Käsemann, *op. cit.* (in n. 63).

142. Cf. Seeberg, *Katech.*, 48-58. The texts cited in the
following are Seeberg's evidence, which today would have to be
examined critically.

143. Cf. *ibid.*, 58-85.

144. Cf. *ibid.*, 59ff.

145. Cf. *ibid.*, 70ff. Between the resurrection and re-
ceiving the title as Son of David, Seeberg naturally sees no
causal connection, but a terminological and topological one.

146. Cf. *ibid.*, 76f.

147. Cf. *ibid.*, 78ff.

148. Cf. *ibid.*, 81ff.

149. Cf. *ibid.*, 86ff.; Seeberg, *Ev.*, 61ff.

150. Cf. *Katech.*, 96ff.

151. Cf. *ibid.*, 125ff.; *Ev.* 63ff.

152. Cf. *Katech.*, 142ff.

153. Cf. *Ev.*, 4ff.

154. Cf. *Katech.*, 174ff., 204; *Ev.*, 11ff., 22ff., 67ff.,
40f.

155. Cf. *Katech.*, 193.

156. *Ibid.*, 83.

157. Cf. *ibid.*, 198ff.

158. Cf. *ibid.*, 200ff.; *Ev.*, 43ff.

159. Cf. *Katech.*, 204; *Ev.*, 56ff.

160. Cf. *Katech.*, 154f.

161. Cf. *ibid.*, 168ff.

162. Cf. *ibid.*, 178f.

163. Cf. *ibid.*, 182.

164. Cf. *Ev.*, 69ff.

165. Cf. *ibid.*, 72.

166. *Ibid.*, 75.

167. For criticism, see F. Hahn, in Seeberg, *Katech.*, xiii; R. Deichgräber, *Gotteshymnus und Christushymnus in der frühen Christenheit*, 1967, 13f.

168. Cf. Hahn, *op. cit.*, xii.

169. Cf. Wengst, *Diss.*, 8.

170. Hahn, *op. cit.*, xiiif.

171. Cf. the bibliography, #5, nn. 17-19.

172. Cf. Hahn, *op. cit.*, xviiff.; Deichgräber, *op. cit.*, 13.

173. This assumption is supported, with various, partly quite questionable, arguments in W. Schmithals, "Paulus und der historische Jesus," *ZNW* 53 (1962) 145-60; Schmithals, *Paulus und Jakobus*, 1963; U. Wilckens, "Hellenistisch-christliche Missionsüberlieferung und Jesustradition," *ThLZ* 89 (1964) 517-20; Schille (see #2, nn. 15, 17).

174. To be sure, Seeberg's design is less explicit in presentation than in terminology, oriented as it is to a linguistic phenomenon. But the individual analysis is *de facto* directed toward the theory of the association-mechanism.

175. Cf. Seeberg, *Katech.*, 174ff.; *Ev.*, 11-22, 69ff.

176. Cf. H. E. Tödt, *Der Menschensohn in der synoptischen Ueberlieferung*, 1959, 134-38; W. Popkes, *Christus traditus*,

1967, 159 (*ibid.*, n. 429: further bibliography); A. Strobel, *Kerygma und Apokalyptik*, 1967, 81.

177. Cf. W. Grundmann, *Das Evangelium nach Markus*, 1965, 166.

178. Cf. J. Schniewind, *Das Evangelium nach Markus*, 1963, 115; E. Lohmeyer, *Das Evangelium des Markus*, 1953, 160f.

179. Schweizer, *EvTh* 24 (1964) 351.

180. Cf. W. Wrede, *Das Messiasgeheimnis in den Evangelien*, 1963-3rd ed., 93ff., 101ff., 229ff.

181. This section can only be specially regarded in terms of the teaching of the disciples. So Tödt, *op. cit.*, 135. However Mk 10:52 is almost universally regarded as the conclusion.

182. Cf. Tödt, *op. cit.*, 135.

183. Cf. *ibid.*, 143.

184. Strobel, *op. cit.*, 82.

185. Tödt, *op. cit.*, 138.

186. Cf. Bultmann, *Syn. Trad.* [Germ. ed.], 164, n. 2; Tödt, *op. cit.*, 134.

187. Cf. Schniewind, *op. cit.*, 118f.; Tödt, *op. cit.*, 131-203; F. Hahn, *Christologische Hoheitstitel*, 1963, 46-53; E. Schweizer, *Neotestamentica*, 1963, 67-70; Schweizer, *Das Evangelium nach Markus*, 1967, 94-96; Vielhauer, *Aufs.*, 118; Strobel, *op. cit.*, 72-84.

188. Cf. Goldammer, *ZNW* 48 (1957) 100.

189. We should not eliminate the functional distinction between missionary proclamation and community preaching, even if perhaps the distinction between kerygma and didache (so Dodd, cf. above, n. 2; Stendahl, *ThLZ* 77 [1952] 716f.) proves too schematic insofar as the community is also cited in memory over against the kerygma (cf. above, #6, n. 57).

190. Cf. Tödt, *op. cit.*, 143: "We cannot speak of a sequence of words if a characteristic and vital main-concept was present, which drew to itself a limited, relatively closed, group of words related in terms of their presentational con-

tents, in a certain exclusivity." -- It is too bad that both
this definition and the actual analysis was pursued according
to this principal without reference to linguistic method.

191. Cf. the bibliography in #10, n. 1. We are taking up
and modifying here a term from K. Bühler, *Sprachtheorie*, 1965-
2nd ed., 165f.: The synsemantic field is the linguistic context in which arises the exclusivity and relative semantic
autonomy (cf. above, #3, n. 89) of the individual "sign" by
means of the "signs" simultaneously produced in the speech
act, and constitutes a relatively closed horizon of "sense".

192. Cf. Goldammer, *op. cit.*, 100f.

193. Cf. K. Stendahl, "Kerygma und kerygmatisch," *ThLZ* 77
(1952) 715-20.

194. Cf. below, p. [214ff.].

195. Differently Strecker, *ZThK* 64 (1967) 18: "A further
compositional element that determines the *total*-framework of
the gospel of Mark is given us by the predictions of the suffering and passion of Jesus." (My emphasis.) However it is
clear that Mark 1:1-8:26 was not compositorially encompassed
by the summaries.

196. Cf. G. Strecker, "Die Leidens- und Auferstehungs-
voraussagen im Markusevangelium," *ZThK* 64 (1967) 16-39.

197. Cf. *ibid.*, 31 on Mk 10:33f.

198. *Ibid.*, 29f. This reservation is also true, naturally,
concerning those linguistic special features of the summaries
which remain unmentioned in what follows because they are not
considered to be decisive.

199. H. Spencer, *Eine Autobiographie*, vol. 2, 1905, ed.
L. and H. Stein, 101, mentions the principle "that the spiritual development strives upwards from the simple to the corpo-
rate, from the indefinite to the definite", so that understanding "develops from homogeneous to heterogeneous, from the indefinite to the definite, and represents a continual integration of its components".

200. On the phantom of the "primal edition" in the oral,
cf. above, #7, n. 236.

201. Here one differentiates between the citation of a
clear form-critical dimension, something such as the "kerygma"
in the sense given it above, and the stylistic comparison of

the peculiar manner of speaking in a traditional *langue* which belongs to form criticism in the extended sense, i.e., to be expanded by means of linguistics, but only actualized by means of the total image of the *langue* that each speaker actualizes in the *parole* (cf. above, p. [51]).

202. Strecker, *op. cit.*, 31.

203. Cf. *ibid.*, 24-31.

204. Cf. *ibid.*, 30ff.

205. Cf. *ibid.*, 24.

206. Cf. Tödt, *op. cit.*, 152 on Lk 17:25 and 9:44: "the shorter and less definite form is...the younger, in contrast with the more extensive sayings."

207. We can be satisfied here with reference to the redactional phrases in Mk 8:31: *kai ērxato* (cf. Mk 4:1; 6:2, 7, 34; 8:11, 32; 10:28, 32, 41; 12:1, and Schmidt, *Rahmen*, 217; Bultmann, *Syn. Trad.*, 357), mostly associated with *didaskein* (cf. however Mk 1:21f., 2:13, 4:1f., 6:2, 6, 34, 9:31, 10:1, 12:35, and Schweizer, *Aufs.*, 95f.; Luz, *ZNW* 56 (1965) 22, n. 60; Strecker, *op. cit.*, 26). Mk 8:32a (*kai parrēsia*) *ton logon elalei* (cf. Mk 2:2, 4:33, and M. Schulze, *ZwTh* 37 (1894) 370; Schweizer, *NTD*, vol. 1, 98). Mk 8:30 (cf. 1:25, 3:12, and Wrede, *Messiasgeheimnis*, 33f.). Mk 8:31 is framed therefore by a strong Markan redaction in 8:30, 32a (so also Strecker, *op. cit.*, 22, n. 16) and 8:31a (cf. Schweizer, *Aufs.*, 93).

208. Cf. Strecker, *op. cit.*, 30.

209. Cf. H. Grass, *Ostergeschehen und Osterberichte*, 1964-3rd ed., 130, n. 4; Schweizer, *NTD*, vol. 1, 108; Popkes, *op. cit.*, 154-69.

210. Cf. Hahn, *op. cit.*, 49f., 52f. On the two types, see Tödt, *op. cit.*, 166f.

211. Cf. the bibliography in Popkes, *op. cit.*, 159, n. 30 as well as in Tödt, *op. cit.*, 164, 186; Schweizer, *Aufs.*, 108.

212. So, restrictively, Strecker, *op. cit.*, 30, in spite of conceding that *eis cheiras anthrōpōn* is a Semitism. But it would also be possible to think of a Septuagintism in the area of Greek language.

213. Cf. Schniewind, *NTD*, vol. 1, 128; Grundmann, *Mk.*, 193; Popkes, *op. cit.*, 159.

214. Cf. Hahn, *op. cit.*, 50; Strecker, *op. cit.*, 30.

215. So Hahn, *op. cit.*, 47.

216. According to Bultmann, *Syn. Trad.*, 288, Mk 14:41b (*idou paradidotai ktl.*) is Markan. (Differently K. G. Kuhn, *EvTh* 12 [1952/53] 273; Tödt, *op. cit.*, 184; Popkes, *op. cit.*, 158f.). Then it must be understood redactionally as a reference back to 9:31, not as a traditio-historical variant, of which *tōn hamartōlōn*, as compared with *anthrōpōn*, is secondary (so Popkes, *op. cit.*, 161). Popkes, *ibid.*, 159, states as a *petitio principii* that a "more stringent proof is not to be had for the Markan origin of v. 41 b", although it is precisely the hypothetical pre-Markan character that must be demonstrated. The structural function of 14:41 for the construction is not disputed (*ibid.*, 160, 181)! But why must a redactional phrase be in its function (cf. also Tödt, *op. cit.*, 184: an interpretative element used by Mark) unconditionally a traditional "kerygma"? -- Mark 14:21 is according to Bultmann, *Syn. Trad. Ergh.*, 38, to p. 285 in the text: "the transformation of a general statement" from Q (Mt 18:7//Lk 17:1), i.e., a theologically reflected level. (Differently Tödt, *op. cit.*, 183). The issue is not a "kerygma" in the exact sense: *ho huios tou anthrōpou paradidotai* is not to be dissolved from its context, already on grammatical grounds. That one may draw from this undertone a conclusion of an older formula is simply capricious. For could Mark have wanted to suggest that it was through Judas that the Son of Man would be "killed, despised, spat upon and scourged"? This type of tradition history is a long way from a contextual elucidation of the sense.

217. Mk 8:31: three times; 9:31: twice; 10:33f.: seven times.

218. So Popkes, *op. cit.*, 163f.

219. So *ibid.*, 164. A hypothetical premise for this further hypothesis is provided by the priority of Mk 9:31.

220. Cf. Tödt, *op. cit.*, 152; Hahn, *op. cit.*, 46, n. 1; Wilckens, *op. cit.*, 115.

221. So Popkes, *op. cit.*, 158. Also Wilckens, *op. cit.*, 116f., assumes a special Lukan tradition related to the speeches in Acts.

359

222. Cf. Kümmel, *Einleitung*, 78ff. Further bibliography there.

223. So Strecker, *op. cit.*, 29.

224. Cf. Hahn, *op. cit.*, 47f., with reference to the dependence of Mk 14f. "up to the point of the words themselves" (47).

225. Cf. Strecker, *op. cit.*, 31, with reference to the prejudice referred to in 9:31, and the extraordinarily meagre differences from the passion, which show "that the redactor is not slavishly tied to his model".

226. Cf. Tödt, *op. cit.*, 186f., with reference to the main reproach of the handing over to the gentiles at the insistence of the Jews, to the enumeration of the abuses of the gentiles, which are not thought to agree with Mk 15:16-20 (*ibid.*, 159-62; similarly already Lohmeyer, *Mk.*, 220) and to the lack of *stauroun* (cf. Mk 15:13, 14, 15, 20, 24, 25, 27, and 16:6).

227. Cf. Wilckens, *op. cit.*, 112f., with reference to the omission of the Barabbas-episode (Mk 15:6-15), of the term *stauroun* in Mk 10:33f., and the term *apokteinein* in Mk 14f., and to the relation of the almost literary agreement only in the second part of the passion. The summary seems "not formulated directly with a glance at the Markan passion, but rather with a glance at an older pre-form of the passion" (113).

228. According to Popkes, *op. cit.*, 160f., Mk 10:33f. (8:31) is secondary, as opposed to 9:31, because of the more precise realization of the description of the recipients, and because of the replacement of the indeterminate *paradothēsetai* by *paradōsousin*. It cannot be known whether or not the later hand that carries out the transformation is that of Mark himself (*ibid.*, 188f.).

229. So also Schniewind, *NTD*, vol. 1, 142.

230. So E. Haenchen, *Der Weg Jesu*, 1966, 361.

231. So Schweizer, *NTD*, vol. 1, 123.

232. So Popkes, *op. cit.*, 160.

233. Tödt, *op. cit.*, 162.

234. *Ibid.*, 159.

235. Cf. Popkes, *op. cit.*, 188f. On the political apologetics in Luke, cf. Conzelmann, *Mitte der Zeit*, 117ff.; Wilckens, *op. cit.*, 118f.

236. Cf. above, p. [164f.].

237. If we pay attention to the structural relations (cf. above, p. [55f.]) and the semantic autonomy thereby relativized (cf. above, #3, n. 89), we will not want to regard the "sense"-content of individual terms as independent in themselves in each case; only after such analysis can we set out an aggregative total sense of the language form that now confronts us.

238. Cf. E. Lichtenstein, *ZKG* 63 (1950/51) 29, 38f.; Tödt, *op. cit.*, 167f., 198; Hahn, *op. cit.*, 48f.; Wilckens, *op. cit.*, 113f., 137ff.

239. Cf. Wilckens, *op. cit.*, 138f.

240. Wilckens, *ibid.*, 139, n. 2, seems to find that I Thess 4:14 is pre-Pauline. But even so the traditio-historical relationship to the summaries is still completely unresolved.

241. On "killing" (not "crucifixion") of the Son of Man, cf. Tödt, *op. cit.*, 162f., who thinks of the polemic against the Jews, because of I Thess 2:15, Mt 23:34//37//, Mk 12:8, Mt 22:6, Acts 7:52, 3:15.

242. Cf. Hahn, *op. cit.*, 49, n. 1; Kramer, *op. cit.*, 16ff.; Wengst, Diss., 21ff.

243. Cf. Tödt, *op. cit.*, 163.

244. Because of the terminological variation, Mk 9:12b is taken as a tradition dependent upon 8:31a (*ibid.*, 181f.). Its fixed terminology is an unproven premise for such. According to Hahn, *op. cit.*, 51f., on the other hand, both 9:12b and 9:9b are redactional.

245. Tödt, *op. cit.*, 186. On the reference to Ps 117:22f. (LXX), cf. *ibid.*, 153, 156f.; Wilckens, *op. cit.*, 112; Strecker, *op. cit.*, 26. Similarly already J. Wellhausen, *Das Evangelium Marci*, 1903, 71.

246. Strecker, *op. cit.*, 26f., takes into consideration *polla pathein* because of the adverbial *polla* in Mk 1:45, 3:12, 4:2, 5:10, 23, 26, 38; 6:20; 9:26, and the tension between *pathein* and the two verses following. If we exclude Lk 17:25

as a Lukan reformulation, and Justin, *dial.* 76:7 as a secondary version, then the *polla pathein* is in fact a *hapax legomenon* for the summaries. But that only demonstrates how well the style of Mk 8:31 suits the Markan language, not a pre-Markan ur-version. Further a Markan insertion of the Son of Man title is considered possible (*ibid.*, 27-29). But then it would be even less clear why Mark must have unconditionally taken over a kerygmatic summary and cannot have shaped it independently in "Christian" style, since the remainder is so seemingly fragmentary.

247. Cf. *ibid.*, 32-34.

248. This exegesis naturally presupposes the questionable association-psychology (cf. above, p. [163f.]) and a traditional "dependence upon presentations" of the term independently of its present context, whereas today we would first have to analyze the "sense" in its present context. Only if *apokokimasthēnai* calls forth associations with Ps 117:22f. (LXX) in an isolated and automatic manner, would the argument be illuminating. But *apodokimazein* is used occasionally within a quotation of Ps 117 (cf. in addition to the parallels to Mk 8:31 and 12:10: I Peter 2:4, 7 and Barn 6:4) and within an echo of the expression in Ps 117 which was proverbial (cf. Herm., Sim., Book 9: 7:4, 12:7, 23:3). However as an isolated term (cf. LXX: Sap 9:4; Jer 6:30, 7:29, 14:19; and Hebr 12:17; Ign. Rom 8:3) it contains no clear and direct reference to Ps 117, but means the rejection on qualitative grounds, especially of a candidate: Herod., *histor.* 6, 130, 1 (cf. Liddell-Scott, 197b). That *dei* implies a reference to scripture (so T. A. Burkill, *NovTest* 2 [1958] 248, n. 1; Burkill, *ZNW* 52 [1961] 191, n. 2; Tödt, *op. cit.*, 174ff.; Hahn, *op. cit.*, 50f.; Strecker, *op. cit.*, 26), so that it has the same significance as *gegraptai* (cf. Mk 9:12b) (so Tödt, *op. cit.*, 177), cannot be drawn from the isolated *dei* but at most from the combination with Mk 9:11f. (redactional!) and from Lk 24:25ff., 44. Cf. E. Fascher, "Theologische Beobachtungen zu *dei*," in *Neutestamentliche Studien für Rudolf Bultmann,* 1957-2nd ed., 228-254. But a particular scriptural passage is not intended by Luke even if we understand *hina polla pathē kai exoudenēthē* in Mk 9:12b as a literal quotation from scripture; then Ps 117:22f. (LXX) cannot have been intended, because of the lack of this phrase, but an apocryphal tradition (cf. Lohmeyer, *Mk.*, 183). Finally there is no contrast between the apocalyptic and the scriptural *dei*, because the latter is the revelation of the will of God which is also contained in the former (cf. Hahn, *op. cit.*, 50, n. 4).

249. It is remarkable how quickly conclusions are drawn from a traditional *langue* to *non*-Markan material, although

Mark himself sets alongside one another in an undifferentiated
manner formulations that are both fixed in form and independent. Was he even *aware* of such a distinction?

250. Cf. above, n. 246.

251. Cf. Schmidt, *Rahmen*, 218.

252. Cf. Haenchen, *Der Weg Jesu*, 295: Mark uses here "an
old kerygmatic formula". "That this formula does not always
appear in the same words, but is sometimes longer and sometimes shorter, says nothing: the evangelist may vary such a
formula." If the freedom in formulation is also valid for
Mk 8:31, then the precise form-critical sense of "kerygmatic
formula" is lost, since it can then only be at most indirectly concluded from its redactional variation.

253. Cf. Strecker, *op. cit.*, 32.

254. So Schmidt, *Rahmen*, 218.

255. Strecker, *op. cit.*, 29.

256. Thereby the concept "sociological setting" is altered
to the contextual field (cf. p. [167ff.]) and at the same time
"historicized": the "sociological setting" for the summary
cannot be the life of Jesus but only the reconstructed context
(cf. *op. cit.*, 32f.).

257. So *ibid.*

258. U. Luz, *ZNW* 56 (1965) 21, n. 60.

259. Cf. Schmidt, *Rahmen*, 19f., 32f.; Bultmann, *Syn. Trad.*,
348f., 363f.

260. Cf. what was mentioned above, p. [202], as well as
Strecker, *op. cit.*, 17, n. 6.

261. Strobel, *op. cit.*, 84.

262. Cf. Strecker, *op. cit.*, 24.

263. Cf. more extensively Grass, *op. cit.*, 127-38.

264. Differently, Strecker, *op. cit.*, 24f.

265. Cf. Grass, *op. cit.*, 136, n. 1; Kümmel, *Verheissung*,
61.

266. Cf. G. Delling, *ThW*, vol. 2, 1935, 952f.

267. Cf. Grass, *op. cit.*, 137f.

268. So Lohmeyer, *Mk.*, 165; W. Michaelis, *ThW*, vol. 5, 1954, 913, *ll.* 22ff.; Grundmann, *Mk.*, 169; Schweizer, *NTD*, vol. 1, 93. Further bibliography in Strecker, *op. cit.*, 19, n. 10.

269. St Strecker, *op. cit.*, 20.

270. So Tödt, *op. cit.*, 151f. Cf. also Kümmel, *Verheissung*, 63.

271. Cf. *ibid.*, 64. Differently: Grässer, *Parusieverzögerung*, 17ff., 33ff.

272. Cf. Bultmann, *Syn. Trad.*, 347-400. Cf. also Dibelius, *Formgesch.*, 219-34.

273. Bultmann, *op. cit.*, 395, my emphasis.

274. *Ibid.*, 396, partly italicized in original.

275. Cf. *ibid.*, 396f.

276. Cf. *ibid.*, 399f.

277. *Ibid.*, 399.

278. *Ibid.*, 393.

279. *Ibid.*, 394.

280. *Ibid.*

281. *Ibid.*, 347f.

282. *Ibid.*, 348.

283. Cf. *ibid.*, 362. Similarly also Dibelius, *op. cit.*, 220, 223; W. Michaelis, *Einleitung in das Neue Testament*, 1954-2nd ed., 47f.

284. Bultmann, *op. cit.*, 363.

285. Cf. *ibid.*, 370.

286. Cf. *ibid.*, 347.

364

287. *Ibid.*, 362.

288. Wellek and Warren, *Theorie der Lit.*, 229.

289. Cf. A. T. Cadoux, *The Sources of the Second Gospel*, 1935; J. M. C. Crum, *St Mark's Gospel: Two Stages in its Making*, 1936; R. Thiel, *Drei Markus-Evangelien*, 1938 (criticism in Kümmel, *ThLZ* 64 [1939] 118ff.); E. Hirsch, *Frühgeschichte des Evangeliums*, vol. 1, 1951-2nd ed. (criticism: cf. Haenchen, *ThLZ* 67 [1942] 129ff.); D. F. Robinson, "The Sources of Mark," *JBL* 66 (1947) 153ff.; B. P. W. Stather Hunt, *Primitive Gospel Sources*, 1951; H. Helmbold, *Vorsynoptische Evangelien*, 1953 (criticism: Bultmann, *Gn* 39 [1958] 274ff.); L. Vaganay, *Le problème synoptique*, 1954 (criticism: cf. Vielhauer, *ThLZ* 80 [1955] 647-52); E. Trocme, *La formation de l'évangile selon Marc*, 1963, 7ff.

290. Cf. Kümmel, *Einleitung*, 37f. Further bibliography there.

291. Cf. *ibid.*, 35.

292. Cf. J. Jeremias, "Zur Hypothese einer schriftlichen Logienquelle Q," in his *Abba*, 1966, 90-92; Dibelius, *Formgesch.*, 236; Vaganay, *op. cit.*, 34ff.; Tödt, *op. cit.*, 224; Kümmel, *op. cit.*, 33-35.

293. So Dibelius, *op. cit.*, 234ff.

294. So Bornkamm, *RGG*-3rd ed., vol. 2, 1958, 759f.; Tödt, *op. cit.*, 224ff.

295. M. Kähler, *Der sogenannte historische Jesus und der geschichtliche, biblische Christus*, ed. E. Wolf, 1956-2nd ed., 60, n. 1.

296. W. Marxsen, *Einleitung in das Neue Testament*, 1963, 120.

297. *Ibid.*, 122. According to Vielhauer, *ThR* 31 (1965/66) 143, we may not on the other hand impute to Mark a "phobia of historicizing".

298. Marxsen, *op. cit.*, 123.

299. Cf. Schreiber, Diss., 11ff.; and *Die Markuspassion*, 1969.

300. Schmidt, *Rahmen*, 303.

301. Dibelius, *op. cit.*, 178.

302. *Ibid.*, 180.

303. Bultmann, *op. cit.*, 297.

304. G. Bertram, *ChW* 38 (1924) 839.

305. Bultmann, *op. cit.*

306. Bertram, *Leidengesch.*, 8.

306a A linguistic criticism of the available traditio-historical and motif-critical studies (cf. #5, n. 121) would have to investigate exactly whether empirically-observable linguistic processes are actually close to the projected composition from various separated "traditions" (better: networks of motifs, language fields). So far as I can already judge here, it seems to me that the proposed reconstructions are too heavily weighted down by the premises of a purist reduction of the motifs within a circle of tradition. However I am consciously not treating individual analysis; a methodologically thought-out analysis cannot be presented too quickly, especially since there is a beginning attempt in J. Schreiber, *Mkpassion*, 40ff., to sketch the thesis that the passion narrative is as a whole a Markan composition. This assumption seems to me also to have been arrived at with the fewest hypotheses.

307. Cf. Bultmann, *op. cit.*, 374.

308. Cf. *ibid.*, 366.

309. *Ibid.*

310. *Ibid.*, 365.

311. *Ibid.*

312. Cf. Schweizer, *Aufs.*, 95f.

313. Cf. Bultmann, *op. cit.*, 226f., 370.

314. *Ibid.*, 167.

315. So Schmidt, *op. cit.*, 104; M. Albertz, *Die synoptischen Streitgespräche*, 1921; Albertz, *Die Botschaft des Neuen Testaments*, I/1, 1947, 172; Bultmann, *op. cit.*, 374.

316. Marxsen, *Einleitung*, 117. Cf. also Bultmann, *op. cit.*, 374.

317. Schmidt, *op. cit.*

318. Dibelius, *op. cit.*, 220.

319. *Ibid.*, 42.

320. Cf. Bultmann, *op. cit.*, 347, n. 2.

321. *Ibid.*, 351.

322. Marxsen, *Aufs.*, 16f.; Marxsen, *Einleitung*, 115, 121.

323. Vielhauer, *ThR* 31 (1965/66) 142.

324. Cf. Bultmann, *op. cit.*, 374; Dibelius, *op. cit.*, 220; Marxsen, *op. cit.*, 121.

325. Cf. L. Bieler, *Theios Aner*, vol. 1, 1967-new ed., 80f.

326. Cf. D. Georgi, *Die Gegner des Paulus im 2. Korintherbrief*, 1964, 213ff. Criticism: Güttgemanns, *ZKG* 77 (1966) 129f.

327. Luz, *ZNW* 56 (1965) 30. Differently: Schweizer, *Aufs.*, 96f.: "The special theological contribution of Mark lies in the emphasis upon the teaching of Jesus, not the driving out of the demons which was transmitted to him. The latter rather serve him to understand and to describe the character of Jesus' teaching as the act of a divine power."

328. Albertz, *op. cit.*, 173; Marxsen, *Einleitung*, 121.

329. Cf. Bultmann, *op. cit.*, 129; G. Hölscher, "Der Ursprung der Apokalypse Mrk 13," *ThBl* 12 (1933) 193-202; J. Sundwall, *Die Zusammensetzung des Markusevangeliums*, 1934, 76-78; Marxsen, *Evglist Mk.*, 108f. Differently: G. Harder, "Das eschatologische Geschichtsbild der sogennannten kleinen Apokalypse Markus 13," *TheolViat* 4 (1952) 71-107; Kümmel, *Verheissung*, 91; Grässer, *Parusieverzögerung*, 153.

330. Cf. Albertz, *op. cit.*, 180f.

331. Cf. H. Conzelmann, "Geschichte und Eschaton nach Mc 13," *ZNW* 50 (1959) 210-21; J. Lambrecht, S.J., "Redactio Sermonis Eschatologici," *VD* 43 (1965) 278-87; "Die Logia-Quellen

von Markus 13," *Bibl* 47 (1966) 321-60; and *Die Redaktion der Markus-Apokalypse*, 1967; R. Pesch, *Naherwartungen: Tradition und Redaktion in Mk 13*, 1968.

#14. *The Illustration of the Kerygma by Narration.*

1. The Christological Recourse to the Phenomenon
   of Narrative.*

In Chapter #1 we pointed out the emminent theological
relevance given to the narrative moment in the position represented by E. Käsemann. Here we refer briefly to a few especially characteristic quotations in order to develop a preliminary answer to the christological questions put forward
in Ch. #1. The gospel form is "as such not preaching but information [Bericht]",[1] i.e., a form sharply distinguished from
myth, which in this respect is also a historical source:[2] It
is only in the form of "history"[2a] with its unique functions
of narration and repetition,[3] indeed of reminiscence of the
historical Jesus,[4] as the linear and temporal securing of the
prevenience and pre-valence of the divine grace[5] that the historical safeguards the history of Jesus in such a way[6] that it
cannot be misunderstood in an Ebionitic way: The form of the
narrative gospel is the bullwark against both gnostic docetism
and Ebionitic historicism.[7] The narrative moment of this "history" marks the gospel form as "information",[8] i.e., as "historicizing repetition" of the "once upon a time",[9] which must
always remain prior to faith,[10] if the gestalt of Jesus is not
to evaporate into a myth.[11] That is to be seen in the tempo-

---

*[+1978: "Generative Poetics" has developed a theory of "nar-
rative theology" in terms of this topic, following a suggestion of H. Weinrich. E. Güttgemanns.]

ral form of the narrative: Since the issue is the unity of the earthly [Jesus] with what is believed [about him], since "faith begins not with itself, but lives from out of a prior-given history", hence "one [may] only speak of" this history "in the time [p. 233] of the past".[12] The temporal form of the narrative past is christologically needy, for it is the linguistic reference to a non-linguistic reality.[13] "Hence the tradition at every level and in every single element is a witnessing of the reality of his history and the reality of his resurrection."[14] Although Jesus' history in the gospels is not presented as a type of history-writing and chronicle, yet the gospels speak "of history as occurrence and event",[15] of a history, to be sure, which is the history of *Christus praesens*: "In the narrative of the history of the days of old they proclaim not who he was, but who he is."[16] Mark wrote his gospel in a world threatened by enthusiasm and symbolization.[17] He was determined "essentially only to relate what Jesus, and what through him, humankind, experienced from God". "For that there is only one real prototype, the Old Testament", so that Mark with his narrative returns fundamentally to the historical theology of the O. T.[18] Hence the phenomenon of narrative represents not only the quintessence of the "post-Bultmannian" recourse to the reality of Jesus, but also the quasi-linguistic brackets of the "salvation history" unity of O. T. and N. T. theology in the so-called "biblical" theology.[19]

Because of the limitations of this work mentioned in my Introductory Remarks, I will have to be satisfied with focusing upon the essential elements in presenting the contemporary christological recourse to the phenomenon of narrative. Apart from the already mentioned reference to the lack of clarity of the concept "to narrate",[20] and the reference to the discussion already begun in O. T. studies concerning [p. 234] a much too rapid adoption of the concept "history" in O. T. theology,[21] it would not be appropriate to the linguistic and literary-critical complex of narrative present here to procede without extensively taking into account so-called poetics,[22] especially with respect to long range research on narrative;[23] the study of folk tales;[24] of epics,[25] with its debate about the "constructional forms of narrative",[26] the "temporal framework" of narrative,[27] and the distinction between "narrative time" and "narrated time";[28] and also the extended area of the so-called fictionality of the narrated[29]--all literary-critical [p. 235] questions without an exact knowledge of which relevant knowledge and analysis of the understanding of time and reality of the various narrative genres according to the contemporary position of literary criticism is no longer possible. If N. T. theology lays any value upon the scientific verification of its theses concerning the narrative of the gospels and the "historicizing" affirmed in the framework of a primitive Christian literary history, it will not be able to ignore literary-critical analysis. Special value would have to be placed upon a corresponding analysis of the structural value of the tense forms, which may not be confused with indications of time.[30] It would then have to investigate whether the fictionality of narrative forms already in hellenistic antiquity possessed its own tense system,[31] something that may not be confused with the absolute tense system of classical grammar, which was developed without reference to the structural value of the linguistic phenomena, e.g., A. Kaegi's paradigms,[32] from which the works referred to above deduce the "significative value" [p. 236] of the tenses. Only then could it be decided whether the theological appeal to particular tense forms in favor of a particular understanding of time and reality in the synoptic gospels is in any way a philological and linguistic argument, and not merely a theological postulate. However it may be, H. Weinrich's stimulating book raises a negative suspicion in this regard. But to undertake such would necessitate our touching upon a difficult inquiry which, in spite of a few attempts,[33] is yet to be satisfactorily resolved today without a longer methodological discussion of the linguistic facts to be considered here. In order not to demand too much from the reader all at once, I will limit my focus here again by referring to one candid question and will discuss extensively only the phenomenon of the "vividness" of narrative, with the qualification that the aspect of narrative fictionality, which is connected to that of "vividness", and the important linguistic connection between language and perception[34] will have to be treated sometime in the future, for similar reasons. All these qualifications, to be sure, mean that the christological problematic cannot be satisfactorily resolved within the framework of this work. But that certainly does not mean that there are no reasons to call into question Käsemann's conception. Rather in the course of this study, in spite of all its qualifications, we have already referred to so many candid questions and noted so much relevant bibliography, that both the distant horizons of a well-grounded confrontation, thought through in every respect, and also the *value* of questioning the problem indicated, have become evident.

[p. 237]   2.   The Illustration of the Kerygma:
           Martin Dibelius.[35]

We have already seen in Ch. #13 that the conceptual model of Dibelius' preaching-theory is more probably oriented to the modern practice of preaching than to the results of an analysis [i.e., a historically-deductive analysis of primitive Christian preaching; W.G.D.]. Here we may perhaps see an orientation of Dibelius' conceptual model to Papias' refer-

ences to Mark (cf. Eusebius, *h.e.* III.39.15), according to
which Mark as *hermēneutēs Petrou* [an interpreter of Peter]
wrote down his gospel following Peter's sermons.[36]   With
reference to this ecclesial tradition, J. Wellhausen suggests:
"Mark is not writing the *vita et moribus Jesu* [life and death
of Jesus], he does not intend to make his person vivid or indeed conceivable."[37]   "Nor have the apostles proclaimed the
gospel in such a manner as Papias appears to present it, bas-
ing individual segments of the gospel history on their preaching."[38]   As already mentioned,[39] Dibelius' conceptual model
equates the relationship of the "small units", especially of
the so-called "paradigms", to the primitive Christian preaching and the relationship of sermon and "text". That can now
be made more precise as the relationship between the non-
graphic kerygma and its illustration by means of the paradigms.

    According to Dibelius, "the Christian missionaries" did
"not preach the plain kerygma in their sermons, but the elucidated, illustrated kerygma, provided with examples and expanded"; in this respect the speeches of Acts contain "more
the skeleton than the body of a speech".[40] Dibelius explicitly develops this conceptual model as representing the origin
of the Jesus-tradition: The paradigms "had to serve the
preaching about Christ". "The tradition was born out of the
desire to illustrate the preaching about Jesus Christ by
examples, and exhortations to the church and to such as wanted
to become Christians, empowering them with the word of the
Lord."[41] "The dependency of the creation of the tradition
upon the proclamation is such that the traditional material
made concrete the preaching of salvation, elucidated and expanded it, and correspondingly was soon introduced into the
preaching [p. 238], was soon preached at its conclusion."[42]
"What was present to the missionaries and preachers in the
oral or written tradition was a tradition which was able to

illustrate, establish, and undergird their preaching."[43] From these quotations it is clear that Dibelius considered the "plain" kerygma, in itself non-graphic, as having been encompassed by the vividness of the tradition of the gospels. Is this conceptual model still usable today? What is the source of the impression that *the kerygma is non-graphic, whereas the tradition of the gospels is vivid?*

3. The Contrast between Paul and Jesus as the Background in the History of Research of the Thesis of the Illustration of the Non-graphic Kerygma in the Tradition of the Gospels.

If we investigate the provenance of the schema referred to, we find such astonishing parallels in our theological forebears that it makes one think of an unrecognized further-transmitted rudiment of liberal hermeneutics. For this hermeneutics, the radical contrast between Jesus and Paul is characteristic, according to which "Jesus" means by and large the Jesus-image of the gospels.[44] The best known example is indeed W. Wrede, with his 1904 book on Paul that was epoch-making in the history of research.[45] Already seven years earlier Wrede had spoken about the Pauline christology: "The image of the human and individual personality has disappeared in the Apostle's presentation."[46] Now he suggests that the personality of the human Jesus which is essential to us today played no more role for Paul: "therefore all the concrete ethical and religious content of his earthly life has no meaning for his Christ-doctrine. The 'humanity' appears to be something purely formal." One might almost have the impression of docetism—naturally not intended by Paul. "Paul lacks the concept of personality, the human individuality. For this reason the humanity of Christ as he conceives it remains for us an impalpable schema."[47] It is only a "transitional peri-

od" of the heavenly Christ "in human form".[48] Along with that
we also hear from Wrede the fateful catchword of the "episode"
of the human phase of the redeemer, which [p. 239] above all
M. Brückner had introduced.[49] In its terms, for Paul the
earthly Jesus is an "episode" in the career of the essentially
heavenly redeemer, since he has had so little recourse to the
image of the "historical" Jesus normative in the tradition of
the gospels.[50] As Wrede represents it, this thesis is only
more generally represented, but is clearly a variant to what,
besides Brückner, almost all critical exegetes conceived.
After the fact we must judge this as being overshadowed by a
peculiar twilight. Namely when Wrede, as did many of his contemporaries, misunderstood Paul's image of the "personality"
of Jesus, this genial discoverer of the dogmatic tendencies
of the gospels[51] had to inquire where then anywhere in the
N. T. an image of the "personality" of Jesus was to be found.[52]
But if there is nothing of the sort in the entire N. T., then
it is not to be observed how this fact should be something
specific to the Pauline christology, unless the category of
"vividness" normalized in the tradition of the gospels is sur-
reptitiously used as a criterion for the comparative schema-
like Jesus-image of Paul. We could also say that the antithesis of the non-graphic kerygma represented by Paul's theology,
and the vivid tradition of the gospels is derived from a particular schematism in the history of research that is no longer a possibility for us today in this form.

4. The Aesthetics of Liberal Exegesis.

Now that form criticism has established that nowhere in
the N. T. is there present a "historical" image of Jesus in
the nineteenth century sense, it is illegitimate, and a rudiment of a pre-form-critical standpoint, to bring together the

category of "vividness", in no matter how reconceived, with that of "history", in order so to conclude from the lack of "vividness" a theologian's lack of interest in the "earthly" Jesus confused with the "historical" Jesus.[53]   Even when R. Bultmann himself still partly represents this misunderstanding, such a procedure involves a fragment stemming from a "pre-Bultmannian era", to be set aside by an immanent tendency-criticism, [p. 240] which goes against Bultmann's expressed intention.[54]   As a matter of fact for the "pre-Bultmannian era" the "vividness" of the tradition of the gospels (especially that of Mark)[55] is actually an indication of their relative historical trustworthiness,[56] in which case "vividness" means especially the eidetic plane of human psyche corresponding to the narrative style-moment,[57] which among other things also [p. 241] emphasizes the human side of Jesus[58] and hence seems to lead one close to his reality:[59]   The "vividness" of the text causes an eidetic image of the reality to arise in the eidetic sensorium of our psyche,[60] and deludes us, by the aesthetic affect through the image-like style, into thinking we have attained a special closeness to reality itself.[61]   Such pictorial traits ostensibly cannot be invented,[62] [p. 242] but indicate the presence of eyewitnesses,[63] although the intensification of the sensual awareness of Jesus' miracles, as for instance in the gospel of John,[64] or the striking increment in "vividness" in the [p. 243] apocryphal gospels,[65] should warn us against drawing this conclusion.[66] Only where in this manner there is an appeal to the eidetic plane of human psyche as the sensorium of reality, do we find ourselves hermeneutically at a fundamentally "pre-Bultmannian" standpoint, because here a sensualistic empiricism and not a hermeneutics nurtured on a criticism of I. Kant and a "critique of historical reason" (W. Dilthey) makes historical "understanding" the norm of the concept of "reality".

5. The Psychologizing of Mark by Johannes Weiss.

We turn now to a conception of the hermeneutics just characterized which is typical of the "pre-Bultmannian" standpoint, as we encounter it in the completely subjective judgments of the psychologizing exegesis of J. Weiss.[66a]

Weiss agrees completely with D. F. Strauss, "that a greater or lesser number of mythical components have been merged into the material of the gospels. But no matter how cautiously we may today approach the conviction that the basic traits of the image of Jesus' character, and especially of a large number of words of the Lord, are stored up for us in essentially true and unblemished fashion."[67]

From the standpoint of our modern biographical interest we naturally miss in the gospel account much "which appears to be necessary for a complete understanding of the personality (*scil.*, of Jesus). We hear nothing of education and culture, nothing of development and life experiences, on the part of the child, the teenager, or the adult. Jesus appears before us complete and mature, in order to take up his true profession and to fulfill his fate. It is impossible to gain an impression of his growth and to grasp his nature from the presuppositions of his actual existence."[68] Weiss sadly bemoans this [p. 244] lack of developmental psychology in the gospel image of Jesus' character, on account of his liberal presuppositions;[69] on the basis of his psychologizing hermeneutic, he does not at all arrive at the later question which broke out in dialectical theology, *whether then our psychological curiosity is at all appropriate to the interest in Jesus that is present in the N. T. with respect to belief in Jesus.* To the contrary, he appeals explicitly to the psychological combinatorics of the exegete, who attempts to reconstruct a "portrait of the soul" of Jesus from the scanty fragments of the

N. T.[70] Although Weiss thinks that the "extraordinary intensification of the pneumatically-intensified nature of Jesus"
contributes to Mark's presentation "a nervousness and lack of
calm" "which has something artificial about it",[71] and although Weiss expressly grounds this judgment in a highly subjective aesthetic by means of our modern psychological sensitivity,[72] on the other hand he considers that "a striving,
psychologically motivated, to characterize, to paint..." is
betrayed by the numerous dramatic and graphic traits of Mark.
"Here lies the kernel of a psychological conception which is
yet lacking in the whole situation."[73] In spite of its impression of artificiality, Mark's sketchy material, in the
sense of modern psychology, is therefore still sufficient to
confirm our modern impulse toward illumination of a soul-pro-
cess that is foreign to us, as a decisive aspect of the category "reality"!

Thereby J. Weiss is thoroughly conscious of the basis
upon which he introduces such a psychologizing hermeneutics.
The appeal to the eidetic level of human psyche is supposed to
provoke our aesthetic power into developing an image of reality.[74] Hence Weiss [p. 245] also scarcely scruples, in spite
of his inclination to the judgment of F. Schleiermacher and
D. F. Strauss concerning the artificiality of Mark's "vividness", to evaluate the same traits positively as an indication
that the original tradents were eyewitnesses. In the process
the subjective and aesthetic character of his judgments is
clearly evident.

Mark's presentation is not consistent, like a diary.
"The narrator has no interest in every-day events, the usual
things, in the Lord's quiet and unapparent effect on the souls
of his surroundings; what are transmitted to us are primarily
highly unusual events, the high points of the communal life,
in which Jesus' greatness forcefully makes itself apparent,

disappointing or exciting scenes, critical days, dramatic dia-
logues--short, life-like images of moments as they may have
been sketched more than once by the apostle (*scil.*, Peter) in
dialogue or in proclamation, important and significant reminiscences, frequently, of the most highly personal nature, as
in the call of the fishermen or the courage of the sons of
Zebedee, or the betrayal. That is the oldest level of the
gospel tradition. In spite of its limitation we cannot be
grateful enough that we have it. By means of its freshness
and vividness, by means of its genuine local color and its
wholly non-theological manner, it is a capital source. Its
value becomes constantly more apparent, the more we enter
more deeply into these scenes with love and understanding.
Certainly their trustworthiness is compellingly proven to no
one; but whoever allows them to work upon oneself without bias
will hardly be able to escape the impression that here are vi-
vacious, experienced, and inconsumate reminiscences of an eyewitness."[75]

After what has been said, it will be sufficient to let
such a salient quotation speak for itself. It is only too
evident that here the category of "vividness" is utilized in
an aesthetic and psychological manner, i.e., pre-form-criti-
cally.[76] The conclusion is close to hand that his categories
have become heremeneutically unusable at least since form
criticism. We will refer here only generally to the fact
that we thereby attain to a result similar to that reached
by a discussion of the relation between demythologizing and
vividness of presentations, or by an excursus on the problem
"language and vividness" discussed in linguistics since G. E.
Lessing's *Laocoon* (1766) and its revival by Th. A. Meyer.[77]
[p. 246] Here we will limit ourselves to an exegetical discussion.

6. The "Vividness" of Mark as an Aesthetic Deception.

An analysis of passages in which liberal exegesis found the "vividness" of the Markan style especially well documented also comes to a negative result with respect to "vividness". We focus here paradigmatically upon J. Weiss' judgment concerning the beginning of Jesus' Galilean ministry.

The vivid tradition begins at the point of the call of the two pairs of disciples (Mk 1:16-20).[78] The narrative is "exceedingly vivid, and there seems to be nothing that would prohibit the assumption that here we are confronted by the first portion of the Petrine narratives that Mark will have utilized".[79] Similarly H. J. Holtzmann remarks concerning the beginning of Jesus' ministry in Galilee (Mk 1:21-34) and its continuation in 1:35-38, that here "the opening day of his ministry...and the reaction which success experienced on other mornings trails..., are imaged with a vividness that can only be put alongside the account of Jesus' last days".[80]

For J. Weiss the "sobriety, liveliness, and decisiveness of this group of narratives" demonstrates that Mark is not "the schematic performer and inventor of his material", but "one who tells a limited, detailed tradition".[81] However since K. L. Schmidt's work, it has been recognized in form-critical research that the impression of a chronological and topological framework, in the sense of a "history" of Jesus, derives from Mark's redaction, which revises the individual passages that were in each case transmitted in isolation, by means of a compositional technique that is not exclusively indebted to "vividness",[82] that therefore in other words the "vividness" of Jesus' life can be confirmed at the most in preliminary and fragmentary fashion. *Therefore with reference to the eidetic image-quality of Jesus' history we secure only occasional* [p. 247] *snapshots, but never an un-interrupted motion picture sequence.*[83]

That is immediately clear when we once leave the eidetic
affect in the individual instance and try to visualize an un-
interrupted motion picture sequence. In the case of Jesus'
beginnings in Galilee that will look something like this:
Jesus called the first pair of disciples, who were standing
by with small hand nets for catching fish (Mk 1:16f.). If we
take this passage by itself it is possible for aesthetically-
gifted persons to gain an idyll-like impression in spite of
the haziness of many details. But this impression is immediately shattered by the terse style with which Mark indicates
the obedience of the two brothers (1:18): What will Simon and
Andrew do with the fish they have caught, and their nets? Do
they throw the whole lot back into the lake, in order vividly
to illustrate their break with their old life? What do they
do while Jesus walks further along the shore and immediately
calls a second pair of brothers (1:19f.)? Indeed they do not
even seem to play the role of mute supernumeraries, since they
are never again mentioned. Where are the two pairs of brothers living when Jesus goes into the synagogue at Capernaum and
performs the first exorcism (1:21-28)? Although according to
1:21b, Jesus apparently goes alone into the synagogue, the
five leave together in 1:29, in order to repair to the house
of Simon and Andrew. But did they view the miracle? What did
their faces look like when they reacted to Jesus' first miracle? Perhaps indeed the first pair did not entirely turn
their backs upon all earthly goods when they followed Jesus,
since they again seek out their dwelling, and indeed invite
Jesus to it. The evangelist is entirely silent about such
matters, since in between there has been a tearing apart of
the eidetic film of "vividness". It seems to be edited together once again when the oriental crowd of people milling
around in front of the door of Peter's house in the evening
is sketched (1:32-34). But already J. Weiss conceded that

the evangelist had gone too far into hyperbole for the sake of "vividness" when he has the entire village gather at the door (1:33).[84] It is not stated what the four disciples did during this whole period, since again we are given only a selective snapshot which omits everything of a subsidiary nature.

In other words: In Mk 1:16ff., "vividness" leads only to quite brief and in each case isolated eidetic impressions; in [p. 248] an aesthetic approach, therefore, only certain traits actually realize a rudimentary "vividness". "But it is the vividness of poetry, not of history. It disappears as soon as we attempt earnestly to put ourselves into the situation and the motive powers and perceptions which have created these scenes are allowed full play."[85] M. Brückner's judgment can also be applied without difficulty in similar analysis to other "vivid" pericopes.[86] Again and again it is apparent that the exegetical interest in "vividness" is a false hermeneutical premise, which is in tension with form-critical findings.[87]

This hermeneutical premise replaces theological reflection by aesthetic affect, i.e., an act of thought is replaced by an act of presentation, which in each case can be more or less intensified, depending upon the aesthetic gift of the exegete.[88] What is experienced as "vivid" is understood in a historicizing procedure as a mirroring of reality, so that exegesis hermeneutically weighted in this manner *eo ipso* "historicizes" the texts instead of inquiring about their theological intention. The category of "vividness" in this sense is also hermeneutically too heavily weighted by a fragmentary and un-reflective application for it to be able to serve as a form-critical methodology.

But not only hermeneutically but also historically the category of "vividness" is highly questionable, since eidetic "vividness" and a narrative element are also inherent in myth,[89] and hence the often-affirmed opposition between "history" and "myth" in [p. 249] these passages is not present.[90] The "vividness" of linguistic phenomena is by no means an immediate indication of their understanding of reality, all the less so for a particular understanding of reality, and so can no longer be used as an argument in the christological debate. "Vividness" is a rudimentary category of the aestheticizing and psychologizing hermeneutics of romanticism or idealism[92] already found in J. G. Herder,[91] and it is no longer applicable as a form-critical dimension or in a form-critical context. The N. T. phenomena intended with such an approach need most of all to be described by means of hermeneutically-unweighted categories which are more appropriately in harmony with the form-critical procedure.

Hence once again a candid question has arisen, especially because what has been discussed here needs to be expanded and perhaps also modified by means of the aspects of narrative fictionality and the relevance of tenses, mentioned above. In view of the difficulties demonstrated it seems better to me to reject completely Dibelius' preaching theory and to cease interpreting the moment of narration as a form-critical "illustration" of the "non-graphic" kerygma,[93] since in such a way narrative is "derived" as a historically-secondary variant of the kerygma, although the linguistic function of narrative "description" cannot be reduced to the other language functions.[94] The [p. 250] "vividness" of Mark is an aesthetic deception which diverts our attention from the thought processes implicit in the language forms toward eidetics. Insofar as theology is not an eidetic presentation but an act of thought,[95] our interest in the theology of the gospels should not be dazzled by the aesthetic deception of narrative fictionality, but we should seek to conceive *the language form as a "gestalt" of a christological understanding.* In this

manner it is also conceded that language always implies understanding,[96] even if this "understanding" is not simply a phenomenon of consciousness.

Notes to #14

1. Käsemann, *Aufs.*, vol. 2, 54. Taken up and developed further by S. Schulz, *Die Stunde der Botschaft*, 1967, 9ff., 31, 35ff., 41ff.

2. Cf. P. Althaus, in H. Ristow and K. Matthiae, [eds.], *Der historische Jesus und der kerygmatische Christus*, 1960, 240f.

2a [+1978: The German term "Geschichte" is ambiguous: it means "history" as well as "story", at least where it is used by the authors quoted. If one has in mind the distinction recently made between "historicness" and "historicality" (J. M. Robinson), a complete translation gets even worse. The reader should bear in mind Käsemann's--philosophical--presupposition that "story" and "history" are correlated epistemologically.]

3. Cf. Käsemann, *op. cit.*, 61 (cited in #1, n. 46).

4. Cf. *ibid.*, 68 (cited #1, n. 52).

5. Cf. *ibid.*, 66. Similarly already Käsemann, *Aufs.*, vol. 1, 202f.

6. Cf. Käsemann, *Aufs.*, vol. 2, 61, 67.

7. Cf. *ibid.*, 95.

8. Cf. *ibid.*, 66.

9. Cf. Käsemann, *Aufs.*, vol. 1, 195-99.

10. Cf. Käsemann, in *BEvTh* 15, 151: "Faith always lives out of the revelation which has already preceded it."

11. Cf. Käsemann, *Aufs.*, vol. 1, 196, 203. Similarly G. Bornkamm, *Jesus von Nazareth*, 1956, 20.

12. *Ibid.*, my emphasis.

13. Cf. however Bornkamm, *Aufs.*, vol. 3, 18: "Even when the gospels narrate in past time, this time is not for the gospels precisely the past, but presently-powerful, the breaking-in of the eschaton, the epiphany of God, and therefore a history which breaks through the boundaries of Then and Now."

14. Bornkamm, *Jesus*, 18.

15. *Ibid.*, 22.

16. *Ibid.*, 15.

17. Cf. E. Schweizer, *EvTh* 24 (1964) 337f.

18. *Ibid.*, 339.

19. On the concept of a "biblical theology", see: M.
Barth, *Vom Geheimnis der Bibel*, 1962; F. J. Cwiekowski, S.S.,
"Biblical Theology as Historical Theology," *CBQ* 24 (1962) 404-
11; E. O'Doherty, "The Unity of the Bible," *Bible-Today* 1
(1962) 53-57; N. Lohfink, S.J., "Ueber die Irrtumslosigkeit
und die Einheit der Schrift," *StZ* 174 (1963/64) 161-81; L.
Krinetzki, O.S.B., "Das Verhältnis des Alten Testamentes zum
Neuen Testament," *Lebendiges Zeugnis* 1 (1964) 81-99; R. E.
Murphy, O. Carm., "The Relationship between the Testaments,"
CBQ 26 (1964) 349-59; D. Hill, "What is 'Biblical Theology'?",
Biblical Theology 15 (1965) 17-23; H. Schmid, "Die Einheit der
Testamente," *Judaica* 21 (1965) 150-66; H. Seebass, "Der Beitrag des Alten Testaments zum Entwurf einer biblischen The-
ologie," *WuD* 8 (1965) 20-49; D. Barthélemy, *Gott mit seinem
Ebenbild: Umrisse einer biblischen Theologie*, 1966; H. Ca-
zelles, "The Unity of the Bible and the People of God," *Script*
18 (1966) 1-10; E. Jacob, "Possibilités et limites d'une Théologie biblique," *RHPhR* 46 (1966) 116-30.

20. Cf. above, p. [29].

21. See E. Sellin and G. Fohrer, *Einleitung in das Alte
Testament*, 1965-10th ed., 102ff.; J. Barr, *Alt und Neu in der
biblischen Ueberlieferung*, 1967, 11ff., 61ff.

22. Cf. E. Hirt, *Das Formgesetz der epischen, dramatischen und lyrischen Dichtung*, Diss., Zürich, 1922; R. Petsch,
Wesen und Formen der Erzählkunst, 1942-2nd ed.; J. Pfeiffer,
Wege zur Erzählkunst, 1953; W. Kayser, *Das sprachliche Kunstwerk*, 1965-11th ed., 176ff., 349ff.; H. Seidler, *Die Dichtung*,
1965-2nd ed., 456ff.; R. Wellek and A. Warren, *Theorie der
Lit.*, 88ff. (*ibid.*, 303ff.: further bibliog.); Bausinger,
op. cit., 142ff.

23. Cf. K. Friedemann, *Die Rolle des Erzählers in der
Epik*, 1920; E. Berend, "Die Technik der 'Darstellung' in der
Erzählung," *GRM* 14 (1926) 222-33, and "Noch einmal: Die Tech-
nik der Darstellung in der Erzählung," *GRM* 16 (1928) 248-52;
A. Schaeffer, "Die Technik der 'Darstellung' in der Erzäh-
lung," *GRM* 15 (1927) 13-18; O. Brinkmann, *Das Erzählen in*

einer Dorfgemeinschaft, Diss., Münster, 1933; G. Henssen, "Stand und Aufgaben der deutschen Erzählforschung," in *Festschrift Richard Wossidlo*, 1939, 133-37; E. Kahler, "Die Verinnerung des Erzählens," *Die Neue Rundschau* 68 (1957) 501-46.

24. Cf. H. Steinthal, "Mythos, Sage, Märchen, Legende, Erzählung, Fabel," *Zeitschr. für Volkerpsychol. u. Sprachwiss.* 17 (1887) 113-39; E. Bethe, "Mythus, Sage, Märchen," *Hessische Blätter für Volkskunde* 4 (1905) 97-142; W. Wundt, "Märchen, Sage und Legende als Entwicklungsformen des Mythus," *ARW* 11 (1908) 200-22; F. Heyden, *Volksmärchen und Volksmärchen-Erzähler*, 1922; M. Lüthi, "Märchen und Sage," *DVjs* 25 (1951) 159-83; Lüthi, "Gattungsstile (Sage und Märchen)," *WW* 4 (1953/ 54) 321-27; Lüthi, *Das europäische Volksmärchen*, 1960-2nd ed.; K. Ranke, "Betrachtungen zum Wesen und zur Funktion des Märchens," *Studium Generale* 11 (1958) 647-64; S. Sudhoff, "Die Legende," *Studium Generale* 11 (1958) 691-99; F. von der Leyen and K. Schier, *Das Märchen*, 1958-4th ed.; L. Röhrich, "Die deutsche Volkssage," *Studium Generale* 11 (1958) 664-91; Röhrich, *Märchen und Wirklichkeit*, 1964-2nd ed.; Röhrich, *Sage*, 1966; H. Rosenfeld, *Legende*, 1964-2nd ed.; L. Dégh, *Märchen, Erzähler und Erzählgemeinschaft*, 1962; H. von Beit, *Das Märchen*, 1965. [+1978: Cf. also the complete analysis of all oral genres made by H. Jason, *Ethnopoetry*, 1977.]

25. Cf. C. M. Bowra, *Heldendichtung*, 1964; J. de Vries, *Heldenlied und Heldensage*, 1961; A. B. Lord, *Der Sänger erzählt*, 1965.

26. Cf. E. Lämmert, *Bauformen des Erzahlens*, 1967-2nd ed.; M. Weiss, "Einiges über die Bauformen des Erzählens in der Bibel," *VetTest* 13 (1963) 456-75.

27. Cf. G. Müller, *Die Bedeutung der Zeit in der Erzählkunst*, 1947; "Ueber das Zeitgerüst des Erzählens," *DVjs* 24 (1950) 1-31; and "Zeiterlebnis und Zeitgerüst in der Dichtung," *Studium Generale* 8 (1955) 594-601; A. A. Mendilow, *Time and Novel*, 1952; H. Seidler, "Dichterische Welt und epische Zeitgestaltung," *DVjs* 29 (1955) 390-413; R. Ingarden, *Das literarische Kunstwerk*, 1960-2nd ed., 247ff.

28. Cf. G. Müller, "Erzählzeit und erzählte Zeit," in *Festschrift Paul Kluckhohn und Hermann Schneider*, 1948, 195-212.

29. Cf. P. Lubbock, *The Craft of Fiction*, 1957-rev. ed.; C. Brooks, Jr., and R. P. Warren, *Understanding Fiction*, 1943; G. Storz, "Ueber die Wirklichkeit von Dichtung," *WW SH* 1 (1952/ 53) 94-103; H. Levin, *Symbolism and Fiction*, 1956; R. Brink-

388

mann, *Wirklichkeit und Illusion*, 1957; W. C. Booth, *The Rhetoric of Fiction*, 1963-3rd ed.; Ph. Wheelwright, *Metaphor and Reality*, 1964-2nd ed.; K. Burke, *Dichtung als symbolische Handlung*, 1966; Seidler, *Dichtung*, 61ff. Cf. also N. Frye, *Analyse der Literaturkritik*, 1964, 73ff.

30. Cf. H. Weinrich, *Tempus*, 1964, 7ff., 26ff. Cf. also "Der Begriff 'Tempus'--eine Ansichtssache?", *WW BH* 20.

31. For fictionality in German, cf. E. Lerch, "Die stilistische Bedeutung des Imperfektums der Rede ('style indirect libre')," *GRM* 6 (1914) 470-89; K. Hamburger, "Zum Strukturproblem der epischen und dramatischen Dichtung," *DVjs* 25 (1951) 1-26; "Das epische Praeteritum," *DVjs* 27 (1953) 329-57; "Die Zeitlosigkeit der Dichtung," *DVjs* 29 (1955) 413-26; and *Die Logik der Dichtung*, 1957, 21ff.; H. Seidler, "Zum Stilwert des deutschen Praeteritums," *WW* 3 (1952-53) 271-79; F. K. Stanzel, "Episches Praeteritum, erlebte Rede, historisches Praesens," *DVjs* 33 (1959) 1-12; W. Rasch, "Zur Frage des epischen Praeteritums," *WW SH* 3 (1961) 68-81. In particular K. Hamburger has developed the thesis that the preterite does not have the same structural *valeur* in narrative fictionality as in the "actual account"; hence it does not serve as a means of style for the past-character of what is narrated, but as a means of style of fictionality. This differentiation of the abstract grammatical function and the structural function of the tenses associated with particular language forms is in essential agreement with H. Weinrichs' findings--it was the latter that brought my attention to these linguistic contexts some time ago. But it was primarily my knowledge of structural linguistics that led me to grasp the complete, fundamental relevance of such information. Since E. Käsemann parallels "narration" and "account" (cf. #1, n. 68) and the theological theses quoted above draw upon the tense of the narrative with respect to its view of reality, it is quite clear that the bibliographic references we have cited are relevant in this context. That such questions have been dealt with more extensively in German and Romance language studies can only be an incentive for biblical exegesis.

32. See for instance E. Koschmieder, *Zeitbezug und Sprache*, 1929; and "Zu den Grundfragen der Aspekttheorie," *IF* 53 (1935) 280-300; G. Guillaume, *Temps et verbe*, 1929; and *L'architectonique du temps dans les langues classiques*, 1945; J. Brunel, *L'aspect verbal et l'emploi des préverbes en Grec, particulièrement en Attique*, 1939; E. Hermann, "Die altgriechischen Tempora, ein strukturanalystischer Versuch," *NGG* 1943, phil.-hist. Kl., 583-649; M. S. Ruipérez, *Estructura del sis-*

tema de aspectos y tiempos del verbo griego antiquo, 1954;
Weinrich, *op. cit.*, 290ff.

33. Cf. M. Williams, "Das historische Präsens, ein wesent-
liches Merkmal des evangelischen Erzählungsstiles," *BZ* 21
(1933) 309-19; M. S. Enslin, "The Perfect Tense in the Fourth
Gospel," *JBL* 55 (1936) 121-31; M. Zerwick, S.J., *Untersuchungen zum Markus-Stil*, 1937, 49-74; C. S. Emden, "St Mark's Use
of the Imperfect Tense," *ET* 65 (1953/54) 146-149; Schreiber,
Diss., 87-90, 91-93. Cf. also D. Michel, *Tempora und Satz-
stellung in den Psalmen*, Diss., Bonn, 1960; K. Beyer, *Semi-
tische Syntax im Neuen Testament*, I/1, 1962, 86ff., 240ff.;
Rundgren, *op. cit.*; E. Jenni, *Das hebräische Pi'el: Syntak-
tisch-semasiologische Untersuchung einer Verbalform im Alten
Testament*, 1968.

34. Cf. below, p. [245f.].

35. The following sections contain material from my previously unpublished promotion-lecture, "Die Kategorie der 'An-
schaulichkeit' in der Hermeneutik des Neuen Testaments," 12
November 1966. Cf. the note in Güttgemanns, *Der Leidende Apostel*, 291, n. 55. I still plan a reworking of this complex in
terms of an expanded range of questions on given "times".

36. I can only refer to the following interesting articles: J. Kürzinger, "Das Papiaszeugnis und die Erstgestalt
des Matthäusevangeliums," *BZ* 4 (1960) 19-38; Kürzinger, "Ire-
näus und sein Zeugnis zur Sprache des Matthäusevangeliums,"
NTS 10 (1963) 108-15.

37. J. Wellhausen, *Einleitung in die drei ersten Evangelien*, 1911-2nd ed., 44.

38. *Ibid.*, 148.

39. Cf. above, p. [193f.].

40. Dibelius, *Formgesch.*, 23.

41. Dibelius, *Aufs.*, vol. 1, 316.

42. Dibelius, *Formgesch.*, 14.

43. Dibelius, *Aufs.*, vol. 1, 307.

44. Cf. Güttgemanns, *Der leidende Apostel*, 370ff.

45. W. Wrede, *Paulus*, 1907-2nd ed.

46. Wrede, *Ueber Aufgabe und Methode der sogenannten Neutestamentlichen Theologie*, 1897, 67f.

47. Wrede, *Paulus*, 55.

48. *Ibid.*, 56.

49. M. Brückner, *Die Entstehung der paulinischen Christologie*, 1903, 32. Cf. on this, Güttgemanns, *op. cit.*, 335ff.

50. The gospels are still treated here as relatively trustworthy historically, while in Paul "non-historical" traditions about Jesus are criticized. Cf. M Brückner, "Zum Thema Jesus und Paulus," *ZNW* 6 (1907) 112f., 115, 117.

51. W. Wrede, *Das Messiasgeheimnis in den Evangelien*, 1963-3rd ed.

52. Just this question is placed by R. Bultmann, *Glauben und Verstehen*, vol. 1, 1954-2nd ed., 250f.

53. Cf. the evidence in Güttgemanns, *op. cit.*, 34ff., 351ff.

54. Cf. the examples listed in *ibid.*, 32, n. 161; they prove that Bultmann's peculiar boundary here is determined by his liberal dialogue partner.

55. Chr. H. Weisse, *Die evangelische Geschichte*, vol. 1, 1838, 68, establishes the historical priority of Mark by means of clearly aesthetic categories: It is "sketched from out of a living total perception of the object, from an image that is in spirit contemporary as a whole, and hence awakens a corresponding total image of its contents in a way that is unique among the gospels, one that is present already at a simple, free reading, whereas in the case of the other gospels, one must first puzzle out such an image". On the other hand D. F. Strauss, *Das Leben Jesu für das deutsche Volk*, vol. 1, 19th ed., n.d., 64f., agrees with F. Schleiermacher, who sees something artificial in the "graphic nature" of Mark. Cf. below, n. 64. Strauss recognizes here a characteristic of the reflection of a later author, since "graphic nature" may not be naively connected with "history".

56. "Vividness" was used by the rationalists as a means of explaining miracles. Cf. A. Schweitzer, *Geschichte der Leben-Jesu-Forschung*, 1951-6th ed., 89f. Already D. F. Strauss, *op. cit.*, 16b, stated especially with reference to A. W. Neander, *Das Leben Jesu-Christi*, 1837: "What is to be

praised in Mark is called his vividness: but basically that
is the back door he seems to keep open as a means of making
room for a naturalistic explanation of many miracles in the
material means and other matters of his presentation." B.
Weiss, *Lehrbuch der Einleitung in das Neue Testament*, 1889-
2nd ed., 505, argues against the tendency criticism of the
Tübingen school with respect to Mark: "To a gospel which so
apparently intended to present images, to make visible, in
which the completely unrestrained joy in narrative and portraiture is still so momentarily dominant, it is only possible to impress a tendentious character if its historical
description is arbitrarily allegorized and its intentions
cast onto the most artificial ways, which are as far as possible from the naivete of the narrator." Cf. the agreement
in H. J. Holtzmann, *Lehrbuch der historisch-kritischen Einleitung in das Neue Testament*, 1892-3rd ed., 384.

57. F. Chr. Baur, *Das Markusevangelium nach seinem Ursprung und Charakter*, 1851, 150: The authorial talent of
Mark "consists quite specially in the skill with which he
paints individual details, and thereby knows how to give to
his description life and color". B. Weiss, *Einleitung*, 500:
"The most striking uniqueness of the second gospel is its
imagic character." "Where an individual story is told, the
local details are given as exactly as possible, the situation
is as vividly sketched as possible, a wealth of concrete details enliven the presentation, Jesus' method of salvation is
made visible." Th. Zahn, *Einleitung in das Neue Testament*,
vol. 2, 1899, 223: The narratives following Mk 1:16 are conveyed "by means of graphic vividness and by means of a trea-
sure of indispensible individual details". Mark has "not only
a partiality but indeed an eminent aptitude for lively and
vivid narrative". These "give the presentation the effect of
a drama". (A. Kuby, *ZNW* 49 [1958] 54, also refers to a dramatic illustrativeness.) R. Drescher, *ZNW* 17 (1916) 243:
"Doubtless Mark in his gospel hits the right narrative tone.
He narrates vividly, imagically." A. Jülicher and E. Fascher,
Einleitung in das Neue Testament, 1931-7th ed., 305: "Mark is
characterized by a lively presentation, oriented toward vividness and complete portraiture of the images." Ch. H. Weisse,
op. cit., 67, already suspected that these judgments were dependent upon the aesthetic experience of the individual.

58. H. Frhr. v. Soden, *Die wichtigsten Fragen im Leben
Jesu*, 1909-2nd ed., 39: "The image of Jesus himself bears
human contours in every respect. He is excited and astonished,
he gets irritated and trembles, he has need of recreation, and
feels himself deserted by God, he rejects for himself the
thoughtless, conventional designation 'good', and confesses

that he does not know when all that he sees as coming will be
fulfilled." Cf. F. Barth, *Einleitung in das Neue Testament*,
1914-3rd ed., 180: "Mark is happy to narrate the stories
about Jesus with a popular appeal and does not spare the
imagic details for that purpose." "And since the emphasis of
the *human* traits of Jesus belong especially to the vividness
of his presentation, the evangelist in his painting of human
qualities goes quite a ways without damaging his faith in
Jesus as the wonderful Messiah." Already Strauss, *op. cit.*,
3b, comes to conclusions similar to those of J. J. Hess, *Geschichte der drei letzten Lebensjahre Jesu*, 3 vols., 1768/72,
in seeing that the spirit of a time "can be identified alongside moralistic predications of the worth of the deity in the
beauty of the gospel story, its effect on aesthetic feeling".

59. Cf. E. Schick, *Formgeschichte und Synoptikerexegese*,
1940, 49: "Mark narrates with a natural freshness, the liveliness of his presentation breathes the breath of reality, the
local coloring and the convivial sketching of individual scenes
...has a natural and genuine effect."

60. Cf. J. Rohr, *ThQ* 101 (1920) 276f.: In Mark 4 "we
have a charming example of a peaceful popular-sermon, untouched by party strife, and its appropriate framework has
been developed in the magical scenery: the crowd gathered
around the Lord, he himself sitting on a little boat by the
lake, and everything visible and audible; Jesus teaching from
that place, the people lying on the beach and listening. The
evangelist turns away from detailed portraiture. No detail
draws attention away from the great design of the primary
scene. And yet it is not difficult to imagine the clear reflection of the Galilean lake, the luxuriant colors of the
fruitful terrain, and the sublime majesty of the mountains in
the blue distance. And what the clouds heard and what the
waves gave back, that was worthy of the grandiose setting."

61. C. S. Emden, "The Gospel of Mark Made More Vivid,"
ET 64 (1952-53) 334-36; and "St Mark's Use of the Imperfect
Tense," *ET* 65 (1953-54) 146-49, gives in this respect an especially characteristic exposition: "St Mark's Gospel is...
the most graphic and life-like of all the books in the New
Testament" (*ET* 64 [1952-53] 334). "All commentators on St
Mark's Gospel tell their readers that St Mark has a style
that is vivid, but inelegant. They say that, while he is remarkable for enabling us to visualize an incident, he lacks
literary skill and polish" (*ET* 65 [1953/54] 146). A sense of
greater actuality can be gained by precise observation of the
way tenses are used (*ibid.*, 148f.). Every example (Mk 1:32,
45, 4:37, 5:32, 6:41, 48, 8:29, 9:15, 11:9, 15:14, 36, 47)

"enables us to imagine with new vividness scenes in the Gospel
story. Some of them suggest the excitable behaviour of an
Oriental people, and the tension produced by our Lord's ministry" (*ibid.*). "Furthermore, the acceptance of the fact that
St Mark knew how to manage his tenses would enable readers to
have a truer appreciation of the extent and significance of
the eyewitness passages in the only account of the beginnings
of Christianity which includes first-hand recollections"
(*ibid.*, 149). Cf. also R. G. Bratcher, *Review and Expositor*
55 (1958) 363: "Mark's narrative of the events of Christ's
life is vivid, unpolished and life-like." "Such vividness in
details makes the narrative all the more trustworthy."

62. This is especially so for John: E. Renan, *La vie de
Jésus*, 1863. Cf. A. Schweitzer, *op. cit.*, 182. Similarly already W. F. Wilcke, *Tradition und Mythe*, 1837, 223. The abstract teaching of Paul was not enough for primitive Christianity. "Since the word of salvation is presented concretely in Jesus' person and deeds, the simple knowledge thereby
received vividness and warmth and divine breath" (*ibid.*, 8).
"Everywhere parables, gnomic sayings, and allegories contributed to the gospel saga-cycle a festivity, uniformity, freshness, and interest; these lightened the tradition, determined
with their inner content and gave to the uniform conception
of Jesus' speeches an uncommon countenance..., since they
likewise replaced the abstract, systematic manner of teaching as an occurrence of teaching, and so made God's word
available in the garb of the popular and practical" (*ibid.*,
109). So it is self-evident for Wilcke, *ibid.*, 51-53, that
Mark utilized Petrine sources. H. Frhr. v. Soden, *Urchrist-
liche Literaturgeschichte*, 1905, 72, still states, with respect to the presumed Petrine narratives of Mark (cf. on this,
below, n. 66): "The colors of Palestine stand forth sharply,
we see the characteristically incomprehensible forms of Judaism floating before us." These stories "desire to do nothing
other than to relate what goes on. And in spite of the vividness with which the images and circumstances confront us, the
narrator is actually only interested in Jesus' words spoken
on these occasions." According to Michaelis, *Einleitung*, 52,
the traits mentioned do not rest upon the personal reminiscence
of Peter but they are "a unique form of the unrestrained manner
of narration in the early period", and "witness to the great
age of the tradition present in Mark". Already Wellhausen,
Einleitung, 159, spoke out ironically against such aesthetic
and psychological judgments of the "inner worth" of the tradition with reference to authenticity: "The *testimonium spiritus sancti* is raised to a critical principle: what penetrates
to one's heart, what lifts up, grasps us, and shakes us to the
core, is itself demonstrated as genuine. Thereafter the exe-

getical and literary-historical investigation is superfluous."

63. So M. Meinertz, *Einleitung in das Neue Testament*, 1933-4th ed., 205; D. M. Stanley, S.J., *ThSt* 20 (1959) 575, n. 50. More cautiously Weisse, *op. cit.*, 65f.: To be sure the detail portraiture is not a completely genuine emanation of Peter's eyewitness accounts, but Mark could not have written differently, given his circumstances. D. E. Nineham, "Eye-Witness Testimony and the Gospel Tradition," *JThS* 9 (1958) 13-25, 243-52; *JThS* 11 (1960) 253-64, analyzes the possible veracity of the tradition that the narrator or his correspondent was an eyewitness, with thoroughly negative results.

64. According to Weisse, *op. cit.*, 125ff., the "graphic power" of John is of an authorial nature, hence not an indication of the historicity or eyewitness quality. On the other hand Wilcke, *op. cit.*, 223, defends the eyewitness veracity of John precisely because of the "vividness". According to B. Bauer, *Kritik der evangelischen Geschichte der Synoptiker*, vol. 1, 1841, xivf., in their pragmatism the synoptic gospels are just as much as John (cf. Bauer, *Kritik der evangelischen Geschichte...des Johannes*, 1842) of a purely authorial origin, i.e., an "artistic work", where primarily the "form" is intended, but which is related to the "content" dialectically: Even the content of the gospels is of authorial origin, stemming from the free sense of beauty of the self-conscious, so that there is no other criterion for an immanent differentiation between the pure literary tradition and the original bricks of history any longer. Cf. J. Mehlhausen, *Dialektik, Selbstbewusstsein und Offenbarung*, Diss., Bonn, 1965; Mehlhausen, "Die religionsphilosophische Begründung der spekulativen Theologie Bruno Bauers," *ZKG* 78 (1967) 102-29. [+1978: I must confess my sympathies with my colleague in Bonn in the last century: Bruno Bauer.]
F. Schleiermacher, *Ueber die Schriften des Lukas*, 1817, finds the "vividness" of Mark artificial, and therefore secondary in contrast to his additional resources. Also Bauer, *Markusevangelium*, 152, drew this other conclusion from the "vividness" of Mark. D. F. Strauss, *Das Leben Jesu*, kritisch bearbeitet, 2 vols., 1835/36, emphasizes the connection of the imagic sensibility of myth: The presentational form of biblical accounts "similar to history" comes from the forms of presentation in myth. Cf. Chr. Hartlich and W. Sachs, *Der Ursprung des Mythosbegriffes in der modernen Bibelwissenschaft*, 1952, 124.

65. Cf. Nineham, *JThS* 9 (1958) 21f.

66. Mostly the "vividness" is derived from the so-called Petrine narratives which are considered to have formed the his-

torical kernel of Mark. Cf. for instance J. Weiss, *Das älteste Evangelium*, 1903, 346ff.; v. Soden, *Die wichtigsten Fragen*, 25ff. Criticism: M. Brückner, "Die Petruserzählungen im Markusevangelium," *ZNW* 8 (1907) 48-65.

66a Criticism: Güttgemanns, *Der leidende Apostel*, 351ff.; *VF* 12/2 (1967) 42f. Exegetical criticism of details: Brückner, *art. cit.*, 53ff.

67. J. Weiss, in *Die Schriften des Neuen Testaments*, ed. Weiss, vol. 1, 1907-2nd ed., 39.

68. *Ibid.*, 40. Similarly Weiss, *älteste Evgl.*, 14f., 21f.; Weiss, *Das Urchristentum*, ed. posth. R. Knopf, 1917, 546.

69. Weiss, *Schriften des NT*, vol. 1, 41: "The evangelists did not understand themselves to be painters of souls. We would be happy to see more deeply into Jesus' disposition; but the narrators offer us only certain lively processes from which we can at the most draw information about a particular circumstance of soul."

70. *Ibid.*: Mark portrays many things simply, "without concerning himself about painting Jesus' experience. It is up to the imagination of the listener to grasp this activity on the basis of his own soul."

71. Weiss, *älteste Evgl.*, 18f. Cf. *ibid.*, 114f.: The liveliness and vividness of Mark's portrayal of details has something schematic and mannered about it. *Ibid.*, 118: The impression of artificiality "lies in the fact that here a charmingly authorial manner prevails instead of a sleek art grown up out of a sound, complete emotionality".

72. *Ibid.*, 117: "The impression Jesus gives in these portrayals as a whole is a very arousing one, but not exactly a pleasing one; he stirs up the emotions." *Ibid.*, 118: Mark is "not exactly a gifted and impressionable representationalist; he has very few colors on his palette which he uses again and again without peevishness. His manner of perception in this presentation of Jesus has something forceful about it, something exciting".

73. *Ibid.*, 18.

74. Weiss, *Urchristentum*, 548: Mark's material contains many traits "that must have worked directly upon the emotions of Christians of his day". "Whoever reads such narratives

cannot avoid thinking of the heavenly Lord as being much like
the earthly Jesus: mild, full of love, ready to help."

75. Weiss, *Schriften des N.T.*, vol. 1, 43. Similarly
Weiss, *älteste Evgl.*, 360. Criticism: Brückner, *ZNW* 8 (1907)
54.

76. Weiss, *älteste Evgl.*, 5ff., is concerned with the
form criticism of the gospel, without using its terminology.
But what he develops in the process is something entirely
other than form-critical observations.

77. Th. A. Meyer, *Das Stilgesetz der Poesie*, 1901, as
well as the rich store of material in F. Kainz, *Psychologie
der Sprache*, vol. 1, 1967-4th ed., 125-42. *Ibid.*, 353f.:
further bibliography. [+1978: Meanwhile I have demonstrated
the semiotic background of Lessing's distinctions. Cf. Güttgemanns, "Die Funktion der Zeit in der Erzählung," *LingBibl*
32 (1974) 56-76.]

78. Weiss, *älteste Evgl.*, 137f.

79. *Ibid.*, 138. At the same time J. Weiss senses, on the
basis of particular form and material traits, "that here we
have before us no longer an initial primitive narration, but
a developed type of presentation" (*ibid.*, 139).

80. H. J. Holtzmann, *Die Synoptiker*, 1901-3rd ed., 11.

81. Weiss, *älteste Evgl.*, 149.

82. Schmidt, *Der Rahmen der Geschichte Jesu*, 1964-2nd ed.

83. In a somewhat different connection, R. A. Bartels,
Kerygma or Gospel Tradition...Which Came First?, 1961, 39,
suggests with respect to Mark that "his Gospel moves the reader in rapid strides with little comment from its beginning to
its end. Its portrait of Jesus is like a series of snapshots
depicting only major episodes from Jesus' career."

84. Cf. Weiss, *älteste Evgl.*, 148.

85. So Brückner, *art. cit.*, 55.

86. In a somewhat different connection, R. Bultmann, *ThBl*
2 (1923) 124, asks with respect to G. Dalman, *Orte und Wege
Jesu*, 1921-2nd ed.: "Are not the author's investigations and
reflections based to a large extent upon a false ideal of historical vividness?" Similarly Schmidt, in *Eucharisterion*, vol.

2, 129: "Whoever describes the 'Orte und Wege Jesu' ["the places and byways of Jesus"--the title of Dalman's famous book on specific details of Palestinian life; W.G.D.] on the basis of secondary fragments of the framework, is following the idealistic vision of a vividness that is simply not present."

87. "Vividness" is also not simply denied as a whole in my thinking. But the issue is rather that it may not be interchanged with a naive and non-theological relationship to reality. A positive evaluation of "vividness" could only succeed in the framework of a linguistic and literary-critical study which recognizes the connection between the complex "language and perception" (cf. above, n. 77) and fictionality (cf. above, n. 29).

88. The subjective aesthetics to which this can lead is shown by M. S. Enslin, *JBL* 66 (1947) 390, concerning "Mark's rough-and-ready style": "Conscious rhetoric and polished periods are absent; but in their place is a tremendous vitality, a vividness and intensity which is at times positively painful. The man who can read this gospel through at a sitting--the only way to sense its vigor and drive--without a feeling of near exhaustion at the end is strangely callous."

89. Cf. above, Ch. #1, n. 66. Already Wilcke, *op. cit.*, 133, judged: "A myth is the narrative presentation of an idea made graphic by an image."

90. E. Troeltsch, *Der Historismus und seine Probleme*, vol. 1, 1922, 30, emphasizes "that history is actually the concrete, graphic presentation of the individual images of history according to general practice, and that no narrator can sketch the whole". The generalizing disciplines have not been able to suppress the form of the historical presentation. "Quite naturally, since the actual interest and the reality lies precisely in the graphic, un-ending manifold nature of events."

91. J. G. Herder, *Von Gottes Sohn, der Welt Heiland*, 1797, 18ff., for example, understands the Miracles of Jesus in John as symbolic allusions and figurations. On the form-critical beginnings in Herder, see Fascher, *formgesch. Methode*, 11-17.

92. Chr. H. Weisse, *Die evangelische Geschichte*, vol. 2, 1838, 476ff., expressly affirms a connection between historical valuation and aesthetic vividness in religion. F. A. Krummacher, *Ueber den Geist und die Form der evangelischen*

Geschichte in historischer und ästhetischer Hinsicht, 1805,
offers an aestheticizing stepping stone to form criticism.
Cf. Fascher, *op. cit.*, 17-20.

93. It is not to be seen how the kerygma is "non-graphic"
if at the same time the graphic "presentations" in it are emphasized by research. It is clear that this "vividness" is of
a different linguistic type than narrative. But only in that
way are we properly referred to the linguistic question about
the medial possibilities of the various language forms.

94. On the doctrine of language functions, cf. Ch. #10,
n. 1. K. Bühler, *Sprachtheorie*, 1965-2nd ed., 28ff., distinguishes three functions of the linguistic sign: Expression
(giving of information), appeal (resolution), and presentation. The representational function of language thereby is
given emphasis. H. Dempe, *Ueber die sogenannten Funktionen
der Sprache*, Diss., Jena, 1929 (= *Was ist Sprache?*, 1930) and
Kainz, *Sprachpsychol.*, vol. 1, 172-266, describe the representational function as the basic function for all other language functions, even if they have different accentuation and
foundation.

95. Cf. Güttgemanns, *Der leidende Apostel*, 46ff.

96. Cf. above, p. [41f.].

This chapter briefly summarizes the inquiries and results of our work. At the same time it emphasizes particular aspects of the new tasks which future research must anticipate, tasks toward which some of my own contributions, now in preparation, may contribute further.

1.   What is intended in this work is what G. Strecker characterized as "urgently needed" attempts toward a "working-up of the methodological problem of redaction criticism".[1] The particular methodological positioning of the task determines even our essentially non-analytical inquiries and procedures. Only if the problematics with respect to foundations, which becomes increasingly clear today in form and redaction criticism, is methodologically considered with respect to its own dimensions and to the possibilities for un-raveling it, can we reach a perspective leading to a more productive advance of the recognized exegetical methods within the history of research, methods which in spite of their fundamental victory in Germany, seem to be shot through with a certain stagnation (Ch. #2). For this reason my main assignment was to work rigorously, by means of a methodological sketch of this problematics with respect to the foundations, on those candid questions which still encumber an analysis of the gospel form that will be both clear and materially sufficient. However the analysis of the still-unexplained form of the gospels itself does not belong to the task of the present preliminary study, but to future research, where the larger framework of our her-

meneutical interest in the form of the gospels within the history of theology (which we sketched in #1) can be resumed.

2.   The projected working-up demonstrated itself as impossible without a simultaneous and resolute treatment of inquiries stemming from general linguistics and literary criti-
cism--not something customary within the framework of earlier
form and redaction criticism--inquiries stemming from a shared,
fundamental sociological attitude in the disciplines related to
the study of language. Chapter #3 demonstrates the extent to
which the justification and boundaries of the sociological
treatment of linguistic phenomena can be argued only by overcoming the atomistic co-existence of the linguistically-related disciplines and methods. [p. 252] A self-restriction
with respect to the scope of this work meant that we often had
to refer to forthcoming publications.[1a] There we intend to
describe *in extenso* the literature referring to linguistic and
literary-critical matters which could only be mentioned here.

3.   The main problem with respect to the methodological difference between earlier form criticism and contemporary redaction criticism lies in the traditio-historical continuity or
discontinuity between the oral and the written nature of the
genres transmitted (#4; #5, Sects. 1 & 2). The traditional
and present-day acceptance of extensive identity in the traditio-historical laws of the oral and of the written has never
been empirically and analytically proved. Such an identity is
found in M. Dibelius' "constructive" method, where it is actually an unproved conceptual premise (#5, Sects. 3 & 4; #13
Sect. 1; #14, Sect. 2). The assumption of identity meets with
justified scepticism, in light of the crisis in modern folkloristics and the metaphysical foundations of "folk poetry"
stemming from the "romantic school" resident in it, and in

the older school of folkloristics which influenced early form
criticism (#7, Sect. 2); and it meets with scepticism in the
light of certain findings of modern linguistics (#7, Sects.
3a-b), and especially in view of A. B. Lord's empirical literary-critical results with respect to "oral literature" (#7,
Sect. 4b). The scepticism arises from asking whether its conceptual model is anything more than a serviceable and inter-
mittently very useful hypothesis, which however possesses
relevance today only as part of the history of research, due
to the powerful counter-arguments that have been raised. According to Lord we may not, because of the different natures
of oral and written genres, transfer relationships prevailing
in the written mode onto the oral, as by investigating an ur-
version which has been modified historically in its different
variants (something like a "small unit"), since textual stability and normativity is a phenomenon of the written. *Thereby for the first time the sociological discontinuity between
the oral and the written mode of tradition has been empirically demonstrated with respect to "oral literature"*, so that
form-critical premises must now be harmonized with this finding.

4.   Consequently, in connection with F. Overbeck's (#6) and
H. Gunkel's (#8) discoveries with respect to distinctions between the oral and the written modes, the extensive destruction of the conceptual model customary within traditional form
criticism corresponds to inner tensions present from the start,
and to a marked dependence upon the fragmentary character of
the "pre-literature", which makes it seem that a scientifi-
cally-grounded reconstruction of the "pre-literary" tradition
history and redaction criticism of the gospel form [p. 253]　is
hardly to be ventured any longer; we may have to be satisfied
with I. Engnell's focus upon structural analysis of the compo-

sition as we now have it (#13).

5.   The central problem of gospel redaction criticism in
contrast to form criticism is the written nature of the "Kleinliteratur", which according to the form-critical conceptual
model that is still relatively valid, is to be identified in
terms of its limited public and its "non-literary" character.[2]
The written is not conceived as a writing-down of language in
order to utilize the media-possibilities of writing,[3] but like
the tradition of the gospel material, as a sociological phenomenon, namely as the surrogate record of the movements of
life of a collective.[4] However we demonstrated that the sociological and folkloristic conceptual model (used for instance
by M. Dibelius) is empirically and analytically unprovable, and
(in light of the empirical research of A. B. Lord) indeed highly doubtful. Further, we established that appeal to the "non-
literary" character of the "Kleinliteratur" by reference to the
apocalyptic and eschatological posture of primitive Christianity was mistaken because of the failure of the historical analogy of Jewish apocalyptic (#5, Sect. 4). Hence we should substitute for the term "Kleinliteratur", which is too strongly
burdened by a particular sociological conception, F. Overbeck's
term "pre-literature" ["Urliteratur"], since it is more directly oriented to the problematics and the historical consequences
of the written nature of the form of the gospels (#6, Sect.
3c). Hence we become conscious of the candid question *whether
the written nature of the form of the gospels is a surrogate
for the oral in the same sense that the Pauline letter may be
(with limitations)* (#6, Sect. 3b). With that the accent of
the sociological orientation of form criticism is transferred
from the sociological relationships of the primitive Christian
collective which created or sanctioned language--which are no
longer recoverable--to the sociological implications of the

linguistic media themselves (the oral and the written). (Sociological here means behavior-creative and behavior-carrying.)[5] The specific theological problematics of such a sociology of language have already been expressly recognized (#3, Sect. 6).

6.   Our reference to F. Overbeck is the foundation for our unenthusiastic attitude toward a naive use of hypotheses with respect to the primitive Christian history. Hundreds of apparently proven hypotheses (which together constitute an impressive argument), a number of accumulated probabilities: all these still do not produce historical certainty or security. The opposite impression often develops, due to a scholastic commitment to a particular [p. 254] line of thought, or by means of a scientifically-diffuse atmosphere of confidence (E. Troeltsch), i.e., by means of a psychological *circulus vitiosus* [vicious circle] of scientific nature. Often this circle also determines what in each case is experienced as "illuminating" or "probable". With the reference to the fragmentary character of the "pre-literature" and to the untenable "cat's eyes" for seeing into the "ur-historical" obscurity (#13, Sect. 2b), the question about the usefulness of scientific hypotheses is set out in its full acuity. These hypotheses are mostly dependent upon unexpressed and often even unrecognized premises, which were not reached analytically, nor are they free from methodological objections. As soon as these premises are concentrated by interconnection into a single network of hypotheses forming a fundamental prior-decision about the framework and the gestalt of possible results, the vicious circle of scientific confidence mentioned above can only out-maneuver the methodological scepticism that likewise belongs to science.

7.   The atmosphere of scientific confidence vanishes as
soon as the traditional boundaries of the disciplines are
overstepped and it is discovered that general linguistics and
literary criticism deal with problems similar to those of form
and redaction criticism, but with a completely different methodology. *But what if, in the long run and against our will,
something like a* hermeneutica sacra [*sacred hermeneutics*]
should turn up, because the linguistically-related exegetical
disciplines (form criticism, redaction criticism, the history
of religions, motif criticism, tradition history, etc.)—in
spite of simultaneous emphasis upon their own secular character—have developed quite apart from intensive inner confrontation with linguistics and literary criticism, although they
frequently advance theses (e.g., concerning the understanding
of reality in particular language forms, concerning systems of
verb tenses, the relevance of narrative, etc.), whose justification by the related disciplines has either not been examined
or is only very critically regarded? If theology is actually
motivated by the question of truth, it can only enter resolute-
ly into dialogue with the likewise linguistically-related disciplines and seek to determine the methods most appropriate to
the subject matter by means of the most possibly universal re-
integration of the aspects of the inquiry, in order to re-es-
tablish H. Gunkel's intended union of form criticism and the
history of religions (#8, Sect. 4), and the union of the history of religions and linguistics already demanded by A. Harnack (#13, Sect. 2b). *Since the linguistic phenomenon present
in the N. T. "texts" does not disintegrate into unrelated individual aspects, the development of a non-atomistic methodology is an unavoidable obligation for a science for which the
question of truth or material appropriateness is central.* We
have undertaken an initial attempt in this direction in the
[p. 255] present work, and provided foundations for individual

details. In the process of our investigations the following
fundamental questions were drawn from related disciplines.

8.   The methodological distinctions between linguistic
structure, linguistic *shape*, linguistic *work*, linguistic *form*
(*langue*), and linguistic *act* (*parole*), introduced into general
linguistics by F. de Saussure, are very important for form
criticism (#3, Sect. 3), in that it needs to clarify the sociological structural laws of the linguistic genres (#3, Sect.
4; #7, Sects. 2g & 4), as well as the dialectical interaction
between linguistic "gestalt" and literary individuality within the *history* of the genre (#11, Sect. 2; #12, Sect. 2). We
have explained in detail (Part II.) how by means of this distinction one can explain the methodological difference between
form criticism, which is primarily interested in the collective and oral, or surrogate-like and oral, genres (#4, Sect.
1; #6, Sect. 3a), and redaction criticism, which is primarily
interested in the more strongly individualistic and "literary"
processes. Along the way we referred to the tensions that
exist, with respect to the written nature of the primitive
Christian "pre-literature", between the surrogate-character
of this written nature which may have been intended, and the
objectifying tendency of the written which more and more
evades the "intentional act" (E. Husserl, R. Ingarden, H.
Dempe, F. Kainz; #7, Sects. 3b & 4a). The tendency of the
written toward objectification, which after all also implies
a different relevance of the "sociological setting" for the
oral and for the written (#9, Sect. 2), is to be regarded,
following F. Overbeck (#6, Sect. 3c), as the *a posteriori*
condition which causes *the process by which the gospels become literature and canon* appear to be *a possible* a priori
consequence of their written nature.

9.   One further candid question for future research concerns the justification and limits of the sociological *foundation* of form criticism (#3, Sect. 6). If we are able to distinguish between the *sociological* pre-history of the cultural model (consisting of a co-existence of various "sociological settings"), or of the historical sequence of various "sociological settings", and the pre-history of the *linguistic* and traditio-historical materials;[6] if further the "sociological setting" itself is not a quasi-"non-linguistic" phenomenon prior to language (*langue*), but itself belongs immediately to *langue* as the cultural context-situation for the speech-event (*parole*), even for behavioral linguistics (#10), then it is questionable to what extent linguistic phenomena (the super-structure) may be "derived" as a secondary human activity from ostensibly primary activities.[7] [p. 256] We need only refer to the fact that with that one of the most essential supports of the form-critical method is rocked by inner crisis. Future research will have to clarify in detail the sense in which form criticism should be understood as a method of the *sociology* of language: Is the main issue a recourse to the sociological (social and commercial, *structurelle*) milieu, in which the primitive Christian genres originated, were shaped, and passed on, in order thus to probe the history of primitive Christianity "constructively"? Is it crucial to describe the linguistically-normative types of behavior of primitive Christianity which manifest themselves as culture models produced by "sociological settings", within the larger framework of a linguistic behaviorism that studies both the collective types of behavior of groups (form criticism) as well as the more individual achievements (redaction criticism), in that it incorporates them as behavioral reactions to the stimulus of the culture model? Or are the boundaries of sociological and behavioristic description accepted because understanding inter-

course with the world at the basis of the culture model is itself of a linguistic nature and therefore first of all founds
the allegedly primary sociological law as the secondary consequence of a world which culturally shapes understanding? In
this case the "sociological setting" as the linguistic content
of the genres, would merely be their *accompanying* linguistic
context, which is hermeneutically important everywhere, but
is not a phenomenon *establishing* linguistic genres, something
in itself "non-linguistic", since the distinction between sociological structures that are in themselves "non-linguistic"
and the "linguistic" phenomena established in them has been
destroyed as linguistically beside the point. According to
the self-understanding of modern structural sociology of language, the relation between "sociological" and "linguistic"
phenomena is one of identity, not of one establishing the
other. It is clear that thereby the form-critical conceptual
model presently practiced must undergo fundamental transformation. The process of creation of the primitive Christian
genres is certainly not free from objections, nor is it described in terms of sociological categories that are clear in
themselves. At any rate for traditional form criticism we
must now refer to the scientific duty finally to clarify its
methodological foundations in dialogue with the other disciplines in the sociology of language, if it is to participate in
the advance in knowledge that has occurred in these disciplines as a whole.

10.   Another matter unfamiliar to traditional form criticism
[p. 257] is the gestalt-theoretical inquiry (Part III.). With
its help we can explain why the gospel form is not a simple
aggregate, but a gestaltist unity that can have a linguistic
function or effect, such as a christological relevance. In
the process it becomes clear that the gospel form, because of

its "trans-summitivity" (Chr. von Ehrenfels), cannot be explained as an addition or summation of individual elements ("small units"), or genetically derived, because that is not how a unified "gestalt"-sense arises (#12, Sect. 1). In *this* respect the traditio-*historical* genealogy of the so-called "final redaction" turns out to be too one-sided and insufficiently reflective, so that one task for the future is to modify the analytical method in such a way that it does more justice to the gestaltist unity of the form of the gospels: Neither the "material" ("small units") nor the redactional act ("framework") may be non-dialectically over-emphasized, since then the gestaltist unity of the present form is lost. The gospel form, as a linguistic "gestalt", is an indissoluble dialectical unity of traditio-historically transmitted "material" and an intentional, enacted shaping of the linguistic "form" which "takes up" ["aufhebt"] the "material", in that it serves as a means of presentation to the fabric of signification given with the new "sense"-horizon of the gospel form (#12, Sect. 2), and hence also alters the linguistic context of the "materials" ("sociological setting") (#9, Sect. 2).

There are two sub-questions in the gestalt-theoretical inquiry: The first concerns the form-*historical* derivation of the gospel from the primitive Christian kerygma (Part IV.), which is connected with the literary-critical problem of whether and to what extent linguistic "gestalts" can have a history, if the unity of structure and effect of any individual "gestalt" is not to be derived in an evolutionary manner (#11, Sect. 2). The other question concerns the christological understanding of time implied by the "gestalt" of the gospel, which first and foremost constitutes this "gestalt".[8] The two questions are closely inter-related.

Methodological analysis with respect to the first question suggests that the form-*historical* derivation of the gospel from the "kerygma", because of the fragmentary character of the "pre-literature", and the "ur-historical" obscurity, is inapplicable and cannot be proved, since the development of the brief, formulaic primitive Christian "kerygma", as the historically-primary language form for the production and tradition of "small units", and then larger complexes as far as the final form of the gospels, can only be hypothetically postulated, but not analytically [p. 258] demonstrated (#13). The opposite type of analysis operates too rapidly, too readily, and above all too uncritically with "kerygma", that imprecise term used in form criticism that often merely designates the theological impressiveness of the content, the history-of-religions presentational background of a language form, when it actually should designate, within the necessary form-critical precision, a brief, formulaic, and traditional formulation primarily serving missionary proclamation, and having a mostly stereotyped "synsemantic field" (K. Bühler; #13, Sect. 2, e, ii). That the christological events of salvation appear as motifs both in the "kerygma" in this precise sense as well as in the form of the gospels, proves only that there is a common language background, but not that the form of the gospels can be reduced in traditio-*historical* terms, which otherwise has become analytically unprovable as a result of U. Wilckens' dismantling of M. Dibelius' preaching-theory (# 13, Sect. 1). After showing that the thesis that the narrative moment of the form of the gospels "visualizes" the "non-graphic" kerygma is exegetically, hermeneutically, and linguistically questionable (# 14), we laid out the strongly hypothetical character of the form-critical *premise* concerning the evolution of language forms. Their relation to one another needs to be described by future form criticism more appropriately in terms of the subject matter, especially with respect to the linguistic precision of its concepts and approaches. Partly such precision en-

tails theologically-unprejudiced analysis of the language
function of the gospel narration, which today, often without
the least confrontation with linguistic and literary-critical
research concerning the "function of presentation" in language
in general[9] and narrative fictionality in particular,[10] is
simply identified with the [informational] "account" ["Be-
richt"], and further with "historicizing",[11] although the
commonality of the narrative moment within all "elementary
forms" (A. Jolles)[12] would also permit the qualification of
the narrative as "mythologizing". So long as the form-critical specificity of gospel narration has not been made precise
over against something like mythological narration, the description of the gospel as "history" and as antithetical to
myth appears to be merely a *petitio principii* (#14, Sect. 1).
*Hence the gospel form has been presented in this work as an
autosemantic language form*, whose fabric of signification cannot be derived from its aggregative sense, i.e., as a gradual,
collectively-guided summation of "sense"-units (Part IV.).

   With respect to the second question, the task ahead [p.
259] likewise involves gestalt-theoretical analysis of the
gospel form concerning construction or literary structure,
namely how the gospel was created by Mark, and [also] belongs
to the decisive criteria of the form.[13] This structural analysis encompasses not only the question about the temporal disposition of narrative fictionality in the "time frame" ("the
time of the narrative" in relation to "narrated time") and
tense-composition,[14] but also the old question about the compositional relevance of Mk 8:27ff.,[15] and especially P. Vielhauer's newly-argued thesis concerning the christological understanding of time stratified within the three "stages" of
the ancient Egyptian enthronement schema (Mk 1:9-11: Apothe-
osis, 9:2-13: Presentation, 15:16-39: Enthronement), as a
determinant of the organizational structure of the form:[16]

"In this composition the three-fold predication of Jesus as
the Son of God receives great significance as the baptism,
transfiguration, and crucifixion."[17] "In that the evangelist
gives coherence to and breaks up the disparate material of the
Jesus tradition by means of the enthronement ritual, he interprets the history of Jesus from the baptism to the crucifixion
as a process of enthronement, by which Jesus is installed as
eschatological king, as heavenly cosmocrator."[18] This christological "time frame" carried by the composition is determined
by the Markan parable theory.[19] Not only in the sense that
the chronological development "is the stage-by-stage disclosure of the messianic secret",[20] [p. 260] but in such a way
that the "history" of Jesus, as the "history" of the *huios
tou theou*[21] which issues in "secret epiphanies" (M. Dibelius)
can first be recognized, made public, and especially proclaimed in the *euangelion* (cf. Mk 9:9) from the conclusion of
the enthronement process,[22] since only at the conclusion of
the enthronement process can it be perceived, recognized, and
proclaimed by human beings (gentiles!): *alēthōs houtos ho an-
thrōpos huios theou ēn* (15:39).[23] Whether, to be sure, this
is to be understood: *a*) in the sense of a historicization
process projected from the resurrection as the turning point
between two periods in the history of Jesus,[24] to be made
more specific as the justification and boundary of the understanding of Jesus' history and that of the believer as a cos-
mic battle,[25] which is the significance of the transfiguration
narrative not only within its own context, but especially with
respect to the Markan construction (especially in relation to
8:27ff., and the passion narrative);[26] or *b*) as the drawing of
the soteriological arc between temptation and crucifixion;[27]
or *c*) as the closer determination of the relation between geo-
graphical and material [p. 261] structural media;[28] or in
brief, *d*) as the constructional arrangement of Exordium (1:

1-13), Part 1 (1:14-3:6), Part 2 (3:7-6:6), Part 3 (6:7-8:26),
Part 4 (8:27-10:52), Part 5 (11:1-13:37), and Part 6 (14:1-
16:8),[29] in relationship to the "three-stage-enthronement":
all these possibilities can and must be explained in detail
within the structural analysis which is demanded here as the
primary assignment with respect to the subject matter. And
so at the end of this methodological sketch of the essential
problematics of gospel form and redaction criticism, we are
referred even more emphatically to specific theological tasks.

Notes to #15

1. G. Strecker, *ZThK* 64 (1967) 17, n. 5.

1a [+1978: Many of these were published in *Linguistica Biblica*; see references in these additional notes.]

2. Cf. p. [94].

3. Cf. p. [108f.].

4. Cf. p. [73f.].

5. Cf. p. [60f.].

6. Cf. p. [84f.].

7. Cf. p. [225f.], and J. Stalin, *Der Marxismus und die Fragen der Sprachwissenschaft*, 1951, against N. J. Marr.

8. Cf. p. [34].

9. Cf. #14, n. 94.

10. Cf. #14, nn. 23, 29.

11. Cf. #14, n. 1.

12. Cf. #1, n. 67.

13. Cf. the bibliography in I. de la Potterie, S.J., "De compositione evangelii Marci," *VD* 44 (1966) 135-41, and especially H. U. Meÿboom, "Een plan in het Marcus-Evangelie," *Theologisch Tijdschrift* 1 (1867) 651-90; M. Schulze, "Der Plan des Marcusevangeliums in seiner Bedeutung für das Verständnis der Christologie desselben," *ZwTh* 37 (1894) 332-73; J. Rohr, "Der Aufbau des Markusevangeliums," *ThQ* 101 (1920) 272-306; J. Sundwall, *Die Zusammensetzung des Markusevangeliums*, 1934; G. Hartmann, S.J., *Der Aufbau des Markusevangeliums*, 1936; E. Lohmeyer, *Mk.*, 5*f., 8f.; W. Hillmann, *Aufbau und Deutung der synoptischen Leidensberichte*, 1951; H. Riesenfeld, "Tradition und Redaktion im Markusevangelium," in *Neutestamentliche Studien für Rudolf Bultmann*, 1954, 157-64; G. Schille, "Bemerkungen zur Formgeschichte des Evangeliums, I.", *NTS* 4 (1957/58) 1-24; A. Kuby, "Zur Konzeption des Markus-Evangeliums," *ZNW* 49 (1958) 52-64; E. Trocmé, *La formation de l'évangile selon Marc*, 1963, 59ff.; E. Best, *The Temptation*

and the Passion, 1965, 112ff.; E. Schweizer, *Aufs.*, 100, n. 32; Schweizer, *EvTh* 24 (1964) 342ff.; N. Q. Hamilton, "Resurrection Tradition and the Composition of Mark," *JBL* 84 (1965) 415-21.

14. Cf. p. [234].

15. Cf. Wellhausen, *Einleitung*, 70; Riesenfeld, *op. cit.*, 160; Taylor, *Formation*, 40; T. A. Burkill, *ZNW* 51 (1960) 31; Best, *op. cit.*, 121.

16. P. Vielhauer, "Erwägungen zur Christologie des Markus- evangeliums," in his *Aufs.*, 199-214.

17. *Ibid.*, 211. Cf. also E. Hoskyns and N. Davey, *Das Rätsel des Neuen Testaments*, 1957, 108: "Since he..., pre- cisely at the high points of his narrative, more than once transcribes the title 'Christ' with 'Son of God' and comments upon it, it is clear that his gospel as a whole offers a Son- of-God-Christology."

18. Vielhauer, *op. cit.*, 213.

19. Cf. *ibid.*, 213f.

20. So K. Grobel, *Formgeschichte und Synoptische Quellen- analyse*, 1937, 7.

21. Cf. especially S. Hoekstra, "De Christologie van het canonieke Marcus-Evangelie, vergeleken met die van de beide andere synoptische Evangeliën," *Theologisch Tijdschrift* 5 (1871) 129-76, 313-33, 407-40; Weiss, *älteste Evgl.*, 42-52; M. Werner, *Der Einfluss paulinischer Theologie im Markus- evangelium*, 1923, 45-51; S. Lösch, *Deitas Jesus und antike Apotheose*, 1933, 106-21; J. Dupont, "'Filius meus es tu'," *RechSR* 35 (1948) 522-43; P. E. Davies, *JBL* 73 (1954) 197f.; B. M. F. van Iersel, S.M.M., *"Der Sohn" in den synoptischen Jesusworten*, 1961; Hahn, *Hoheitstitel*, 280ff. (criticized by Vielhauer, *Aufs.*, 187ff.); Best, *op. cit.*, 167f.

22. Cf. Wrede, *Messiasgeheimnis*, 66ff.; Güttgemanns, *VF* 12/2 (1967) 44.

23. Cf. Schreiber, Diss., 37ff., 212-15; Schreiber, *Theologie des Vertrauens*, 1967, 113f.

24. So G. Strecker, "Zur Messiasgeheimnistheorie im Markusevangelium," in *TU* 88 (1964) 87-104. Cf. also S. Schulz, "Die Bedeutung des Markus für die Theologiegeschichte

des Urchristentums," in *TU* 87 (1964) 135-45; Schulz, *Die Stunde der Botschaft*, 1967, 9ff.

25. Cf. J. M. Robinson, *Das Geschichtsverständniss des Markus-Evangeliums*, 1956. Criticism: Best, *op. cit.*, 18ff.

26. Cf. A. T. Fryer, "The Purpose of the Transfiguration," *JThS* 5 (1904) 214-27; E. Lohmeyer, "Die Verklärung Jesu nach dem Markus-Evangelium," *ZNW* 21 (1922) 185-215; S. Hirsch, *Taufe, Versuchung und Verklärung Jesu*, 1932; J. B. Bernardin, "The Transfiguration," *JBL* 52 (1933) 181-189; J. Blinzler, *Die neutestamentlichen Berichte über die Verklärung Jesu*, 1937; E. Dabrowski, *La Transfiguration de Jésus*, 1939; G. H. Boobyer, "St Mark and the Transfiguration," *JThS* 41 (1940) 119-40; H. Riesenfeld, *Jésus transfiguré*, 1947; G. B. Caird, "The Transfiguration," *ET* 67 (1955/56) 291-94; A. Kenny, "The Transfiguration and the Agony in the Garden," *CBQ* 19 (1957) 444-52; H. Baltensweiler, *Die Verklärung Jesu*, 1959; A.-M. Denis, O.P., "Une théologie de la Rédemption. La Transfiguration chez Saint Marc," *La Vie Spirituelle* 101 (1959) 136-49; H.-P. Müller, "Die Verklärung Jesu," *ZNW* 51 (1960) 56-64; Ch. Masson, "La Transfiguration de Jésus," *RThPh* 13/xiv (1964) 1-14.

27. Cf. Best, *op. cit.*

28. Cf. E. Lohmeyer, *Galiläa und Jerusalem*, 1936; R. H. Lightfoot, *Locality and Doctrine in the Gospels*, 1938; W. Marxsen, *Evglist Mk.*, 33ff.; Schreiber, *Theol. des Vertrauens*, 158ff.

29. On this division which cannot be more adequately argued here, see Lohmeyer, *op. cit.* (in n. 13); Trocmé, *op. cit.*, 65f.; Schweizer, *op. cit.* (in n. 13).

Author's Epilogue to the English Translation*

I began working on this book in the winter of 1967, com-
pleting it within four months. At that time I could not know
that it would stimulate a scientific revolution, nor did I
even dream of the possibility of an English translation.

I sat in my lonely work room, impressed by the sudden
discovery of a hidden library of which I had never heard before. I was struck by the foreign nature of a professional
science of language and literature which destroyed my self-
conscious adaptation of a Bultmannian hermeneutics and my dependence upon form criticism. I would have been quite astonished had someone stated at that time that in those four
months a new "text" science was being born in German New
Testament scholarship. And I would have been a "doubting
Thomas" indeed, had someone added that this new science would
evoke interest in the United States some ten years later.

And then shortly after publication a very serious contro-
versy--and sometimes even a war of "resistance"!--began to
develop, tensed between blaming me for having assaulted the
whole "guild" of New Testament scholars, and the commendation
that no contemporary could afford to overlook my book. I
stood in the middle of the struggle, somewhat like Parcifal
awakening with no consequence of what he had set in motion.

---

*[Text provided by the author in English, but edited and
styled by the translator.]

418

I took up the quarrel, and developed, in another four-month period, the kernel of my conception of "Generative Poetics", the initial parts of which were first published along with this book, in the winter of 1970.

The eleven years from 1967 to now represent a long period of time, particularly since "Generative Poetics" has been developed extensively within the last five years. Since I could not rework my original text--nor did I intend to--there remained only the possibility of short replies to some critics of the German edition within the footnotes to this translation, thereby taking into account the history of the reception of this book. These replies are all marked [+1978....]. That I chose to reply to some harsh criticisms of a former teacher will surprise no one who knows about our German theological situation: no one being mis-interpreted systematically may keep silence forever.

William G. Doty became known to me several years ago as a congenial interpreter of my projects when he sketched some of my concepts in a technical journal [*JournAmerAcadRelig* 40 (1972) 521-27; 41 (1973) 114-21]. Now that he has completed his excellent translation of my book, to be sure by means of hard work, I am very satisfied and grateful for his having rendered my sometimes dense courses of thinking. May the reader be as "candid" as I was in writing the book!

                              E. Güttgemanns

Bonn-Röttgen, 1 August 1978